CONCEPTS

Philosophical Issues, 9, 1998

PHILOSOPHICAL ISSUES

Edited by Enrique Villanueva
(Universidad Nacional Autónoma de México)

EDITORIAL ADVISORY BOARD

Ned Block (Massachusetts Institute of Technology)
Paul Boghossian (New York University)
Jerry Fodor (Rutgers University)
Richard Foley (Rutgers University)
James Higginbotham (University of Oxford)
Jaegwon Kim (Brown University)
Brian Loar (Rutgers University)
Christopher Peacocke (University of Oxford)
Sydney Shoemaker (Cornell University)
Ernest Sosa (Brown University)
James Tomberlin (California State University, Northridge)

Previously published volumes:

CONSCIOUSNESS
    (*Philosophical Issues*, 1, 1991)
RATIONALITY IN EPISTEMOLOGY
    (*Philosophical Issues*, 2, 1992)
SCIENCE AND KNOWLEDGE
    (*Philosophical Issues*, 3, 1993)
NATURALISM AND NORMATIVITY
    (*Philosophical Issues*, 4, 1993)
TRUTH AND RATIONALITY
    (*Philosophical Issues*, 5, 1994)
CONTENT
    (*Philosophical Issues*, 6, 1995)
PERCEPTION
    (*Philosophical Issues*, 7, 1996)
TRUTH
    (*Philosophical Issues*, 8, 1997)

Forthcoming volumes:

SKEPTICISM, EXTERNALISM, CONTEXTUALISM
    (*Philosophical Issues*, 10, 1999)

Philosophical Issues, 9, 1998

CONCEPTS

edited by

Enrique Villanueva
SOCIEDAD FILOSÓFICA IBERO AMERICANA

Ridgeview Publishing Company • Atascadero, California

Copyright © 1998
by Enrique Villanueva
All rights reserved.
No part of this book may be reproduced
or utilized in any form or by any means,
electrical or mechanical, including
photocopying, recording or by any
informational storage or retrieval system,
without written permission from the
copyright owner.

Paper text: ISBN 0-924922-30-3
Cloth (library edition): ISBN 0-924922-80-X

The typesetting was done by José Luis Olivares.

Published in the United States of America
by Ridgeview Publishing Company
Box 686
Atascadero, California   93423

Printed in the United States of America
by Thomson-Shore, Inc.

Contents

Preface
Enrique Villanueva ix

1 There Are No Recognitional Concepts; Not Even RED
Jerry Fodor 1

2 Concept Constitution
Paul Horwich 15

3 Recognitional Concepts and Compositionality
Richard Grandy 21

4 Recognitional Concepts and the Compositionality of Concept Possession
Terence Horgan 27

5 A More Plausible Kind of "Recognitional Concept"
Ruth Garret Millikan 35

6 Implicit Conceptions, Understanding and Rationality
Christopher Peacocke 43

7 Doubts about Implicit Conceptions
Stephen Schiffer 89

8 What Implicit Conceptions are Unlikely to Do
Georges Rey 93

9 Implicit Conceptions and The Phenomenon of Abandoned Principles
Eric Margolis 105

10 The Implicit Conception of Implicit Conceptions
Josefa Toribio 115

11 Implicit Conceptions, the *A Priori*, and the Identity of Concepts
Christopher Peacocke 121

12 Conceptual Competence
  James Higginbotham 149
13 The Significance of the Distinction between Concept Mastery and Concept Possession
  Genoveva Martí 163
14 Conceptual Competence and Inadequate Conceptions
  Pierre Jacob 169
15 On Concepts and Conceptions
  Josep Macià 175
16 The Concept–Conception Distinction
  Maite Ezcurdia 187
17 Response to Commentators
  James Higginbotham 193

18 What the Externalist Can Know *A Priori*
  Paul Boghossian 197
19 Is There a Good Epistemical Argument against Concept–Externalism?
  Brian Loar 213
20 Self–Knowledge & Semantic–Luck
  Stephen Yablo 219
21 A Challenge to Boghossian's Incompatibilist Argument
  Josep E. Corbí 231
22 Boghossian's *Reductio* of Compatibilism
  Carlos J. Moya 243
23 Replies to Commentators
  Paul Boghossian 253

24 A Theory of Concepts and Concept Possession
  George Bealer 261
25 Bealer's Intuitions on Concept Possession
  Jaegwoon Kim 303
26 Concepts and Ontology: A Query for Bealer
  James E. Tomberlin 311
27 Getting Clear on the Concept
  David Sosa 317
28 Some Critical Remarks on an Explanation of Concept Possession
  Eleonora Orlando 323
29 Concept Possession
  George Bealer 331

30 What Might Nonconceptual Content Be?
Robert Stalnaker 339
31 Grain and Content
Stephen Neale 353
32 Non–Conceptual Content, Subject–Centered
Information and the Naturalistic Demand
Juan José Acero 359
33 Report of an Unsuccessful Search for Nonconceptual
Content
Mario Gómez-Torrente 369
34 Information and Content
David Pineda 381
35 Replies to Comments
Robert Stalnaker 389

Contributors 397

Preface

The papers in this volume are concerned with issues in recent developments in the topic of Concepts. The present volume follows the structure of two previous volumes of Philosophical Issues, namely, *Perception* and *Truth* that proved to be most appropriate.

Philosophical Issues aims at publishing original papers by leading philosophers on topics of fundamental importance within the tradition of Western Philosophical Thought. We aim to bring about the dialectics surrounding a unified topic in a number of symposia for each volume. A significant number of Ibero and Latinoamerican participants concur in the present and previous volumes. We intend to publish volumes annually.

Philosophical Issues could not be possible without the collaboration of Ernest Sosa, Jim Tomberlin and Lourdes Valdivia; my gratitude by their generous assistance and advice throughout the composition and publication of the present volume.

SOFIA is indebted specially to Dr. Daniel Reséndiz Núñez, head of the Subsecretaría de Educación Superior e Investigación Científica (SESIC) for his academic solidarity in providing funds (through Anexo 97-01-09-160-135) that did help to cover the typesetting and coordination of the present volume.

Again, my thanks to my Universidad Nacional Autónoma de México and to the Centro de Neurobiología, where I continue working, for their permanent support in providing an academic environment where I can gladly discharge the tasks implied in the publication of this series.

José Luis Olivares did the typesetting again; thank him.

Enrique Villanueva
Juriquilla, Querétaro, August 1998

There Are No Recognitional Concepts; Not Even RED*

Jerry Fodor

Introduction. Let it be that a concept is *recognitional* if and only if:

(1) It is at least partially constituted by its possession conditions; and

(2) Among its possession conditions is the ability to recognize at least some things that fall under the concept *as* things that fall under the concept.

For example, RED is a recognitional concept iff it numbers, among its constitutive possession conditions, the ability to recognize at least some red things as red.

In this paper, I propose to argue —indeed, I propose to sort of *prove*— that there are no recognitional concepts; not even RED.

Lots of philosophers are sympathetic to the claim that there are recognitional concepts. For one thing, insofar as *recognitional* capacities are construed as *perceptual* capacities, the claim that there

---

*Thanks to Ned Block, Paul Horwich, Chris Peacocke, Stephen Schiffer and Galen Strawson for helpful comments on an earlier draft.

are recognitional concepts preserves the basic idea of Empiricism: that the content of at least some concepts is constituted, at least in part, by their connections to percepts. For philosophers who suppose that Empiricism couldn't be *all* wrong, recognitional concepts can therefore seem quite a good place to dig in the heels. More generally, the claim that there are recognitional concepts is a bastion of last resort for philosophers who think that semantic facts are constituted by epistemological facts, a doctrine that includes, but is not exhausted by, the various forms of Empiricism. If you have ever, even in the privacy of your own home among consenting adults, whispered, hopefully, the word 'criterion', then probably *even you* think there are recognitional concepts.

Philosophers who hold that there are recognitional concepts generally hold that it's important that there are; for example, a familiar line of anti–skeptical argument turns on there being some. The idea is that, if a concept is recognitional, then having certain kinds of experience would, in principle, *show with the force of conceptual necessity* that that the concept applies. If, for example, RED is a recognitional concept, then having certain kinds of experience would, in principle, show with the force of conceptual necessity that there are red things. Ditto, mutatis mutandis, SQUARE, CHAIR, IS IN PAIN and BELIEVES THAT P, assuming that these are recognitional concepts. So, if you think that it's important that skepticism about squares, chairs, pains, beliefs or red things be refuted, you are likely to want it a lot that the corresponding concepts are recognitional. Nevertheless, it's sort of provable there aren't any recognitional concepts; so, at least, it seems to me.

I pause to mention a kind of argument against there being recognitional concepts to which I am sympathetic, but which I am *not* going to pursue in what follows. Viz. that it's truistic that the content of ones experience underdetermines the content of ones beliefs, excepting only ones beliefs about one's experiences. No landscape is so empty, or so well lit —so the thought goes— that your failure to recognize that it contains a rabbit *entails* that you haven't got the concept RABBIT. So, it couldn't be that your having the concept RABBIT requires that there are circumstances in which you couldn't but recognize a rabbit as such.

I think this is a good argument, but, notoriously, lots of philosophers don't agree; they think, perhaps, that the connection between concept possession and recognitional capacities can be relaxed enough to accommodate the truisms about rabbits without the claim that there are recognitional concepts lapsing into vacuity. I propose, in any event, not to rely upon this sort of argument here.

Compositionality. The considerations I will appeal to are actually quite robust, so a minimum of apparatus is required to introduce them. It will, however, be useful to have on hand the notion of a *satisfier* for a concept. The satisfier(s) for a concept are the states, capacities, dispositions, etc. in virtue of which one meets the possession condition(s) for the concept.[1] So, if the ability to tell red from green is a possession condition for the concept RED, then *being able to tell red from green* is a satisfier for the concept RED. If a disposition to infer P from P&Q is a possession condition for the concept &, then *being so disposed* is a satisfier for the concept &. And so forth. Since, by assumption, concepts have their possession conditions essentially, and possession conditions have their satisfiers essentially, the exposition will move back and forth among the three as convenience dictates.

I propose to argue that there are no concepts whose satisfiers are recognitional capacities; hence that there are no recognitonal concepts. I need a premise. Here's one:

Premise P: S is a satisfier for concept C if and only if C inherits S from the satisfiers for its constituents concepts.[2] (I'll sometimes call this the 'compositionality condition' on concept constitution.

Consonant with my general intention not to have the argument turn on its details, I leave it open how 'inherited from' is construed in premise P, so long as fixing the satisfiers for constituent concepts is necessary and sufficient for fixing the satisfiers for their hosts.

Why premise P is plausible: Unless P is true, we will have to give up the usual account of why concepts are systematic and productive; and, mutatis mutandis, of how it is possible to learn a language by learning its finite basis. Consider, for example, the concept-constitutive possession conditions for the concept RED APPLE. If *Premise P* is false, the following situation is possible: The possession conditions for RED are ABC and the possession conditions for RED APPLE are ABEFG. So denying P leaves it open that one could have the concept RED APPLE and not have the concept RED.

But, now, the usual compositional account of productivity requires that one satisfy the possession conditions for complex concepts, like

---

[1] Whereas, by contrast, the satisfiers *of* a concept are just: whatever is in its extension. This is not, admittedly, a very happy way of talking, but it's no worse, surely, than intention/intension, and nothing better came to mind.

[2] If C is a primitive concept, the condition is trivially satisfied.

RED APPLE, *by* satisfying the possession conditions for their constituent concepts. That is, it requires that one's having a grasp of the concept RED is *part of the explanation* of one's having a grasp of the concept RED APPLE. So accepting the usual compositional account of productivity is incompatible with denying *premise P*.

Likewise the other way around. The usual compositional account of productivity requires that if one satisfies the possession conditions for the constituents of a complex concept, one thereby satisfies the possession conditions for the concept.[3] But, suppose that *premise P* is false, and consider, once again, the concept RED APPLE. Denying P leaves it open that the concept–constitutive possession conditions for RED APPLE are *not* exhausted by the concept–constitutive possession conditions for RED and APPLE. For example, the former might be ABCDE and the latter might be AB and CD respectively. But then grasping the concepts RED and APPLE would not be sufficient for grasping the concept RED APPLE, and, once again, the standard account of conceptual productivity would be undermined.

So much for the bona fides of premise P. The next point is that the condition that compositionality imposes on concept constitution is highly substantive. A brief digression will show the kind of theory of concepts that it can rule out.

Consider the idea that concepts are (or are partially) constituted by their stereotypes, hence that *knowing its stereotype* is a satisfier for some concepts. *Premise P* says that this idea is true only if, if you know the stereotypes for the constituents of a complex concept, then you know the stereotype for that concept. Which, in some cases, is plausible enough. Good examples of RED APPLES are stereotypically red and stereotypically apples. Let's assume that that's because *the stereotype of RED APPLE is inherited from the stereotype for RED and the stereotype for APPLE.* (This assumption is concessive, and it may well not be true. But let's let it stand for the sake of the argument.) So then, as far as RED APPLE is concerned, it's compatible with premise P that knowing their stereotypes should be possession conditions for RED and APPLE.

Still, concepts can't be constituted by their stereotypes (knowing its stereotype can't be a satisfier for a concept). That's because RED

---

[3]This isn't quite right, of course; you also have to know how the constituents are 'put together'. Suppose a satisfier for RED is being able to identify red things and a satisfier for SQUARE is being able to identify square things. Then, presumably, the corresponding satisfier for RED SQUARE is being able to identify things in the intersection of RED and SQUARE. The fact that it's the intersection rather than, say, the union, that's at issue corresponds to the structural difference between the concept RED SQUARE and the concept RED OR SQUARE.

APPLE isn't the general case. In the general case, complex concepts don't inherit their stereotypes from those of their constituents. So, in the general case, stereotypes don't satisfy *premise P*.

Consider such concepts as PET FISH, MALE NURSE, and the like.[4] You can't derive the PET FISH stereotype from the FISH stereotype and the PET stereotype. So, if stereotypes were constitutive of the corresponding concepts, having a grasp of FISH, and having a grasp of PET (and knowing the semantics of the AN construction; see fn. 3) would *not* suffice for having a grasp of PET FISH. So, the usual story about how PET FISH is compositional would fail.[3]

So much for stereotypes. If premise P is true, it follows that they can't be concept-constitutive. I will now argue that, if premise P is true, then it likewise follows that there are no recognitional concepts. In fact, most of the work is already done since, for all intents and purposes, the notion of a recognitional concept is hostage to the notion that concepts are constituted by their stereotypes. Here's why. Nobody could (and nobody does) hold that the possession of a recognitional concept requires being able to identify *each* of its instances as such; if that *were* the requirement, then only God would have any recognitonal concepts. So, the doctrine must be (and, as a matter of fact, it always is) that possession of a recognitional concept requires the ability to identify good instances as such in favorable conditions. (There are various variants of this in the literature; but it doesn't matter to what follows which you choose.)[5]

But, now, unsurprisingly, the ability to recognize *good instances* of Fs doesn't compose, and this is for exactly the same reason that *knowing the stereotype of F* doesn't compose; good instances of F&Gs needn't be either good instances of F or good instances of G. See PET FISH, once again: Good instances of PET FISH are, by and large, poorish instances of PET and poorish instances of FISH. So a recognitional capacity for *good instances of PET and good instances of FISH is not required for,* and typically does not provide,

---

[4]The immediately following arguments are familiar from the cognitive science literature on stereotypes, so I won't expand on them here. Suffice it to emphasize that the main point —that stereotypes don't compose— holds whether stereotypes are thought of as something like exemplars or as something like feature sets. For reviews, see Fodor and Lepore, 1992; Fodor, forthcoming, 1997.

[5]The intended doctrine is that having the recognitional concept F requires being able to recognize good instances of F as instances of F, not as *good* instances of F. It's concessive of me to insist on this distinction, because it requires the Empiricist to defend only the weaker of the two views.

[1] Stereotype will be a dog or cat
[2] NURSE stereotype will be a woman
[3] For a defense of this argument, see Osherson, D. & E. Smith, "Gradedness and Conceptual Combination," *Cognition* 12 (1982): 299-318.

a *recognitional capacity for good (or, indeed, any) instances of PET FISH.*

Somebody who is good at recognizing that trouts are fish and that puppies are pets *is not thereby good at recognizing that goldfish are pet fish.* The capacity for recognizing pet fish as such is not conceptually, or linguistically, or semantically connected to capacities for recognizing pets as such or fish as such. The connection is *at best* contingent, and it's entirely possible for any of these recognitional capacities to be in place without any of the others.

This doesn't, of course, show that the semantics of PET FISH are uncompositional. What it shows is that recognitional capacities aren't possession conditions for the concepts that have them. If recognitional capacities were possession conditions, PET FISH would not inherit its satisfiers from those of PET and FISH. So if recognitional capacities were possession conditions, PET FISH would fail premise P. So recognitional capacities aren't possession conditions. So there are no recognitional concepts.[6]

Objections:

Q1: You're, in effect, taking for granted not only that compositionality is needed to explain productivity, but that it is therefore a test for whether a property is constitutive of the concepts that have it. Why should I grant that?

A1: I suppose I could just dig my heels in here. Compositionality is pretty nearly all that we know about the individuation of concepts. If we give that up, we will have no way of distinguishing what *constitutes* a concept from such of its merely contingent accretions as associations, stereotypes and the like.

But though I do think it would be justifiable to take that strong line, I really don't need to in order to run the sort of argument I'm endorsing. If push comes completely to shove, the following exiguous version will do for my polemical purposes:

If you know what 'pet' and 'fish' mean, you thereby know what 'pet fish' means. But you can be able to recognize pets and fish as such but be quite unable to recognize pet fish as such. So recognitional capacities can't be meanings, and they can't be constituents of meanings, all varieties of Empiricist semantics to the contrary notwithstanding.

---

[6]This assumes, of course, that what holds for PET and for FISH holds likewise for *any* candidate recognitional concept: viz. that there will always be *some* complex concept of which it is a constituent but to which it does not contribute its possession condition. The reader who doubts this should try, as an exercise, to find a counterexample. For starters, try it with RED and APPLE.

As far as I can see, that formulation doesn't need much more than the distinctness of discernibles, so it seems to me that it cuts pretty close to the bone.

Q2: But couldn't an Empiricist just *stipulate* that recognitional capacities, though they demonstrably don't satisfy P, and are thus demonstrably not constituents of meanings, are nevertheless to count as essential conditions for the possession of primitive concepts?

A2: Sure, go ahead, stipulate; and much joy may you have of it. But nothing is left of the usual reasons for supposing that any of the concepts we actually have comply with the stipulation; in particular, nothing is left of the idea that the *content* of our concepts is constituted by our recognitional capacities. Whatever content is, it's got to be compositional; so it's got to come out that the content of RED APPLE includes the content of RED, and the content of PET FISH includes the content of PET.

It may be worthwhile to reiterate here an argument I gave for the plausibility of premise P. Suppose a primitive concept has a possession condition which is not inherited by one of its complex hosts; suppose, for example, that being able to recognize good instances of pets is a possession condition for PET but is *not* a possession condition for PET FISH. Then it is presumably possible that someone who has the concept PET FISH should nonetheless not have the concept PET. I take this to be a *reductio*, and I think that you should too.

Here's a closely related way to make the same argument: Perhaps you're the sort of philosopher who thinks it's a possession condition for RED APPLE that one is prepared to accept the inference RED APPLE → RED (i.e. that one finds this inference 'primitively compelling').[7] If so, that's all the more reason for you to hold that the possession conditions for RED APPLE must *include* the possession conditions for RED. Hence, it's all the more reason for you to hold that the satisfiers for RED are inherited under composition by RED APPLE. But if that's right, then, once again, it couldn't be that a recognitional capacity is a satisfier for RED *unless* it's a satisfier for RED APPLE. But the capacity to recognize pets as such is not a satisfier for the concept PET FISH, so it can't be a satisfier for PET. Since sauce for the goose is sauce for the gander, the ability to recognize red things is likewise not a satisfier for RED.

---

[7]Even conceptual atomists like me can hold that inferences which relate a syntactically complex concept to its parts are typically analytic and concept constitutive. See Fodor and Lepore, 1992.

Q3. Couldn't we split the difference? Couldn't we say that the satisfiers for the *primitive* concepts include recognitional capacities, but that the satisfiers for complex concepts don't?

A3. Simply not credible. After all, people who have the concept PET FISH do generally have a corresponding recognitional capacity; for example, they are generally good at recognizing goldfish as pet fish. And, surely, being able to recognize (as it might be) a trout as a fish stands in *precisely* the same relation to having the concept FISH as being able to recognize a goldfish as a pet fish does to having the concept PET FISH. So, how could that relation be constitutive of concept possession in the one case but not in the other? Is it, perhaps, that the concepts FISH and PET FISH have content in different senses of 'content'?

This sort of point is probably worth stressing. Some philosophers have a thing about recognitional capacities because they want to tie meaning and justification close together (see the remarks earlier about antiskeptical employments of the idea that there are recognitional concepts). But if recognitional capacities are constitutive only of primitive concepts, then the connection between meaning and justification fails in infinitely many cases. It will thus be concept–constitutive that (ceteris paribus) *it's troutlooking* is evidence for 'it's a fish', but *not* concept constitutive that (ceteris paribus) *it's goldfishlooking* is evidence for 'it's a pet fish'. What possible epistemological use could such a notion of concept constitutivity be put to?

Q4. FISH and PET are only *relatively* primitive (they're only primitive relative to PET FISH). What about absolutely primitive concepts like RED? Surely the concept RED is recognitional even if neither FISH nor PET FISH is.

A4. It's just more of the same. Consider RED HAIR, which, I will suppose, is compositional (that is, not idiomatic) and applies to *hair that is red as hair goes*. This view of its semantics explains why, though red hair is arguably not literally red, still somebody who has RED and has HAIR and who understands the semantic implications of the syntactic structure AN, can figure out what 'red hair' means. So, prima facie, RED HAIR is compositional and the demands of productivity are satisfied according to the present analysis.[8]

---

[8]Let it be that an AN concept is 'intersective' if its extension is the intersection of the As with the Ns. The standard view is that being intersective is sufficient but not nececessary for an AN concept to be compositional: RED HAIR is *compositional* but not *intersective*, and PET FISH is both. (For a general discussion, see Kamp and Partee, (1995)). Actually, my guess is that RED HAIR, BIG ANT,

But notice, once again, that the productivity/compositionality of the concepts does not imply the productivity/compositionality of the corresponding recognitional capacities. Somebody who is able to say whether something is a good instance of HAIR and whether something is a good instance of RED is not *thereby* able to recognize a good instance of RED HAIR. Well then, what *does* 'red' contribute to the semantics of 'red hair'? Just what you'd suppose: it contributes a reference to the property of *being red* (as such). It's just that its doing that isn't tantamount to, and doesn't entail, its contributing a recognitional capacity for (good instances of) redness.

One's recognitional capacity for RED doesn't compose. So one's recognitional capacity for red things is not a satisfier for the concept RED. So not even RED is a recognitional concept.

Q5. What do you say about intentional concepts?

A5. Nothing much for present purposes. They have to be compositional, because they are productive. If they are compositional, then there are, to my knowledge, three theories (exhaustive but not exclusive) of what they inherit from their constituents:

— they inherit the *extensions* of their constituents.

— they inherit the *senses* of their constituents

— the inherit the *shapes* of their constituents. (Notice that shape is compositional; 'red hair' contains 'red' as a morphosyntactic part; and the shape of 'red hair' is completely determined given the shape of 'red', the shape of 'hair', and the morphosyntactics of the expression.)

But, invariably a theory of intentional concepts that says that any of these are *inheritable* properties of their constituents will also say that they are *constitutive* properties of their constituents. So, as far as I can tell, nothing that anybody is likely to want to say about intentional concepts will deny my argument the premise it requires.

Conclusion. The moral of this paper is that recognitional capacities are contingent adjuncts to concept possession, much like knowledge of stereotypes; *a fortiori*, they aren't *constitutive* of concept possession. How, indeed, *could* anyone have supposed that recognitional capacities are satisfiers for concepts, when recognitional capacities patently don't compose and concept satisfiers patently do?

---

and the like are the general case. Excepting the 'antifactive' adjectives ('fake', 'imitation', etc.) AN usually means *A FOR (an) N*, and the *intersectives* are just the limiting case where things that are A for (an) N are A. But it doesn't matter for present purposes whether this is so.

I think what went wrong is, after all, not very deep, though it's well worth attending to. Content, concept–constitutivity, concept possession, and the like, are connected to the notion of an *instance* (i.e. to the notion of an *extension*). The notion of an instance (extension) is semantic, hence compositional, through and through; idioms excepted, what is an instance of a syntactically complex concept depends exhaustively on what are the instances of its parts. The notion of *a recognitional capacity*, by contrast, is connected to the notion of a *good* (in the sense of a typical, or a reliable) instance; the best that a recognitional capacity can promise is to identify good instances in favorable conditions. It's a mistake to try to construe the notion of an instance in terms of the notion of a good instance;[9] unsurprisingly, since the latter is patently a special case of the former, the right order of exposition is the other way around.

Recognitional capacities don't act like satisfiers: What's a satisfier for a complex concept depends on what's a satisfier for its parts; but what's a good instance of a complex concept doesn't depend on what's a good instance of its parts. Why should it? What's a good instance of a concept, simple or complex, depends on *how things are in the world*.[10] Compositionality can tell you that the instances of PET FISH are all and only the pet fish; but it can't tell you that the *good* instances of pet fish are the goldfish; which is, all the same, the information that pet fish *recognition* (as opposed to mere PET FISH *instantiation*) is likely to depend on. How could you expect semantics to know what kind of fish people keep for pets? Likewise, what counts as red hair depends, not just on matters of meaning, but also on what shades hair actually comes in (i.e. because red hair is hair that is *relatively* red.) How *could* you expect semantics to know what shades hair actually comes in? Do you think that semantics runs a barber shop?[11] How, in short, could you expect that relations

---

[9]Indeed, it's a venerable mistake. I suppose the Platonic theory of Forms was the first to commit it.

[10]It also depends on how things are with us. What the good instances of RED are almost certainly has to do with the way the physiology of our sensory systems is organized (see, for example, Rosche, 1973; Berlin and Kaye, 1969). Likewise, it's no accident that the good instances of ANIMAL are all big enough for us to see (i.e. big enough for *us* to see). It does not follow that a creature whose range of visual acuity is very different from ours would *thereby* have a different concept of animals from ours.

[11]The cases in the text are not, of course, exceptional. What counts as an average income depends not only on what 'average' and 'income' mean, but also on what incomes people actually earn. Semantics tells you that the average income is in the middle of the income distribution, whatever the distribution

among recognitional capacities would exhibit the compositionality that productivity requires of semantic relations?

Oh, well; so what if there are no recognitional concepts?

For one thing, as I remarked at the outset, if there are no recognitional concepts we lose a certain class of antiskeptical arguments; ones that depend on the connection between percepts and concepts being, in some sense, constitutive of the latter. We will no longer be able to say to the skeptic: 'If you don't think that *this* experience shows that *that's* a chair, then you don't have the concept CHAIR'. But maybe this isn't a great loss; I've never heard of a skeptic actually being convinced by that kind of argument. I sure wouldn't be if I were a skeptic.

I'm not, however, meaning to deny that the issue about recognitional concepts goes very deep. To the contrary, I'm meaning to claim that it goes very much deeper than (mere) epistemology. Close to the heart of the last hundred years of philosophy is an argument between a Cartesian and a Pragmatist account of concept possession. Though the details vary, the essentials don't: According to Cartesians, having the concept X is being able to *think about* Xs; according to Pragmatists, its being able to *respond differentially* or *selectively* to Xs (for short: it's being able to *sort* Xs.) I doubt that there's a major philosopher, anyhow since Peirce —and including, even, the likes of Heidegger—, who hasn't practically everything at stake on how this argument turns out.

Notice that the issue here isn't 'Naturalism'. Sorting is just as intentional as thinking, and in the same way: *Neither* coextensive thoughts *nor* coextensive sorts are *ipso facto* identical. A Pragmatist who isn't a behaviorist can (and should) insist on this. The issue, rather, is whether the intentionality of thought derives from the intentionality of action. Roughly, Pragmatists think that it does, whereas Cartesians think that the metaphysical dependences go the other way around. It's the difference between holding, on the one hand, that whether you are sorting Xs is a matter of how you are thinking about what you are doing; or, on the other hand, that whether you are thinking about Xs depends on (possibly counterfactual) subjunctives about how you would sort them.

Well, the minimal Pragmatist doctrine (so it seems to me) is the claim that there are recognitional concepts; i.e. that at least some concepts are constituted by one's ability to sort their instances. And

---

may be. But if you want to *recognize* an average income, you need the facts about how many people actually earn how much. Semantics doesn't supply such facts; only the world can.

the present arguments (so it seems to me) show that even this minimal Pragmatist doctrine isn't true. Thinking centers on the notion of an instance; recognitional capacity centers on the notion of a *good* instance. Unless you are God, whether you can recognize an instance of X depends on whether it's a good instance of an X; the less good it is, the likelier you are to fail.[12]

But you can always *think* an instance of *X*; viz by thinking *an instance of X*. So thinking is universal in a way that sorting is not. So thinking doesn't reduce to sorting. That is bed rock. To try to wiggle out of it, as so many philosophers have drearily done, by invoking ideal sorts, recognition under ideal circumstances, the eventual consensus of the scientific community, or the like, is tacitly to give up the defining Pragmatist project of construing semantics epistemologically. *Being an ideal sort* always turns out not to be independently definable; it's just being a sort that gets the extension right.

Or, to put the point with even greater vehemence: The question whether there are recognitional concepts is really the question what thought is *for*; whether it's for directing action or for discerning truth. And the answer is that Descartes was right: The goal of thought is to understand the world, not to sort it. That, I think, is the deepest thing that we know about the mind.

Afterward. This paper was presented at the 1997 meeting of the Central Division of the American Philosophical Association. Stephen Schiffer commented, and what he said was typical of the reaction I've had from a number of philosophical friends. So I include here my reply to Steve's reply:

Steve asked, in effect: 'What's wrong with a mixed view, according to which recognitional capacities are constitutive for (some) primitive concepts but not for their complex hosts?' Steve thinks that my reply must be either aesthetic (mixed theories are ugly) or an outright appeal to the 'agglomerative principle' that if the conjuncts of a conjunctive proposition are recognitional, then so too is the conjunctive proposition. Since Steve takes this principle to be not better than dubious, he thinks that I haven't a better than dubious argument against there being recognitional concepts.

---

[12] Analogous remarks hold for other epistemological capacities like, e.g., drawing inferences. Unless you are God, whether, in a particular case, you are disposed to infer P from P&Q depends, *inter alia*, on whether the logical form of the proposition is perspicuous. This sort of consideration strongly suggests that the considerations that rule out recognitional capacities as concept-constitutive apply, *mutatis mutandis*, to rule out *any* epistemological candidate.

Now, it does seem to me that somebody who holds that there are primitive recognitional concepts should also hold the agglomerative principle (see the discussion of Q3). But my thinking this isn't an essential part of my argument. I tried to make clear in the text what the essence of my argument is; but, evidently, I didn't succeed. This hasn't been my century for making things clear.

Here it is again:

A theory of compositionality should explain why, in the standard case, anybody who has a complex concept also has its constituent concepts. (Why anybody who has RED TRIANGLE has RED and TRIANGLE; why anybody who has GREEN HAIR has GREEN and HAIR... and so forth.) This is tantamount to saying that a compositionality principle should be so formulated as to entail that satisfying the possession conditions for a complex concept *includes* satisfying the possession conditions for its constituents.

Now look at Steve's proposal, which is that "It is reasonable to hold that the possession conditions of complex concepts are determined by those of their constituents concepts. But for the case at hand this simply requires F-&-G to be such that to possess it the possessor must be able to recognize good instances of F and good instances of G."

As stated, Steve's theory is wrong about PET FISH: It's true, of course, that to have the concept PET FISH you have to have the concept FISH. But it's certainly *not* true that to have the concept PET FISH you have to have a recognitional capacity for good instances of fish. To have a concept, conjunctive or otherwise, you have to have the concepts that are its constituents. But you *don't* have to have recognitional capacities corresponding to its constituents; *not even if, by assumption, the complex concept is itself recognitional.* So, having the constituents of a concept can't require having a recognitional capacity in respect of their instances. If it did, you could have a complex concept *without* having its constituents; which is not an option. So concepts can't be recognitional capacities.

Can Steve's proposal be patched? Well, if he is to get the facts to come out right, he'll presumably just have to stipulate that for *some* F-&-G concepts (RED TRIANGLE) "the possessor must be able to recognize good instances of F and G", but that for others (PET FISH, MALE NURSE) that's not required. And he'll have to say, in some general and principled way, which concepts are which. But, surely, you don't want to have to stipulate the relations between the possession conditions for a complex concept and the possession conditions for its constituents; what you want is that they should just fall out of the theory of compositionality together with the theory of concept constitutivity.

Which, indeeed, they do if you get these theories right. What's constitutive of FISH, and hence what PET FISH inherits from FISH, is (not a capacity for recognizing fish but) *the property that FISH expresses: viz the property of being a fish.* Likewise, mutatis mutandis, what's constitutive of RED, and hence what RED TRIANGLE inherits from RED, is (not a recognitional capacity for red things but) the property that RED expresses, viz. the *property of being RED*. Because what is constitutive of a concept determines its possession conditions, it follows that you can't have the concept PET FISH unless you know that pet fish are fish, and you can't have the concept RED TRIANGLE unless you know that red triangles are red. This is, of course, just what intuition demands.

Explanations are better than stipulations; and they're a *lot* better than stipulations that misdescribe the facts. So there *still* aren't any recognitional concepts.[13]

REFERENCES

Berlin, B. and Kaye, P. (1969): *Basic Color Terms: their Universality and Evolution*, University of California Press, Berkeley.
Fodor, J. and Lepore, E. (1992): *Holism, a Shopper's Guide*, Blackwell, Oxford.
Kamp, H. and Partee, B. (1995): "Prototype theory and compositionality, *Cognition*, 57, 129-181.
Rosche, E.H. (1973): "Natural categories," *Cognitive Psychology*, 4, 328-350.

---

[13]Steve also suggested that maybe PAIN is a recognitional concept, even if RED is not. I won't, however, discuss the notion that sensation concepts might be recognitional since I guess I don't really understand it. Does one recognize one's pains when one has them? Or does one just have them? If I can, indeed, recognize good instances of MY PAIN, I suppose it follows that I have the concept PAIN. Does it *follow*, as compositionality would require if PAIN is a recognition concept, that I can also recognize good instances of YOUR PAIN? Hard cases make bad laws. Sensation concepts are too hard for me.

Concept Constitution

Paul Horwich

Jerry Fodor defines a 'recognitional' concept as one whose possession requires the ability to recognize at least some of its instances: thus RED is recognitional if, and only if, in order to have that concept one must be able (in favourable circumstances) to identify certain red things as red. His argument that there are in reality no such concepts has two main premises. One, which he, calls "the compositionality principle", is that the possession condition of a complex concept (such as PET FISH) will be satisfied by anyone who satisfies the possession conditions of its constituents and who appreciates how those constituents have been combined. The other, to which he does not give a name but which we might call "the principle of uniformity", is that if the constituents of a certain complex concept are recognitional then that concept must itself be recognitional.

In a more general form, this principle would require that if the constituents of a concept have possession conditions of a certain type, K, then the concept must also have possession conditions of that type. From this pair of premises Fodor reaches his conclusion without difficulty. Given any concept A (e.g. PET) we can always find another one N (e.g. FISH) such that our being able to recognize certain instances of A and certain instances of N does not ensure that we will be able to recognize any instances of AN; therefore, the assumption that there are recognitional concepts leads to a conflict between the uniformity principle (which implies that the complexes they form are recognitional) and the compositionality principle (which implies that not all such complexes could have possession conditions characteristic of recognitional concepts); therefore, there are no recognitional concepts.

So the situation is uncontroversially this: the principle of compositionality, the principle of uniformity, and the belief in recognitional concepts, form an inconsistent triad. Moreover, no one wants to give up the principle of compositionality. Therefore the issue boils down to whether we are to give up uniformity or recognitional concepts. Fodor thinks there is good reason to hold on to the principle of uniformity —so recognitional concepts must go. His critics (amongst whom I must count myself) don't agree with (or don't understand) his reason for wanting to hang on to the principle of uniformity. Therefore, whether or not they themselves have any time for recognitional concepts, they think that his argument against them is no good.

In support of this scepticism about Fodor's position I'd like to offer three considerations. The first responds to his allegation that to give up the principle of uniformity is *ad hoc*. The second is the admittedly *ad hominem* point that Fodor's own 'informational' view of concept constitution would fall foul of uniformity just as blatantly as do recognitional concepts. And the third consideration sketches a *prima facie* plausible rationale for the principle of uniformity and identifies where that rationale goes wrong.

1   Is It *Ad Hoc* to Abandon Uniformity?

In the face of Fodor's argument, one might try to preserve recognitional concepts by denying the principle of uniformity and maintaining instead that, although *primitive* concepts A and N may be recognitional, the condition for possessing the *complex* concept AN is simply possessing A and possessing N and seeing how they are put together. To this, however, Fodor objects that it would make the principle of compositionality true by stipulation —which is not as explanatorily deep and plausible as having it derive from general principles of concept constitution. But this complaint strikes me as unjust. For the situation is really that we are faced with two competing general accounts of concept constitution. One (which Fodor prefers) says that all concepts —both simple and complex— have possession conditions of type K. The other (which I am recommending) says that the possession condition for any simple concept is of type K, and for any complex concept is 'possessing the constituent concepts and knowing how they are combined'.[1] Both of these are substantive proposals. Neither is merely a stipulation. Granted, one of them trivially entails compositionality, whereas showing that the other entails it will take a bit of work. But since when was it an objection to a theory that it obviously entails an obvious fact?

2 There Are No Informational Concepts; Not Even RED!

Fodor's own view of concept constitution (which he does not talk about in the paper under discussion) is that a person has the concept F if and only if he has a term (of mentalese) whose tokening would, in appropriate circumstances, be caused by the presence of Fs.[2] Thus

x means RED = the presence of something red would, in appropriate circumstances, cause a tokening of x

x means COPPER = the presence of copper would, in appropriate circumstances, cause a tokening of x

and so on. But now we are in a position to argue, on the basis of the generalized uniformity principle, that there can be no such 'informational concepts'.

Actually, there are two such arguments. In the first place, if the informational account is to have any plausibility at all then we cannot suppose that the 'appropriate circumstances' for red things to cause tokenings of "red" are exactly the same as those for copper to cause "copper": precisely how the qualifier is filled in will have to depend on the concept in question. But that means that the different meaning-constituting properties are not especially uniform. We do not have a general theory of the form

$$x \text{ means } F = T(x, F)$$

where T is the same for every F. What we have, rather, is

$$x \text{ means RED} = T_1(x, \text{red})$$

---

[1] For articulation and defence of this approach to compositionality, see my "The Composition of Meanings", *Philosophical Review*, 1998.

[2] See J.A. Fodor, *Psychosemantics*, Cambridge, Mass., MIT Press, 1987; and *A Theory of Content and Other Essays*, Cambridge, Mass., MIT Press, 1990.

$$x \text{ means COPPER} = T_2(x, \text{copper})$$
$$x \text{ means DOG} = T_3(x, \text{dog})$$

which is not truly uniform.

In the second place consider concepts such as ROUND SQUARE and HOT SNOW which, for either semantic or physical reasons, *cannot* have any instances at all. In the case of such concepts there are no 'appropriate circumstances' in which instances would cause some expression or other to be tokened. Consequently the possession conditions for those concepts cannot be informational; so, given the generalised uniformity principle, there can be no informational concepts. It would seem then that Fodor has to chose between his theory of concept constitution and his principle of uniformity.

3 A defective case for uniformity

One natural line of thought leading to the uniformity principle goes like this. Surely all predicative concepts belong to the same ontological category —in particular, they might well all be *properties.* But then, for a simple or complex term to express a concept is for it to stand in some specific non-semantic relation to one of these entities. And this is surely the same relation in each case; for it is whatever constitutes the relation 'x means (or expresses) property y'. Consequently, what constitutes the property 'x means F' is the same sort of thing whatever F may be. Therefore, what constitutes '(Ex)(Person S has x and x means F)' —or, in other words, 'Person S possesses concept F— must be constituted by the same sort of thing regardless of which concept F is (and, in particular, regardless of whether it is simple or complex).

The flaw in this reasoning, it seems to me, is the implicit assumption that any relational fact, $a\,R\,b$, must be constituted by combining whatever constitutes its three components, a, b, and R. That is the general rationale for assuming, in particular, that facts of the form 'x means F' must consist in facts of the form 'x bears relation R to the property of F-ness'. However, to see that this need not be so, consider the relational properties 'x exemplifies redness', 'x exemplifies doggyness', etc. What constitute these properties are simply 'x is red', 'x is a dog', and so on. Thus properties of the form 'x exemplifies F-ness' are not constituted by properties of the form 'x bears relation R to F-ness'. Similarly, we cannot take for granted that properties of the form 'x means F' (or, if concepts are properties, 'x means F-ness') are constituted by properties of the form 'x bears

R to F-ness'. But if they needn't be, then the argument for uniformity collapses. It becomes quite possible that 'x means RED' and 'x means RED DOG' are constituted by properties of very different kinds. Thus there is a line of thought leading to the uniformity principle, one which is *prima facie* plausible —but which on reflection should not persuade us.

I think the moral of this discussion is that Fodor is absolutely right to stress that compositionality, being one of the very few things we really know about concepts, can be put to useful work in helping us develope a general account of them. But its real import is not to rule out recognitional concepts, informational concepts, stereotype concepts, or indeed any theory of *primitive* concept constitution;[3] but rather to show that the principle of uniformity is false and that the possession condition for a complex concept can perfectly well be *possessing its constituents and knowing how they are combined*.

---

[3] Arguments against the constitution of word-meanings either by conceptual roles or by prototype structures are given by Jerry Fodor and Ernie Lepore in their "Why Meaning (Probably) Isn't Conceptual Role" (*Mind and Language* 6, 4, 1991) and their "The Pet Fish and The Red Herring: Why Concepts arn't Be Prototypes" (*Cognition* 58(2), Feb 1996, 243-276). But these arguments take for granted the uniformity principle, and so they are subject to the criticisms developed above.

Recognitional Concepts and Compositionality

Richard E. Grandy

Fodor's arguments against recognitional concepts appear very simple, but I will argue this simplicity is only superficial. Just below the surface lurk deep and complicated issues. I actually agree with him on his conclusion and title, but disagree about the validity of his arguments, and even over how many arguments he is putting forth.

The "Principle of compositionality" seems an obvious and deep insight. Yet giving a formulation of it that is:

1. relatively precise,

2. not obviously false,

3. not trivially true,

is extremely difficult and has hardly been addressed in the literature.

One major problem to contend with is that any serious statement of compositionality will have to take context into account —both the context of the sentence, but also the environment in which the sentence is uttered.

Compositionality is a word with strong connotations. It at least suggests that the meaning of a complex phrase is **composed** of the meanings of the parts, that it contains them. This metaphor invokes the sense in which a brick wall is composed of the bricks (plus the mortar). This analogy is also suggested by the fact that a complex linguistic phrase literally contains the words of which it is composed, at least in some cases. Even some syntactic cases are a little more complex. Most plurals are formed by combining a basic unit with a plural unit —the plural of "table" is "table" + "s", but there are the deviant cases such as "mouse" + "s" = "mice", "wolf" + "s" = "wolves", and so on. Is semantics as simple as syntax is in the standard cases? I think we should not assume so.

Actually Fodor suggests a more sophisticated version of compositionality —the meaning of the complex phrase is composed of parts of the meanings of the parts. I think that this view, while more sophisticated is still too simple. I was going to criticize him for having too simple a view of compositionality, but I now think that question is irrelevant to evaluating his arguments. The arguments fail, I will argue, on even the strongest view of compositionality,

Nonetheless, I want to wave a red flag about this kind of view of compositionality, which is widespread, whether Fodor holds it or not.

There seem to be some combinations which work by simply combining the meanings of the taking their conjunction as truth conditionis for the new term: pet fish, perhaps, red triangle, almost certainly. But I suggest that even 'red', and other color words, in many other combinations are not nearly so straightforward. A triangle is, typically, red if it is red all over. But a red apple is red only on the surface, while a pink grapefruit is pink only inside (and not all of the inside!) A car or house is red if a certain part of its exterior is red —windows don't count for either of them. The roof does not count for houses, but it does for cars unless they are convertibles!

A pen can be red by being red all over the surface, or, more commonly, by having red ink inside. The two conditions clearly diverge in many cases. But in context, e.g., if you have a bunch of pens in front of you —all of the mostly white on the surface and all with green ink but with varying colored caps, then if I ask for the red pen you will know in that context that I want the one with the red cap, even though in other contexts all of the pens are white and in other contexts they are all green!

In fact, we can readily imagine a red pen whose surface is entirely green and whose ink is blue when in the pen but which turns red when it leaves the pen and combines with oxygen in the atmosphere. I submit that if it writes red in a normal environment, it is red.

3. Recognitional Concepts and Compositionality

Returning more specifically to Fodor's arguments, first, let me note that there are two targets, neither very explicitly developed. One is the "prototype" or "stereotype" theorist of meaning, who holds that some/many/most/all concepts have as an essential element the ability to recognize prototypical examples of the concept.

The second target is all empiricists, including everyone and anyone who has ever whispered "criteria". I confess to being part of the latter group, though I would claim, that I did not inhale while whispering.

But no sane empiricist currently thinks that **all** concepts are recognitional, probably not even **most**, just enough to get us started. So it is only the end claim, that there are **NO** recognitional concepts that gets the attention of the sane empiricist. And of course the arguments must be much sharper to show that there are NO recognitional concepts, than is required to show that not ALL concepts are recognitional or that MOST concepts are not, or that even that ALMOST NO concepts are.

And notice an important ambiguity in the phrase "recognize good examples". The prototype theorist is committed to our being able to recognize good examples of red **as good examples**. The empiricist, however, is only committed to our recognizing good examples **as examples**.

Let's look at the arguments in more detail, again giving the most generous construal of compositionality:

> Strong Compositionality Assumption: The truth conditions of the compound "an F G" are formed by conjoining the truth conditions of F, call them A,B,C, and those of G, call them D,E.

> Fodor's Compositionality argument: If A is the recognitional capacity for Fs, then it follows that anyone who understands "an F G" has all of A-E, and thus has a recognitional capacity for F Gs.

While, given the Strong compositionality assumption, it follows that anyone who understands "an F G" has all of A-E, it does not follow that they must have a recognitional capacity for 'an F G" because that is not part of the conjunction. You can't "inherit" a recognitional capacity for the complex from the parts because it isn't there. Now if you have two recognitional concepts and conjoin them, you get recognitional capacities for both parts, but empirically it is known that you don't necessarily get the recognitional capacity for the complex by combining those for the parts. In fact, this is part of Fodor's argument.

The (insanely) strong prototype theorist, who holds that ALL concepts are recognitional and who holds that knowing the meanings of the parts suffices for knowing the meanings of the whole is refuted by this argument/observation.

But the moderate prototype theorist, who holds that many concepts are recognitional is not touched by this argument. Such theorists are at most in danger if such investigations tend to show that few concepts are recognitional, but given the vagueness of "few" the danger seems slight.

And the empiricist need not claim that you do get the recognitional, capacity, and the sane empiricist should not make that claim.

Against Steve Schiffer's comments at the APA, Fodor asked for a principled explanation of when the combination produces a recognitional concept and when it doesn't. I don't know Schiffer's answer, but I would suggest that the recognitional condition is **never required** to be a constitutive part of the complex expression. The default condition is the complex expressions are not recognitional —the exceptional case is when they are. And further details are a matter of empirical investigation.

In the paper Fodor presented at the APA meeting in Pittsburgh, he only presented the compositionality argument. But as an afterword, in response to Schiffer's comment, he presented a decompositionality argument, which he repeats here. He apparently believes it is the same argument, but I respectfully disagree.

> Decompositionality argument: Someone who grasps the concept "pet fish" may have the ability to identify prototypical examples of pet fish, but does not necessarily thereby have the ability to identify prototypical pets or prototypical fish. More abstractly, if someone grasps the concept associated with "an F G", on our supposition, knows that it has as conditions A-E. It does not follow that they know that A-C are associated with F and D,E with G.

The second argument seems more persuasive, but I think a large part of its persuasiveness depends on an identification of concepts and linguistic expressions. It seems clear that to understand the meaning of the phrase "red hair" it is necessary to understand the meanings of "red" and "hair". If we project from this that the meaning of "red hair" is a concept RED HAIR, then it is tempting to think that the concept must be complex for the linguistic expression is.

3. RECOGNITIONAL CONCEPTS AND COMPOSITIONALITY 25

But it is evident that someone can understand the concept RED HAIR without knowing the meaning of either 'red' or 'hair' —many billions of non–English speakers manage this feat quite well. What Fodor needs is a stronger premise that to grasp a complex concept requires not only knowing the conditions of the complex but knowing which conditions come from which component. He probably has arguments for this, but we haven't heard them, yet. Also in this neighborhood is the assumption that the concept associated with a linguistically complex expression is therefore a complex concept. I see no reason why a language might not be inefficient, or inept or indifferent and only have a complex expression for a simple concept. I doubt that the concept of an analog watch is shown to be cognitively complex by the fact that it now can be referred to by a complex expression. Many of us understood this concept under the simple designation "watch" before it acquired the complex designation as a new kind of watches was developed.

Recognitional Concepts and the Compositionality of Concept Possession*

Terry Horgan

1. Let me begin by reconstructing Fodor's argument, as I understand it. Premise P1 in the following argument is my reconstruction of Fodor's premise P. For me, the core argument is clearer if we dispense with talk of "inheritance," and with talk of states, capacities, and dispositions as "satisfiers" for a concept. The core idea involved in Premise P seems to be this: In order for a person to satisfy the possession conditions for a complex concept C, it is necessary and sufficient that the person satisfy the possession conditions for C's constituent concepts and also satisfy the possession conditions for C's mode of composition. (The rationale for this is that otherwise, the usual account of productivity fails.) I find it clearer to reformulate the Premise P as an expression of this idea —and to reconstruct the overall argument accordingly. So here's my reconstruction:

---

*I thank David Henderson, Michael Lynch, Matjaz Potrc, John Tienson, and Mark Timmons for helpful discussion and comments in a reading group on Jerry Fodor's recent work on concepts.

P1. One satisfies the possession conditions for a complex concept C iff: (i) one satisfies the possession conditions for each of C's constituent concepts, and (ii) one satisfies the possession conditions for C's mode of composition.

C1. If the possession conditions for PET include the capacity to recognize good instances of PET, and the possession conditions for FISH include the capacity to recognize good instances of FISH, then the possession conditions for PET FISH include the capacity to recognize good instances of PET FISH. [From P1.]

P2. The possession conditions for PET FISH do not include the capacity to recognize good instances of PET FISH.

C2. It's not the case that both (i) the possession conditions for PET include the capacity to recognize good instances of PET, and (ii) the possession conditions for FISH include the capacity to recognize good instances of FISH. *I.e.*, it's not the case that both PET and FISH are recognitional concepts. [From C1 and P2]

P3. Either PET and FISH are both recognitional concepts, or neither is.

C3. PET is not a recognitional concept. [From C2 and P3.]

P4. For every putative recognitional concept C, there is another putative recognitional concept C* such that the preceding argument for C3 applies, mutatis mutandis, to C and C*.

C4. There are no recognitional concepts. [From P4 and the argument for C3.]

2. I turn now from exposition to commentary. First, someone might claim that only one of the concepts PET and FISH are recognitional, and that this fact alone suffices to explain why PET FISH is not recognitional. More generally, someone might claim that whenever a complex concept fails to be recognitional, at least one of its constituent concepts is not recognitional. I won't pursue this line of thought here, but I note it for the record.

Second, the argument is not valid. Conclusion C1 does not follow from the principal premise P1, because P1 does not imply that for every cognitive capacity included in the possession conditions of all the constituent concepts, the possession conditions for the complex concept must include a matching cognitive capacity involving the complex concept itself. Thus, P1 does not exclude the possibility

4. RECOGNITIONAL CONCEPTS AND THE COMPOSITIONALITY... 29

that the possession conditions for a complex concept's mode of composition work in such a way that the property *being recognitional* does not "transfer" to the possession conditions of a complex concept from the possession conditions of its constituent concepts. To make the argument valid, Fodor would need to fill this logical lacuna with a suitable additional premise, and would need to defend that premise.

Now, in effect Fodor addresses this logical hole in the argument when he discusses the third objection he considers. Here's the objection, in his words: "Couldn't we just split the difference? Couldn't we just say that the satisfiers for the *primitive* concepts include recognitional capacities, even though the satisfiers for complex concepts don't?" (p. 8). The core of his reply is this:

> Simply not credible. If one's grasp of PET FISH isn't constituted by one's ability to recognize its instances, then, surely, one's grasp of FISH isn't constituted by one's ability to recognize *its* instances. And vice versa: if recognizing good instances like goldfish isn't a satisfier for the concept PET FISH, then recognizing good instances like (as it might be) trout, isn't a satisfier for the concept FISH. Surely, being able to recognize goldfish as pet fish must stand in *precisely* the same relation to having the concept PET FISH that being able to recognize trout as fish stands in to having the concept FISH. So, how could that relation be constitutive of concept possession in the one case but not in the other? (p. 8)

I have several preliminary comments about this reply, and then I'll turn to my main comment and some considerations it prompts. First, the claims in which the term 'surely' occurs are question-begging in this dialectical context. Someone who claims that PET and FISH are recognitional concepts, but who holds that recognitionality does not transfer from recognitional concepts to complex concepts of which they are the constituents, will deny these very claims.

Second, the plausibility of the claims in which the term 'surely' occurs seems to depend in part on the fact that it's somewhat dubious whether concepts like PET and FISH really *are* recognitional concepts. Concepts like RED seem like more plausible candidates for this status.

Third, in the quoted passage Fodor talks about whether or not the ability to recognize good instances *constitutes* a given concept, rather than talking about whether or not that ability *partially* constitutes the concept. This rhetorical move is important to notice, because (a) someone who holds that a given concept is recognitional is only committed to saying that the ability to recognize good instances is *part* of the possession conditions for the concept, and (b) the fact that there might be other conditions too is potentially relevant to whether or not the property *being recognitional* transfers from primitive constituent concepts to complex concepts. (Claim (a) is evidently built into the notion of a recognitional concept, as Fodor characterizes it; see clause (2) of his definition at the beginning of the paper.)

Fourth, in the quoted passage Fodor slides back and forth between talk of the ability to recognize *instances*, and talk of the ability to recognize *good* instances. This rhetorical move is worth noticing too, because (a) someone who holds that a given concept is recognitional is only committed to holding that the ability to recognize *good* instances is among the concept's possession conditions, and yet (b) the statements containing 'surely' in the above passage gain at least some of their air of plausibility from the fact that they trade on 'instance' rather than 'good instance'.

Fifth, in the quoted passage —and throughout the paper— Fodor under–emphasizes the role played by the possession conditions for a complex concept's *mode of composition*. When one keeps that role clearly in mind, it is easier to have doubts about whether the property *being recognitional* transfers from primitive concepts to complex concepts of which they are constituents.

In the end, though, it seems to me that none of these preliminary remarks matters very much. The crucial part of the passage lately quoted (and this is my principal comment on it) comes in the final sentence, where Fodor throws down a *challenge* to the fan of recognitional concepts, viz.: *How could* recognitionality be constitutive of certain primitive concepts but not constitutive of complex concepts composed from them, *given that concept possession is compositional in a way that makes it productive*? The passage raises this challenge, and the rhetorical force of the passage is to suggest that the fan of recognitional concepts has very little chance of being able to meet the challenge.

3. Let me now say something about how this challenge might be addressed, by someone who holds that although the possession conditions for certain concepts include the capacity to recognize good instances of the concept, this feature doesn't transfer to complex concepts of which the recognitional concepts are constituents. For concreteness, suppose that this hypothetical fan of recognitional concepts holds that PET and FISH are recognitional concepts, but that PET FISH is not one. (As I said earlier, concepts like RED seem like more plausible candidates for being recognitional than do PET or FISH. But leave that aside for now.)

4. RECOGNITIONAL CONCEPTS AND THE COMPOSITIONALITY... 31

The general idea involves two principal elements. First, articulate possession conditions for recognitional concepts in a way that incorporates something more than —something in addition to— the ability to recognize good instances of the concept. Second, articulate possession conditions for the *modes of composition* of complex concepts in a way that (i) draws upon these additional possession conditions for the constituent concepts, and (ii) does so in such a manner that the property *being recognitional* does not transfer from the constituent concepts to the complex concept.

Concerning the first element: A fan of recognitional concepts could say that the possession conditions for a recognitional concept include not only the ability to recognize good instances, but also the disposition to apply the concept to things by taking them to be *sufficiently relevantly similar* to good instances of that concept. This latter capacity involves some kind of "similarity metric" that is employed in applying the concept, a metric that is specific to the given concept (or perhaps to a genus–concept of which the given concept is a species). So the idea is that when one classifies something as a fish, one does so by taking the thing to be sufficiently relevantly similar to good, prototypical, instances of FISH. Likewise, when one classifies something as a pet, one does so by taking the thing to be sufficiently relevantly similar to good, prototypical, instances of PET.

Concerning the second element: Consider the complex concept PET FISH. Three factors are in play here: the concept PET, the concept FISH, and the relevant mode of combination —call it the *conjunctive* mode of combination. Plausibly, the possession conditions for the conjunctive mode of concept combination will involve cognitive dispositions of this sort: one will classify something as an instance of PET FISH by (i) taking it to be sufficiently relevantly similar to prototypical instances of PET, *and* (ii) taking it to be sufficiently relevantly similar to prototypical instances of FISH. (For some modes of combination, things can get more complicated. In the case of RED HAIR, for instance, the possession conditions presumably include this disposition: one will classify something as an instance of RED HAIR only if one takes it to be sufficiently relevantly similar, *for an instance of HAIR*, to prototypical instances of RED.)

Admittedly, the story as so far described is very sketchy indeed. Obvious worries arise about whether it can be carried through in adequate detail. In particular, it might or might not be possible to produce a detailed and workable theoretical account of how the concept–specific similarity metric works psychologically. There are also worries about whether this notion will turn out to be vitiatingly circular —that the only satisfactory way to explain what the similarity metric for PET is would be by appeal to the individual's prior, up-and-running, possession of the concept PET. In addition, theoretical problems certainly could arise (and *have* arisen in the psychological literature) in attempting to work out a suitable account of concept composition, especially in a way that is sufficiently general with respect to the kinds of concepts and the kinds of concept–combination that would need to be considered. But it's not obvious —not to me, anyway— that such problems couldn't be surmounted by some specific way of filling in the details theoretically.

Suppose, then, that the sketchy two–part story I've been telling can be elaborated in an adequate way. Well then, we thereby have an answer to Fodor's challenge to explain how the ability to recognize good instances could be part of the possession conditions for PET and for FISH but not part of the possession conditions for PET FISH. Explanation: The above–described possession conditions for the conjunctive mode of concept combination, together with the above–described possession conditions for PET and for FISH, just don't entail that someone who satisfies the possession conditions for PET FISH has the ability to recognize good instances of PET FISH —even though the stated possession conditions for PET and for FISH *do* include the ability to recognize good instances of those concepts.

And that's as it should be. For, what counts as a *good* instance of PET FISH depends on more than what is knowable just by virtue of being a competent user of this concept. A competent user does know, tacitly anyway, that something is an instance of PET FISH just in case (i) it is sufficiently relevantly similar to prototypical pets, and (ii) it is sufficiently relevantly similar to prototypical fish. But which kinds of fish are *good* instances of PET FISH is something that depends on additional facts about the world —in particular, what kinds of fish are typically used as pets, and what kinds are not.

Let me add that nothing I have said here should be taken to indicate that I actually *believe* the sort of story about concept–possession I have been sketching, or that I actually believe that there are recognitional concepts. I don't have developed opinions on these matters. I have been explaining why it seems to me, as someone who is agnostic on the issues, that Fodor's argument against recognitional concepts is not persuasive.

4. Even so, the question remains whether there is any good reason to believe in recognitional concepts. Speaking for myself, concepts like PET and FISH don't seem like especially credible cases. For, I don't really see why one couldn't learn these concepts *by description*,

4. RECOGNITIONAL CONCEPTS AND THE COMPOSITIONALITY... 33

so to speak, without thereby acquiring the ability to recognize good instances when confronted with them.

On the other hand, it seems to me much more plausible that concepts like RED are recognitional. Imagine someone blind from birth. Although such a person could certainly learn a lot about physics, about electromagnetic radiation of various wavelengths, about the effects of light of different wavelengths on the human visual system, about the uses of color words, etc., there remains a question whether such a person could actually acquire the concept RED. Many people, myself included, would be strongly inclined to say no. But if the answer is no, then contra Fodor, there is at least one recognitional concept, namely RED.

A More Plausible Kind of "Recognitional Concept"

Ruth Garrett Millikan

I find Fodor's argument against "recognitional concepts" very peculiar indeed. But I find the view that there are any "recognitional concepts" *of the kind he* (most directly) *impugns* equally peculiar. So I will take this opportunity to say a few words about another more plausible sort of concept that might actually better deserve the title "recognitional", and I will discuss the issue of compositionality for these concepts. In doing so, although I will not be defending the narrow target of Fodor's paper, I will be defending its broader target, the "epistemological" and/or "pragmatic" construal of what concepts are. But first I should say at least a word about why Fodor's argument seems to me so peculiar.

It's a sort of moebus strip argument. Rather than circularly assuming what it should prove, it assumes one of the things Fodor says he has disproved. It assumes that the extensions of those concepts thought by some to be recognitional are in fact controlled by stereotypes. Why do I say that? Because Fodor assumes that what makes an instance of a concept a "good instance" is that it is an average instance, that it sports the properties statistically most commonly found among instances of that concept. But that the "good instances" are always the common instances is remotely plausible only if we take concepts to be organized by stereotypes. True, a goldfish is not an average or stereotypical fish (*is* that true?) and the nursing profession is not average for a male and maleness is not average for a nurse. But there is surely is nothing *borderline* about the fishiness of a goldfish nor, typically, about the maleness of a male nurse or the petness of a pet fish. Notice also that good examples of some kinds of things are very hard to find, for example, good examples of the fallacy of accent, and good examples of wild children, and (nowadays) good examples of scurvy are hard to find. If good instances had to be instances that were average, including in respects having nothing to do with the point of the category being defined, and if recognitional concepts had to recognize by attending to average properties, then I suppose the recognitional ability defining the concept "sphere" would have to include the ability to tell whether a thing bounces!

Fodor says that a concept is recognitional if (1) it is at least partially constituted by its "possession conditions" (2) among which conditions is the ability to recognize some things that fall under it as such. But he also tells us that "if a concept is recognitional, then having certain kinds of experience would, in principle, show with the force of conceptual necessity that the concept applies". It is clear from this, and also from the text that follows, and also from the tradition that he is addressing, that the possession conditions for a recognitional concept are assumed to include more than just having some–ability–or–other to recognize those things that fall under the concept. They must include an ability to recognize those things *in some particular manner or manners*, these *manners* being what are really definitive of the recognitional concepts. That is, you cannot have the same recognitional concept that I do unless you rely on the same manner of recognizing. This leaves Helen Keller with very few recognitional concepts expressible in the English language.

Also, what the recognitional concept is *of* is supposed to be, just, whatever–it–happens–to–be–that–gets–recognized–by–using–this–criterion. That is, although the recognitional concept is said to be an "ability", it is not the sort of ability that entails a success in contrast to a failure. It would be clearer not to muddy things this way but to call it a plain old "disposition".

I wish to contrast this description of "recognitional concepts" with another possible description that conforms equally well to Fodor's original definition but has quite different consequences.

Suppose that we adopt a flatfooted realist ontology, admitting certain objectively ("theory independently") repeatable properties

5. A More Plausible Kind of "Recognitional Concept" 37

and Aristotelian–like substances to own these properties. Let the substances be things such as (1) people, pebbles and bridges (*c.f.*, Aristotle's primary substances), (2) water, gold, and peanut butter, (3) kinds such as dog–kind, geode–kind (*c.f.*, Aristotle's secondary substances) and phillips–screwdriver–kind. In the case of the kinds, just as in the case of the individuals and stuffs, although philosophers and sometimes even Nature can construct borderline cases, "for the most part" (as Aristotle was fond of saying) whether or not one has encountered or collected an example of a certain one of these kinds is written in nature itself, not just in English or !Kung. These kinds are real, not nominal. I will say more to back up this ontology soon. Right now I wish only to argue that its introduction makes possible another interpretation of Fodor's definition of "recognitional concepts".

A recognitional concept, Fodor said, is "partially constituted by... the ability to recognize some things that fall under it as such". Now how are we to interpret the phrase "as such"? Does it mean, say, that one is to recognize red as red rather than as green? And what would it be, exactly, to recognize red as green? Or what would it be, say, to recognize a cat as a dog? Would it be to apply the concept *green* to something red, or the concept *dog* to a cat? But then the definition is circular: it defines the concept *red* by reference to applications of the concept *red*, the concept *cat* by reference to applications of the concept *cat*. On the other hand, if the idea is that one should not confuse red with green, nor confuse dogs with cats, this cannot be made to fit with the notion that recognitional concepts are of just whatever they in fact recognize. This will not fit with the idea that "having certain kinds of experience would, in principle, show with the force of conceptual necessity that the concept applies". If the recognitional concept is taken to *define* its own extension, if its extension is whatever gets recognized under it, if it is whatever one is disposed to apply it to in using its criterion or criteria, surely the "as such" in the definition is entirely vacuous.

Suppose, on the other hand, that we take it that recognitional concepts recognize real properties, real individuals, real stuffs and real kinds. How *now* do we interpret the phrase "the ability to recognize some things that fall under "the concept— as such"? To re–cognize is to know again. To know something again *as such* must be to know that it *is* the same again, to identify it *as being* the same thing again. And one can be said to have an *ability* to do this only if it is possible to fail to do it, only if there are requirements on doing it that need not necessarily be met. But this will be the case exactly and only in so far as what one is trying to recognize has an objective identity independent of one's dispositions to recognize its identity. To make sense of Fodor's definition, we need a strong realist ontology.

Before asking whether we can have one, notice this consequence. If the methods that one uses to identify better, perhaps, "reidentify" an objective individual, property, stuff or kind do not determine the extension of one's concept of it but, rather, have the task of correctly locating that extension, then there may be room for alternative methods of recognizing the same thing, alternative ways to have the same conceptual ability, the same concept. It is easy here to get hung up on words. If I peel potatoes easily with a paring knife while you demand a proper potato peeler, do we have "the same ability", or not? We can both peel potatoes. That is what I have in mind. And it is that kind of ability that constitutes having "a concept" in the fundamental sense, of an Aristotelian substance. Identifying things the same *way* that someone else does is an added frill, more clearly labeled as having the same "conception" rather than the same "concept". The advantage of talking this way is that then Helen Keller gets to know English, assuming that speaking English requires having the concepts that correspond to English words.

How then do we do the ontology? I have said quite a lot on this elsewhere (Millikan 1983 chapters 14-17, forthcoming a, forthcoming b, forthcoming c) but if we are to tackle the question about compositionality, I must give a sketch. I'll only talk about "substances", where the idea is roughly this. A substance is the sort of thing that one can learn about on one occasion of meeting, various things that will be applicable also on other occasions of meeting, and where this is no accident, but the result of some principle of real connection. Thus if I meet Sam today and discover that he is strong and a good violinist, there is a good chance that if I meet him tomorrow or next week he will be strong and a good violinist. This is not a dead certainty, of course, but if it is true it is true for good reason, not by accident. Sam today causes Sam tomorrow, conserving many of his properties over time, in accordance with principles of conservation and principles of homeostasis. Of course there are only certain kinds of grounded inductions one can make over encounters with Sam. The fact that he is sitting today or angry today or playing tennis today does not mean he will be when I meet him tomorrow. Indeed, an important part of having a hold on Sam's identity, of having an adequate concept of Sam, is knowing roughly what kinds of inductions to draw over instances of meeting him. Understanding that he is a human person is in large part understanding which kinds of inductions these are. It is understanding not so much what

5. A More Plausible Kind of "Recognitional Concept" 39

properties he has, but what kinds of questions can sensibly be asked and answered about him.

Similarly, meeting gold on one occasion I can learn about its luster, malleability, density, color, tastelessness, conductivity, chemical inertness, and so forth, and when I encounter it again it will have these exact same properties, all of them. On the other hand, its shape, its size, its owner are none of them things that will carry over to the next meeting with gold, or if they do happen to carry over it will be an accident, not a grounded connection. Similarly, from one flat worm in the lab tray I can learn a great deal about other flat worms of the same species, as I spend perhaps hours dissecting it. And there is a good reason for this, for the genes in the gene pool from which the flat worm comes produce copies of themselves, and homeostatic principles operate in the dynamics of that gene pool to keep variety among the individuals of the species within strict limits.

Now try phillips screwdrivers. They are made to fit extant phillips screws which were made to fit then extant phillips screwdrivers and so forth, thus reproducing themselves in an indirect sort of way. Someone invented the phillips screwdriver possibly Phillips? And people have been copying that general design ever since, copying those aspects of it that were serviceable for certain purposes. There is a reason why phillips screwdrivers are much alike, why one can recognize them as a kindand draw rough inductions over them not many inductions to be sure, but the ones there are are well grounded. Compare also Gothic cathedrals and 1995 Nissan Sentras. The members of each of these kinds are alike for good reason too, and here the variety of possible well–grounded inductions is larger.

The broad picture is this. Basic concepts are concepts of real properties and real substances. They involve (I do not say "are") real, though inevitably fallible, abilities (not mere dispositions) to recognize these real entities. But typically the ability to recognize a substance or property is useful only if one can recognize it under a variety of different conditions: when it is near and when it is far; under various mediating conditions such as different lighting conditions and sound–carrying conditions; despite interference of static of various kinds. Think how many ways you have of recognizing manifestations bearing information about any member of your immediate family. You can use looks from a thousand angles, voice through many mediating conditions, handwriting, characteristic habits, clothing, and probably thousands of tidbits of identifying information. And notice two things.

First, these methods do not constitute a *definition* of that family member. Concepts of ones friends are not analytical concepts, but synthetical ones. The same is true for the ordinary person's concept of water and of cat–kind. The abilities to recognize that partially compose these concepts are not composed of prior concepts, not built on analytical definitions.

Second, though you have many ways of identifying each family member, similarly for water and cats, there will always be many conceivable conditions under which you wouldn't recognize them, conditions under which manifestations bearing information about them are not or would not be apparent to you. Moreover, in the case of less familiar substances it is quite possible to have recognitional concepts of them, in this sense, while lacking the ability to recognize them in their most common manifestations. For example, at the beginning of term I often have concepts of various students that I am not yet able to recognize anywhere outside my classroom. And I have a concept of the metal nickel, though I can only recognize it in the form of U.S. five cent pieces.

How now does Fodor's demand for compositionality fare when applied to this sort of recognitional concept? What happens when concepts of this sort are combined? Consider conjunctive concepts built on base substance concepts. Unlike the base concepts that compose them, typically these concepts will not themselves be concepts of substances of individuals, stuffs or real kinds. For example, black cats do not form a real kind. There is probably nothing to be learned (nonaccidentally) from one black cat about other black cats that does not follow independently either from their both being black or from their both being cats. From this it follows also that there is no way to recognize black cats without recognizing independently that they are black and also that they are cats. Putting this in Fodor's terms, the concept *black cat* "inherits all its satisfiers from its constituent concepts".

It does not *follow*, however, although it may happen to be true in this case, that if one has the concept of black and the concept of cat then one can recognize typical (Fodor says "good examples of") black cats, or recognize black cats under typical conditions. Try this example for illustration. Little Johnny is quite good at recognizing Daddy, and also quite good at recognizing Santa Clause costumes. It does not follow that he will recognizing Daddy in a Santa Clause costume. On the other hand, if he approaches Daddy in a Santa Clause costume from a certain special perspective, if he sees Daddy put on the costume, then he will recognize that it is Daddy in a Santa Clause costume. And that is all that is necessary for him to have a recognitional concept of Daddy in a Santa Clause costume. Parallel is recognizing male nurses and pet fish. Being able to recognize the most common cases straight off is not a requirement on a recognitional concept (in this sense) of anything.

But there is another sort of example to consider. Take red sulphur. It is an allotropic form of sulphur, having many of its own properties not characteristic of sulphur generally. It is an (Aristotelian) substance in its own right. It also happens to be the only substance that is both red and (pure) sulphur. So is the concept of red sulphur a compositional concept? For some people yes and for others no. Not knowing that sulphur that is red is a substance in its own right, one would only have an analytical concept of red sulphur. That is, one would never identify red sulphur in any other way than by noting that it was sulphur and noting that it was red. And one would not attempt inductions from one sample of red sulphur to another that would not have been attempted either from any sample of red to another or any sample of sulphur to another. On the other hand, one might instead have a synthetical concept of red sulphur, in which case it is conceivable that one wouldn't know it was red or even, perhaps, that it was sulphur. One might recognize it as the sticky so-smelling stuff typically found in such-and-such context. Similarly, I suggest, conceivably there are two ways to have a concept of Californians, though I'm sure even Fodor will admit that their status as a real kind is a bit looser than the status of red sulphur as a real stuff.

BIBLIOGRAPHY

Millikan 1983, *Language, Thought, and Other Biological Categories*, (Bradford Books/MIT Press, 1984).

———, forthcoming a, "A Common Structure for Concepts of Individuals, Stuffs, and Basic Kinds: More Mama, More Milk and More Mouse", *Behavioral and BrainSciences*.

———, forthcoming b, "Historical Kinds and the Special Sciences", *Philosophical Studies*.

———, forthcoming c, "With Enemies Like These I Don't Need Friends", replies to commentaries on (Millikan forthcoming a), *Behavioral and BrainSciences*.

Implicit Conceptions, Understanding and Rationality*

Christopher Peacocke

I will be advocating the importance of what I will call *implicit conceptions* in the theories of linguistic understanding, of concepts and of rationality. I will try to say something about why we need implicit

---

*Earlier versions of this material were presented as an Invited Lecture at the 1996 Barcelona meeting of the European Society for Philosophy and Psychology, and as seminars at the Universities of Hamburg and St. Andrews, and at New York University. At a presentation at the Pittsburgh meeting of the Central Division of the American Philosophical Association in 1997, my commentator was Tyler Burge; and at a presentation at the 1997 meeting of the Conference on Methods in New York, my commentators were Georges Rey and Gideon Rosen. I am very grateful for all their comments, from which I have learned much. It will soon be apparent to those who have followed my earlier efforts that the present paper involves a significant change of view. In grappling with these issues, I have been helped too by the comments and advice of Paul Boghossian, Ned Block, Bill Brewer, John Campbell, Martin Davies, Hartry Field, Wolfgang Künne, Barry Loewer, Stephen Schiffer, Stewart Shapiro, John Skorupski and Crispin Wright. I have also taken the opportunity to correct a mistake pointed out to me by Eric Margolis in private discussion at the SOFIA meeting. Once again, I acknowledge with gratitude the support of the Leverhulme Trust. Without one of their Research Professorships, none of this work would have been possible.
© Copyright C. Peacocke 1998.

conceptions; how we can discover them; what they explain; and what they are. Implicit conceptions also seem to me capable of furthering our understanding of some classical and recent issues in the theory of meaning and knowledge.

Several forces pulled me towards this position on implicit conceptions. One was a growing dissatisfaction with the treatment of primitive axioms and rules given in *A Study of Concepts* (1992). Another was reflection on what is involved in rational acceptance of new principles which do not follow from those a thinker already accepts. A third force was my attraction to the conception of sense expounded and developed in Tyler Burge's paper "Frege on Sense and Linguistic Meaning" (1990).

1 Implicit Conceptions

Consider someone who is introduced to a primitive logical axiom, or to a primitive logical rule. This person might be yourself, when you were first taught logic at around the age of eighteen. Your introduction might be to an axiom $A \supset (A \text{ or } B)$, or it might be to the inference rule 'From A, the conclusion A or B can be inferred'. There is such a phenomenon as a thinker in your situation reflecting, drawing on his understanding of the expressions in the rule, and coming to appreciate that the axiom or rule is valid. What is going on when such reflection takes place?

The example is specified as one in which the axiom or principle is a primitive one: it is not something which is derivable from other axioms or rules. So the movement of thought in which our rational, reflective thinker is engaged cannot be one of straightforward inference. Nor is it a matter of accepting a stipulation involving some newly introduced symbol. The axiom or rule is appreciated, on reflection, as correct when taken as involving the very same words, such as "or", which an eighteen-year old learner of logic, for instance, will have understood for more than fifteen years. Nor is it plausible that our thinker has to draw on memories of his own previous uses of the word "or" on particular occasions. The logical principle is not about his use of the word. In any case, if he is like me, he will not remember any particular occasions as ones on which he used that very word. All the same, he can still reflect, drawing on his understanding of the word, and come to appreciate that the axiom or principle is valid.

Our thinker's knowledge cannot always be explained as a result of his having explicitly inferred the validity of the axiom or principle from his explicit knowledge of the truth-tables for the connectives involved. This cannot be a fully satisfying explanation for two rea-

6. IMPLICIT CONCEPTIONS, UNDERSTANDING AND RATIONALITY

sons. First, our thinker can reflect and rationally appreciate the validity of these principles before having been explicitly taught any truth tables. Second, and crucially, we must also think about rational acceptance of the truth–tables themselves. Each of us, when first presented with the truth–tables for the unproblematic connectives, was able to reflect, and come rationally, on the basis of our understanding of the expressions, to appreciate that the particular truth–table is correct. This is itself a further illustration of the kind of phenomenon we are trying to explain.

No doubt there are various different detailed ways in which reflection may proceed in the original case of the axiom or principle, but one of them is as follows. Like the other variants in which the details differ, the reflection involves a simulation exercise. The thinker imagines —to start with one of the cases— that A is true and B is false. His aim is to address the question of whether the alternation 'A or B' should be regarded as true or false in the imagined circumstances. As in any other simulation exercise, he then exercises a capacity off–line. This capacity is the very same, understanding–based capacity he would be exercising in a real case in which he had the information that A is true and B is false and has to evaluate the alternation 'A or B'. As in the corresponding real case, in the imaginative exercise he goes on to hold that 'A or B' will be true in the imagined circumstances. In coming to hold that 'A or B' is true in the simulated circumstances, our thinker employs only the information about the truth–values, within the simulation, of A and of B, together with his understanding of alternation. He does not draw on any other resources.

Next our thinker proceeds to consider imaginatively another case, say that in which A is true and B is true .. As he goes through the cases, he is eventually in a position rationally to accept that there will be no cases in which the antecedent, or premiss, is true, and the consequent, or conclusion, is false for the axiom or inference–rule respectively. Thus he comes rationally to accept the axiom or rule as valid. The same procedure and resources will equally allow him to come to accept rationally each line of the truth–table for some connective he understands. When axioms, inference rules, or lines of truth–tables are reached in this way, it seems to me that the resulting judgements constitute knowledge.[1]

---

[1] *A Study of Concepts* claimed that certain axioms are found primitively compelling by those who understand their terms. The description I have just given in the text does not contradict that claim. The problem with *A Study of Concepts* is rather that it gives no elucidation of the rationality of accepting primitive axioms.

This account of the reflection gives a clear explanatory priority to the thinker's understanding-based capacity to evaluate particular alternations, such as "Either he went left or he went right", and particular conjunctions, and other complex statements, on the basis of information about their components. This is a capacity which a thinker can possess and exercise, and normally does do so, prior to having any explicit knowledge of general logical principles or of truth–tables. It is this capacity which is run off–line in the simulation. It is a capacity involved in the very understanding the connectives. Its role in the imaginative exercise makes the case one in which the thinker draws upon his own understanding of the expressions in coming to appreciate, via this reflection, that the axiom or principle is valid.

I suggest further that the thinker's understanding of the connective "or" involves (and perhaps is even to be identified with) his possession of an implicit conception, a conception with the following content: that any sentence of the form 'A or B' is true if and only if either A is true or B is true. Similarly at the level of thought: a thinker's grasp of the concept of alternation involves (and is perhaps to be identified with) his possession of an implicit conception with the content that any Thought (content) of the form A or B is true if and only if either A is true or B is true. Such implicit conceptions are influential in the thinker's evaluation of alternations given information about the truth–values of their components. The influence is exerted not by the thinker inferring something from the content of the implicit conception. He need not have any explicit knowledge of its content. Rather, his having the implicit conception explains his particular patterns of semantic evaluation of the complex, given information about the truth–values of its constituents. Derivatively, it is this implicit conception which is influential in the simulational part of the reflection which eventually leads him to accept certain primitive axioms and inferential rules involving alternation.

This, then, is a description at the personal level of a way in which a thinker may come rationally to accept a logical principle, a way which is not simply a matter of inferring it from other previously accepted object–language principles. Before I give other examples of implicit conceptions, I want to clarify certain features of this non–inferential but rational means of acceptance.

Simply saying that they are noninferentially accepted is much too undiscriminating. Adding that they are noninferentially accepted on the basis of the thinker's understanding at least makes clear that understanding plays an explanatory role. It does, though, still fail to say what 'on the basis of' amounts to here, or to say how rationality is implicated.

6. IMPLICIT CONCEPTIONS, UNDERSTANDING AND RATIONALITY

(a) The very simple description I have given of the rational acceptance of a logical axiom is not meant to enable us to resolve the dispute between classical and constructivist, or any other, interpretation of the logical constants. Nor could it provide such a resolution. The phenomena cited in this simple description of the case are phenomena of a general kind which would equally need to be mentioned in an account how it is that an ordinary, nonphilosophical thinker can come to appreciate that certain axioms are valid, even if a constructivist theory of meaning were correct. The constructivist is likely to elucidate validity of a transition as the transformabilility of any means of establishing its premises into a means of establishing its conclusion. To work out whether this definition applies to a particular form of transition, the ordinary thinker will have to use simulation to gain knowledge of the ways in which he takes statements of certain forms to be established. Imaginative simulation will be involved in any case in which the thinker is drawing, at least on early occasions, on the understanding he exercises in ordinary, real-world applications. This is something common to classical and to constructivist approaches. Any resolution of the dispute between them must appeal to a quite different body of considerations.

(b) The described means of rationally coming to accept a primitive law is a fallible means. A thinker may overlook a combination of truth-values, or may perform the simulation incorrectly. He may fail to run the very same procedure for evaluation off-line as he would exercise on-line. He may misremember information derived from earlier simulations in which he was checking cases. He may use a procedure in imaginatively assessing particular cases which is not just understanding-based, but draws on auxiliary information specific to those particular cases. Much, then, may go wrong. Nonetheless, when the procedure is properly executed, the resulting belief in the logical law has an *a priori* status. No perceptual state, nor the deliverance of any other causally sensitive faculty for finding out about the world, is playing an essential *justificational* role in the thinker's rational acceptance of the logical law when it is arrived at in this way. This combination of fallible capacities which, when exercised properly, are nevertheless capable of yielding *a priori* knowledge, is something with which we are very familiar in other routes to *a priori* knowledge.

(c) An objector may protest that simulation can never give knowledge of what would be true in the circumstances imagined in the simulation, but can only give knowledge of what the simulating thinker would judge or believe in the imagined circumstances. This, though, seems to me to be false. Simulations, properly executed, can give information about the world, as well (of course) as information about the thinker's mental state in various hypothetical circumstances. Suppose you are asked the question: "If you walk south down Whitehall, and turn left over Westminster Bridge, when you are on the bridge, what building is slightly to the left of straight ahead of you?". You answer this by imagining yourself following the described route. When, by this means, you reach the conclusion that when on the bridge, the former County Hall would be slightly to the left of straight ahead, this is a means of obtaining information about the world. If they are knowledgeable states which the thinker is drawing upon in performing the simulation, it is also a means of obtaining knowledge about the world. It is important to emphasize that the conditions initially specified to hold in the simulation, both in this spatial example and in our logical case, concern not merely what the subject believes in the simulated circumstances, but what is true in the simulated circumstances.

Of course this spatial example involves sensory imagination, and such experiential imagination does not need to be involved in the simulations I have been considering in the logical case. It is rather a form of suppositional imagining in the logical cases. It is important, though, that even imagining what else would be the case when something is suppositionally imagined to hold still involves simulational capacities. It is a constraint on suppositionally imagining properly, and indeed in reasoning properly from a supposition, that one carry over to the supposed state of affairs the holding of certain transitions that one would be prepared to make in the actual world, in non–suppositional cases. Thus there is a first–personal element which does not simply disappear when we consider non–sensory, merely suppositional imagination.

(d) A thinker of a certain frame of mind sometimes classified as neo–Wittgensteinian may wonder whether there is really any objectivity in what is obtained by the simulation procedure as applied in the logical case. This is not the point in this paper to take on central Wittgensteinian issues, and for present purposes I just note the plausibility of the following biconditional. The results of the simulation, properly carried out, will have the required objectivity if and only if there is objectivity in a thinker's corresponding response to a new case in the real, non–simulational, world. If there is objectivity of the latter, that is if it goes beyond merely an impression of correctness, then the capacity exercised on–line in the real–world cases can be drawn upon in carrying through the simulation.

That concludes the preliminary remarks on the nature of the simulation in this first example. It is not hard to reach, by reflection,

6. IMPLICIT CONCEPTIONS, UNDERSTANDING AND RATIONALITY 49

principles distinctive of alternation, and in doing so to be appropriately influenced by one's underlying implicit conception. It is not even hard, in that particular example, to make the content of the implicit conception explicit. In other examples, neither of these things is so. There are some cases in which a thinker has an implicit conception, but is unable to make its content explicit. The thinker may even be unable to formulate principles distinctive of the concept his possession of which consists in his possession of that implicit conception.

One of the most spectacular illustrations of this is given by the famous case of Leibniz's and Newton's grappling with the notion of the limit of a series, a notion crucial in the explanation of the differential calculus. It would be a huge injustice to Leibniz and Newton to deny that they had the concept of the limit of a series, or to deny that they had propositional attitudes describable by using the word 'limit' within the 'that...' clauses. What they could do was to differentiate particular functions, and they had no difficulty in saying what the limit of a particular series of ratios was. I would say that each of these great thinkers had an implicit conception which explained their application of the phrase "limit of..." in making judgements about the limits of particular series of ratios. What they could not do, despite repeated pressing by critics and well–wishers, was to make explicit the content of their implicit conceptions. When pressed for explications, Leibniz spoke of values that were infinitely close to one another. This is something we can now make sense of in the theory of infinitesimals, but was quite illegitimate within the ontology of real numbers within which Leibniz was working. Newton spoke of 'limiting values', 'ultimate ratios', and the like, but these were not given a steady explanation. Sometimes the procedures given even seem to require dividing by zero. Newton comes extremely close to a correct explication at one point, but gives that explanation no special salience amongst the others. If their explications were really the best that could be given, it would be hard not to sympathize with Berkeley's critique of the calculus. Even John John Bernoulli, in trying to sort the matter out, wrote sentences like this:

[...] a quantity which is diminished or increased by an infinitely small quantity is neither increased nor decreased.[2]

As is well–known, it was not until Bolzano, Cauchy and arguably even until Weierstrass in the mid–nineteenth century that a com-

---

[2] Quoted by Ian Stewart in *From Here to Infinity* (1996, p. 77).

pletely clear, unproblematic explication of the limit of a series was achieved, the familiar epsilon–delta definition. L is the limit of the function $f(x)$ as x approaches a if for any positive number e, there is some number d such that $f(x)$ minus L is less than e whenever x minus a is less than d. In this explication there is, famously, no unexplained talk about ultimate ratios, infinitely small values, nor anything which even appear to involve dividing by zero. To make an implicit conception explicit can, then, on occasion be a major intellectual achievement.[3]

The case of Leibniz, Newton and limits also serves to illustrate another point. We do sometimes ascribe attitudes to contents containing a concept to a thinker, even when a thinker has only a partial understanding of the expression for the concept, provided that the thinker defers in his use of the expression to others in the community who understand it better, and provided that the thinker has some minimum level of understanding. That phenomenon has been very well described by Burge (1979). But we ought not assimilate the example of early uses of the limit–concept to cases of deference, for the facts explained by implicit conceptions cannot be explained away by appealing to deference. To whom were Leibniz and Newton supposed to defer? There was no one else who understood the notion better. Nor, one may conjecture from each of their characters, was either of these two gentlemen of a mind to defer to anyone else on these (or any other) matters.

Leibniz's and Newton's use of the limit–concept is rather a non–deferential example of what Frege called grasping a definite sense, whilst also failing to grasp it 'sharply' —that is, an example whose philosophical explanation does not involve social elements. The present paper is in effect an exploration of what is involved in employing concepts which are not 'sharply grasped', and in which the social/individual divergences are not the crux of the matter. Actually, the very example of the limit–concept occurs in a list in the first section of Frege's *Foundations of Arithmetic*: "The concepts of function, of continuity, of limit and of infinity have been shown to stand in need of sharper definition" (1953, §1). The early use of the concept of a limit in Leibniz and Newton is a concrete historical illustration

---

[3]Did Newton and Leibniz actually operate with different, but equivalent, implicit definitions of the limit? Newton's informal explications are closer to the Bolzano–Cauchy–Weierstrass definition, while, at first blush, Leibniz's seem like those one would give in the theory of infinitesimals. Ishiguro (1990, chapter V), however, argues that "infinitely small" was regarded as contextually defined by Leibniz, and so not thought by him to be referential vocabulary.

6. IMPLICIT CONCEPTIONS, UNDERSTANDING AND RATIONALITY

of a state of affairs whose possibility is articulated by Burge. In the course of elaborating Frege's conception of grasp which is not sharp, Burge writes: "The striking element in Frege's view is his application of this distinction to cases where *the most competent speakers, and indeed the community taken collectively,* could not, even on extended ordinary reflection, articulate the 'standard senses' of the terms" (1990, p. 46, Burge's italics). That was precisely the position of Leibniz and Newton in relation to terms for limits. So the Fregean view, Burge's account, and the description I am in the course of developing would all firmly distinguish this phenomenon from that of attributions of concepts legitimized by the existence of deference in the use of expressions.

Some of the intellectual skills required to succeed in making an implicit conception explicit will be skills useful in any enterprise of building an explanation from instances. Choosing the right classification of cases matters. The right classification of cases is a relatively trivial matter for the logical connectives (or at least, it is so once one has settled on a particular kind of semantic theory). It is somewhat less trivial to articulate the implicit conception involved in understanding the word "chair". It is definitely non-trivial to make explicit what is involved in being the limit of a series. Equally, skill in appreciating the full range of cases matters too, as those failed attempts to define "chair" which omitted ski-lift chairs showed. So, even though in trying to articulate one's own implicit conceptions, one is trying to articulate what is influencing one in making judgements involving the concept in particular cases, the skills and methodology involved are those pertinent to any abductive investigation. Achieving such an articulation is not simply a matter of passively allowing the content of some implicit conception to float into consciousness from the subpersonal level.

Since it can be hard to make explicit the content of one of one's own implicit conceptions, we should equally not be surprised if thinkers sometimes mischaracterize the content of their implicit conceptions. A thinker's explicit endorsement of an incorrect definition does not mean that he does not have an implicit conception whose content is the correct definition. The attribution of a content to an implicit conception is fundamentally answerable to its role in explaining the thinker's ordinary applications of the concept in question. Examples are primary in the attribution of content to the implicit conception. Thinkers can be good at classifying cases, and bad at articulating the principles guiding their classifications. Ordinary thinkers, who understand the predicate "chair" perfectly well, often give an incor-

rect definition when pressed for one. And if Leibniz and Newton can mischaracterize their own grasp of a concept, how can the rest of us expect never to be in error on such matters?
How wide is the range of concepts and expressions with which implicit conceptions are associated? The examples of implicit conceptions I have offered so far have been associated with logical and mathematical concepts, and have involved definitions. Implicit conceptions involving definition may, though, be found in almost any domain. A significant segment of moral and political thought, for example, consists in making explicit the implicit conceptions and constraints which explain our applications of such notions as fairness, equality and opportunity. At the other end of the spectrum, I think we need to employ implicit conceptions in characterizing the mastery even of some observational concepts. In mastering the concept *cube*, taken as an observational concept, a thinker must have an implicit conception with a content which includes this: that cubes are closed figures formed from square sides joined at right angles along their edges. Not all examples will be so trivial. In the case of any philosophically interesting concept, the question of the content of the implicit conception underlying it will be highly substantive. Answering the question will in such cases involve making some substantive advance in the subject–matter in question.[4]

The benefits of successfully making explicit the content of some previously merely implicit conception are multiple and various. Since having a merely implicit conception is fundamentally tied to judgements about particular examples, the first benefit of an explicit statement is that of generality. Leibniz and Newton had no difficulty giving the limits of particular series of ratios. What they did not knowledgeably formulate was the general, universally quantified biconditional stating the relation in which a number had to stand to a series to be its limit. The generality brings much in its wake. In particular, it provides a crucial tool needed to prove general theorems about limits. A second benefit of making the conception explicit, one for which the generality also matters, is the possibility of fully defending the legitimacy of the notion. Only with a general, explicit statement of what it is to be the limit of a series is a theorist in a position to give a fully satisfactory answer Berkeley's critique of the notion. A third benefit is which Frege notes that proofs can also bring: correct definition can help to establish "the limits to the

---

[4] I do not hold that all concepts involve implicit conceptions. That threatens to be regressive. It is also quite unmotivated in the case of the more basic observational concepts.

validity of a proposition" (*Foundations of Arithmetic*, §1 again). In general, proof and definition will do this hand–in–hand. Proofs usually require some definition of the notion in question. Equally, the fruitfulness of the definition can be established only by investigating what can be proved from it. A fourth benefit, like the second, also has to do with justification. Someone who knows the explicit characterization can give a rationale for his classification of particular examples. This applies both in mathematical and logical cases, and in the moral and political examples. Any general constraints on fairness, for instance, which we can discover and formulate with generality will allow us to argue much more forcibly that some particular procedure or arrangement is, or is not, unfair.[5]

If a thinker has an implicit conception, there will be a certain psychological relation in which he stands to a content which specifies the content of that conception. The nature of that psychological relation is something which I will be discussing imminently. I do, though, want to distinguish sharply between this relation which is under investigation, and at least one familiar notion of tacit or virtual belief. This is the notion of tacit belief which is most trivially illustrated by such examples as an ordinary person's belief that cars are not edible, and perhaps less trivially by an ordinary person's beliefs about an interlocutor with whom he is engaged in a conversation —his rationality, or perhaps some of his higher–order attitudes. Mark Crimmins seems to me to have made a good case that these examples of tacit belief can be elucidated as ones in which for a person to at–least–tacitly believe that p is for it to be as if the person has an explicit belief in p (1992, p. 248). In paradigmatic cases, Crimmins says, this elucidation could be paraphrased more specifically by saying that the tacit believer's cognitive dispositions are relevantly as if he has an explicit belief in p (1992, p. 249). However, the case of Leibniz and Newton having an implicit conception of the correct definition of the limit of a series is a case in which their cognitive dispositions are not relevantly as if they had an explicit belief in the correct definition. For the explicit believer, the correct definition is not news; whereas the Bolzano–Cauchy–Weierstrass definition was certainly news. (The point applies even to the modest case of the correct definition of "chair".)

---

[5]Here too I am at one with Burge's elaboration of the Fregean position: "I think that Frege's conception attempts to bridge the gap between actual understanding and actual sense expression by means of a normative concept —that of the deeper foundation or justification for actual understanding and usage" (1990, p. 47).

It follows that the sense of 'limit' as used by Leibniz and Newton —its contribution to cognitive value— cannot be identified with the correct explicit definition of 'limit'. Burge has made the same point forcefully for a different range of examples (1986, p. 715-7). It is worth noting that the distinction between cognitive value and correct explicit definition applies both in cases which have no externalist character, such as the case of limits, and in cases like 'chair', which do. In both kinds of case, it is plausibly the close tie between ordinary employment of the sense and the ability to correctly classify examples which brings with it the distinction between the ordinarily used sense and the more theoretical explicit definition. The close tie with particular examples can be present both in cases where there is external individuation of the concept, and in cases where there is not.

Maybe some substantial restriction on the range of phenomena considered in verifying the "as if" clause in Crimmins' characterization would capture tacit conceptions as a special case of a generic notion of virtual belief.[6] The natural restriction would cut the range of phenomena down to certain canonical applications of the concept for which an implicit conception is being given. In the case of the limit example, we might be restricted to considering the thinker's ability to calculate the limits of particular series. My point at present, however, is that some such substantial restriction is required. There may be a spectrum of tacit and virtual beliefs here, but implicit conceptions are not at the same point along it as many more familiar examples of tacit belief.[7]

2 Deflationary Readings Rejected

What I have said so far can be greeted with varying degrees and kinds of scepticism. One important deflationary reaction is the complaint that the implicit conceptions of which I have spoken are simply projected backwards from the actual inferential and classificatory dispositions of thinkers. The complaint would run thus: insofar as it is

---

[6]Crimmins considers a range of grades of "as if" clauses at p. 257.

[7]Near the start of his paper (p. 241), Crimmins also says that the notion of tacit belief may be needed to explain the relation between thinkers and non-trivial analyses of concepts. The Bolzano–Cauchy–Weierstrass definition is a non-trivial analysis of a concept. It is, then, a question whether it is quite the same standard, or grade of strictness, of "as if" clause that we need to accommodate both the more trivial examples of tacit belief and the non-trivial analyses.

6. IMPLICIT CONCEPTIONS, UNDERSTANDING AND RATIONALITY   55

legitimate to speak of implicit conceptions at all, they serve simply to summarize the actual classificatory and inferential propensities of those who understand the expressions in question. But, the complaint continues, the implicit conceptions neither explain nor justify anything. What constitutes understanding are the particular inferential and classificatory dispositions, rather than anything which underlies them.

The first consideration I offer in reply is that a person's understanding of an expression may outrun natural generalizations of all the principles he has ever encountered, or could be expected to come up with. A natural illustration of the point is provided by non–standard models of first–order arithmetic, which contain blocks of 'non–natural' numbers which follow after all the genuine natural numbers. It seems clear that an ordinary person's understanding of the expression "whole number" definitely counts non–standard models *as* non–standard. One principle whose truth excludes non–standard models is the w–rule: in one form, this is the rule that if '$F(0)$', '$F(1)$', '$F(2)$',... are all provable in the given system, then so is 'All natural numbers are F'. Another such principle is a second–order induction axiom with a quite specific and highly general understanding of the range of the second–order quantifiers. Now ordinary thinkers, who use and understand the expression "whole number", have no conception of any such principles. Nor, for many hundreds of years, did anyone else. All the same, it seems to me that the ordinary thinker's understanding of the expression "natural number", and that of everyone more than a century–and–a–half ago, would count the non–standard models as non–standard. That these models of first–order formulations exist would hardly have been striking otherwise. Their designation as non–standard was not simply a matter of stipulation, convention or a resolution of some indeterminacy.

It is at this point in the discussion that the deflationist about implicit conceptions may be tempted to appeal to counterfactuals. He may suggest that what matters is that our ordinary thinkers would acknowledge these principles as correct on their understanding of "whole number", were they to be presented with these principles. This seems to me to be a decidedly optimistic view of the person in the street (or many other places) when we imagine that person presented with the w–rule, or with unrestricted second–order induction. But let us waive that. We will waive it by allowing, more specifically, that there may some non–question–begging restriction R such that if someone has the ordinary concept of a whole number, and meets this restriction R, then he would acknowledge such principles as the w–rule, or unrestricted second–order induction, as correct.

The important issue here is: does that help the deflationary reading of implicit conceptions?

It seems to me that it does not. Intuitively, a person's prior understanding of the predicate "is a whole number" *explains* why the counterfactual is true of him. When all is working properly, a person who understands the predicate "is a whole number" uses that understanding to work out that the w–rule is correct. The present deflationist is wrongly offering a kind of identification rather than an explanation.

This first deflationist is also vulnerable to a near–ubiquitous problem with counterfactual analyses of categorical notions. We must be able to distinguish between someone who has an understanding of "is a whole number" in advance, and someone who gains it in the course of his coming to meet the antecedent of the counterfactual. This distinction is incompatible with identifying understanding with something which simply has his satisfaction of the counterfactual as one primitive constituent.

I would say that the counterfactuals, when they are true of a thinker, and properly result from his prior understanding of the predicate "is a whole number", are explained by his possession of a specific implicit conception of the range of that predicate. My own view is that the content of that particular implicit conception should make essential use of primitive recursion with a limiting clause. Its content is given by three primitive principles:

(1) "is a whole number" is true of 0

(2) "is a whole number" is true of the successor of anything it is true of; and

(3) nothing falls under "is a whole number" unless it can be shown to do so on the basis of rules (1) and (2).

Clause (3), on its intuitive understanding, excludes the non–standard models. It is worth noting that no explicit use of the notion of finiteness, or second–order properties, or reference to reasoning by arithmetical induction, occurs in this statement of the implicit conception.[8]

---

[8]Here I diverge from Field (1996), who brings in cosmological considerations to make sense of a determinate notion of finiteness, and to rule out non–standard models. On the position I am advocating, primitive recursion with a limiting clause like (3) is explanatorily more fundamental than the general notion of finiteness. We do not need to rely on any empirical truths about the physical universe

6. IMPLICIT CONCEPTIONS, UNDERSTANDING AND RATIONALITY

These points may just encourage our deflationist further, to say that a thinker's understanding of "is a whole number" consists in no more than his willingness to accept as correct an explicit statement of *this* primitive recursion with a limiting clause. But the distinctions of two paragraphs back remain. The implicit conception explains acceptance, when there is rational acceptance based on the thinker's own understanding. This deflationist would also, of course, have to grapple with the problem of the willingness of some thinkers to accept incorrect explications of particular concepts.

This first deflationist view I have been considering may seem like a no-nonsense position, opposed to mysterious views of understanding which transcend the knowable. But in fact nothing in what I have said should encourage the view that implicit conceptions are somehow transcend the knowable. There would be a commitment to such transcendence if it were allowed as a possibility that there could be two thinkers whose rational judgements about particular applications of an expression, and about principles involving it, are in actual and counterfactual circumstances identical, and who yet have differing implicit conceptions. Nothing I have said entails that that is a possibility. I have, on the contrary, been emphasizing the role of implicit conceptions in the explanation of particular judgements involving the expression or concept. The upshot is, then, that insofar as we see rejection of this sort of transcendence as desirable, its rejection is not unique to the deflationist. Rejection of transcendence cannot be used in support of the deflationist's view.

So far I have been concentrating on points about explanation; but I also promised a second point in reply to the deflationist's objection that what I say about implicit conceptions is no more than a summary of truths about inferential dispositions. The second point emerges from the question: how is the deflationist to specify the inferential dispositions of which he says that implicit conceptions are not more than a summary? The second point starts from the fact not any old inferential disposition can be included. Ordinary logical inferences are rational transitions. They are not blind leaps into the dark, inclinations to make transitions in thought which just grip and take over the thinker's rational self. (On this, I am totally

---

to classify the non-standard models as non-standard. It has of course to be part of this position that the modal 'can' which occurs essentially in (3) is not itself to be elucidated in arithmetical terms not governed by an implicit conception — otherwise the problem of non-standard interpretations would be with us again. I also note for the record that it is an obligation of the present position to say why the modal approach is to be preferred to second-order characterizations of the natural numbers.

in agreement with Brewer (1995).) I tried at the start of this paper to say something about how a thinker's implicit conception can make rational acceptance of even a primitive axiom or inference rule. The phenomenon we highlighted was not merely that our learner of logic is unable to see how a primitive logical law might fail to hold in the actual world. It is rather that he has a quite specific positive means of rationally reaching the view that the particular law in question will always be true. How might our deflationist try to account for the rationality of accepting primitive axioms or inference rules?

He may just say that the rationality of acceptance is explained by the fact that these axioms and inference rules are evidently correct for the truth–functions, or higher–level functions, expressed by logical vocabulary. They are indeed evidently correct; but the point cannot serve the deflationist's purpose, again for two reasons. One reason is that the deflationist had better say *why* these are the correct truth–functions and higher–level operations to associate with the logical expressions. Those specific semantic assignments are hardly given in advance, and what makes them the correct assignments must have something to do with what is involved in understanding these expressions.The theorist of implicit conceptions will insist that they are the correct assignments because they capture precisely the contribution of the expression to truth–conditions given in the content of the implicit conception associated with the expression by one who understands it.

The other reason the deflationist's purposes are not served by this response is that the rationality of the acceptance of a logical principle must also somehow connect up the truth–function, or higher–order function, which is the semantic value of the expression with the thinker's own understanding. Saying the principles are correct for a certain semantic value does not explain the rationality of accepting the principles unless we make this semantic value something the thinker knows about. How is this connection with the thinker's knowledge to be effected on the deflationist's view? It cannot always be a matter of explicit knowledge of the semantic value. As we noted, the thinker who comes rationally to accept a logical principle does not always have such explicit knowledge. It is also the case that such explicit knowledge seems obtainable by rational reflection on the part of one who understands the expression. If the deflationist tries, at this point, to retreat to the position that the thinker has implicit knowledge of the semantic value, he would thereby be embracing implicit conceptions after all.

The deflationist might respond by taking a different route. He may say that the semantic value of a logical constant is simply fixed

6. IMPLICIT CONCEPTIONS, UNDERSTANDING AND RATIONALITY 59

as that which makes truth–preserving the axioms and principles the thinker is willing, in some specially primitive way, to accept. This was the line I myself took in some earlier work (1987,1992). It involves what is sometimes called a form of thinker–dependence. On the view proposed, what makes an axiom or principle correct is, as a constitutive matter, dependent upon whether thinkers actually accept it (in some designated, specially primitive way) or not. This is sometimes advertized as a virtue of the view. I think, however, that it makes it impossible to give a satisfactory account of the rationality, the non–blind, acceptance of logical principles and axioms. The rationality of accepting some proposed axiom or principle containing already understood expressions involves aiming at correctness which is, as a constitutive matter, explained independently of acceptance of that particular principle. That sort of independence must be an illusion on a judgement–dependent view of these matters.

Alternatively, a thinker–dependent view may mention not judgement, but rather how the principle strikes the thinker. How the principle strikes the thinker is quite properly to be distinguished from judgement, for a thinker's judgement may either endorse or overrule how it strikes him. But we still conceive of validity as something which is equally neither constituted nor guaranteed by conditions involving how the principles strikes the thinker. A proposed new logical principle may strike a thinker as correct. But he is not entitled to accept it until he has engaged in rational reflection on it, reflection of the sort we have been discussing. One of the points which distinguishes the logical case from that of colour is that it is not plausible that, before a thinker makes a colour predication of a perceived object, further rational reflection is required, of a thinker who experiences something as a shade of a certain colour, and who has no reason to doubt that environmental and his own perceptual mechanisms are favourable. There is then no blanket objection in what I am saying which would apply to any thinker–dependent treatment of any concept whatsoever. My point is only that we have a conception of validity, and correspondingly of what is required for rational acceptance of logical principles, which makes thinker–dependent treatments of the validity of ordinary (nonmetalinguistic) principles inappropriate.

A second, more persistent deflationary objector may still press his case. He may say:

> Everything you explain by appeal to implicit conceptions can be explained by use of inferential dispositions run off–line. For

instance, the lines of the truth–table for "or" can be reached as follows. Our new student of logic treats any sentence A of English as inter–inferable with "A is true", or, as we may say, he has the disquotational inference for truth. We can consider the thinker's disposition to infer either 'A or B', or its negation, from each of the sets of premisses {A, B}, {A, ¬B}, {¬A, B}, {¬A, ¬B}. These inferential dispositions, when exercised off–line, and employed in conjunction with mastery of the disquotational inference, allow him to attain each line of the classical truth table for alternation. From this he can also infer the validity of the schema A ⊃ (A or B). So we can explain all the phenomena without any appeal to implicit conceptions.[9]

I reply that an inference such as that from the premisses {¬A, ¬B} to ¬(A or B), is —though no doubt automated for even elementary logicians— one which our student of logic has to work out to be correct on the basis of his existing understanding of alternation. It seems to me that this working–out must involve use of the concept of truth. It must involve reasoning tantamount to: "The premisses imply that neither A nor B is true. 'A or B' to be true, though, only if at least one of A and B is true; so when these premisses hold, 'A or B' won't be true, that is '¬(A or B)' will be true". If this is right, then, even for students who do have the disposition to make the inference from the premisses {¬A, ¬B} to ¬(A or B), that disposition cannot be part of the explanation of his knowledge of the truth–table for alternation. On the contrary, appreciation of the principles which fix the truth–value of an alternation is part of the rational explanation of the student's appreciation of the validity of the transition. I have made the point with a more complicated inference, for the point is perhaps more vivid there. In fact I suspect it applies equally to the rational acceptance of the general schema of alternation–introduction.

In response to this, our second deflationary objector may shift his position slightly. He may say that it suffices for his purposes to consider a conceptual role mentioning metalinguistic transitions involving predications of truth and falsity themselves. It is metalinguistic inferential dispositions which are run off–line, he may say, and which generate the truth–table for 'or'. Given the metalinguistic premiss that A is true and B is false, for instance, the thinker will immediately be willing to infer that 'A or B' is true. I have some

---

[9] I thank Stephen Schiffer for helping me improve on an earlier formulation of this objector's position.

6. IMPLICIT CONCEPTIONS, UNDERSTANDING AND RATIONALITY 61

incidental doubts about this strategy for other lines of the truth-table. Unlike us experienced (elementary) logicians, I suspect that a transition from the falsity of A and the falsity of B takes a bit of thinking about for an eighteen-year old. I suspect he has to reason that if A and B are both false, then neither A nor B is be true, that is neither of the conditions at least one of whose truth is required for the truth of *A or B* holds. But let us waive the incidental doubts. After all, I agree that the corresponding metalinguistic transitions are immediately compelling in the case of conjunction. So what do I say about this second variant of the deflationary objection?

I say that, in moving to the metalinguistic level, it is not presenting a competitor to the theory of implicit conceptions. Finding such a metalinguistic transition as is cited in this objection to be a compelling transition is a manifestation of an implicit conception with the content that any sentence of the form 'A or B' is true iff either A is true or B is true. Our objector may protest, saying "Well that's a spurious explanation: the alleged explanans is simply summarizing what needs to be explained". But I dispute the objector's claim that the attribution of an implicit conception simply summarizes the dispositions to be explained. The explanation makes quite specific commitments. One of these commitments is that what explains the transition is it's having a certain form —rather, than, say the Gödel-numbers of its components standing in a certain relation, which is equally something which might be computed.

This last issue is equally one which arises about the implicit conception underlying understanding of the predicate 'chair', and reflection on that case may help to make this part of the reply to the second objector more plausible. Implicit knowledge of the definition of 'chair' can explain a person's applying the word correctly in central cases. To say that a person has a disposition to correct application in central cases is not by itself yet to specify *which* features of chairs in his environment are operative in leading him to apply the term. Saying that the thinker's performance is explained by a specific implicit conception commits one to saying that his performance involves the identification of backs, seats, and the rest —the features mentioned in the content of the implicit conception involved in his understanding.

I myself am very sceptical that there is one set of inference schemata acceptance of instances of which is absolutely constitutive of understanding classical alternation. Some thinkers are better at inferring to alternations, some are better at making inferences from them, some may have a better grasp of the way alternations interact with conditionals, others may find their interactions with negation easier. They may all nevertheless have the same core understanding of alternation and the same implicit conception of its contribution to truth conditions.

In other parts of the philosophy of mind and language, we have become quite comfortable with the idea that there are states which are not definitionally tied to one kind of manifestation, but which produce their effects only in combination with several other factors. A perceptual state's having a particular spatial content is one such example. Such spatial content may explain all sorts of actions, in combination with other attitudes, abilities, and enabling conditions. It is, though, quite implausible that there is some privileged possible kind of explanandum which is canonical in legitimating that attribution of a spatial content. Seeing something as at a certain distance and direction from oneself may, in the presence of other attitudes, produce action directed at that position. But it may, as in the case of the prisoner in *The Count of Monte Cristo*, equally produce a certain sequence of winks of any eyelid as a message in code; or may just result in the updating of some mental map on the part of someone incapable of movement at all.

Another example of a psychological state not individuatively tied to just one kind of explanandum is that of a psychologically real grammatical rule. Its psychological reality may explain features of a person's perception of heard utterances; or of his own productions; and the same rule may be real both for one thinker who can understand but not produce, and for another who can produce but not understand. I suggest that this feature, of having explanatory power which is not canonically or definitionally tied to one privileged kind of manifestation, is present also in the state of understanding logical expressions, and in having an implicit conception with a semantic content.

There is yet a third deflationary critic to be considered, one who takes a rather different tack. He will say that we have no need of implicit conceptions. He will say that it suffices, in attaining the correct interpretation, to note that we maximize intelligibility of Newton and Leibniz, for instance, if we attribute to them the concept of the limit of a series.

Now the description 'maximizing intelligibility' is a term of art, but on any natural reading, I doubt whether the reasons offered by this third critic are really incompatible with the existence of implicit conceptions. It cannot be a cosmic coincidence that interpreting Newton and Leibniz as having the concept of the limit of a series counts them as getting the answers to questions about series and gradients right. Interpretations must be counterfactually projectible, or they would be no use in either the explanation or the prediction of thought and action. If the interpretation of an expression which maximizes intelligibility is said to have no implications or commitments for the psychological explanation of why the expression is applied to the cases it is, the charge of cosmic coincidence would, it seems to me, be just. Indeed, I would make the charge even in the humble case of the concept *chair*. If someone is said to be interpretable as meaning *chair* by an expression, and gets its application correct, but is said not to have any tacit knowledge of its definition, then the charge of unexplained coincidence would stick against that view too. The coincidence in question is that of his applying the expression to all and only things which fall under the definition (independently certifiable illusions aside). Extending the coincidence to counterfactual circumstances would only increase the mystery. If, by contrast, the definition, either of 'chair' or of 'limit', is regarded as the content of an implicit conception which is contributing to the psychological explanation of why the expression is applied to the cases it is, there is no coincidence at all.

The astute theorist who says that correct interpretation is to be elucidated in terms of maximizing intelligibility would do better to say the following. When we think through the consequences of maximizing intelligibility, we are forced by the need not to postulate massive cosmic coincidences —one indeed for each thinker and each such concept— to recognize the existence of implicit conceptions. This more astute position is then of course not in conflict with what I have been advocating. It is reaching some of the same conclusions by a (possibly) different route.

It is not always the case that later theory simply articulates a concept which at an earlier time was not fully understood by its users. Sometimes later theoretical developments are refinements, precisifications which resolve earlier indeterminacies. This can happen as much in the physical and other empirical sciences as in the mathematical. Whether an example is one of articulation of a conception which was earlier merely implicit, or is rather one of refinement, has to be examined case–by–case, and is often a complex and intriguing matter. It would be a brave soul who claims that we have a unique pretheoretical notion of set. Though the matter needs much argument, it would equally be a brave soul who denies that there was a determinate notion of whole number prior to the theoretical developments of the past hundred years. The theorist of implicit conceptions needs only the recognition that not all cases of theoretical development are resolutions of indeterminacies. I turn now to some further ramifications of the point.

3 Personal–Level Conceptual–Role Theories and the Phenomenon of New Principles

If we accept the existence of implicit conceptions, what are the consequences for conceptual–role theories of meaning? Conceptual–role theories were proposed by Sellars (1974), and were developed in one variety or another by Harman (1972), Block (1986) and Field (1977). It is consistent with the existence of implicit conceptions that in at least some cases, some part of the conceptual role of an expression or concept contributes to making the expression have the meaning it does, or contributes to the identity of the concept. I have emphasized the answerability of the content of implicit conceptions to their role in the explanation of particular judgements in particular instances. A concept for which there is a specific type of instance of which it is true that the thinker must be willing to make certain judgements of such instances —involving certain logical transitions, or certain perceptions, as it might be— then conceptual role will contribute to the individuation of the concept.

If possession of the concept also consists in possession of an implicit conception with a certain content, it will also follow that having the implicit conception explains the concept's having that particular aspect of its conceptual role. Though it would take further detailed argument to establish the point, it would also seem that this explanatory link is in some cases an *a priori* matter. (It seems to be so in some logical cases, for instance.) The existence of an *a priori* connection between the content of the implicit conception and certain of its consequences should not, however, be taken to mean that the implicit conception cannot be genuinely explanatory. The idea that certain states are individuated in ways which connect them *a priori* with what they are capable of explaining is one we have, quite properly, happily lived with in the philosophy of mind and psychology for many years now. The claim that a thinker's practice with the concepts *chair* or *limit* is explained by his having a certain implicit conception is also one with quite specific import and other explanatory consequences too. In saying that an implicit conception with a certain content explains the practice, we are committing ourselves, for instance in the case of the concept *chair*, to the explanation of particular judgements implicating the thinker's ability to distinguish seats, backs, the relation of support, and something with a certain function for human beings.

Let us call label as 'purely personal–level conceptual–role theories' those conceptual–role theories of meaning and content which restrict themselves to the role of an expression or concept in such personal–level phenomena as thought, acceptance or action. The general phenomenon which seems to me to preclude acceptance of purely personal conceptual–role theories is that of the rational, justified acceptance of new principles involving a given concept, new in the sense that these principles do not follow from those principles (if any) immediate acceptance of which is required for possession of the concept. I label this 'the Phenomenon of New Principles'. I am inclined to think that the Phenomenon of New Principles is as decisive an argument against personal level conceptual–role theories as the phenomenon of understanding sentences one has never encountered before is decisive against theories of meaning which do not proceed compositionally. Rational acceptance of the w–rule was one example of the Phenomenon. Another, arguably, is the rational acceptance by a 14–year old of the ordinary principle of arithmetical induction, as correct for the universal quantifier over natural numbers which he has used for several years. We do not even have to go as far as axioms to find examples. Even definitions can provide examples of the phenomenon. For the ordinary user of the concept, the definition of *chair* is something which does not follow from those judgements about instances which he must immediately be able to make if he is to possess the concept *chair*. The same applies once again to the definition of *limit* in relation to Leibniz's and Newton's use of the concept.

The Phenomenon is also displayed by so basic a concept as that of negation. What might a purely personal–level conceptual–role theorist offer as the meaning–determining role for classical negation? He might include the conditions for assertion of the negations of observational sentences. He would need to do more, because negation must be fixed for all contents to which it can be applied, whether observational or not. At this point, the purely personal–level conceptual role theorist is likely to be tempted to reach for and include the classical logical inferential principles for negation: that from $\neg\neg A$ one can infer A, and that if one can derive a contradiction from A, one can infer $\neg A$. Yet again, it seems clear that these classical logical rules for negation (and their instances) are ones whose correctness can be, and needs to be, attained by rational reflection from some prior understanding of negation. The prior understanding is simply possession of the implicit conception that a sentence prefixed with "It is not the case that" is true just in case the sentence is not true. In fact in the very special case of negation, it seems to me that possession of this implicit conception does not involve drawing on anything new which was not involved in the understanding of sentences not containing negation. To understand the sentences not containing negation, the thinker must know their truth–conditions; and that is, ipso facto, to know their falsity conditions. As Geach once emphasized, to know the truth conditions of a sentence is in effect to know the location of the boundary between the cases in which it is true and those in which it is not (1972). There is no such thing as knowing the location of this boundary without possessing knowledge of the falsity-conditions of the sentences. The implicit conception associated with the understanding of negation simply links the expression for negation with these already appreciated falsity conditions. That this is the subject's implicit conception may be manifested in all sorts of different ways.

A conceptual–role theorist of meaning and content need not be a purely personal–level conceptual–role theorist. In the case of functionalism, we regularly distinguish, following Block (1978), between analytical functionalism, and 'psychofunctionalism', which takes into account information from an empirical psychology in individuating functional roles. We should make a similar distinction between types of conceptual–role theory. A conceptual–role theory may be a 'psycho–conceptual–role theory'. It may state that what is involved in possessing a particular concept includes the requirement that certain of the thinker's personal–level applications of that concept be explained by subpersonal representational states, ones which could be regarded as realizations of what I would say is an implicit conception. Nothing I have said tells against psycho–conceptual–role theories of meaning and content. The Phenomenon of New Principles tells only against pure personal–level conceptual role theories. If I am right, some concepts are such that any conceptual–role theory which treats them adequately must be at least a psycho–conceptual–role theory.

Purely personal–level conceptual–role theorists have not wholly neglected the Phenomenon of New Principles. The sorts of moves they have made to attempt to accommodate it, though, do not seem to me fully to resolve the problem. One move that suggests itself, and which I made in earlier work (1987), is for the theorist to say that a new principle, whose correctness can be rationally appreciated, is fixed by those which are mentioned in the conceptual role in some less direct way than that of: being determined as a consequence of other principles which must be accepted for possession of the concept. In that earlier work, I spoke of the new principle as being determined as one made correct by, for instance, the strongest semantical assignment that validated some introduction rule mentioned in the conceptual role. In this way, for instance, one can

6. Implicit Conceptions, Understanding and Rationality

explain why the natural deduction rule of or–elimination is correct, even though it is not found immediately obvious by all those who understand "or". Corresponding moves can be made for elimination rules too. This strategy, however, even if it succeeds in fixing the right set of new principles as correct, leaves at least three problems unresolved.

The first problem is that the resources it employs give no credible description of the ordinary thinker, like our new learner of logic, who works out the correctness of a new principle which does not follow from (say) the logical principles he already accepts for a given constant. When you worked out that or–elimination is a valid rule, you did not employ any premiss, or tacit simulation which committed you to the proposition, that the semantical value of a constant is the strongest which validates an introduction rule, or the weakest which validates an elimination rule. You had no such thought or commitment. If we are going to explain the rationality of acceptance of a new principle, we must appeal to something which is plausibly operative with a thinker engaged in rationally accepting it.

The second problem is that in some cases, *all* of the inference rules distinctive of a concept have to be worked out by a thinker. We noted that this was plausibly the case for the natural–deduction rules of negation–introduction and negation–elimination. So in some cases, this strategy does not have the initial materials on which it needs to operate.

The third problem with the strategy of appealing to the strongest semantical assignment which validates an introduction rule is the most fundamental. It is that the strategy gives no rationale for this requirement itself. I do not think it can be founded in considerations of tightness of ascription of contents and semantical values. Suppose, for the sake of giving the view the best chance, we grant that if someone is using an introduction rule correctly, and that if the logical expression is meaningful, there must be some semantical assignment that validates it. It still does not follow that we must take as the semantic value the strongest such assignment. On the contrary, if we are appealing to considerations of tightness, with only that data, we should consider as semantical assignments only the whole class of those assignments which make valid the introduction rule, rather than the strongest. To select the strongest is actually to go beyond what is justified by the inferential practice.

I conclude, then, that once we acknowledge the full range of phenomena explained by implicit conceptions, including the Phenomenon of New Principles, purely personal–level conceptual roles cannot fully determine meanings, nor fully individuate concepts.

For someone who occupies the Fregean standpoint, and regards the examples as evidence of incompletely grasped —but nevertheless determinate— senses, none of this should be surprising. The Phenomenon of New Principles is only to be expected from that standpoint. The new principles which are rationally accepted reflect those aspects of the determinate sense which is already employed in thought, but whose nature needs theoretical thought on the part of its ordinary users if it is to become 'sharply grasped'.

In criticizing purely personal–level conceptual role theories as constitutive theories of understanding and concept–possession, I have not committed myself to the view that meaning can go beyond the full range of correct personal–level conceptual roles for an expression. Equally, a realist about theoretically postulated magnitudes in a physical science should not assert that truths about them go beyond everything determined by possible observational consequences, when we are considering the full range of possible experimental setups. It would, however, also be almost universally agreed that acceptance of this last point does not mean that statements about the theoretically postulated magnitudes can be reduced to those about possible observations. Something analogous seems to me to be true of meaning and concept–possession, and their relation to personal–level conceptual roles. Indeed the very notion of a *correct* conceptual role is precisely one which I have been claiming the conceptual–role theorist cannot fully elucidate. In some cases, what is correct can be explained only by appeal to an underlying implicit conception.

I also add a remark for enthusiasts who have followed the debates about conceptual role theories of meaning and concepts. For some years now I have argued that not every coherent conceptual role determines a meaning or concept. Only those roles which naturally correspond to a certain contribution to truth–conditions do so (1993, forthcoming).[10] If not every conceptual role determines a meaning, it would hardly be surprising if the specific contribution made to truth conditions also played a role in understanding. On the proposal I have been advocating, the content of an implicit conception involved in understanding is given by a rule specifying a contribution to truth (or satisfaction) conditions. For conceptual roles for which there is

---

[10]It is not only inconsistent conceptual roles, like that which Prior assigned to 'tonk', which fail to determine contributions to truth–conditions (Prior, 1960). There can also be a failure to determine truth–conditions in the case of a consistent conceptual role, if the specification of the role also states that certain rules are invalid for the connective being explained. There are examples in Peacocke (1993).

no corresponding contribution to truth (or satisfaction) conditions, there is no content available to be the content of any corresponding implicit conception. Conceptual roles which correspond to no contribution to truth–conditions are, under the conception I am advocating, automatically excluded.

4 Explanation by Implicit Conceptions

Explanation by implicit conceptions raises a host of queries and doubts. There are doubts about the particular kind of psychological explanation in which they are said to be implicated. There are also more general philosophical doubts about whether implicit conceptions can ever properly be involved in a description of what is involved in possessing a concept or understanding an expression. Let us take first the issue of what kind of psychological explanation an explanation which appeals to implicit conceptions might be.

An explanation by an implicit conception is a species of explanation by a content–involving state, the content being the content of the implicit conception. So the usual features of content–involving explanation apply. An explanation of a judgement involving a particular concept by citing the person's implicit conception is not an explanation of a syntactic state by a syntactic state, not even if both implicit conception and judgement are realized in subpersonal syntactic states. An implicit conception contributes to the explanation of a judgement under its content–involving description as a judgement that p, for some particular p. The implicit conception does not explain the judgement under a merely syntactic description. Nor could we regard the explanation as one which is covered by a *prima facie* law relating some syntactic realization of the implicit conception to the occurrence of content–involving judgements. Explanations by content–involving conceptions can be the same across persons who realize contents in different subpersonal systems of representation, different mental 'notations' if you will. It is also not at all clear that a 'syntax to content' *prima facie* law would be adequate to explain the knowledgeable status of the resulting judgements.

The model, then, to illustrate it for the simple case of *chair* would run thus. One of the thinker's perceptual systems, say, identifies some object in the environment as having a supporting area and a back, and the subject has the background information that the object is used for sitting on. This information from the perceptual system, together with the background information, is combined, at a subpersonal level, with the content of the implicit conception involved in possession of the concept *chair*. It is computed, from this body of information, that the presented object is a chair. This in turn explains the thinker's willingness to judge that that object, demonstratively given in perception, is a chair. In the case of other concepts, the role just played by the perceptual system will be played by some informational source or other. This source yields a content which, together with the content of the implicit conception underlying the concept, and possibly some background information or presupposition, permits computation of a content to the effect that some given object falls under the concept in question. Of course, in both perceptual and non–perceptual cases, we can expect all sorts of short–cuts to be used in reaching particular judgements. The full content of the implicit conception need not be on–line in every classification the thinker makes. As Susan Carey emphasized, to say that a concept has a definition is not to say that the constituents of the definition are computationally primitive, nor is it to say that they are developmentally prior (1982, pp. 350-351).

All the implicit conceptions I have considered so far have contents which are correct. It is not impossible for there to be an implicit conception with an incorrect content. A thinker may misunderstand some word in the public language. False presuppositions about certain kinds of objects or events in his environment may also enter the content of his implicit conceptions. Nonetheless, there is a core of cases in which one can expect that the content of the implicit conceptions within that core will be correct. It is very plausible, on grounds having to do with the theory of interpretation and content, that there will be a core of cases in which a thinker will make judgements correctly, and will do so also in a range of counterfactual circumstances. If we accept any theory of content or interpretation on which that is so, then we can expect that any implicit conceptions explaining the applications of the concepts in those judgements will also be largely correct. If the implicit conceptions were not largely correct, the judgements would not be largely correct either.

Having squarely accepted that explanation by implicit conceptions is content–involving explanation, there is still the question of whether the content of the implicit conception is, at the level of subpersonal mental representations, implicitly or explicitly represented. As with other kinds of tacit informational state, what has here been deemed important to an implicit conception is *prima facie* compatible both with explicit and with implicit representation, at the subpersonal level, of the content of an implicit conception (see Davies 1989). In the example of the limit of a series, the informational content might be explicitly formulated in a language of thought. There would be

6. IMPLICIT CONCEPTIONS, UNDERSTANDING AND RATIONALITY   71

some stored formula which states the definition of a limit. But the content of the implicit conception could equally be grounded in the operation of a processor which does not involve, at the subpersonal level, explicit representation of the content of the implicit conception. We can certainly conceive of a processor which takes information about the numerical values approached by a function at a given point, and delivers as output information about the differential at that point. It must be at least partly an empirical question which kind of representation is operative in a given thinker.

Whichever way the issue is resolved for a given subject and implicit conception, I would like to note one constraint which a fuller theory ought to satisfy. Thinkers can know that certain general principles hold for some concept for which they have only an implicit conception. Even though a rigorous justification for these principles would need to draw on an explicit statement of that conception, it seems that these principles are known even though the conception is not explicitly known. An example would be the multiplication principle that $(dx/dy).(dy/dz) = dx/dz$. I think Leibniz and Newton knew this general multiplication principle. Again, they did not learn it by being told it by someone else. Though they did not know any adequate explicit definition of a limit, they had sufficient insight into what it must be to realize that this principle is correct. Any theory which characterizes their implicit knowledge as simply serving up the value for the differential of a particular function, and then claiming that such general principles as the one just mentioned are extracted inductively would be inadequate to the phenomena. Indeed, one does not have to be a Leibniz or a Newton to appreciate that the rate of change of one magnitude with respect to a third magnitude is identical with the rate of change of the first with respect to a second magnitude, multiplied by the rate of change of the second with respect to the third. Perhaps the correct description of the situation is that though they had only an implicit conception of the definition, they did know that limits are instantaneous rates of change of one magnitude (as one loosely writes) with respect to another; and they knew that relative rates of change respect that multiplication principle. This phenomenon, of knowledge of some general principles involving a concept in the absence of knowledge of any explicit definition is found outside the mathematical and logical cases. It applies in cases from the more interesting moral and political examples, right up to the humble case of the definition of 'chair'.

While we are on the topic of the nature of explanation by implicit conceptions, it may be helpful if I locate the position I have outlined in relation to the well-known theory of the psychology of inference expounded by Johnson–Laird in his book *Mental Models* (1983). Evidently I am committed to agreement with him on two of the distinctive claims of his approach. Like him, I have held that the validity of logical principles has to be worked out by thinkers on the basis of their prior understanding of the expressions they contain. I am also in agreement with him that this prior understanding takes the form of knowledge of contribution to truth conditions. Thus Johnson–Laird writes: "What children learn first are the truth conditions of expressions: they learn the contributions of connectives, quantifiers and other such terms to these truth conditions. And, until they have acquired this knowledge about their language, they are in no position to make verbal inferences" (1983, p.144). Some aspects of his theory of mental models could be integrated further with the position I have outlined. However, I do part company with any claim that there is no 'mental logic', that no form of mental reasoning is needed to explain explicit logical inference.[11] There is, on the view I have put forward, inference at one, and possibly two, levels. First let us recall the example in which we envisaged the subject as working out, via a simulation procedure, at the personal level, the validity of some simple truth-functional principle. There the thinker had to use logical reasoning, for instance in drawing conclusions from the premiss that these were all the truth-values that could be taken by the atomic components. Second, at the subpersonal level, in the explanation envisaged a few paragraphs back of a judgement "That's a chair", for instance, some form of subpersonal inference is essential. It was employed in moving from the information that the presented object has certain properties together with the content of the implicit conception to the conclusion that the presented object is a chair. Perhaps Johnson–Laird would say, as I think in consistency he should say, that the mental models should be used at that subpersonal level too. But it does become a real question then whether the procedures for constructing and operating on mental models should not be regarded as just the way the system is, subpersonally, encoding various inferential principles. It is true that the inferential principles need not be explicitly represented in a language of thought. (Perhaps that is all Johnson–Laird really wanted to claim about the subpersonal level, in which case our positions would not diverge.) But we noted only a few paragraphs back

---

[11] "Explicit inferences based on mental models, however, do not need to make use of rules of inference, or any such formal machinery, and in this sense it is not necessary to postulate a logic in the mind." —Johnson–Laird (p. 131, 1983).

6. IMPLICIT CONCEPTIONS, UNDERSTANDING AND RATIONALITY

that absence of explicit representation at the subpersonal level does not mean that there are no psychologically real states which contain the content of those principles. The theory of implicit conceptions which I have started to outline is committed to holding that there are some such psychologically real states whose content is that of the implicit conceptions.

I turn now to two principled objections to the enterprise of employing implicit conceptions in explaining understanding. They could both be considered at some length, but here I will just try to indicate the lines of a response to them. The first set of concerns revolve around the 'A(C) form', the noncircularity constraint of *A Study of Concepts*. The other set starts from the views of the later Wittgenstein about meaning and understanding.

What I have said about implicit conceptions is incompatible with adoption of the A(C) form of *A Study of Concepts*, and involves abandonment of that constraint on the philosophical explication of concept–possession. The A(C) requirement on explicating possession of a given concept F was that the concept not feature in the explication, as the concept F, within the scope of attitudes attributed to the thinker. Implicit conceptions of the sort I have advocated violate this principle. I have been advocating implicit conceptions with such contents as "Any sentence of the form 'not–A' is true iff A is not true", and "Any sentence of the form $A \vee B$ is true iff either A is true or B is true". Here the occurrences of 'not' and 'or' on the right–hand side of these biconditionals violates the A(C) restriction when implicit conceptions with these contents are offered as explications of possession of the concepts of negation and alternation. There are various ways in which one might try to qualify the A(C) form to avoid an incompatibility, but I can only report that I have not been able to find any that are well–motivated and also cover the ground.

Violations of the A(C) form are unobjectionable in the explication of a concept F because one can use one's own mastery of the concept F to assess what someone with an implicit conception involving F could be expected to think or do in any given state of information. This is why a statement about what is involved in possession of a concept, and which does not respect the A(C) form, is not vacuous. It still makes an assessable claim. Each one of us, in evaluating the claim it makes, draws on his own mastery of the concept F being explicated. One draws on that mastery, and engages in simulations to assess what one would be obliged, or rational, to think or do in any given state of information. With information from these simulations, one is then in a position to assess the claim about possession of the concept in question. It is in just this way that one can evaluate the various claims I have made in this paper about the content of the implicit conceptions underlying various particular concepts.

Drawing on one's own mastery and using simulations in this way is sharply to be distinguished from making assessments by inference from any theoretical beliefs one may have about the conditions for possession of the concept F. Though of course if one uses the simulations, and draws on one's own mastery of the concept, one will eventually end up with some such theoretical beliefs, the route by which they are attained essentially involves simulation.

We could of course equally proceed this way in assessing what sentences someone would, in various circumstances, be likely to accept on the simple hypothesis that by 'chair' they mean *chair*. We did, though, have given specific motivations in the case of the logical constants for going beyond the disquotational form, and actually introducing semantic notions into the content of the implicit conception. Equally in the case of 'chair' too, there are facts about a thinker's relations to seats, backs and supporting humans in a seated position which make it important to recognize an implicit conception underlying mastery of the predicate.

To keep this paper within reasonable bounds, I will not pursue here the many issues involved in adopting a theory of mastery of a concept which cannot be fitted into the A(C) form. A fuller development is owed. It would have to say much more about the constraints on the ascription of content to implicit conceptions, and about the nature of explanation by content–involving subpersonal states.

I should also note explicitly that offering, for a given concept F, an implicit conception which violates the A(C) form is consistent with the existence of an A(C)–conforming conceptual role which individuates F. The case of logical conjunction arguably shows the consistency of this combination. From the standpoint of the present theory, however, this is just a special case from which no general conclusions can be drawn.

A defender of the A(C) form may be inclined to ask the following question. Why cannot we proceed as follows? First, using our own understanding of negation, or alternation, or whatever is the target concept in question, we work out the inferential and transitional patterns distinctive of the target concept. These patterns will in general involve other concepts with which the target concept interacts in valid transitions, and may involve complex principles. Then, this objector continues, we just take this totality of transitional patterns, and say that what is distinctive of the target concept is this: it makes rational that totality. By putting a variable in place of reference to the target concept in the specification of this total-

6. IMPLICIT CONCEPTIONS, UNDERSTANDING AND RATIONALITY 75

ity, can we not then attain something which instantiates the A(C) form?

I make three interrelated points in reply. First, the A(C) form was meant to be a form of account of concept–*possession*, or of understanding. It is crucial in this area to distinguish between principles which must be acknowledged for possession of the target concept, and the wider class of correct principles which are rationally held (perhaps even knowable *a priori*). There are principles and transitions involving a concept which can be rationally endorsed by a thinker, but acknowledgement of which is not required for possession of the concept. That was a point I was pressing in the earlier sections of the paper. Ignorance, or even rejection, of correct definitions or principles for a concept is consistent with possession of the concept defined. Not everything involving a given concept which can be rationally accepted has be to be accepted, even conditionally, by a thinker who possesses the concept.

Second, even if we could, without begging the question, specify circumstances in which the principles it would be rational to hold would in fact be held be a possessor of the given concept, there would still be something unexplained in the proposal. If the target concept makes rational the totality of transitions mentioned by this defender of the A(C) form, there ought to be an answer to the question: *how* does it make these transitions rational? What aspect of possession of the concept makes it rational to accept a primitive principle involving the concept, a principle the thinker had not thought of before? The theorist of implicit conceptions has an answer to this question. The correctness of the new principle follows from the content of the implicit conception which is involved in the thinker's possession of the concept. The implicit conception can influence, for instance via the outcome of simulations, which principles the thinker rationally comes to accept. The defender of the A(C) form does not, it now seems to me, have an answer to these questions about the rational acceptance of new primitive principles.

The third reply to the proposal is that the totality of rational transitions distinctive of a concept is in any case quite open–ended. There is no limit to the valid interactions even of so simple an operator as negation or alternation not only with other logical concepts, but with any other concept, such as that of probability, evidence, arithmetical quantification, observational concepts... or indeed any other new concepts we may introduce. If we ask what unifies this open–ended totality, for instance in the case of negation, it seems to me that there is essentially only one answer we can give. It is that these are all the transitions which we would expect as consequences of possession of an implicit conception with the content that any sentence of the form 'not–A' is true iff A is not true. That is the only way of fully capturing the open–ended class of transitions whose rationality is distinctive of negation. If that is so, the way of capturing the totality is incompatible with, rather than supporting, the A(C) form.

I promised also to discuss the relation of implicit conceptions to Wittgensteinian views on understanding and rule–following. The views I have been presenting are clearly incompatible with some parts of his thought.

(a) They are incompatible with his thesis that one's understanding of an expression does not exceed what one can explain (*Philosophical Investigations* 209-10). The considerations we developed earlier do seem to me to show that some thinkers' understanding of 'chair', 'limit' and even 'natural number' exceeds what they can in fact explain.

(b) The view I have been outlining would also endorse one reading of such a claim as 'Once you have got hold of the rule, you have the route traced out for you' (*Remarks on the Foundations of Mathematics*, VI, 31). Wittgenstein rejected that claim, though of course he was considering 'rules' of a sort available to guide a thinker at the reason–giving level in his intentionally making one application rather than another of the expression in question. Implicit conceptions as understood here are not rules of that sort.

(c) Finally, the whole idea of explaining rule–application was anathema to the later Wittgenstein. I am committed to the possibility of content–involving subpersonal computational explanations of thinker's applications of expressions they understand. Wittgenstein's objections to the possibility of explanation in 'bedrock' cases where, Wittgenstein says, the person has nothing which is his reason for going on the way he does, are addressed either to the reason–giving level of explanation, or, on occasion, to physiological explanations. It would be wrong to assimilate content–involving subpersonal computational explanation to either of those very different cases. I have not myself found anything in Wittgenstein which can be extrapolated to give a sound argument against the possibility of subpersonal computational explanation.

It is equally striking, however, how wide the area of agreement may be between a defender of implicit conceptions and the considerations marshalled in Wittgenstein's arguments about rule–following. That one's reasons for saying that something is the result of adding 2, or is a chair, may in a certain sense give out eventually is entirely compatible with the existence of a content–involving computational

6. IMPLICIT CONCEPTIONS, UNDERSTANDING AND RATIONALITY 77

explanation of why one applies these expressions in the cases one does. The existence of implicit conceptions as understood here is consistent with Wittgenstein's arguments that rule–following in the fundamental cases does not involve consciously consulting anything —as Crispin Wright puts it, there is "no essential inner epistemology of rule–following" (Wright 1989, p. 244).

There is even a point of positive agreement, rather than mere consistency, between the present view and Wittgenstein's. Wittgenstein insists at various points in his argument that the relation between understanding and correct application is not merely contingent.[12] The way the account of implicit conceptions has been developed here involves a commitment to precisely what Wittgenstein is here insisting upon. An implicit conception has as its content a certain condition for falling under the expression it treats. We said that the principles for ascribing content to an implicit conception would ensure that, in certain basic and central applications, an expression associated with that implicit conception would be applied to things satisfying the condition in its content. So indeed the connection between possession of an implicit conception, in cases in which that is the nature of understanding, and correct application, is not merely contingent. Hence we have a point of agreement with Wittgenstein. Indeed once the noncontingency is acknowledged, it even becomes possible for what a thinker finds compelling —the way he goes on— to enter the individuation of a concept, consistently with the theory of implicit conceptions. The content of the implicit conception can be fixed in part by the properties of the cases which the thinker finds it compelling that the concept applies.[13] So one should not exaggerate the divergence between implicit conceptions and Wittgenstein on rule–following.

It is, though, only fair to add that if one can consistently accept these most recent points about rule–following whilst rejecting

---

[12]For instance, in *Remarks on the Foundations of Mathematics*(1978), VII §26 (p. 328):

"But, *if* you have seen this law in it [a series of numbers – CP], that you then continue the series in *this* way —that is no longer an empirical fact.

But how is it not an empirical fact? —for "seeing *this* in it" was presumably not the same as: continuing it like this.

One can only say that it is not an empirical proposition, by *defining* the step on this level as the one that corresponds to the expression of the rule."

[13]This is a point of contact between the theory of implicit conceptions and the position of *A Study of Concepts*.

Wittgenstein's claims about the extent and the explanation of understanding, we have to drawn a certain conclusion. The conclusion must be that the correctness of these most recent points, about the phenomenology of rule–following and about the noncontingent relation between understanding and application, offer no support for his positions on the extent and the explanation of understanding.

5 Rationalism Supported

What I have said so far about implicit conceptions, together with the use to which I have put them, has the distinctive flavour of a classical rationalist position. Here, for instance, are six principles which can be supported by appeal to implicit conceptions, and which were held by that paradigm rationalist Leibniz.

(1) The evidentness of particular axioms is grounded in the understanding of the terms they contain.

In the *New Essays*, Leibniz's protagonist quotes with approval the views of those philosophers who held that axioms "are evident *ex terminis* —from the terms— as soon as they are understood. That is, they were satisfied that the 'force' of their convincingness is grounded in the understanding of the terms" (1981, p. 406; Book IV, Chapter vii, 'Of the propositions which are named maxims or axioms'). The description I gave at the start of this paper of the way in which our logic student comes rationally to accept a logical axiom conforms to the description given by the philosophers with whom Leibniz's protagonist agrees. According to that description, the student's implicit conception is drawn upon in the simulations which lead to rational acceptance of the axiom. In the account given, possession of the appropriate implicit conception was also identified with understanding. So acceptance of the axiom is grounded in understanding. The content of the student's perceptual experience is justificationally irrelevant to his acceptance of the axiom.

(2) Concerning the Thought expressed by an axiom: finding the axiom evident, when that is properly grounded in the understanding, is a way of coming to know that Thought.

The legitimacy of attributing knowledge when acceptance is reached via the understanding was essential to Leibniz's case against Locke's empiricism. Leibniz would hardly have had an anti–empiricist account of knowledge of these axioms if this understanding–based evidentness did not amount to knowledge. I noted early on in this

6. IMPLICIT CONCEPTIONS, UNDERSTANDING AND RATIONALITY

paper that the reflections which can lead to rational acceptance of an axiom or inference rule plausibly yield knowledge.

The innateness of axioms and inference–rules is not, however, something I am advocating. Chomsky, in his book *Cartesian Linguistics*, insisted that the rationalists were right in wanting a psychology which is "a kind of Platonism without preexistence" (1966, p. 63). In a similar spirit, I offer implicit conceptions as a rationalist account of understanding and certain kinds of knowledge, but without any commitment to innateness. Implicit conceptions can be acquired.[14] In fact I think there are strands in Leibniz which suggest that what really mattered to him was independent of innateness taken literally. At one point in the *New Essays*, he writes that

[...] quite often a 'consideration of the nature of things' is nothing but the knowledge of the nature of our mind and of these innate ideas, and there is no need to look for them outside oneself. Thus I count as innate any truths which need only such 'consideration' in order to be verified (1981, p. 84).

The distinctively purely understanding–based 'consideration' can be applied whether or not the understanding is, in the literal sense, innate. Leibniz's here saying that he counts as innate any truth which can be attained by a certain kind of consideration suggests that this part, at least, of the rationalist position may not need to involve literal innateness. The talk of verification in this passage also emphasizes Leibniz's conception of this sort of consideration as a route to truth and knowledge.[15]

(3) Logical axioms can be known *a priori*.

This was the burden of Leibniz's dispute with Locke: we can have an entitlement or justification for accepting a logical axiom which is

---

[14] Correspondingly, beliefs rationally explained by the possession of an implicit conception may be innate only in C.D. Broad's "negative sense of internally generated" (1975, p. 138).

[15] I am, though, uneasy about Leibniz's implication that a priori knowledge is really knowledge about the thinker's own mind. The content of a thinker's understanding —the content of his implicit conceptions— can explain a thinker's a priori knowledge without that knowledge being about his understanding. What his understanding makes available is not itself about his understanding. A later rationalist like Frege is clearly, and in Frege's case explicitly, free of any commitment to the idea that a priori knowledge concerns the thinker's own mind. Leibniz's position may have been influenced by his other doctrines about the metaphysics of minds, which are not commitments of the position I have been defending.

justificationally independent of perceptual experience or sensation, even if experience is an enabling condition for our attaining such an acceptance. The procedure by which, at the start of this paper, I envisaged someone coming to accept rationally a primitive logical axiom is also one which yields *a priori* knowledge. Nothing in that rationale for the subject's belief involves perceptual experience or sensation.

Of course Leibniz had what in our post–Fregean time we would regard as a very rudimentary conception of logic. The logical laws to which, according to him, all *a priori* truths could be reduced by means of substituting correct definitions were of such forms as "All As are As", or "All AB's are A's", "All ABC's are A's", and the like. The 'trifling' character of these axioms was a topic of some discussion in Leibniz's writings. By contrast, someone acquainted with modern logic would be unlikely to characterize all of its axioms as trifling. Yet it seems to me that an understanding-based, non-empirical procedure for attaining knowledge of axioms, even when they are not merely trifling, still lies squarely within the spirit of the rationalists' conception. Moreover, even on his simpler conception of logic, Leibniz still needs to rely on some of the apparatus I have been employing. Correct definitions, to which Leibniz repeatedly appeals in his characterization of demonstrations, are precisely definitions which correctly articulate the implicit conception involved in understanding the term being defined.

To say, as I have, that knowledge of the axioms is grounded in understanding of the expressions in them, and is also *a priori*, is not at all to endorse the Carnapian view that they are true solely in virtue of the meaning of their constituent expressions. On the contrary, the sort of rationale I envisaged a thinker going through at the start of this paper is one which shows that, for any instance of a logical axiom schema, what it is true in virtue of is its disquoted truth condition (as indeed would be the case for any other true sentence). I have been trying to develop the present view in a way which respects that point throughout, and which regards the phrase "true purely in virtue of meaning" as applying to no sentences whatever.[16] For this reason, the views I am developing here are not in the target area of Quine's formidable attack on Carnap's views on truth–purely-in–virtue–of–meaning (particularly in 'Carnap on Logical Truth', in his 1976). The truth–condition for any sentence containing a logical operator, including primitive logical axioms, is determined in the

---

[16]In this respect at least, my views have not changed since my paper "How Are A Priori Truths Possible?" (1993).

6. IMPLICIT CONCEPTIONS, UNDERSTANDING AND RATIONALITY

same uniform way, by application of the clauses of a Tarskian truth–theory. In fact the ways of coming to know these axioms which I have been identifying clearly rely on states whose informational content involves what is stated in the clauses of a truth–theory.

(4) Logical axioms are necessary.

This was a view Leibniz expressed repeatedly, and was another plank of in his criticism of Locke. Leibniz thought, rightly in my view, that Locke could explain neither the necessity nor our knowledge of the necessity of the axioms. Indeed Leibniz repeatedly endorses the much stronger claim that for every necessary truth there is a reduction of it to logical axioms by means of substitution of definitions for defined terms.[17] It would take us much too far afield to go into (4), or the stronger claim, in detail. It can be assessed only in the presence of a substantive theory of necessity. For now, let me simply say dogmatically that I think a correct account of the truth conditions of necessity statements has the consequence that the semantical rules for logical operators hold not only in the actual world, but in any possible world.[18] (Of course a theory must explain why this is so.) If it is so, then the sorts of rationale I have been considering for primitive logical axioms can be extended to show not only the validity of these axioms, but also their necessity.

(5) Reflection is needed to discover the axioms of logic: it would "be wrong to think that we can easily read these eternal laws of reason in the soul, as the Praetor's edict can be read on his notice–board, without effort or inquiry" (*New Essays* p. 50).

Leibniz in many places emphasizes that we need to reflect, to attend, to discover logical axioms. I have also emphasized that it can take reflection to appreciate that an axiom or primitive inference–rule is correct. If anything, I think Leibniz still overstates their ease of discovery, as in the passage quoted above in which he says they are evident as soon as their terms are understood. He writes as if reflection may be needed to discover the axioms, but that once stated, it will evident that they are correct. This is too strong. I suspect that if Leibniz had been acquainted with modern logic, he would have

---

[17] Cp. Loemker (1969, p. 646). Also in the *New Essays* p. 86, of the kind of truths which are innate in Leibniz's sense, he writes "and among necessary truths no other kind is to be found".

[18] For a theory of the truth–conditions of statements of necessity which I think can serve this purpose, see 'Metaphysical Necessity: Understanding, Truth and Epistemology' (Peacocke 1997).

withdrawn this point. As far as I can see, nothing in the rationalist conception rules out revision on this point.

(6) There is an important distinction to be drawn between clear ideas and distinct ideas.

A clear idea, for Leibniz, is one which enables one at least to recognize instances of the concept in question. A clear idea may nevertheless be indistinct, that is, "I am not able to enumerate separately the characteristics required to distinguish the thing from others, even though such characteristics and distinctions are really in the thing itself and the data which enable us to analyze the notion" ('Reflections on Knowledge, Truth and Ideas', 1951, p. 284). It seems to me that the way to elucidate the distinction between someone whose clear idea is indistinct, and someone whose clear idea is distinct is to use the notion of an implicit conception. The thinker with the distinct idea is one who has succeeded in achieving an explicit formulation of the implicit conception which was all he had when he had only an indistinct, though clear, idea.

Beyond this agreement on six particular theses, there is also an underlying sympathy between the approach I have been adopting and the general rationalist conception of knowledge. The views I have been putting forward are at home in a conception of knowledge as rationally or reasonably attained. No doubt, historically, the rationalists overshot in their enthusiasm for this idea. Nonetheless, if there is something in it, it would be a quite unstable position theoretically to hold that it applies to much of our knowledge, but fails to hold when we consider the case of primitive axioms and inference rules. If there are rationality or reasonability conditions for knowledge, they must apply in these basic cases too; and in effect I have been trying to argue that they do.

6 Consequences for the Theory of Justification, Rationality and Understanding

What makes it rational to accept some logical truth of which one has a proof? The considerations canvassed earlier in this paper suggest that the rationality of accepting it cannot be fully elucidated philosophically just by citing the proof. For what is at the start of this derivation? There are two sorts of case to consider. In one type of case, the proof starts with primitive axioms and/or inference rules. The primitive axioms and/or inference rules may be universally quantified, as in Frege's own formulations, or they may be schemata, as in current approaches. But whichever way the starting point of the proof is set out, under this first type of case the starting point of the proof itself does not involve metalinguistic notions. The notion of truth does not occur in the first line of the proof itself. Proofs of this first type we can call *unsupplemented* derivations. Proofs of the second type, by contrast, start with semantic principles, stating the contribution of particular logical connectives to the determination of the truth–conditions of sentences or contents or Thoughts containing them. They will start from such principles that "Any sentence of the form A ∨ B is true iff either A is false or B is true". Proofs of this second sort then move from these semantic premisses to the logical axioms or primitive inference rules, which the semantics validates. They then proceed as in the unsupplemented case. Proofs of this second kind we call *supplemented* derivations.

Nothing in derivations of the first kind, the unsupplemented derivations, explains the rationality of accepting their starting point, their primitive axioms or inference rules. This state of affairs is especially perplexing for anyone who holds the highly intuitive and (it seems to me) correct view that it is something about the nature of the senses of the expressions in the primitive axioms and inference rules, and correspondingly about the thinker's understanding, that makes it rational to accept them. So we may be tempted to turn to derivations of the second type. Yet it does not seem that they fully explain the rationality of accepting a logical truth, for two reasons. One is that a person can come to recognize the non–semantic axioms as valid, even someone who has no previous explicit knowledge of semantics. It is no doubt partly this point which attracted the classical rationalists to the view that axioms are known independently of other truths. Some prominent logicians, such as Russell, developed logical systems, and knew their axioms, before having been introduced to explicit semantical statements (in his case, by Wittgenstein). The other reason is that the rationality of accepting the semantic axioms is of course itself still unexplained.

The problem is very sharp in Frege himself. Frege held that "it is part of the concept of an axiom that it can be recognized as true independently of other truths" (1979, p. 168). In conformity with this, in the formal system of the *Basic Laws of Arithmetic*, we have a system with primitive, non–semantic axioms and inference rules. It was derivations in this system which were supposed to give the "ultimate justification" for arithmetical propositions. Yet there are many pressures in Frege to want a different position, and these pressures are reflected in the way Frege himself proceeds in the *Basic Laws of Arithmetic*. You might expect someone who holds the quoted rationalist doctrine that axioms can be recognized as true independently of other truths not to derive them from other truths. Yet at every point at which Frege introduces a new primitive axiom or inference rule in the formal language, he actually gives it, in the German, a justification. Indeed a word meaning "therefore" immediately precedes the statement of the axiom or inference rule. And what precedes the "therefore" is a statement of the semantic rule — the rule giving the contribution to truth conditions— of the crucial expressions in the new axiom or inference rule. The very first axiom is introduced by a simple argument that it must always have the truth–value *true*, given the truth–rule for the material conditional. Frege writes —I change to a more modern notation for the material conditional and for the variables—

> By §12 [which states which truth–function the conditional denotes], (A ⊃ (B ⊃ A)) could be the False only if both A and B were true while A was not the True. This is impossible; therefore (A ⊃ (B ⊃ A)) (I)"

Here "(I)" is Frege's notation for his first axiom. He does something similar for every other axiom and inference rule. This, incidentally, shows that it is quite false to say, as Ricketts (1996) does, that Frege never attempts any informal soundness proofs. These are precisely informal soundness proofs.

Frege's giving an informal soundness proof is not a mere quirk of exposition. It has deep roots in his, and indeed I think in the proper, conception of the relations between sense, justification and truth. Frege held, like Leibniz, that "the truth of a logical law is immediately evident from itself, from the sense of the expression" ('Compound Thoughts', 1984, p. 405). There ought, if the evidentness of a logical law depends on the sense, to be some explanation of *how* it depends on the sense. Now Frege famously held that the sense of a sentence is given by its truth–conditions, and that the sense of its components by the contribution they make to these truth–conditions. So an explanation of the evidentness of an axiom should start from the contribution made by its components to its truth–conditions. This is precisely how Frege's soundness proofs proceed. Moreover, in proceeding this way, he is giving a justification for thinking that the truth–condition for the axiom is fulfilled. So we are not, after all, lacking at the very foundation the sort of justification which it was the task of the rest of the structure to provide.

Frege did not recognize the tension, given his account of axioms, nor did he resolve it. It is not only a problem for him; it is a problem for us too. Even if we do not accept his characterization of what an

6. IMPLICIT CONCEPTIONS, UNDERSTANDING AND RATIONALITY 85

axiom is, and so have no problem with a semantic derivation of the truth of an axiom, there is an unresolved issue. Why is it rational to accept the semantic premisses? There must be some answer to this. For if a logical derivation is not an example of a justified, rational route to a conclusion, then what is? And how can it be so unless its premisses are justified?

I suggest that both the supplemented and the unsupplemented derivations have a role to play in explaining the thinker's justification, and that the way of solving the problem is to distinguish two very different relations a single thinker bears to derivations of each of the two kinds. Every step in the unsupplemented derivation corresponds to some transition explicitly made by a thinker who is inferring some logical truth from the primitive logical axioms. The thinker finds those axioms compelling, and does so by proceeding along the lines we envisaged for our eighteen–year old early on in this paper. Equally, when we consider the supplemented derivation, with its semantic premisses, its earliest parts also capture something psychologically real, but they do so in a different way. The semantic premisses of the supplemented derivation give the content of those of the thinker's implicit conceptions which are operative in his rationally coming to appreciate that the nonsemantic axioms are valid. A statement of the implicit conception associated with understanding a truth–functional connective, for instance, would be a statement which determines its truth–table. When our imagined thinker goes properly through the simulation–involving steps I described at the start of this paper, he will come to accept as valid the same principles as someone who is explicitly inferring from a statement of the truth–tables. Moreover, the explanation of his doing so will be that his implicit conceptions entail the content stated in those truth tables. If we regard understanding the logical expression as involving association of the expression with the right implicit conception, we also see on this account how semantic understanding is the source of the thinker's appreciation of the validity of the logical axioms (and primitive rules).

I should add that in making these points, there is no commitment to the possibility of some level of theory at which everything, including all logical transitions, can be justified. Even the mental activities of someone whose thought is captured by the supplemented derivation is still using logic at the very early stages, for instance in moving from information gleaned by simulating the various cases to acceptance that an axiom or inference rule is valid. He will be making such transitions as: if these are possible combinations of truth–values, and there are no others, then this axiom (say) will always be true. We need some form of logic in any theoretical thought. So it seems to be incoherent to suppose that there is some level at which everything can be justified. What this shows is that an $\exists\forall$, an existential–universal, proposition is false: it is false that there is a level at which everything can be justified. That is consistent with a weaker, coherent proposition of $\forall\exists$ form being true: that for every axiom and inference rule, there is some level at which is can justified. This $\forall\exists$ proposition is much more plausible. It may be a requirement of reason.

I draw two conclusions from these points. The first conclusion is that even in the area of logic, the rationality of accepting a proposition or schema on the basis of one's understanding of the expressions it contains cannot be explained solely in terms of proofs, not even supplemented proofs. For whence does our rational understander obtain his knowledge of the semantic premisses? If he has that knowledge because others have informed him of these premisses, then he is not obtaining his knowledge from his own understanding of the logical vocabulary. It is only if the knowledge is obtained ultimately by the simulation means we outlined that the source of the knowledge is his own understanding of the expressions. Of course he does not have to go through the simulation every time he needs to use a semantic premiss. Knowledge obtained by the simulation can be stored for later use without the thinker having to rehearse its origins, just as knowledge obtained by any other means can be stored without rehearsing *its* origins. But the status of the stored information as knowledge derived from his own understanding rests upon its having been reached by the simulation method.

On this view, then, a full account of the rationality of accepting a logical law, when that derives from the nature of the thinker's own understanding, has to mention implicit conceptions, and the way in which reflective simulation provides a means of extracting the informational content of implicit conceptions.

The other conclusion concerns the possibility of explicating Frege's notion of sense in part by appeal to some ideal understander, and the axioms which an ideal understander would accept. Probably Frege was attracted to such an explication, and there are aspects of his thought and presentation which square with it. But it does not follow that we (nor that he) should accept that explication in terms of what ideal understanders would accept. The resource to which I have appealed in explaining rational acceptance of the axioms is that of implicit conceptions of the semantic contributions of certain expressions. I have emphasized that these implicit conceptions play a part in ordinary thinkers' evaluations of sentences. They are something possessed by ordinary, and not only idealized, thinkers. Insofar as a proposed axiom can be recognized as true, it is recognized on a basis which is rooted in the ordinary, non–idealized understanding of the expressions in the axiom.

REFERENCES

Block, N. "Troubles with Functionalism". In W. Savage, ed., *Perception and Cognition: Issues in the Foundations of Psychology, Minnesota Studies in the Philosophy of Science*, vol. IX: 261-326.
Brewer, B. "Compulsion by Reason". *Aristotelian Society: Supplementary Volume* LXIX (1995): 237-253.
Broad, C. *Leibniz: An Introduction.* Cambridge: Cambridge University Press, 1975.
Burge, T. "Individualism and the Mental". *Midwest Studies in Philosophy* 4 (1979): 73-121.
——— "Intellectual Norms and Foundations of Mind". *Journal of Philosophy* LXXXIII (1986): 697-720.
——— "Frege on Sense and Linguistic Meaning". In *The Analytic Tradition*, ed. D. Bell and N. Cooper. Oxford: Blackwell, 1990.
Carey, S. "Semantic development: state of the art". In *Language acquisition: the state of the art* ed. E. Wanner and L. Gleitman. Cambridge: Cambridge University Press, 1982.
Chomsky, N. *Cartesian Linguistics: A Chapter in the History of Rationalist Thought.* ed. N. Chomsky and M. Halle. New York: Harper & Row, 1966.
Crimmins, M. "Tacitness and Virtual Beliefs". *Mind and Language* 7 (1992): 240-263.
Davies, M. "Connectionism, modularity and tacit knowledge". *British Journal for the Philosophy of Science* 40 (1989): 541-55.
Field, H. "Which Undecidable Mathematical Sentences have Determinate Truth Values?" forthcoming (1996).
Frege, G. *The Foundations of Arithmetic.* Translated by Austin, J.L. Oxford: Blackwell, 1953.
——— *The Basic Laws of Arithmetic.* Translated by Furth, M. Berkeley, California: University of California Press, 1964.
——— *Posthumous Writings.* Translated by Long, P. White, R. Oxford: Blackwell, 1979.
——— "Compound Thoughts". In *Collected Papers on Mathematics, Logic and Philosophy*, ed. B. McGuinness. Oxford: Blackwell, 1984.
Geach, P. *Logic Matters.* Oxford: Blackwell, 1972.
Ishiguro, H. *Leibniz's Philosophy of Logic and Language.* Second edn. ed., Cambridge: Cambridge University Press, 1990.

Leibniz, G. *Leibniz Selections*. Translated by Wiener, P. New York: Charles Scribner's Sons, 1951.

——— *Philosophical Papers and Letters*. Translated by Loemker, L. Dordrecht: Reidel, 1969.

——— *New Essays on Human Understanding*. Translated by Remnant, P. Bennett, J. Cambridge: Cambridge University Press, 1981.

Peacocke, C. "Understanding Logical Constants: A Realist's Account". *Proceedings of the British Academy* 73 (1987): 153-200.

——— *A Study of Concepts*. Cambridge, Mass.: MIT Press, 1992.

——— "How Are A Priori Truths Possible?" *European Journal of Philosophy* 1 (1993): 175-99.

——— "Content, Computation and Externalism". *Mind and Language* 9(1994): 303-335.

——— "Metaphysical Necessity: Understanding, Truth and Epistemology". *Mind* 106 (1997) 521-574

Prior, A. "The Runabout Inference–Ticket". *Analysis* 21 (1960): 38-9.

Quine, W. "Carnap and logical truth". In *The Ways of Paradox and Other Essays*, second ed., Vol. Cambridge, Mass.: Harvard University Press, 1976.

Ricketts, T. "Logic and Truth in Fregre". *Aristotelian Society: Supplementary Volume* LXX (1996): 121-40.

Stewart, Ian. *From Here to Infinity*. Oxford: Oxford University Press, 1996.

Doubts about Implicit Conceptions

Stephen Schiffer

According to Chris, most, but not all, concepts are underlain by *implicit conceptions*. These are subpersonal propositional attitudes whose contents are definitions of the concepts they underlie. For example, the implicit concept underlying one's concept CHAIR would be a definition of what it is to be a chair, the proposition (if it exists) expressed by the correct completion of

Necessarily, a thing is a chair iff. . . .

Implicit conceptions are supposed to do at least two very important jobs. First, they explain the Phenomenon of New Principles: they explain how we're able to come to know new principles involving a concept when those principles don't follow from already accepted principles involving that concept. Second, the implicit conception underlying a thinker's concept both individuates that concept and explains the thinker's possession of the concept. In a fuller commentary, I would question exactly *how*, and *whether*, implicit conceptions manage to perform these two jobs. But here I'll merely raise, without attempting to resolve, five *prima facie* problems for Chris's theory of implicit conceptions.

1. As I said, it would seem that for Chris, the content of the implicit conception underlying one's concept CHAIR is the proposition expressed by the displayed definition form. If so, there's an apparent problem: How can that implicit conception explain my possession of the concept CHAIR when it itself uses that concept? The answer must be that while possession of the concept at the *personal* level must be underlain by an implicit conception whose content involves that concept, that's not true of possession of the concept at the *sub*personal level, the one manifested in one's possession of the implicit conception involving the concept CHAIR. But if we don't need an implicit conception involving the concept CHAIR to explain one's subpersonal possession of that concept, why should one need it to explain one's personal possession? The problem here can be usefully elaborated via the metaphor of a language of thought. Suppose we think in English. Then 'chair' in my language of thought means the concept CHAIR. What accounts for this? I gather that Chris would have to say that it's accounted for by the fact that the relevant subpersonal belief box contains a sentence whose propositional content defines what it is to be a chair, some completion, that is, of 'Necessarily, a thing is a chair iff ...'. But then 'chair' must already mean CHAIR in my language of thought, and what accounts for its meaning can't be an implicit conception whose expression involves use of 'chair'. Chris seems forced to say either that an implicit conception defining chairhood isn't required at all for my having the concept CHAIR or else that we need two separate accounts of how 'chair' comes to mean CHAIR in my language of thought: one for its use in sentences that find their way into my personal propositional-attitude boxes, and one for its use in sentences that occur in my subpersonal boxes. I suspect I may be missing something here, and I look forward to Chris's clarification. One should also note, as was in effect noted to me by Paul Boghossian, that the problem here is exacerbated when one considers the implicit conception underlying one's concept of conjunction, the concept expressed by one's use of 'and'. Evidently, the content of that implicit conception is some refinement of the idea that

> Necessarily, a proposition of the form p *and* q is true iff p is true and q is true.

The additional problem raised by this definition is that the concept being defined occurs, as being used, in the *definiens*, as well as in the *definiendum*.

I might note a further problem, also pointed out to me by Boghossian, which arises for *any* implicit conception that *uses* the concept

7. DOUBTS ABOUT IMPLICIT CONCEPTIONS 91

it's supposed to underlie. This is that it will secure, by virtue of the fact that its content contains the concept in question, that the thinker possesses that concept, *whatever* the further content of that implicit conception is, no matter even if that content is a false proposition.

2. My use of 'chair' —its meaning what it does for me— is to be explained by my implicit conception whose content defines 'chair'. Now, the words that express the concepts that occur in that definition —SEAT, BACK, etc.— evidently need their own implicit conceptions. But this regress can't go on forever, which is why, according to Chris, we eventually reach words and concepts that aren't underlain by implicit conceptions. The total picture is eerily reminiscent of logical atomism: every term either expresses a simple, unanalyzable concept or else is definable as a truth-function of such simples. This isn't Chris's view, for his words and concepts not requiring implicit conceptions may be analyzable via what in *A Study of Concepts* Chris calls 'local holisms'. Nevertheless, the structure of Chris's theory is remarkably similar to that of logical atomism, and it seems to me that the good reasons for doubting the extreme reductionism of logical atomism are equally good reasons for doubting Chris's own heavily reductionist program.

3. The following argument is related to the preceding point. (i) Many concepts are not definable, and among them are MEANING, DOG, LOVE, INTELLIGENCE, and so on. (ii) These concepts would have to be definable if Chris were right, since these are concepts he must say are underlain by implicit conceptions. (iii) Ergo, Chris isn't right.

4. According to Chris, not all concepts are underlain by implicit conceptions. Perhaps RED is such a concept. Yet it would seem that the New Principle Phenomenon can arise for such concepts; e.g., one can come to know a necessary truth about RED which doesn't follow from already known truths involving the concept. But if implicit conceptions aren't needed to explain the New Principle Phenomenon in these cases, why should it be needed in any cases?

5. Where do implicit conceptions come from, and what justifies them? Suppose I have an implicit conception whose content is that necessarily, something is a chair iff.... This can hardly be innate. How did I obtain it? It must count as a piece of subpersonal knowledge, so I must have acquired it via some very reliable knowledge producing mechanism. Evidently, this mechanism doesn't require implicit conceptions, and that again has to make one wonder.

What Implicit Conceptions are Unlikely to Do

Georges Rey

Premature obituaries to the contrary notwithstanding, interest in *a priori* knowledge seems still to be with us. I think some of us find that the supposed Quinian "holistic" alternative view that dispenses with *a priori* knowledge entirely hasn't quite panned out: justifications in terms of, e.g., overall simplicity, generality, conservativism of theory are all very well and good, but they remain pretty vague, and certainly are not sharp enough to rule out more local justificatory means, some of which may well turn out to be "independent of experience" in the way that logic, mathematics and much philosophy have always appeared to be. Indeed, there is this reason to think they will: insofar as claims in these disciplines concern pure (non-indexical) necessities, it is difficult to see how they could actually *depend* upon actual sensory experience with *this* particular world, as opposed to any other. Experience would seem only to serve to call to mind possibilities we had imaginatively neglected to consider, but which, as mere *possibilities*, do not depend upon that experience in order to be established.

Of course, what led to the obituaries about the *a priori* was the apparent lack of any account of how such knowledge was possible. The great Positivistic hope of this century, that it was due to arbitrary conventions, *was* shown by Quine to be pretty inadequate. And traditonal accounts, which seemed to insist upon some special, intuitive insight into the structure of concepts, or transcendental conditions for the possibility of experience, seemed to many both mystical and demonstrably unreliable.

Christopher Peacocke wants to have another go at at least one of the traditional accounts. In a number of papers and a book, he has begun to develop an admirably detailed theory of concepts that might provide a basis for the Rationalist idea that *a priori* knowledge can be based merely upon a thinker's grasp of the content of certain thoughts. In a 1993 paper, he advances "the idea that an account of *what makes* a concept have the semantic value it does is also sufficient to generate a set of *a priori* truths" (1993: p. 181). Indeed:

> The *a priori* status of a content... is fundamentally explained by the fact that the possession conditions for the concepts from which these contents are composed, together with the corresponding determination theories,... guarantee that the content is true in the actual world. (1993: p. 178)

And today he has tried to sketch an account in support of Leibniz's contention that "the evidentness of particular axioms is grounded in an understanding of the terms they contain" (p. 78).

Now, while I don't think Quine has offered a satisfactory account of either empirical or apparent *a priori* knowledge, I do think he raised a serious challenge to strategies of this sort. As one reads Peacocke, it is difficult not to hear Quine whispering at one's back, wondering what makes something a possession or understanding condition, and so presumably "analytic", and a fit basis for *a priori* knowledge. In my remarks today, I want to play devil's —or, anyway, Quine's— advocate, if only to get Peacocke to be clearer than I have found him on this score.

In *A Study of Concepts*, Peacocke can be regarded as having tried to answer Quine's challenge by appeal to what thinkers find "primitively compelling". Such appeals he now recognizes are insufficient, since they are "much too undiscriminating" (pp. 45-46, fn. 1), by which I take him to be noticing that people can be primitively compelled by non–possession conditions, e.g. outright fallacies. Indeed, not only are they not sufficient, they are not necessary: people may *fail* to be compelled, at least ordinarily, by transitions that *are* possession conditions: e.g. appreciation of some correct analysis of knowledge, justice, freedom, causation, or just some logical device may require attaining a state of "reflective equilibrium" (Rawls

8. WHAT IMPLICIT CONCEPTIONS ARE UNLIKELY TO DO 95

1970) with regard to *all* of one's knowledge and intuitions, whereby the appreciated transition could no longer qualify as "primitive". The problem is that primitive compulsions are too *superficial*: they rely upon the surface of a person's psychology, and this can involve all manner of transition in thought, primitive or otherwise, that we might have good explanatory reason not to regard as constitutive of their grasp of the concepts they are nevertheless competent to use.[1]

Instead of primitive compulsions (or perhaps in addition to them; he's not explicit), Peacocke today does dig deeper, offering us his "Implicit Conceptions" (hereinafter, "ICs"). They are contents that are supposed to play a certain explanatory role in explaining an agent's judgments and intuitions, particularly those run "off line" in logical simulations. For example, in the case of a person's understanding of a logical connective:

[...] his having the implicit conception explains his particular patterns of semantic evaluation of [a logically] complex [expression], given information about the truth–values of its constituents. (P. 46.)

Indeed, in a particularly interesting application, ICs are supposed to explain rational acceptance of "new principles which do not follow from those the thinker already [presumably explicitly] accepts" (p. 44). ICs are able to perform this explanatory role by virtue of their being encoded either by subpersonal mental representations or by being "grounded in the operation of a processor" (p. 71).

Now, I entirely agree with Peacocke that *something* non–explicit needs to be posited as an explanation of the judgments people make and the patterns of reasoning in which they engage. We have every reason to think that what Chomsky observed in the case of grammars applies equally to concepts: they are governed by hidden rules that psychology and/or philosophy might reveal.[2]

ICs may well provide the content of these rules. However, do they do so in a way that will fit into Peacocke's strategy for the *a priori*? Merely finding an implicit conception that *explains* a person's judgments won't be enough unless the ICs can be identified as *possession conditions* for the constituent concepts as well. What reason do we have to regard them in that way?

---

[1] I discuss superficialism as a general problem in Twentieth Century approaches to mind and meaning in my discussion of Quine (Rey 1993) and of the work of Dennett (Rey 1994, 1997).

[2] I develop this suggestion on behalf of the analytic and *a priori* in Rey 1993 and forthcoming.

Interestingly, the phrase 'possession conditions', so prominent both in *A Study of Concepts* and in the above mentioned (1993) paper on the *a priori*, doesn't appear in the present paper. Instead, Peacocke writes slightly more guardedly that:

> [...] the thinker's *understanding* of [a particular concept] involves (and perhaps is even to be identified with) his possession of an implicit conception. (P. 46, italics mine.)

Moreover, influenced by Burge's (1990) interesting discussion of Frege's view of senses, Peacocke emphasizes throughout his paper how, where a conception is only implicit, one's understanding of a concept may be imperfect: as Frege phrased it, "we do not have a clear grasp of the sense... its outlines are confused as if we saw it through a mist" (1906/1979: p. 211). So perhaps ICs do not supply *possession* conditions, but only the contents involved in a full, clear understanding of a concept. But, if this is so, then the (1993) strategy for establishing *a priori* knowledge will have to be modified, in such a way that the process of going from mere, misty *possession* of a concept to a full clear *understanding* of it can also be shown to provide a basis for *a priori* claims. Peacocke seems to suggest such a modification today in his sketch of a "simulation" procedure (which we might call "semantic simulation"), by which, by reflecting on the semantic conditions for a concept in a way that Peacocke claims is governed by an IC, a thinker comes to a full, explicit understanding of the IC.

In what follows I want to examine the prospects of recruiting ICs as a basis for the *a priori*. In §I, I shall consider the problem of actually pinning philosophically interesting ICs on a thinker's cognitive states. In §II, I shall argue that, partly in view of the problems raised in §I, it is doubtful that philosophically interesting ICs could serve as possession conditions. And in §III, I shall argue that, if ICs aren't possession conditions, Peacocke needs to say more than he has about why we should regard a process of semantic simulation as affording the basis for the kinds of *a priori* knowledge that have been traditionally sought.

1 Pinning ICs to People

1.1 THE LIMIT OF A SERIES

After his uncontroversial example of a pupil's grasp of disjunction, Peacocke proceeds immediately to the rather more startling example

8. WHAT IMPLICIT CONCEPTIONS ARE UNLIKELY TO DO 97

of Newton and Leibniz's concept of the limit of a series. Peacocke claims:

> It would be huge injustice to Leibniz and Newton to deny that they had the concept of a limit of a series, or to deny that they had propositional attitudes describable by using the word 'limit' within the 'that' clauses.... I would say that each of these great thinkers had an implicit conception which guided their application of the phrase "limit of..." in particular applications. (P. 49.)

This implicit conception Peacocke identifies (p. 49) with Weierstrauss's familiar "delta–epsilon" analysis of two centuries later. What startles me about Peacocke's claim here is its boldness as an historical conjecture. Why on earth should we believe that Weierstrauss' analysis is properly regarded as what Newton or Leibniz implicitly had in mind?

One answer I fear Peacocke may have in mind is his endorsement in his earlier (1993) article of Russell's "regressive method", "of finding general axioms from which truths already known to be *a priori* follow" (p196). However, the only constraint on an IC can't be merely that it serves as an adequate axiom for a body of claims. If Quine has taught us nothing else, it's that we have little reason to think such axiomatizations are unique. Indeed, as Peacocke well knows with respect to the definition of a limit, Robinson's (1966) "nonstandard analysis" offers an alternative to Weierstrauss' by developing a coherent account of "infinitesimals" as legitimate "hyper–real" numbers.

Now, we could enter into detailed historical conjecture about whether to pin Weierstrauss' or Robinson's proposals on Newton or Leibniz. Robinson (1966) provides considerable textual support for thinking his account captures many of Leibniz's claims. In a passing footnote (p. 50, fn. 4), Peacocke cites Ishiguro on behalf of pinning Weierstrauss instead. But a year ago Peacocke (1996: p. 450) also cited Morris Kline's remarks to the effect that both Newton and Leibniz, at least on this issue, seem hopelessly confused. In this earlier article, Peacocke went on (1996: p. 451) to stress the importance of attributing some IC or another as "causally influential". But neither there nor in his paper today does he present any serious evidence for thinking that the Weierstrauss conception really was influential in this way —that, to recall his claim about the reality of ICs (p. 71), they really were either represented explicitly or "grounded in the operation of a processor" in Leibniz's brain.

1.2 POSTULARY CONCEPTIONS

Why, indeed, think it was *determinate* just which conception Leibniz had in mind? I think a more realistic approach to the case of Newton and Leibniz, one that Peacocke dismisses too quickly, is afforded by a "deferential" account of concepts, of roughly the sort proposed by Putnam (1975) and Burge (1979). To put their point as I see it: many ICs are not full analyses, but what might be called "postulary" conceptions. Thinkers construct concepts that have to satisfy certain *constraints*, but for which they may have no defining conceptions at all, explicit or implicit. Like Democritus and Boyle, who postulated atoms as ultimate explanatory constituents of matter, Newton and Leibniz postulated infinitesimals and limits without knowing their precise natures, or, in their case, even how to rid the postulation of paradox. We may do them the justice of attributing them the same concept, leaving it a matter of theory what the best explication of that concept might be.

Peacocke rejects a deferential proposal:

> [...] the facts explained by implicit conceptions cannot be explained away by appealing to deference. To whom were Leibniz and Newton supposed to defer? There was no one else who understood the notion better. Nor, one may conjecture from each of these characters, was either of these two gentlemen of a mind to defer to anyone else in these matters. (P. 50.)

(He makes the same argument in his 1996: p. 450.) But this seems to me to misconstrue the plausible kind of deference to which I take Putnam and Burge to have been pointing.[3] Surely, to take some of Putnam's (1962/1975) best examples, when scientists wonder how best to define a term like 'cancer' or 'multiple sclerosis', they are deferring *not to other scientists*, living or even yet to be born, but rather to the *world*. The usage of other living experts may further *constrain* that definition (as in Burge's case of 'arthritis'); but I see no reason to think that it *exhausts* it. Thinkers *postulate* that there is some phenomenon that happens to play (most of) the explanatory roles that interest them, whose nature would be provided by some optimal theory of the phenomenon. After all, we all know that our grip on optimal theories, and the definitions they may provide, is hampered by our accidental evidential relation to the world, and by the difficulties in actually thinking through the demands such

---

[3] I waive the scholarly point of what exactly *they* had in mind.

8. WHAT IMPLICIT CONCEPTIONS ARE UNLIKELY TO DO   99

a theory might impose.[4] This seems a sensible thought not only for obviously empirical concepts, like [water] and [cancer], that are usually invoked as part of an explanatory account of the world, but also for mathematical concepts like [limit] that are needed in those explanatory accounts.

Notice that postulary conceptions of this sort are precisely what we ought to appeal to in the kind of case that Peacocke admits *is* indeterminate, the example of [set]: "it would be a brave soul who claims that we have a unique pre–theoretical notion of set" (p. 63). Perhaps we are only disagreeing about cases, but I do worry that many of the philosophically interesting cases are ones, like that of [set], in which it is the further development of *theory* that influences our analyses, and not merely the making explicit what in some way or other a thinker implicitly thought all along. That the theory may itself be mathematical or more obviously empirical is of no moment for the psychological point. The fact is that, for various historical reasons, we often come to think in ways that we hadn't thought before.

I suspect that Peacocke might not be too happy with mathematical ICs turning out to be postulary and deferential, since that would render the *a priori* knowledge they are supposed to underwrite fairly anemic, and would threaten the *a priori* status of the substantive analyses philosophers have typically sought. But we need to ask how even fully pinned ICs are actually supposed to help out with the *a priori* in the first place.

2 Could ICs be Possession Conditions?

Well, one might suppose that they do so by being enlisted as possession conditions in Peacocke's (1993) strategy. But could ICs plausibly play such a role? Quite apart from whether we could actually pin either the Weierstrauss or Robinson analysis of [limit] on Newton and Leibniz, would their possession of that concept actually *depend* upon our so pinning? Surely the magnitude of the "injustice" Peacocke claims would issue from denying them the [limit] concept isn't proportional to his confidence that they both had the Weierstrauss analysis as an IC. Suppose it turned out that Newton had it, but

---

[4] It is for this reason that I have suggested elsewhere replacing Putnam's (1975) principle of the "Division of Linguistic Labor" by a "*Hypothesis of External Definition*: the correct definition of a concept is provided by the optimal account of it, which need not be known by the concept's competent users" (Rey 1983: p. 255).

Leibniz didn't: should we now say that Newton did, but Leibniz didn't have the concept [limit], so much for injustice to Leibniz? For what it's worth, I'm inclined to think that what would be more just, as well as more germane to whether Newton or Leibniz possessed the concept, would be precisely whether they were prepared to defer, not personally to Weierstrauss or Robinson, but to optimal theory (or, in this case, theories). The deference to the world seems to me part and parcel of possession conditions with such concepts. Were a person *not* inclined to so defer in at least explanatorily important cases like [water] and [cancer], that would strike me as a good reason to suppose that they didn't have the same concepts that I (and I presume most scientists) have. Were Newton and Leibniz to be actually as imperious and non–deferential as Peacocke claims, that *would* strike me as a reason to suspect they might *not* have had quite the concept of limit that later mathematicians defined.

But who am I say? I have my intuitions about possession conditions, Peacocke has his. The problem, as Quine would remind us, is that it's unclear what depends upon deciding between us. Of course, in a way, a lot depends: whether Newton, Leibniz, Weierstrauss, Robinson and the rest of us are "thinking the same thoughts" or not. But the problem is whether *that* question can be answered in a principled way. I earnestly hope it can be, even along internalist lines of the sort Peacocke suggests. But I don't see that he, or anyone, has yet isolated the crucial explanatory role such conditions can be held to play.

It's hard not to be reminded here of what Quine (1954/1976) wrote with regard to considering stipulative definition (what he calls "legislative postulation") as a source of analytic truths:

> Might we not [speak] of a sentence as forever true by convention if its first adoption as true was a convention? No; this, if done seriously, involves us in the most unrewarding historical conjecture. Legislative postulation contributes truths which become integral to the corpus of truths; the artificiality of their origin does not linger as a localized quality, but suffuses the corpus. (1954/1976: pp. 119-20)

I take it, the point here might be put this way: even if it turned out that Newton had written, "and by 'F' I just *mean* 'ma' and its occurence in other equations is to be regarded as substantive": what makes us hold him to it? We will take Newton's theory as a whole, the division between stipulations and mere truths be hanged. Now the question is: why couldn't essentially the same thing be claimed *mutatis mutandis* against Peacocke's implicit conceptions?

I think the table needs pounding in this regard. Quine did make a number of attacks on the analytic and *a priori* that, I have argue elsewhere, are *not* very powerful. For example, no defender of the *a priori* need claim that *a priori* claims are immune from even empirical revision. Nor need a defender reject holistic confirmation —in addition to a local *a priori* sort. What Quine *did* do, however, was to challenge a defender of the analytic or *a priori* to provide for it *a principled, non–question begging explanatory basis*, a basis on which one could claim that our understanding of the world, or of a thinker, would be defective if we didn't treat such and such claim as a possession condition for a concept. It is this challenge that defenders of the *a priori* (among whom I count myself) need to meet.

Here I'd like to enter a sympathetic suggestion: in meeting the Quinian challenge, I think it may be more promising to focus less on procedures that lead thinkers to *accept* some claim, and instead on what explains thinkers finding certain claims *unintelligible*. Quine's holistic epistemology, after all, has what seems like a reasonable story to tell about people's *acceptance* of purportedly analytic claims. What it conspicuously lacks is an account of the peculiar difficulty we often have in understanding their *denials*. At any rate, we have a difficulty with understanding the denial that squares are four–sided, or material objects extended, that we don't have with understanding the denial of something equally "central", such as that the earth has existed for millions of years, or that most people have noses.

The problems of Peacocke securing the principled possession conditions he seeks seem to me exacerbated by the Burge–Fregean proposal to which he is drawn (pp. 44, 50), whereby concepts (or "senses") are abstract entities, *independent of us*, "grasped" sometimes only dimly, whose actual structure is revealed only by careful analysis. Perhaps ICs are to be understood not as possession conditions, but as the contents of a full understanding of a concept. But then we may ask again: what basis is there for regarding the full understanding a thinker might achieve as *a priori*? If concepts are independent of us in the way that Frege's mist metaphor suggests, how is our coming to understand them any more privileged than our coming to understand any other objective phenomenon? Notice that in such cases their denials are more likely to be perfectly intelligible. On the postulary conception, coming "to fully understand" the concept of a limit might be like a doctor coming fully to understand the concept [arthritis] via an optimal, in that case obviously empirical theory of it. Or perhaps, to take up a different, more "constructive" model that Dworkin (1977: p. 160) suggests for [justice], one tries to accommodate intuitions in the way that judges try to accommodate precedents, not as "clues to a moral [or mathematical] reality", but "out of a sense of responsibility for consistency with what has gone before" (p. 161), with different judges making different judgments about how that consistency should be effected (I daresay, this latter alternative seems to me to fit better indeterminate cases like [limit] and [set]. After all, do we really know *a priori* Weierstrauss' analysis to be *correct*, as opposed to merely adequate?).

3 A Priori Knowledge?

Peacocke apparently hopes that the *a priori* status of "full understandings" can be secured by the semantic simulation procedure with which he introduces ICs. A logic student comes to appreciate the rule of addition for disjunction by imagining its different truth conditions, and:

> [...] it dawns on him that there will be no cases in which the antecedent...is true, and the consequent... is false... Then he rationally comes to accept the axiom... as valid.... When axioms, inference rules, or lines of truth–tables are reached in this way, it seems to me that the resulting judgments constitute knowledge. (P. 45.)

This procedure Peacocke regards as

> [...] one which yields *a priori* knowledge. Nothing in that rationale for the subject's belief involves perceptual experience or sensation. (P. 80.)

To the sceptic who wonders what gives this knowledge any objectivity, Peacocke likens such semantic simulation to spatial simulation, by which one imagines what one would see walking across a certain bridge:

> When by this means, you reach the conclusion that when on the bridge, the former County Hall would be slightly left of straight ahead, *this is a means of obtaining information about the world*. If they are knowledgeable states which the thinker is drawing upon in performing the simulation, *it is also a means of obtaining knowledge about the world*. (P. 48.)

But how does this analogy with spatial simulation actually help the *a priori* case? A simulation is at best merely a means of tapping knowledge already possessed; it is not a *further* "means of obtaining information or knowledge about the world". And a "semantic"

8. WHAT IMPLICIT CONCEPTIONS ARE UNLIKELY TO DO   103

simulation would issue in *a priori* knowledge only if the knowledgeable states on which it is based are themselves known *a priori*: but how do we establish *that*? Well, maybe also by simulation; but this can't go on forever. Ultimately, we are driven back to possession conditions, and to Quine's problem of picking these out in a principled way, and pinning philosophically interesting ones on standard thinkers.

Perhaps one shouldn't argue with Peacocke's case of disjunction: as Quine pointed out, disagreement about logic is as basic as disagreement can get, and apparent deviation from the standard norms is probably better understood as poor translation. But how are we to generalize to cases beyond truth–functional logic? What are the possession conditions for quantifiers? Are they substitutional or objectual? Moreover, are the considerations that might enter into a semantic simulation in all cases really devoid of any reliance on empirical knowledge —on whether, for example, space is actually continuous or not, or whether languages are discrete? And passing beyond logic, what about concepts of number, space, time, causation, and material objects, or (to take examples Peacocke anticipates including) "fairness, equality and opportunity" (p. 52)? Consider in this regard Hartry Field's explicit efforts to tie mathematics to actual physics, or Rawls' informing his theory of justice by patently empirical considerations. Is Peacocke really confident that the semantic simulation procedure for arriving at interesting analyses of them doesn't depend upon any empirical considerations? I think he needs to share the basis for this confidence with those of us who are still uncomfortable with the challenge we keep hearing Quine whispering in our ears.

REFERENCES

Burge, T. (1979), "Individualism and the Mental", *Midwest Studies in Philosophy*, 4, pp. 73-121.

——— (1990), "Frege on Sense and Linguistic Meaning", in *The Analytic Tradition*, ed. by D. Bell and N. Cooper, Oxford: Blackwell, pp. 30-60.

Dworkin, R. (1977), "Justice and Rights", in *Taking Rights Seriously*, Cambridge: Harvard University Press.

Frege, G. (1906/1979), "Logic in Mathematics", in *Posthumous Writings*, ed. by H. Hermes, F. Kambartel, and F. Kaulbach, translated by P. Long and R. White; Chicago: University of Chicago Press, pp. 203-50.

Peacocke, C. (1993), "How Are *A Priori* Truths Possible?" *European Journal of Philosophy* 1:2, pp. 175-99.

——— (1992), *A Study of Concepts*, Cambridge: MIT Press.

―― (1996), "Can Possession Conditions Individuate Concepts?", *Philosophy and Phenomenological Research*, LVI(2), pp. 433-60.

―― (1998??), "Implicit Conceptions, Understanding and Rationality", delivered at Conference on Methods in Philosophy and the Sciences, The New School, 3 May 1997 (manuscript).

Putnam, H, (1962/1975), "Dreaming and Depth Grammar", in *Philosophical Papers*, vol. 2, Cambridge: Cambridge University Press, pp. 304-324.

―― (1975), "The Meaning of 'Meaning'", in *Philosophical Papers*, vol. 2, Cambridge: Cambridge University Press.

Quine, W. (1954/1976), "Carnap and Logical Truth", in *Ways of Paradox and Other Essays*, pp. 107-132.

Rey, G. (1983), "Concepts and Stereotypes", *Cognition*, 15, pp. 237-62.

―― (1993), "The Unavailability of What We Mean: a Reply to Quine, Fodor and Lepore", *Grazer Philosophica*, pp. 61-101.

―― (1994), "Dennett's Unrealistic Psychology", *Philosophical Topics*, vol. 22 (#1-2), pp. 259-289.

―― (1996), "Resisting Primitive Compulsions", *Philosophy and Phenomenological Research*, Vol. LVI #2 (June), pp. 419-424.

―― (1997), *Contemporary Philosophy of Mind: a Contentiously Classical Approach*, Oxford: Blackwell.

―― (forthcoming), "A Naturalistic *A Priori*", *Philosophical Studies*.

Robinson, A. (1966), *Non-Standard Analysis*, Amsterdam: North-Holland.

Implicit Conceptions and The Phenomenon of Abandoned Principles*

Eric Margolis

In this paper, I consider the relation between implicit conceptions and conceptual identity. Since Peacocke's reliance on implicit conceptions marks a novel development in his views on concepts, it's understandable that the notion remains unclear on certain points. One of these is whether implicit conceptions are supposed to be constitutive of the concepts that are associated with. I take it to be a natural reading of Peacocke that he thinks they are, in which case his view resembles a standard version of conceptual role semantics. I argue, however, that Peacocke's notion of an implicit conception needn't be tied down in this way; it needn't involve the claim that implicit conceptions are constitutive of the concepts they are associated with. What's more, I argue that there are grounds to deny a constitutive relation between implicit conceptions and their concepts. My argument turns on the need to explain what I call the Phenomenon of Abandoned Principles.

---

*I'd like to thank Richard Grandy, Stephen Laurence, and Michael Strevens.

1 Implicit Conceptions and Conceptual Role Semantics

Peacocke's central claim is that theories of content need to come to grips with an important fact about concepts —his Phenomenon of New Principles. This is the fact that people can be rational in accepting a new principle that involves a concept, even though this principle doesn't follow from other principles whose immediate acceptance is required to possess the concept. What impresses Peacocke is the situation where a person possesses a concept, and applies it accurately in particular cases, yet fails to accept a correct analysis of the concept. Moreover, with a prior grasp of a concept, the same person may be able to reason her way to an analysis, so that she can come to formulate a definition of a concept she'd been using all along. From these observations, Peacocke finds the motivation for introducing a new theoretical tool, implicit conceptions. Implicit conceptions are supposed to be tacit contentful states that are associated with various concepts. The content of an implicit conception isn't readily accessible, so it may take considerable work to elicit. Nonetheless, implicit conceptions are responsible for certain judgments about whether a concept applies in a given circumstance.

One of Peacocke's conclusions is that the principal motivation for implicit conceptions —his Phenomenon of New Principles— also provides grounds for rejecting certain versions of conceptual role theories of content. So it may seem odd for me to describe his commitment to implicit conceptions as being tantamount to his accepting a version of conceptual role semantics. The key to this puzzle, however, is the distinction between personal-level conceptual roles and psycho-conceptual roles. Implicit conceptions may not involve personal-level inferences, but they do involve the sorts of inferences that are familiar from psycho-conceptual role theories.

Here's Peacocke describing how an implicit conception operates in the larger cognitive economy (pp. 69–70):

> The model, then, to illustrate it for the simple case of [the concept] *chair* would run thus. One of the thinker's perceptual systems, say, identifies some object in the environment as having a supporting area and a back, and the subject has the background information that the object is used for sitting on. This information from the perceptual system, together with the background information, is combined, at the subpersonal level, with the content of the implicit conception underlying understanding of [the word] 'chair', and by some form of subpersonal computation it is computed, from the given contents, that the presented object is a chair.

This in turn explains the thinker's willingness to judge that that object, demonstratively given in perception, is a chair. In the case of other concepts, the role just played by the perceptual system will be played by some informational source or other. This source yields a content which, together with the content of the implicit conception underlying the concept, and possibly some background information or presupposition, permits computation of a content to the effect that some given object falls under the concept in question.

The thing to notice is that this description implicates psychological processes among semantically evaluable states. In this respect, processes that access implicit conceptions fall squarely under the rather general characterization of an "inference" that is commonplace among psycho–conceptual role semanticists. Assuming, then, a view of implicit conceptions where they are also constitutive of their concepts, the result is that part of the psycho–conceptual role of a concept is constitutive of its identity. The only difference between Pecocke's brand of conceptual role semantics and more standard psycho–conceptual role theories (such as Block 1986) is Peacocke's interesting suggestion that a crucial part of the conceptual role of such concepts as CHAIR is relatively inaccessible.

Let me say again that it is unclear whether Peacocke does commit himself to the claim that implicit conceptions are constitutive of the concepts they are associated with. To this extent, it's unclear whether Pecocke's theory should be likened to a conceptual role semantics. Nonetheless, in the rest of this paper, I argue against the conceptual role theory that I see in Peacocke. If it turns out that Peacocke doesn't want to endorse a constitutive relation between implicit conceptions and their concepts, then my critique should be read, instead, in the spirit of an exploratory investigation. What I'm really interested in is clarifying the most plausible relation between implicit conceptions and their concepts.

2 Conceptions vs. Constitutive Conceptions

Implicit conceptions do several things for Peacocke. One is that they are supposed to explain people's judgments about whether a concept applies in a given case. Where a concept is associated with an implicit conception, it's the content of the implicit conception that is responsible for judgments about whether something falls under the concept. Another is that they are supposed to explain the Phenomenon of New Principles —the fact that people can be rational in accepting a new principle that involves a concept. Of course, these two *explananda* are linked for Peacocke. What makes the acceptance of a new principle rational is precisely that is based on judgments about which things do, and which things do not, fall under a concept. But let's keep them separate for the moment. An issue I'd like to pursue is whether the first *explanandum*, by itself, motivates the existence of a constitutive relation between an implicit contentful state and the concept it is associated with. The answer is that need not. To see this, it might help to consider some alternative models where judgments involving a concept's application depend upon implicit contenful states.

One departure from Peacocke's model is a variation on the prototype theory in psychology.[1] According to this sort of theory, judgments that something falls under a concept are to be analyzed in terms of the similarity between the candidate item and a prototype. A common way of developing this idea is to analyze a prototype as a set of weighted features and to define the similarity–comparison process in terms of feature matching. On this version, chairs might be judged to be furniture because a sufficient number of the features that are associated with CHAIR are themselves associated with FURNITURE. Now usually, as this model is understood, the features that go into a prototype are assumed to be fairly accessible. In fact, the way psychologists typically arrive at a feature list for a concept is to have subjects report what they take to be crucial properties of the category in question ("write down all the important properties of chairs..."). Yet there is nothing in the prototype theory that requires that features be construed this way. One can easily imagine a variation on the theory in which the features aren't so accessible to reflection, so that they explain certain judgments involving a concept yet resist articulation by a thoughtful person.

There are several ways this might work. One is that the prototype might incorporate low–level perceptual information that isn't in the normal course of things available to reflection. To learn about such structures, one would have to learn about the science of visual processing. Ray Jackendoff adopts a model much like this, in that he appeals to Marr's notion of a 2 1/2 D sketch in distinguishing particular concepts within certain families of concepts (Jackendoff 1987). He proposes, for instance, that the difference between the concepts CAT and DOG can be accounted for by the fact that each

---

[1] The term "prototype theory" is actually used to pick out a family of psychological theories, but we needn't go into the differences among them here. For reviews, see Smith & Medin (1981) and Margolis (1994).

9. IMPLICIT CONCEPTIONS AND THE PHENOMENON... 109

is associated with a different 2 1/2 D sketch, which is partly responsible for whether someone will judge, of a new instance, whether it falls under its respective concept.

In short, the model we are envisioning is one where an implicit contentful state explains judgments about the application of a concept in much the same way that an implicit conception does. The main difference, however, is that for Peacocke, implicit conceptions give constitutive definitions for their concepts.[2] But with the prototype theory, none of the features that characterize a concept need be necessary for the concept's application. An item falls under a concept, and is judged to fall under a concept, not because it satisfies all of the features of the concept, or even any specific ones, but because it satisfies some sufficient number of them. Still, one could argue that the prototype structure, taken as a whole, is constitutive of the concept with which it is associated. So, while the prototype model offers an alternative to Peacocke's implicit conceptions, it's hardly a radical alternative.

But radical alternatives do exist. Perhaps the clearest of these is to be found in certain version of the information–based semantics (IBS) approach to conceptual content. On such accounts, the content of a mental representation is determined by its standing in a nomic relation to the property it expresses. Roughly, the mental representation CHAIR is said to express the property *chair* because chairs cause CHAIR–tokenings (see, e.g., Fodor 1990).[3] What distinguishes this sort of account from both Peacocke's view of concepts and the prototype theory is that, according to IBS, the content of a concept is not at all (metaphysically) determined by its relation to other contentful states. In particular, the inferential relations that are recruited in judgments about whether something falls under a concept are not

---

[2] To be fair, Peacocke never says that implicit conception must specify *definitions*, that is, necessary and sufficient conditions for the application of a concept. Yet all of his examples of implicit conceptions are definitional, and throughout he seems to imply that this is to be expected. For instance, even though he never explicitly says what the implicit conceptions is for CHAIR, he does say that the implicit conception embodies a definition. "Implicit knowledge of the definition of 'chair' can explain a person's applying the word correctly in central cases" (p. 61). Also: "For the ordinary user of the concept, the definition of *chair* is something which does not follow from those judgments about instances which he must immediately be able to make if he is to possess the concept *chair*. The same applies again to the definition of *limit* in relation to Leibniz's and Newton's use of the concept" (p. 65).

[3] This is rough because different version of information–based semantics build on this account in different ways.

constitutive of the concept's content. All that matters to content is that the appropriate mind–world relation obtains.

Still, just because the inferential dispositions for a given concept aren't constitutive of its content doesn't mean that they are psychologically inert. Far from it, they will still be responsible for judgments involving the concept, including judgments that the concept applies in particular circumstances. And, as with the prototype theory, we could add the further assumption that these dispositions aren't easily accessible to reflection. In this case, then, we'd have a clear model where implicit contentful states are responsible for judgments about the application of a concept yet where the content of these states fail to be constitutive of the concept.

Let's call the contentful states that are responsible for judgments about the application of a concept the concept's "conception". The point I've been emphasizing, then, is that one could endorse the existence of conceptions, and one could add that conceptions are sometimes difficult to articulate. Yet accepting all of this doesn't require that one hold that the conception associated with a concept is constitutive of its content.

3 The Phenomenon of Abandoned Principles

Perhaps at this point Peacocke would cite the Phenomenon of New Principles and appeal to his stock examples. In these cases —largely, examples of logical and mathematical concepts— it may seem plausible that their conceptions are constitutive of them. But it's an interesting question whether one should generalize from these concepts, or treat them as special cases. After all, even staunch critics of conceptual role semantics are likely to admit that logical, and perhaps mathematical concepts, are the best candidates for a conceptual role theory.[4] And as I emphasized at the outset, Peacocke's theory of implicit conceptions is a variation on standard conceptual role theories. It's no surprise, then, that the theory appears to work for the stock examples.

But maybe not for all. Consider Peacocke's discussion of the concept CHAIR. He doesn't actually say what he thinks the implicit conception for CHAIR is, but the text I've already cited does suggest that he thinks CHAIR has an implicit conception and that it

---

[4] Jerry Fodor, for example, is widely regarded to be the most forceful and consistent critic of conceptual role semantics and yet even he adopts a conceptual role semantics for the logical concepts.

incorporates information about the function and design of chairs — that they are used for sitting on and that they have, among other features, backs and supporting areas. Arguably, though, not all of these features are necessary for something's being a chair. It's doubtful, for example, that chairs have to be used for sitting on. I can easily imagine a "collector's chair", an object prized for its representing a distinctive style of design, yet one that no one is allowed to touch, better yet sit on. Perhaps one might argue, that it's still taken to be a chair because its structure is aimed to accommodate sitting, even though no one is allowed to sit on it. Yet one could add to the scenario that while the object's construction involves the paradigmatic appearance of a chair —a back, four legs, arms, etc.— that, nonetheless, the construction is such that it can't support any substantial weight and that this was even part of the design under which the object was executed. My own intuitions regarding this case is that the object is still a chair; it's just not a chair you'd want to sit on.

Now I don't want to put too much weight on this one example. Again, Peacocke doesn't say what the implicit conception for CHAIR is; all we have to go on is his remark about how an implicit conception combines with other information in the processes that underlie judgments that certain objects are chairs. However, this example is useful in that it illustrates an important phenomenon which is more or less the flip–side of Peacocke's Phenomenon of New Principles, viz., the situation where someone is rational in coming to *reject* a principle that she once took to be constitutive of a concept. We might call this the Phenomenon of Abandoned Principles.

I suppose that Peacocke might try to explain the Phenomenon of Abandoned Principles in much the same way he explains the Phenomenon of New Principles, that is, by appealing to implicit conceptions. The suggestion is that an implicit conception is responsible for judgments about the application of a concept and that these judgments may be available to correct a flawed analysis of a concept. But once again, it's fitting to consider other models.

Returning to the prototype theory, there is a natural explanation of why a principle might be rejected. As psychologists are apt to emphasize in discussions of the theory, people are often committed to the idea that concepts have definitions, even when they are incapable of specifying one. If this is so, then it might be that people are prone to misconstrue the more central and salient features in a prototype as being defining features of a concept. When faced with an atypical example that they judge to fall under the concept, the fact that the feature is only central, or salient, becomes manifest. They find themselves in the situation where they have to retract their initial definition. I think it's fair to say that most psychologists who favor the prototype theory favor it, in part, for this reason. They are impressed by people's inability to specify a definition of a concept that holds up to a variety of imagined cases.

On the other hand, the prototype theory doesn't fully embrace the Phenomenon of Abandoned Principles. Recall that the big difference between the prototype theory and Peacocke's model of implicit conceptions is that, on the prototype theory, each feature, taken separately, is contingent in its relation to the concept associated with the prototype. At the same time, the cluster of features, together with a metric for defining similarity to the prototype, is constitutive of the concept. So a single principle framed in terms of a single feature, or some small number of them, might be abandoned on the prototype theory. But one shouldn't be able to rationally abandon the entire cluster of features. Similarly, a model that relies upon implicit conceptions is limited in how far it can deal with the Phenomenon of Abandoned Principles. If an implicit conception is responsible for the judgments involving a concept, then one shouldn't be able to rationally abandon a principle that the implicit conception specifies. In this regard, the IBS model is the more radical theory. It fully embraces the Phenomenon of Abandoned Principles because it permits the rejection of entire conceptions. In principle, IBS allows that a person at one time could have the very same concept at another time, despite massive changes in her inferential dispositions.

Here I think it's worth emphasizing the robustness of the Phenomenon of Abandoned Principles. The point isn't just that people have rationally rejected a number of purported analyses. Rather, the interesting fact is that, to a large extent, deeply held principles appear to be susceptible to revision, given sufficient ingenuity and sufficient theoretical motivation. What may have looked like an obvious conceptual truth is all too often revealed to be epistemically contingent. Hilary Putnam, for example, has asked us to imagine the situation where the things we normally think of as cats are discovered to be Martian controlled robots (Putnam 1962). In this case, intuition strongly suggests that the thing to say is that cats aren't animals. If this is right, then the link between the concept ANIMAL and the concept CAT isn't constitutive. One might even possess the concept CAT without thereby possessing the concept ANIMAL. At least, nothing in the nature of the concept CAT requires that, to possess it, one would have to possess ANIMAL as well.

Perhaps a less-fantastical example —one that derives from a scientific theory currently under debate— is the claim that there are more than four dimensions (i.e., the usual three plus time) and that light and matter and the ordinary objects we experience are nothing but vibrations in higher dimensions. This is a view that sounds preposterous at first, but, in the context of hyperspace theory, is perfectly coherent (see, e.g., Kaku 1994). The history of philosophy is filled with comparable cases. Bishop Berkeley, to take another example, argued that material objects are actually mental phenomena —collections of ideas in the mind of God. That this notion is coherent —that a chair might be a collection of ideas— is a testament to Berkeley's ingenious theoretical position. What's more, the fact that it's coherent suggests that one could, under certain theoretical pressure, *rationally* abandon even the principle that material objects are mind–independent entities. In what sense would it be rational? In the same sense that Peacocke would say that the acceptance of a new principle is rational. The rationality of the process derives from the data given by judgments of whether various things fall under the concept in question.

In my view, examples like these offer strong support for the significance of the Phenomenon of Abandoned Principles. They also suggest that the Phenomenon is best explained by a model where the contentful states that are responsible for judgments involving a concept aren't constitutive of the concept.

4 Conclusion

In sum, Peacocke's Phenomenon of New Principles provides some reason to think that part of the conception associated with a concept is tacit, or not readily accessible to reflection. But we have been given no reason to think that tacit conceptions are constitutive of their concepts, and the Phenomenon of Abandoned principles suggests that they are not. One way to describe the situation is that the existence and significance of implicit conceptions has yet to be established. Alternatively, we could say that implicit conceptions do exist, but that they are nothing more than tacit contentful states that are responsible for judgments about the application of a concept: In particular, they don't generally specify definitions for their concepts, and they aren't constitutive of their concepts. I'm not sure if Peacocke will find this alternative to be a friendly amendment to his theory. If not, he can view it as a challenge to supplement his defense of implicit conceptions.

References

Block, N. (1986). "Advertisement for a Semantics for Psychology". In P.A. French, T.E. Uehling Jr., & H.K. Wettstein. (Eds.), *Midwest Studies in Philosophy, Volume X: Studies in the Philosophy of Mind*. Minneapolis: University of Minnesota Press.

Fodor, J. (1990). "A Theory of Content II". In his *A Theory of Content and Other Essays*. Cambridge, MA: MIT Press.

Jackendoff, R. (1987). *Consciousness and the Computational Mind*. Cambridge, MA: MIT Press.

Kaku, M. (1994). *Hyperspace: A Scientific Odyssey through Parallel Universes, Time Warps, and the Tenth Dimension*. New York: Oxford University Press.

Margolis, E. (1994). "A Reassessment of the Shift from the Classical Theory of Concepts to Prototype Theory". *Cognition*, 51.

Putnam, H. (1962/1975). "It Ain't Necessarily So". In his *Mathematics, Matter and Method: Philosophical Paper, Vol. 1*. New York: Cambridge University Press.

Smith, E., and Medin, D. (1981). *Categories and Concepts*. Cambridge, MA: Harvard University Press.

The Implicit Conception of Implicit Conceptions

Josefa Toribio

1 Introduction

Peacocke's characterization of what he calls implicit conceptions recognizes the significance of a subset of contentful states in making rational behavior intelligible. What Peacocke has to offer in this paper is an account of (i) why we need implicit conceptions; (ii) how we can discover them; (iii) what they explain; (iv) what they are; and (v) how they can help us to better understand some issues in the theory of meaning and the theory of knowledge. The rationalist tradition in which Peacocke's project ought to be located is concerned with the nature of understanding. His notion of implicit conceptions is invoked to explain non–straightforwardly inferential but rational patterns of concept–involving behavior. We come to know about implicit conceptions because we treat the thinker's practices as having a certain representational content. They are implicit in what the thinker *does*.

I intend to focus on the question of what implicit conceptions *are* (although in doing so some of the other aspects will also come to the fore). I will argue for the following position: that —even at the personal level— certain inferential principles underlie the process that leads to the thinker's reliably differential responses and that subsequently point us in the direction of a notion such as that of an implicit conception. More precisely, I will argue that *practical* inferential processes are involved in the understanding–based capacities that support our ascription of personal–level implicit conceptions to the thinker. If I am right, then Peacocke's implicit conceptions don't preclude acceptance of personal–level conceptual–role theories because that practical inferential articulation, i.e. that conceptual role, is the implicit conception itself.[1]

2 What Implicit Conceptions Are and What They Are Not

Before the presentation of my argument, it might be helpful to rehearse what I take to be the key positive and negative features of implicit conceptions. On the positive side, we find (i) that implicit conceptions are understanding–based *capacities* that the thinker possesses and that lead her to the rational acceptance of certain principles and statements; (ii) that implicit conceptions are *content-involving states* (even though the thinker need not have any explicit knowledge of those contents); (iii) that they *play an explanatory role* in particular patterns of semantic evaluation and of object and property recognition and also *a justificational role* in the thinker's rational acceptance of primitive (logical) principles; (iv) that they involve concepts whose explicit characterization by a speaker *can be incorrect* without affecting the correctness of the implicit content; (v) that implicit conceptions are fundamentally *tied to judgments about particular cases*; and finally (vi) that implicit conceptions are concepts whose legitimacy can't be defended.

On the negative side, we are told that (i) implicit conceptions are not concepts for which the thinker has only a partial understanding of the expression. The thinker doesn't defer in her use of the expression to others in the community who understand it better; (ii) that implicit conceptions are not tacit or virtual beliefs. (iii) that they are not inferential dispositions; (iv) that implicit conceptions are not rules in Wittgenstein's sense; and finally (v) that the rational, justified acceptance of new principles involving a given concept precludes the idea that implicit conceptions can be characterized —at the personal level— in terms of their conceptual role.

---

[1] The notion of conceptual role as inferential role that I have in mind is the one developed by Robert Brandom (1994) following Sellars' original ideas (1963).

10. THE IMPLICIT CONCEPTION OF IMPLICIT CONCEPTIONS   117

Two caveats. First, the position that I am about to defend should not be taken as one in which implicit conceptions are just dispositions to correctly apply concepts in central cases. I agree with Peacocke that the classification of particular stimuli as instances of a general kind by the exercise of regular differential responsive dispositions may be a necessary condition of concept use, but it is certainly not a sufficient one. Second, I also agree that in order for a thinker to count as having what Peacocke characterizes as implicit conceptions, he or she need not *inferentially* justify her claim, or her acceptance, or her recognition. The claim that —even at the personal–level— *practical* inferential processes are involved in the understanding–based capacities that support our ascription of implicit conception to the thinker doesn't imply that those inferential processes play a justificational role *for* the thinker, but only for the theorist who performs the ascription.

3 My Implicit Conception of Implicit Conceptions

My contention is that for a reliably differential response to be a candidate for the expression of knowledge of the content of an implicit concept, the thinker who behaves according to the possession of that concept must have *some grip on its role in reasoning*. Otherwise implicit conceptions could not be characterized as understanding–based capacities at all. They couldn't be characterized this way because part of what 'being rational' means in this context involves displaying states, attitudes and practices that are liable to normative assessment. In other words, to be a thinker (rather than a mere behaver) is to be involved in a web of structured activity with a normative dimension. The movement of thought —as Peacocke likes to phrase the point— in which the rational thinker is engaged need not involve inference. But inference of a practical kind is indeed involved in grasping the normative force of such non inferentially acquired knowledge. That practical kind of inference is what *takes* the thinker from e.g. the utterance of a sentence such as 'This is a chair' to the acceptance of a commitment to the effect that there is a chair there.

What I mean by the thinker having '*some grip on the concept's role in reasoning*' is thus something like this. In order to count as a thinker and not a mere behaver, the agent must embrace, even in *non inferential* applications of the concept, certain normatively pregnant attitudes whose manifestation is a commitment to *act* in a certain (rational) way. This reflection suggests that the content–

involving implicit conceptions underlying the normative aspect embedded in the thinker's rational commitments can only be specified by the conceptual role they play in accounting for her behavior. The inferential commitment is, then, precisely the conceptual role of the thinker's implicit conception. As Peacocke's main argument against the plausibility of personal conceptual–role theories in accounting for implicit conceptions is based on the thinker's rational and justified acceptance of new principles involving a given concept, I'll now concentrate on that issue.

Let's re–consider the case of classical negation, a case that Peacocke examines in order to show how a personal–level conceptual–role theorist might treat the phenomenon of new principles. He claims that the personal–level conceptual–role theorist might

[...] include the classical logical inferential principles for negation: that from ¬¬A one can infer A, and that if one can derive a contradiction from A, one can infer ¬A. Yet again it seems clear that these classical logical rules for negation (and their instances) are ones whose correctness can be, and needs to be, attained by rational reflection from some prior understanding of negation... The implicit conception associated with the understanding of negation simply *links* the expression for negation with these already appreciated falsity conditions (p. 65. My emphasis).

Now, what is the nature of that *link*? It seems to me that the link Peacocke is talking about has an inferential character of the kind I am advocating here, i.e., that to know the truth-, and therefore the falsity–conditions of a sentence already involves the sort of normative commitment that is conferred on that sentence by the role it plays in the thinker's practices. I grant Peacocke's point that the movement of thought in which a rational thinker is engaged when coming to appreciate the meaning–determining role for classical negation cannot be explained as a result of her having explicitly inferred it from *logical* inferential principles. My point is that the understanding of the meaning–determining role for classical negation and its being a potential manifestation of knowledge couldn't be correctly ascribed to the thinker without her having *implicitly inferred* it from the *implicit knowledge* embedded in her rational practices (especially those that contain the connective involved, i.e., negation).

To invoke an implicit conception of negation in personal–level conceptual–role terms doesn't thus necessarily involve the need to appeal to the *logical* inferential principles that Peacocke has in mind, but it does require an appeal to features of the use of that expression that are inferential in a different sense, a sense that affects even our understanding of the truth–conditions of a claim that does not contain

10. THE IMPLICIT CONCEPTION OF IMPLICIT CONCEPTIONS 119

a negation. To see how this works one only has to change the terms of the *link* that Peacocke mentions —the link between the expression for negation and the already appreciated falsity conditions— and say, as e.g. Brandom does, that since 'the content of a claim can be represented by the set of claims that are incompatible with it' (Brandom, 1994, p. 115), its formal negation can be analyzed as '... the claim that is *entailed* [my emphasis] by each one of the claims incompatible with the claim of which it is the negation' (Brandom, 1994, p. 115). This characterization of our grasp of negation involves an implicit conception, but one whose correctness can only be appreciated by paying attention to the personal–level conceptual role it plays in rational practice.

The move I am making here might sound too close to one that Peacocke tries to undermine in his paper. It might sound like a proposal that Peacocke himself made in his earlier work, and that consists, basically, in saying that the rationally appreciated correctness of new principles '... is fixed by those [other principles] which are mentioned in the conceptual role *in some less direct way*' (p. 66. My emphasis). He points out that this strategy leaves three problems unresolved. One is that the strategy cannot be applied to the 'ordinary' thinker. The second is that the strategy lacks the initial materials on which it needs to operate because there are cases in which all of the inference rules distinctive of a concept have to be worked out by a thinker. Finally, according to Peacocke, the strategy gives no rationale for the requirement itself.

However, I don't think these problems arise for the strategy proposed here. Firstly, the practical inferential capacity of the thinker to engage in rational behavior involving negation is not to be identified with mastery of a *logical calculus*, but rather with the usual understanding of sentences (even those not containing negation). This is certainly something we should concede to the 'ordinary' thinker.

Secondly, the case in which *all* the inference rules distinctive of a concept have to be worked out by a thinker is not a case that applies to the concept of negation as it has been characterized in our practical inferential treatment. The reason is again that some of those inferences are already present in the understanding of any claim and, furthermore, they are already embedded in any other kind of non–linguistic behavior that deserves to be called rational. Also, as a general point, I doubt very much that there are cases —other than stipulations involved in newly introduced symbols— in which all of the inference rules for a concept have to be worked out by the thinker.

Finally, the strategy *does* give a rationale for the requirement of appealing to the inferentially articulated attitudes underlying understanding-based capacities (although certainly not to Peacocke's requirement which is the need to invoke the strongest semantical assignment that validates some introduction rule mentioned in the conceptual role). The rationale, one that can be found already in Frege and in a more elaborate way in Dummett (Cf. Dummett, 1973), is that these understanding-based capacities need to account *both* for the circumstances under which they are correctly applied or used *and* the appropriate consequences of their application (Cf. Brandom, 1994, p. 117).

I think the same strategy can be applied to implicit conceptions that lie outside the logical or mathematical domain, i.e., that understanding-based capacities implicitly involve a practical inferential commitment even in the case of empirical concepts that are mainly used in perception and observational reports. To say this, however, is not much of a criticism, as Peacocke himself acknowledges that the possession of those concepts may be explained in terms of conceptual-roles as long as they are characterized in psychofunctionalist terms and adds that '[n]othing I have said tells against psycho-conceptual-role theories of meaning and content' (p. 66). Now, the central point of my argument is that nothing of what Peacocke has said tells against personal-level conceptual role theories either. As a result, it seems hard to discern any residual deep difference between a conceptual-role characterization of implicit conceptions —both at the personal and subpersonal level— and the one that Peacocke is now defending. But, of course, it might just be that the reason the difference seems elusive is that I still possess only an implicit conception of implicit conceptions.

REFERENCES

Brandom, R. (1994) *Making It Explicit: Reasoning, Representing, and Discursive Commitment*, Cambridge, Mass.: Harvard University Press.
Dummett, M. (1973) *Frege's Philosophy of Language*, New York: Harper and Row.
Sellars, W. S. (1963) "Empiricism and the Philosophy of Mind". Reprinted in *Science, Perception and Reality*, London: Routledge & Kegan Paul.

Implicit Conceptions, the *A Priori*, and the Identity of Concepts*

Christopher Peacocke

In my paper 'Implicit Conceptions, Understanding and Rationality', I advocated the importance of the notion of an implicit conception, and attempted to put it to some theoretical work. I claimed that implicit conceptions can help to explain the application of concepts to instances, the rationality of accepting primitive logical laws, and the rational acceptance of new principles involving a concept, principles which do not follow from those which the thinker already accepts. The theory which develops these claims has a classically rationalist flavour. I also claimed that concepts associated with an implicit conception could not be fitted into certain kinds of personal-level conceptual role theories of content. These several claims raise a host of philosophical issues about concepts, including at least the following:

> Is the whole category of implicit conceptions dispensable in favour of a more general recognition of the extent to which

---
*© Copyright C. Peacocke 1998.

use of a concept involves postulation that there is some (often unknown) unifying property underlying our applications of the concept? Do the examples I gave require anything more than that general recognition?

When a concept has an underlying implicit conception, how does the implicit conception help to explain the *a priori* status of principles containing the concept?

Is the implicit conception constitutive of the concept, or just defeasibly associated with it?

Is there an unacceptable circularity in the content of the implicit conceptions I propose? And is the whole idea of an implicit conception committed to some highly questionable general reductionism?

Is the tension I claimed to identify between personal–level conceptual role theories and the existence of implicit conceptions overstated?

These are amongst the many important questions raised by the four commentators on the original paper, Eric Margolis, Georges Rey, Stephen Schiffer and Josefa Toribio.[1] The aim of the present paper is to begin to address the questions they raise. It is striking that there is virtually no overlap between the various challenges the four commentators present: so we have a wide range of interlocking issues to consider. I am very grateful to all of them for such an incisive and interesting set of comments; I have certainly learned much from reflecting on them.

1 Postulation or Implicit Conception?

I start by considering the relations between implicit conceptions and what Georges Rey helpfully calls 'postulary' conceptions. Georges describes postulary conceptions as follows. "Thinkers construct concepts that have to satisfy certain *constraints*, but [for] which they may have no defining conceptions at all, explicit or implicit" (p. 98); "Thinkers *postulate* that there is some phenomenon that happens to

---

[1] E. Margolis, 'Implicit Conceptions and the Phenomenon of Abandoned Principles'; G. Rey, 'What Implicit Conceptions are Unlikely to Do'; S. Schiffer, 'Doubts about Implicit Conceptions'; and J. Toribio, 'The Implicit Conception of Implicit Conceptions', all in the present volume.

play (most of) the explanatory roles that interest them, whose nature would be provided by some optimal theory of the phenomenon" (pp. 98–99). Georges states, and I agree, that concepts which involve postulary conceptions form an important category, one which is instantiated not only by certain everyday concepts, but also by concepts in the empirical sciences and, at least historically, by some concepts in such abstract disciplines as analysis and set theory. Are some of the concepts I described as involving implicit conceptions better described as involving postulary conceptions? Is the whole alleged category of concepts associated with implicit conceptions better seen as involving such postulations?

I want to argue, first, that not all the examples of implicit conceptions I introduced can be properly assimilated to the category of postulary conceptions. Not that Georges asserts that such a general assimilation is possible: but the question of its possibility is important in assessing whether we have any need for the category of implicit conceptions at all.

One of the examples I gave was that of the concept *natural number*. I claimed that some feature of our grasp of this concept makes it determinate, and not merely a matter of decision, that the non–standard 'numbers' which feature in non–standard models of first–order arithmetic are not genuine natural numbers. Could we apply the postulary model to the concept *natural number*? There are indeed well–developed theories about the non–standard numbers which feature in non–standard models of arithmetic.[2] Far from giving a hitherto unavailable explication of the distinction between the standard and the non–standard, however, these theories simply presuppose that it is obvious (as it is) which are the standard natural numbers. They do not give a theoretical explication of what it is to be a standard natural number. They take for granted that certain objects in the domain of a model are the genuine natural numbers, and then go on to theorize about such matters as the structure of the successor–relation on the non–standard elements, and the like.

Certainly one can think of conditions which are necessary for a something to be one of the standard natural numbers. One of the most salient is that any standard natural number has only finitely many predecessors. This necessary condition is not, though, something one needs a developed theory of the nature of the non–standard models to appreciate. A thinker does not even have to have the idea

---

[2] For some information about the nature of non–standard models, see Chapter 17, 'Non–standard models of arithmetic', of G. Boolos and R. Jeffrey, *Computability and Logic* (Cambridge: Cambridge University Press, 1974).

of a non-standard model to know its correctness. Further, that this is a necessary condition for being a genuine natural number seems to be derivative from our underlying conception of a natural number. It is something whose correctness takes a moment's reflection to work out the first time one hears it, rather than something immediate acceptance of which is definitional of possession of the concept *natural number*. All of these points would be explained on the hypothesis I gave, that to possess the concept *natural number* is to have an implicit conception with the content (i) - (iii):

(i) 0 is a natural number;

(ii) the successor of any natural number is a natural number; and

(iii) only what can be determined to be a natural number on the basis of clauses (i) and (ii) is a natural number.

Here the modality in clause (iii) is taken seriously. In particular, it is not to be regarded as shorthand for 'there is a sequence of natural numbers such that...'. Were it to be so regarded, it would not be a non–circular way of fixing the extension of 'natural number'. The same applies to such a phrase as 'finite sequence', when one considers the explication of its meaning. It also seems to me that possession of an implicit conception with the content given in (i) - (iii) explains an ordinary thinker's particular judgements to the effect that particular things fall, or do not fall, under the concept *natural number*. To those to whom they are explicitly known, the principles (i) - (iii) can also justify such principles as ordinary arithmetical induction.[3]

Of course, even a statement of (i) - (iii) may be regarded as an (extremely modest) piece of theory. Certainly it need not be known explicitly by everyone who has the concept *natural number*. I am hospitable to the suggestion that, when we use a concept without knowing its explication, we commonly presuppose that there is some explication. This point does not produce some general collapse of implicit conceptions into postulary conceptions. We should always distinguish, as I expect Georges would also want to distinguish, between the case in which new theory —even very modest theory— is an explicit statement of something which was already the content of an implicit conception, from the case in which it is not.

I would say the same about the concept *chair*. No new theoretical discoveries about the role or nature of chairs in society is needed

---

[3]For more on these and related issues about understanding, see my note 'The Concept of a Natural Number', *Australasian Journal of Philosophy* 76 (March 1998), forthcoming.

11. IMPLICIT CONCEPTIONS, THE A PRIORI... 125

for us to make explicit what is involved in being a chair. We need only to reflect properly on what properties are influential upon the applications of the expression made by an ordinary person who understands the word expressing the concept, and whose applications do not rely on shortcuts, or on auxiliary hypotheses.

Now let us turn to Leibniz, Newton and the concept of the limit of a series. As Georges notes, here we may have just a disagreement about examples. The case in support of the existence of implicit conceptions can be made independently of my treatment of this particular example. All the same, the example is of interest in itself, and it encapsulates many issues about the principles for attributing implicit conceptions with specific contents; so let us pursue the example a little further. Those who are less intrigued, or who wish to move straight to the topic of the *a priori*, should skip to Section 2 below.

Georges holds that it is more realistic to regard the concept of a limit as employed by Leibniz and Newton as underlain by a postulary conception, rather than an involving some implicit conception of a limit. If a postulary conception is involved, then there must, under Georges's characterization of postulary conceptions, be constraints to which Leibniz and Newton regarded the notion of a limit as subject. What could these constraints be? The constraints must be more specific than the very general idea that there is some notion of a limit which we can employ in defining the rate of variation of one magnitude with respect to another at a specific value of the latter magnitude. Leibniz and Newton had moved far beyond that very general thought. The way they conceived of the notion of a limit was sufficient for them to be able to calculate the limits of particular series, and to calculate the differential of particular functions at particular values.

Perhaps we could formulate the needed constraint in the following way? The limit of a series is conceived as being an operation of such a kind that, when one is taking the limit of some function $f(x)$ as δx tends to 0, any terms for δx in calculations of that limit can be treated as 0. This approach might be found tempting because, it might be said, it can explain how the differentials of particular functions could have been computed by Leibniz and Newton without their having any explicit definition of a limit available to them. So, to take a very simple case, they could have worked out the value of dx^2/dx as the limit of

$$\frac{(x + \delta x)(x + \delta x) - x^2}{\delta x} \tag{11.1}$$

which is
$$\frac{x^2 + 2\delta x \cdot x + (\delta x)^2 - x^2}{\delta x} \quad (11.2)$$
This, they could argue, simplifies in turn to
$$2x + \delta x \quad (11.3)$$
and, it would be said under this approach, by the known constraints on the notion of a limit, δx can here be treated as 0.

The problem with this approach is that the constraint is incoherent when applied to the calculations in which it is actually needed to explain Leibniz's and Newton's ability to calculate specific differentials. To get the right answer, Leibniz and Newton must be allowed to treat δx as 0 in line (3). But in the preceding line (2), it must not be treated as 0, on pain of dividing by 0. Treating a term as having one value in one line of a calculation, and as not having that value in the preceding line of the same calculation, is not a good idea. (This is indeed precisely the point which worried Bishop Berkeley.) Not only is the constraint incoherent if applied in this way, I think it also seriously understates Leibniz's and Newton's real understanding of the matter, which did not essentially involve such incoherence.

What one would so like to say at this point is the following: 'the term δx must be understood in this calculation as having an *arbitrarily small* value, and this should not be identified with its being 0, nor with its having any particular finite value, however small'. I think Leibniz and Newton probably would have accepted some formulation of the constraint along these lines. This formulation of the constraint, though, in using the notion of the arbitrarily small, does not after all avoid attributing notions of the same character as that of *limit* itself. 'Arbitrarily small' is here evidently not a predicate of numbers, but is to be explained in context, as it occurs in such phrases as 'the slope of the curve $f(x) = x^2$ has the value $2x$ as we arbitrarily small chords of the curve around x'. I think Leibniz and Newton had some grasp of talk about the arbitrarily small, and that their understanding consisted in possession of an implicit conception governing it. The content of the implicit conception involves a principle explaining the meaning of 'arbitrarily' in contexts in which it occurs. In short, I think that if one tries to follow through the idea that Leibniz and Newton had a concept of limit that involves postulary conceptions, one finds that a proper formulation of the constraints involves attributing to them notions like 'arbitrarily small', which are closely akin to the limit concept, and their grasp of which involves (I would say) possession of an implicit conception. So I doubt that, in this particular case, that the

11. IMPLICIT CONCEPTIONS, THE A PRIORI...

postulary conception provides a viable alternative to the view that Leibniz and Newton had an implicit conception underlying their use of 'limit'.

Georges also presses another pertinent question: why attribute as the content of (say) Newton's implicit conception of a limit the Bolzano–Weierstrass definition, rather than a definition in terms of infinitesimals? We know from Abraham Robinson's work that a careful definition in terms of infinitesimals is mathematically equivalent to the Bolzano–Weierstrass definition. What reasons do we, *could* we, have for one attribution rather than another?

In the case of Newton, I would offer the following three reasons for attributing the Bolzano–Weierstrass definition as the content of his underlying implicit conception, rather than the definition in terms of infinitesimals. To reactivate our memory traces, let us remind ourselves that the Bolzano–Weierstrass definition states that

a is the limit of the series $x_0, \ldots, x_k, \ldots$ iff for each $\epsilon > 0$, there exists some m such that $|x_k - a| < \epsilon$ for all $k \geq m$.

The pivotal idea in this definition is that of a series approaching closer to a number than any given finite amount. Although Newton never articulated the Bolzano–Weierstrass definition, its pivotal idea is used at several points in his *Principia*. For example, Lemma I of Section 1, Book One, together with its justification, reads as follows:

Lemma I

Quantities, and the ratio of quantities, which in any finite time converge continually to equality, and before the end of that time approach nearer to each other than by any given difference, become ultimately equal.

If you deny it, suppose them to be ultimately unequal, and let D be their ultimate difference. Therefore they cannot approach nearer to equality than by that given difference D; which is contrary to the supposition.[4]

The phrase 'approach nearer to each other than by any given difference' is precisely the core idea of the Bolzano–Weierstrass definition. (The passage is also interesting for its very direct linking of that notion with the 'ultimate equality' and 'ultimate ratios' of which Newton spoke.)

Second, as that same passage makes clear, Newton knew explicitly a sufficient condition for a number b *not* to be the limit of a given

---

[4] I. Newton, *Principia: Volume I, The Motion of Bodies* tr. A. Motte, rev. F. Cajori (Berkeley, Ca.: University of California Press, 1966 reprinting), p. 29.

series $x_0, \ldots, x_k, \ldots$. The sufficient condition is that there is some ϵ such for every m, $|x_k - a| \geq \epsilon$, for all $k \geq m$. If (and it is a big if) one already knows the Bolzano–Weierstrass definition, one is in a position to appreciate that this sufficient condition for a number's not being the limit of a series is but a tiny step from the correct general definition. For a number to be the limit of a series, is for there to be no epsilon of the sort mentioned in the sufficient condition for a number not to be the limit of the series. We can see now that the correct definition is only a few quantifier-and-negation interactions away from the sufficient negative condition Newton knew about. He had the resources to hand for answering the critics of the calculus.

Third, I think the attribution to a thinker of an implicit conception of a limit involving Robinsonian infinitesimals would be justified only if there were other evidence underwriting this much richer kind of attribution. The Bolzano–Weierstrass characterization involves only real numbers, and relations between them, of a sort Newton was using anyway. I do not say that there could not be a thinker for whom an attribution of an infinitesimal-involving conception would be correct. For instance, if a thinker were already using infinitesimals elsewhere, for instance in his treatment of utility theory, or in characterizing mathematically the structure of preference (or other) orderings, the case for attributing an implicit conception involving infinitesimals would be made stronger. It would have to be made stronger in a way which connected up his grasp of the limit–concept with the use of infinitesimals elsewhere, and with the principles of reasoning this thinker takes to be valid for them.

The case of Leibniz is more complex than that of Newton. He did indeed speak of infinitely small quantities, and did employ them in reasoning about what we would now call the differential of functions. He was, however, very insistent that this talk of the infinitely small was merely a manner of speaking. He used the phrase 'well–founded fictions' ('des fictions bien fondées') to describe 'our infinites and infinitely small' ('nos infinis et infiniment petits').[5] Leibniz was, therefore, committed to there being some way of stating in more literal terms what, using his well–founded fictions, one expresses by saying that the slope of a curve at a given point is measured by a ratio of certain infinitesimals. Like Newton, he never gave a completely explicit statement of what was literally meant. But, like Newton again, his intuitive explications make use of the core idea of an error less than any error specified in advance —the core idea of the fully

---

[5]Letter to Varignon of 20 June 1702, *Mathematische Schriften* vol. 4 (Halle, 1849-63), pp. 106-110.

11. IMPLICIT CONCEPTIONS, THE A PRIORI... 129

explicit definitions of Bolzano and, reportedly, of Weierstrass. For instance, Leibniz wrote (with a characteristic flourish at the end):

> For in place of the infinite, or the infinitely small, one takes quantities sufficiently large and sufficiently small as is required for the error to be less than the given error, in such a way that one does not differ from the style of Archimedes other than in the expressions, which are more direct in our method and more in accordance with the art of invention.[6]

Leibniz's attitude was then quite unlike that of Gödel, who is reliably reported to have held that infinitesimals should be regarded as numbers in their own right, as we long ago came to regard rational numbers, negative numbers and irrationals.[7]

2 Concept Possession and the *A Priori*

I start with some clarification of my intended position on the relation between concept possession and the *a priori*. Georges acutely notices that the phrase 'possession condition', which featured so often in *A Study of Concepts*, and in my 1993 paper 'How Are *A Priori* Truths Possible?', appears nowhere in 'Implicit Conceptions'.[8] He wonders whether implicit conceptions are meant to supply 'only the contents involved in a full, clear understanding of a concept' (p. 96), rather than anything involved in merely 'misty' understanding. The strategy of the 1993 paper was to aim to explain *a priori* truth involving a set of concepts by features of those concepts' possession conditions. This strategy, Georges notes, would then have to be

---

[6] My translation. The original reads: 'Car au lieu de l'infini our de l'infiniment petit, on prend des quantités aussi grandes et aussi petites qu'il faut pour que l'erreur soit moindre que l'erreur donnée, de sort qu'on ne diffère du style d'Archimède que dans les expressions, qui sont plus directes dans notre méthode et plus conformes à l'art d'inventer'. Leibniz, *Mathematische Schriften* vol. 5, op. cit., p. 350. I owe this and the previous reference to Chapter X of A. Robinson's classic work *Non-Standard Analysis* (Revised edition) (Amsterdam: North-Holland, 1974). That chapter contain further historical material of philosophical interest. For further discussion of Leibniz's attitude to infinitesimals, see H. Ishiguro, *Leibniz's Philosophy of Logic and Language* (Second edition) (Cambridge: Cambridge University Press, 1990), Chapter 5. The differences between Leibniz and Newton are far more extensive and subtle than has been outlined here. For an absorbing account, see D. Bertoloni Meli, *Equivalence and Priority: Newton versus Leibniz* (Oxford: Oxford University Press, 1993).
[7] A. Robinson, op. cit. p. x.
[8] *A Study of Concepts* (Cambridge, Mass.: MIT Press, 1992); 'How Are *A Priori* Truths Possible?', *European Journal of Philosophy* 1 (1993) 175-99.

modified, since *a priori* knowledge involving a concept can be present even when we have not attained a full and clear understanding of it. The starting point of Georges's line of thought here is not a position at which I am located. The explanation for the absence of the phrase 'possession condition' from 'Implicit Conceptions' is that in *A Study of Concepts* 'possession condition' was used, somewhat proprietorially, for conditions for possessing a concept which could be cast in what I there called 'the $A(C)$' form. In simple cases, that form is given by the schema 'The concept F is that concept C to possess which the thinker must meet the condition $A(C)$', where it is required that the concept F not feature, identified as such, within the scope of the thinker's propositional attitudes in the material in $A(C)$. The idea was that the concept is individuated by its role in a thinker's psychological economy, and that if the role really exhausts the identity of the concept, we should need only the variable 'C' within the scope of the thinker's propositional attitudes in individuating that concept.

Now not all the examples of implicit conceptions which I offered can be cast in the $A(C)$ form. Some of them can: the implicit conceptions underlying grasp of the concepts *chair*, *limit* and (under the modal treatment) *natural number* can be so cast. The contents of the implicit conceptions I offered as underlying grasp of those concepts do not re–use the concept in question. Matters stand differently, however, for my current treatment of the logical constants. On that treatment, grasp of classical alternation consists in possession of an implicit conception with this content: that any thought consisting of alternation applied to the thoughts p and q is true if and only if either p is true or q is true. This final occurrence of 'or' means that the formulation is not of the $A(C)$ form: 'or' here occurs within the specification of the content of the implicit conception, a psychological state of the thinker.

There are important issues about this abandonment of the $A(C)$ form: some of them are discussed in Section 4 below. At this point, I want to note just that this abandonment of the form as a requirement does not involve any commitment to the idea that implicit conceptions are needed only for supplying the contents of full understanding available to one who has articulated the nature of the concept. On the contrary, my position is that the ordinary understander of 'natural number' has an implicit conception with the content I offered. This was why its implicit character matters to me: it is not merely the embedded content of the conception which is my concern. The treatment of implicit conceptions is meant to apply to 'misty' understanding too. It is intended to be a contribution to a constitutive

11. IMPLICIT CONCEPTIONS, THE A PRIORI... 131

account of possession of the concepts in question —even if we do not apply the phrase 'possession condition' to these proposed accounts.

As a result, there remains a position which is wholly within the spirit of the 1993 paper on the *a priori*. What I take to be essential to the spirit of that paper is this: that a correct theory of the nature of a given concept can explain why certain truths involving that concept can be known *a priori* (and likewise for sets of concepts). We still conform to that spirit if for certain concepts their nature is to be elucidated not by the earlier possession conditions, but by the implicit conceptions which underlie possession. That is the position I am maintaining.

Before I turn to the relations between implicit conceptions and the *a priori*, I wish to make a few remarks about the task of identifying the nature of a concept. We have so far distinguished three kinds of case: that in which a concept is individuated by something of the $A(C)$ form; that in which it is individuated by an implicit conception not reducible to the $A(C)$ form; and the case in which the concept is governed by a postulary conception. (Instances of this case may also fall under one of the other two). There is nevertheless a huge overlap between these three cases in respect of the methodology appropriate to discovering more about the nature of the concept in question. In all three cases, there has to be an attempt to find general principles which are capable of explaining a certain range of truths. It is virtually never a trivial matter to find the possession condition for a concept, not even one which can be put in the $A(C)$ form. To work out what the possession condition is, one must take a sufficiently wide range of truths about which Thoughts involving the concept are informative, and which Thoughts involving the concept are uninformative, in various circumstances. A correct statement of the possession condition for the concept must be capable of explaining this range of truths about informativeness and uninfomativeness. Similarly, in the case of a concept for which there is an underlying implicit conception, the nature of that conception is, from the standpoint of the ordinary user of the concept, something which has to be worked out. This working out may involve substantive theory about the domain in which the concept applies. In this respect, the case will be close to concepts governed by a postulary conception. Part of the difference flows simply from the fact that the explanatory principles one aims to identify in the case of an implicit conception are answerable to a wider body of data. The explanatory principles must square with the claim that the content attributed to the implicit conception is the content of a psychologically real state.

When a thinker aims to discover the content of one of his own implicit conceptions, information he can obtain from the use of simulation procedures can contribute to identifying the body of truths to be explained by the implicit conception. Answers to such questions as 'Is something with no back a chair?', or 'What is the truth-value of an alternation $A \vee B$ when A is true and B is false?', can be reached by a proper use of simulation. The results of a range of simulations can then be used as evidence which must be explained by a general hypothesis about the content of an implicit conception. Even the statement that an alternation is true iff both its constituents are true is such a general hypothesis, albeit a modest one. Georges is worried that a simulation "is at best merely a means of tapping knowledge already possessed" (section IV, second paragraph). It seems to me rather that a thinker who engages in simulation need not know the answers to these questions in advance. It is one thing to be rationally willing to make certain correct classifications or assignments of truth–value in hypothetical situations; it is another to know that one is.

Whether a simulation procedure is relying on empirical information depends on the nature of the case. In some cases it does; in others it does not. Of course I agree with Georges that it does so depend when one mentally navigates one's way through a city. But it also seems to me that when I imagine myself given the information that A is true and B is false, and am asked to imagine how in those circumstances I would evaluate the alternation, then (provided I reach my answer by running offline the same evaluational ability I would use online) my answer does not rest on any *a posteriori* information. I doubt that it rests on any premisses at all.

Now I turn to consider the cluster of issues about the relations between implicit conceptions and the *a priori*. We can distinguish three tasks, which I shall call respectively the classificatory, the epistemological and the explanatory. Carrying out any one of these tasks would increase our understanding of the *a priori*; but the tasks increase in depth as we move along this list.

The classificatory task is simply that of making clear the traditional elucidation of the *a priori* as that which can be known in a way which is justificationally independent of perceptual experience, and perhaps of the deliverances of other faculties which deliver information about the spatio–temporal world to the thinker. Only if this task can be carried out is there an interesting philosophical topic of the *a priori* at all.

The epistemological task is to explain why some beliefs which have a justification which is independent of experience also amount to

11. IMPLICIT CONCEPTIONS, THE A PRIORI... 133

knowledge. This task goes beyond the classificatory task, for it must appeal to some general principles of epistemology. An epistemology which can explain how axioms are known independently of experience, and how inferential rules are known, and why knowledge is transmissible by valid deduction, would be making the right moves to answer this question for some *a priori* beliefs.

The explanatory task is to explain how *a priori* truths are possible at all, and in particular to explain, of any particular truth which is *a priori*, why it falls under that classification (rather than just elaborating the fact that it does). The explanatory task is to develop a general theory of the *a priori*, one which satisfactorily explains how there can be knowledge which is justificationally independent of experience. My own view is that the explanatory task should be attempted, but that it should not be approached from the direction followed by conventionalism. I would argue that any plausible execution of the explanatory task will rather have to be a metaconceptual theory, one which traces the *a priori* character of a given truth to features of the nature of some of the concepts from which it is composed.

The core idea of my 1993 paper was that *a priori* truths are guaranteed to be true in the actual world by the nature of their possession conditions, taken together with the way their semantic values are fixed from those possession conditions. Part of this core idea can still be retained even if we give up insistence on possession conditions in the strict $A(C)$ form. The idea that certain contents are guaranteed to be true in the actual world by the way their semantic values are fixed is one which remains attractive and available even under a more relaxed account of concept individuation which does not insist on the $A(C)$ form. In particular, it remains attractive and available when some concepts are individuated by the implicit conceptions involved in their possession. Each of the illustrations of implicit conceptions which I have given wears on its sleeve the way in which the semantic values of the corresponding concept is determined. Each example has had as the content of the implicit conception either a biconditional stating the extension of the concept, or a recursion fixing its extension.

The relation between the fundamental explanation of the *a priori* status of a certain content, and an actual thinker's *a priori* knowledge of that content, is however a complex matter. The appeal to the way in which the semantic value of the concept is fixed is something for the philosopher. It is something of which the ordinary thinker need not know anything, even though some of his knowledge is nevertheless *a priori*. What then is the link between the philosophical answer to the explanatory question, and the epistemic status of the judgements of ordinary thinkers? To address this question, I consider three sorts of example.

First, let us consider ordinary applications of a concept in simple predications, by a thinker who has no explicit knowledge of the content of the implicit conceptions involved. Such applications will include those involved in the judgements '997 is a natural number', and '$d(x^2)/dx = 2x$'. These judgements constitute *a priori* knowledge, even for the non–philosophical thinker. According to the present approach, they do so because the thinker is suitably influenced, in making these judgements, by the holding of the conditions which are mentioned in the content of the corresponding implicit conceptions as sufficient for the concept —of natural number, and of first differential, respectively— to apply. He is influenced by the holding of conditions which, given the way the semantic values of the concepts are fixed, are sufficient to ensure that the concept applies. They ensure application without any need for justificational reliance on perception or similar faculties.

Second, let us consider such universally–quantified contents as the Bolzano–Weierstrass definition of a limit, or the recursive definition of a natural number. It seems to me that these can also be known *a priori*. Application of the method of trying to find the best general characterization of what it is to be a limit of a given series, from a set of examples of the limits of particular series, and the procedures used in determining particular limits, can yield *a priori* knowledge of the general characterization. It can do so when the method is properly applied to a body of initial data which itself has an *a priori* status. That *a priori* status is just what we argued for in the preceding paragraph. The general method in question here is presumably the same method by which the general recursive definitions of addition and multiplication were originally reached when they were first discovered. The general definition was reached as the best explanation of a body of information, itself *a priori*, about the results of adding or multiplying various individual numbers (and in that case probably about why one particular number is the sum of two other given numbers).

Third, we can also account for the *a priori* status of some of the new principles of the sort I discussed in the target paper when considering the phenomenon of new principles. Once a theorist has attained *a priori* knowledge of a general characterization of 'natural number', say, he will then be in a position to infer such new principles as that any natural number has only finitely many predecessors. This is a principle which does not follow from the truths he

11. IMPLICIT CONCEPTIONS, THE A PRIORI... 135

had to know explicitly to have an ordinary understanding of 'natural number'. It is, though, correct and attainable *a priori*, once he has worked out what it is to be a natural number, that is, what is involved in falling under that concept which he possessed all along.

There are different varieties of the *a priori*, different subspecies of the general notion 'can be known to be true in the actual world independently of any justificational reliance on experience'. One way of prompting recognition of the two subspecies is by reflection on a puzzle. It is very natural, pretheoretically, to hold that while certain mathematical and logical contents (amongst others) can be known *a priori*, truths about a thinker's psychological states at a particular time are never *a priori*. Yet consider the following example. Suppose someone reaches, in an *a priori* fashion, knowledge that

$$\frac{d(x^2)}{dx} = 2x. \tag{A}$$

Suppose he then moves from this judgement of (A) to

$$\text{I judge that } \frac{d(x^2)}{dx} = 2x. \tag{B}$$

This is a rational transition, indeed one which can result in self-knowledge. The transition does not rely for its justification or legitimacy on the deliverances of any perceptual experience. If (A) is known *a priori*, and the transition to (B) is one to which the thinker is entitled without relying on perceptual experience, and is a transition which can yield knowledge, is not (B) then also known *a priori*? Yet (B) is a thought about the psychological states of a particular thinker at a particular time. One could make the same point about someone who moves more directly from the reasoning which leads to acceptance of (A) to making the knowledgeable judgement of (B).

Does this argument force us to deny that there was anything at all in the idea that attributions of psychological states cannot be *a priori*? It does not. We ought in any case to be wary of leaving matters there. It is a very satisfying explanation of the *a priori* status of a content in many cases that the truth of the content in the actual world is ensured by the conditions for possession of its constituent concepts (and their mode of combination), together with the way the semantic value of the concept is fixed. But the *a priori* status of (B) is not accommodated by that explanation. It is in no way guaranteed by the conditions for possessing the concepts in (B), and their mode of combination, together with the way their semantic values are fixed, that the thinker will in the actual world be judging that $d(x^2)/dx = 2x$.

I suggest that we resolve the puzzle by distinguished two subspecies of the general category of the *a priori*. Let us say that something is *contentually a priori* if it is a content which is guaranteed to be true in the actual world, without any justificational reliance on perceptual experience, and irrespective of whether the content is actually thought, judged, or is the content of any other propositional attitude of any thinker. Classical examples of the *a priori* in logic or mathematics are examples of the contentual *a priori*. The original intuition that thoughts about a person's propositional attitudes at a particular time cannot be *a priori* is correct for the contentually *a priori*. The whole approach to the explanatory task of deriving *a priori* truth from features of conditions for possession of concepts should be regarded as having as its subject matter the contentually *a priori*.

By contrast, something is *judgementally a priori* if it is guaranteed to be true in the actual world whenever it is judged, or comes to be judged for certain reasons, without any justificational reliance by the judging subject on perceptual experience. In the example as described, (B) above is judgementally *a priori*. It is theoretically unsurprising that the judgementally *a priori* should include contents about a thinker's mental states. The very characterization of the judgementally *a priori* ensures that it is concerned with truth in worlds in which certain judgements are made. There is no reason in advance to expect the truth of the generalization that all contents which are judgementally *a priori* to be guaranteed to be true in the actual world by the conditions for possession of the concepts they contain. (B) is a counterexample to any such generalization.

As a coda to this section, I will also respond with extreme brevity to two other concerns expressed by Georges. One of his concerns is that the possibility of attaining full understanding of a concept in an *a priori* way is exacerbated by the conception of concepts as abstract objects, '*independent of us*, "grasped" sometimes only dimly, whose actual structure is revealed only by careful analysis' (final paragraph of his section III).

First, a small clarification: my position is not that the very concept *limit*, for instance, has the structure given in the Bolzano–Weierstrass definition. The concept *limit* as deployed by Newton, and the complex concept deployed in the Bolzano–Weierstrass definition, must be distinct by Frege's criterion of identity for senses, precisely because the definition can be informative —indeed it was a substantial intellectual advance. My position is rather that Newton's and Leibniz's possession of the concept *limit* consisted in his possession of an implicit conception with the content given by the Bolzano–Weierstrass definition.

On the main point, I do not myself see the tension Georges speaks about. There cannot be any general incompatibility between a subject–matter involving abstract objects and its having an *a priori* status, since we are so familiar with that combination in many parts of mathematics. As far as I can see, at no point do any of the explanations of *a priori* status I have given above require that concepts not be abstract objects. What they do require is the existence of links between the abstract ontology of concepts and the properties of thinkers who possess those concepts which makes possible the links between concept–possession and the *a priori*. These links exist both under the approach involving possession conditions of the strict $A(C)$ form, and under the more relaxed notion of an underlying implicit conception. Indeed the very intimate relation which exists on many theories between the identity of a given concept and reasons for making judgements involving that concept should lead one to suspect that a theory of the *a priori* may well be a by–product of a proper statement of the relations between the identity of a concept and such reasons. A content which is knowable *a priori* is one of such a kind that the conclusive reasons for accepting it which are determined by the identity of its constituent concepts (and their mode of combination) are ones which do not involve perception in any justificational way. Maybe Georges has some way of explaining discourse about propositional attitudes without appeal to an ontology of concepts as abstract objects. I do not know whether this can be done; but I cannot see that the possibility of carrying through such a program is a commitment of the present treatment of the *a priori*. My inclination is to believe that the ontology of concepts is fine as it is. The important task is not to reduce concepts to something else: it is rather to understand how they function in epistemology, psychology, the normative and all the other territories in which they feature so distinctively.

The last point in this coda is about Georges's worry that acknowledging the postulary character of a concept would render the *a priori* knowledge involving it 'fairly anemic, and would threaten the *a priori* status of the substantive analyses philosophers have typically sought' (final paragraph of his section I). I am having difficulty seeing an incompatibility here too. Why cannot further development of *a priori* theory lead to *a priori* knowledge involving a postulary concept? The notion of an infinitesimal as used by Leibniz, and everyone else before Robinson, was a postulary concept. Yet Robinson's theory of non-standard analysis is an *a priori* theory. It does not rely for its justification on the deliverances of perception.

3 Concept Identity, Abandoned Principles, New Principles

Georges touches on questions about the identity of thoughts. He worries about whether there is a principled way of answering the question whether Leibniz, Newton, Robinson and the rest of us are thinking the same thought, and he goes on to enter a sympathetic suggestion. His suggestion is that identity of concept is answerable to explanations of what thinkers find unintelligible, particularly which denials they find unintelligible. I agree that this is an important resource. An appeal to the right kind of unintelligibility is also something which would be congenial to theorists who take radical interpretation as fundamental in the philosophical elucidation of intentional content. Interpretations will be constrained to avoid attributions of beliefs in contents which are unintelligible in the special way.

Fixing on instances of the right kind of unintelligibility is important. Georges says that the denial that squares are four-sided has the right kind of unintelligibility. But someone may equally have the reaction "It's unintelligible!" to the claim that a solid sphere can be dissected into a finite number of pieces which can be assembled, by rigid motion, to form two solid spheres each the same size as the original. Yet that is the claim of the Banach–Tarski Theorem, and whatever kind of unintelligibility it may have, it must be consistent with the truth of the claim —since the claim is true. The right kind of unintelligibility is the kind which can be explained by features of the conditions for possessing the concept in question. For the sort of 'unintelligibility' which attaches to the Banach–Tarski Theorem, there can be no such features of the possession conditions of the concepts it involves.

The only other caveat I would add is that, possibly unlike Georges, I do not see the significance of a certain kind of unintelligibility as confined to denials. It is in the same, and proper, sense unintelligible that the conjunction A&B be true when A is false. The right kind of unintelligibility is significant both for concepts individuated by acceptance conditions and for those individuated by their rejection conditions.

It may be that the impression that questions about sameness of thoughts cannot be answered in a principled way stems in part from the fact that one notion of thought and concept we sometimes use serves different purposes than those served by the concepts individuated by accounts of their possession. Consider one person who has only an intuitive understanding of the notion of a limit, without explicit knowledge of any definition, and a second person, introduced to the notion rigorously from the start, who knows the explicit definition. The two persons think of the relation of being the limit of a series in different ways, but still we may correctly predicate exactly the same predicable 'believes that the limit of such-and-such series is so-and-so' of both of them. The looser standards for such identities of attribution are of some importance, and need not be just the result of laziness. Such attributional identity is important in characterizing the communication and the transmission of knowledge. The first of our two imagined persons can communicate information about the right thing —here, the limit-relation— and transmit knowledge about it, to the second person, even if the second person is not thinking of the relation under the same concept as the first. Propositional-attitude attributions in the language must be elucidated in such a way as to accommodate and elucidate this possibility. The treatment of Crimmins and Perry, and of Schiffer, both do this (in somewhat different ways).[9] What is noticeable is that these two treatments both use in their analyses quantifications over some finer-grained modes of presentation or concepts. It is these finer-grained modes of presentation that have been my concern in giving identity conditions for concepts in terms of conditions for possession, rather than anything deriving from the more relaxed, but still important, notion of identity of 'that...' clause.

Eric Margolis wonders whether implicit conceptions are meant to be constitutive of the concepts which they underlie. He notes that a prototype-and-similarity structure could equally explain applications of a concept. He points further to the Phenomenon of Abandoned Principles —as 'Cats are animals' is abandoned in Putnam's well-known example. Eric suggests that information based semantics handles these cases better, and voices the suspicion that the Phenomenon of New Principles may be something special to logical and mathematical cases.

---

[9] M. Crimmins and J. Perry, 'The Prince and the Phone Booth: Reporting Puzzling Beliefs', *Journal of Philosophy* 96 (1989) 685-711; S. Schiffer, 'Belief Ascriptions', *Journal of Philosophy* 89 (1992) 499-521.

An implicit conception is meant to be part of what it is, constitutively, to possess the concept which involves having that implicit conception. The content of an implicit conception does not, however, need to take the form of a definition. One could certainly be forgiven for thinking otherwise, for as Eric notes, all the examples given in the original paper involve definitions of a sort (even if non–reductive ones, as in the treatment of the logical constants). As far as I can see, however, nothing in the functions ascribed to implicit conceptions preclude the possibility that the content of an implicit conception involve the structure of a prototype and similarity relation, or set of similarity relations. As Eric says, this would still be suited to explain applications of the concept. It would also be suited to explain some examples of the Phenomenon of New Principles. The nature of the similarity relation, or the crucial features of the prototype, need not be obvious to ordinary unreflective possessers of the concept. When they are discovered, the result will be new principles which do not follow from any general principles the thinker had to accept to possess the concept.

I agree with Eric at least conditionally: if a principle involving a concept can intelligibly and correctly be abandoned, it cannot be any part of the content of an implicit conception involved in possessing that concept. I do not see how the implicit conception I offered for 'natural number', for instance, could be intelligibly and correctly abandoned. In cases where abandonment is intelligible and correct, as in Putnam's cat example, it does not seem to me that support is offered for informational semantics. As Eric formulates it, informational semantics is a theory only of reference, and not of mode of presentation or concept. (Even Jerry Fodor brings in mental representation–type to account for the phenomena concepts have been invoked to explain.) The way in which one is thinking of cats, when in Putnam's example one rationally rejects 'Cats are animals', involves a perceptual–recognitional way of thinking of cats. Perceptual–recognitional modes of presentation are not implicit conceptions, of course, but the need for modes of presentation is not impugned by the example. On the contrary, it is perceptual–recognitional ways of thinking of Fs which makes even the most modest theoretical claim about Fs rejectible without unintelligibility.

The Phenomenon of New Principles is not confined to logical and mathematical concepts, nor to those of the *a priori* disciplines in general. Consider the concept *running*, and the principle that the difference between running and walking is that in running, as opposed to walking, there is a time at which both of the runner's feet are off the ground. This is a new principle, actually informative to many ordinary users of the concept *running*. One can come to know the principle by reflection on one's own classificatory practice. One thereby comes to know something about what explains one's application of the concept to ordinary instances. The concept *running* is not, though, drawn from any *a priori* discipline.

4 Issues of Circularity, Uniformity, Reduction and Acquisition

Stephen Schiffer elaborates his first cluster of questions about implicit conceptions "via the metaphor of a language of thought". He writes:

> Suppose we think in English. Then 'chair' in my language of thought means the concept *chair*. What accounts for this? I gather that Chris would have to say that it's accounted for by the fact that the relevant subpersonal belief box contains a sentence whose propositional content defines what it is to be a chair, some completion, that is, of 'Necessarily, a thing is a chair iff...'. But then 'chair' must already mean *chair* in my language of thought, and what accounts for its meaning can't be an implicit conception whose expression involves use of 'chair'. (p. 90, section 1; for uniformity, I have replaced Stephen's capitalization of expressions for concepts by italicization.)

The concern that 'chair' is used on the left hand side of the biconditional which specifies the content of the sentence of the language of thought can be met by the following formulation —I follow Stephen in framing the issues in terms of a language of thought. What is involved in a subpersonal expression α in the language of thought meaning *chair* is that the relevant subpersonal box contains some sentence $\Sigma(\alpha)$, where $\Sigma(\_)$ means that necessarily an object is $\_$ iff.... (As in Stephen's Comment, the '...' is replaced by the correct definition of 'chair'.) Here 'α' is a variable over expressions, and the use of this variable does not presuppose anything about a substantive philosophical account of what it is for a subpersonal expression of the language of thought to mean *chair*. Of course, if a particular expression α_0 does meet the condition that the relevant subpersonal box contains some sentence $\Sigma(\alpha_0)$ (etc.), then α_0 will indeed mean *chair*. But we did not need to presuppose that it did in saying what is involved in an arbitrary expression of the language of thought meaning *chair*.

So far, the situation is quite analogous to that which is found in conceptual role theories of meaning. The conceptual role theorist says (for instance) that for an expression α to mean conjunction is for the thinker to be willing to make the transitions $A\alpha B/A$, $A\alpha B/B$, and $\{A, B\}/A\alpha B$ in some specially primitive way which does not depend on other inferences. The use of the variable 'α' is in itself noncommittal about substantive philosophical theories of conjunction. The substantive part the conceptual role account comes in its statement about the complex role that α must play if it is to mean conjunction.

Correspondingly, Stephen is also worried that I will be "forced to say either that an implicit conception defining chairhood isn't required at all for my having the concept *chair* or else that we need two separate accounts of how 'chair' comes to mean *chair* in my language of thought: one for its use in sentences that find their way into my personal propositional–attitude boxes, and one for its use in sentences that occur in my subpersonal boxes" (his section 1). This threat seems to me to disappear if what I have said so far is correct. The single, uniform statement of what is involved in a subpersonal expression α meaning *chair* is that the relevant subpersonal box contains some sentence $\Sigma(\alpha)$, where $\Sigma(\_)$ means that necessarily an object is _ iff... —again the dots abbreviate the correct definition. This statement is applicable both to occurrences of an expression α in subpersonal boxes, and in personal–level boxes. An expression occurring in a personal–level box has the meaning it does because that same expression also features in a certain way in a subpersonal box, the way described by the theory of implicit conceptions. In giving the reply in this simple form I assume the univocality of expressions in the language of thought, but that is a kosher assumption. Stephen was not trading on the possibility of ambiguity.

Stephen goes on to note that some of the implicit conceptions I have suggested have contents which employ the very same concept possession of which is being said to involve that implicit conception.[10] Stephen says that this exacerbates the problem(s) he has already noted. He then goes on to observe that the structure of my approach "is remarkably similar to that of logical atomism, and it seems to me that the good reasons for doubting the extreme reductionism of logical atomism are equally good reasons for doubting Chris's own heavily reductionist program" (p. 91, section 2).

A natural first reaction to this combination of criticisms is that they are inconsistent. If it is desirable to avoid extreme reductionism,

---

[10] Stephen acknowledges Paul Boghossian here (p. 90). The point is also one which I have discussed on several occasions, to my benefit, with Paul.

how can it be a criticism of an implicit conception that it is not reductive?

This first reaction would, though, be unfair. A more sympathetic reading of Stephen's points would take him as saying that an approach using implicit conceptions would need to be reductive, to carry through its own announced goals, and yet we know that such extreme reductionism cannot succeed. This is not inconsistent; but still I disagree with its first part. The crucial locus of disagreement comes at the point at which, under this reading, it is claimed that an approach using implicit conceptions needs to be reductive. Sometimes an implicit conception gives a genuine definition of a concept, as in the cases of *chair*, *limit* and *natural number* (under the modal treatment). When this is possible, well and good. Sometimes definition may even be theoretically necessary for some particular concept, in the face of a challenge to the concept. In the case of the concept of a limit, only a correct definition would have answered Berkeley's challenge. But, contrary to Stephen's claim, I am not committed to holding that *love* or *intelligence* can be defined (I have no idea whether they can be). There is a huge variety of types of concept: definition is a model for only one type. I claim neither that all concepts other than a set of primitives involve implicit conceptions, nor do I claim that those which do involve implicit conceptions have reductive definitions.

It is important to recognise that an implicit conception can serve explanatory purposes without its content amounting to a definition. Consider, for instance, the explanation in the target paper of the rationality of accepting a primitive logical law involving a particular logical constant. That explanation proceeded by reference to an implicit conception with a non–reductive content, a content specifying the constant's contribution to truth–conditions by using that very same concept again. The same applies to the rational acceptance of new principles involving a logical constant. What is required in both these cases is not that the implicit conception be reductive. All that is required is simply that it be true that having the concept in question involves having the implicit conception whose content reuses the concept. That suffices for explanation of the phenomena in question.[11]

---

[11] To address another of Stephen's points: I do not know whether all instances of the phenomenon of new principles can be explained by implicit conceptions. That is an enormously wide–ranging (and very important) issue. All I am committed to is that some instances of the phenomenon of new principles can be explained by implicit conceptions, in the way outlined in the discussion of George Rey's points.

It may seem that if nonreductive implicit conceptions are permitted, we might as well just say that (for instance) to understand 'and' is to know that it means conjunction, and be done with all this philosophy. That statement about understanding is true enough, but it is much less explanatory than attributing the implicit conceptions I have been proposing. From the bare statement that the understander knows that 'and' means conjunction, we do not derive an explanation of the rationality of accepting primitive logical laws, or of new principles. We will obtain such explanations only by at some point invoking the understander's possession of information which involves the notion of truth, and the expression's contribution to truth conditions. This is what the implicit conceptions I offered aim to do.

When an implicit conception has a nonreductive content, there are further matters in need of philosophical theory. For instance, in the case of the logical concept of alternation, the implicit conception has a content containing one particular mode of presentation of the classical truth–function for alternation. That mode of presentation is distinct from one which corresponds to a complex definition of the same truth–function in terms of joint exclusion, for instance. What makes it correct to refer to that mode of presentation in the statement of the content, rather than some other mode of presentation of the same truth–function? It is plausible that the answer to this question will have something to do with the following difference. Someone who understands alternation is able to move from the information that A is true and B is false to the conclusion that 'A ∨ B' is true, without any need for further inference. The same transition from that initial information to the conclusion that some complex formula containing A and B and joint exclusion is true will need a lot more inference. In short, it is very plausible that there will be some aspects of conceptual role which need to be mentioned in answering the question of why one mode of presentation rather than another features in the content of the implicit conception. This is by no means ruled out by the approach I have been developing. The phenomenon of new principles implies only that meaning cannot be exhausted by personal–level conceptual role, and not that conceptual–role plays no part at all in fixing meaning. The whole issue of the relation between conceptual role and meaning needs further investigation. That further investigation would also need to consider the more general issue of the constraints upon the ascription of

---

I am also committed to the view that whatever the correct way of explaining any instance of the phenomenon of new principles involving a given concept, the explanation must trace back to some aspect of the nature of that concept.

contents to subpersonal states in other areas where we engage in content–involving explanation of personal–level phenomena by content–involving subpersonal states. Computational explanations of perceptual experience are one salient domain in which these issues arise.

In the final section of his comments, Stephen asks "Where do implicit conceptions come from, and what justifies them?". On the issue of acquisition, it seems to me that it ought eventually to be possible to do something which is, at present, not much more than a gleam in the eye: to construct a theory which stands to the possession of particular concepts as Chomskyan Universal Grammar stands to the knowledge of a specific language. Such a Universal theory would aim to explain why thinkers extrapolate in the particular way they do from particular examples given as items falling under a concept, and from various principles or transitions involving the concept, to achieve a final state in which they meet a quite specific condition for possessing the concept. This theory would be empirical, though its goals cannot be stated without use of the philosophical notion of the condition for possessing a concept.

Part of Stephen's question asks what 'justifies' implicit conceptions. Outside the very rare cases in which concept–acquisition is something occurring at the level of conscious, rational reflection, the notion of justification seems to me to be inapplicable at the subpersonal level at which such a Universal theory would operate. This is parallel to the case of language, where equally the child does not have personal–level reasons or justifications for constructing the grammar he does from the sample of sentences he encounters. However, though indeed we are here operating at a level below that at which reasons and justification apply, there are still some significant connections with epistemology. We need to be able to explain, both in the case of the acquired language, and in the case at least of a linguistically expressed concept, how the selection of a grammar or a possession condition yields states capable of underlying knowledge of the structure of someone else's sentence, and of which concepts he is expressing in his use of it. Reliability of the acquisition–procedures, in the environments in which the thinker finds himself, must play some part at least in the explanation of the possibility of such knowledge.

I cannot see any threat of regress in the idea of a Universal theory which explains the nature of concept–acquisition in actual thinkers, even when the concept acquired involves possession of an implicit conception. The explanatory states mentioned in the Universal theory of acquisition need not involve implicit conceptions. Even if they do, their innateness would as a philosophical matter be no more problematic in principle than the innateness of the states mentioned in Universal Grammar. General theories of acquisition of concepts seem to me to be not so much a threat as a huge challenge for further thought and investigation, a challenge which is necessarily of an interdisciplinary character.

5 Implicit Conceptions and Personal–Level Conceptual Role Theories

Josefa Toribio writes that, contrary to one of my claims, nothing I have said about implicit conceptions "tells against personal–level conceptual role theories" of meaning (her final paragraph).

To discuss these issues, we need to sharpen the characterization of what it is to be a conceptual role theory. At one point, Josefa describes one proposal with which she has sympathy as being one "whose correctness can only be appreciated by paying attention to the personal–level conceptual role it plays in rational practice" (p. 119). Attribution of the implicit conceptions I have proposed is however equally something whose correctness can only be appreciated by paying attention to the personal–level conceptual role of the concept which is underlain by the conception. I emphasized that the ascription of one content rather than another to an implicit conception is fundamentally answerable to truths about the personal–level application of the concept underlain by the proposed implicit conception. Any theory which did not take some account of personal–level conceptual role in its account of meaning will be a non-starter, for it would be separating meaning from the domain of reasons, judgement and propositional attitudes. Recognition of the importance of personal–level role is a general point which does not discriminate between the more restricted class of conceptual-role theories of meaning, and their competitors.

We trivialize conceptual role theories of meaning if we count the following as individuating the meaning of negation by giving its conceptual role:

> O which has the conceptual role appropriate in a thinker who appreciates that Op is the strongest proposition that is entailed by all propositions with which p is incompatible.[12]

---

[12]This formulation is adapted from the passage of quoted by Josefa from Robert Brandom, *Making It Explicit* (Cambridge, Mass.: Harvard University Press,

11. IMPLICIT CONCEPTIONS, THE A PRIORI... 147

This specification uses the notion of incompatibility within the scope of 'appreciates that __', and the notion of incompatibility could hardly be elucidated without employing the notion of negation or falsity. This specification picks out a role only by taking for granted we know what it is for the thinker to have some grasp of negation or falsity. It does not succeed in individuating the meaning of negation by specifying a conceptual role which does not at any point take for granted the thinker's grasp of negation or falsity. The phrase 'the conceptual role appropriate in a thinker meeting such–and–such conditions' can succeed in picking out a conceptual role without thereby providing something which supports conceptual-role *individuation* of meaning.

The kinds of materials which can, from the standpoint of a conceptual role theory of meaning, feature in a meaning–determining conceptual role will depend upon the species of conceptual role theory being advocated. There are almost as many varieties of conceptual role theory as there are advocates thereof. For instance, suppose we were concerned with a very pure kind of conceptual role theorist, one who says that truth and reference have no part to play at any point in the individuation of meaning.[13] This theorist would face some challenges even for such concepts as that of logical conjunction. If conjunction is explained by its inferential role, and that role is defined over a relation *follows from*, it is a real question whether that relation can be elucidated without at some point employing the notion of truth.

In the case of concepts, a specification of conceptual role is a candidate for being individuating, by the terms of a conceptual-role theory of content, only if it meets the $A(C)$ form of *A Study of Concepts*. If we are concerned with the roles of expressions (external or internal), rather than concepts, then a specification of conceptual role is meaning–individuating, with the terms of a conceptual-role theory of meaning, only if it meets the analogue of the $A(C)$ condition: that the individuating condition at no point mention expressions which are presupposed to have the particular meaning the condition is intended to individuate. The displayed specification of a

---

1994), at p. 115. The point that the negation of p is the strongest proposition incompatible with p is also made and exploited in section 4 of my 'Understanding Logical Constants: A Realist's Account', *Proceedings of the British Academy* 73 (1987) 153-200, pp. 163-5.

[13] This theory would be purer than that advocated in *A Study of Concepts*, where there is a substantive, non–vacuous requirement that a determination theory exist if something written in the form appropriate to a possession condition is really to succeed individuating a concept.

conceptual role for negation does not meet this condition, and nor do the conditions for possessing logical concepts mentioning the implicit conceptions I proposed in the target paper.

Perhaps Josefa might reply that these arguments I am offering apply only to her particular suggested personal–level specifications of conceptual roles. May there not be others to be found, and which are consistent with the existence of the phenomena by which I tried to motivate the postulation of implicit conceptions? However, the arguments against explaining meaning purely in terms of personal–level conceptual role were quite general. In the case of the phenomenon of rationally accepted new principles, the basic dilemma runs as follows. If we try to individuate meaning in terms of personal–level conceptual role, do we include, amongst the principles that a thinker must accept in order to grasp that meaning, any new principles of the sort I talked about? Or do we exclude them? Neither option is acceptable. To include them leaves us with no explanation of the very phenomenon we were discussing, that these principles have to be worked out as correct. Their acceptance is not properly written into an understanding–condition for expressions they contain (they are not mere stipulations). On the other hand, to exclude them is to provide us with no explanation of why the new principles are *a priori* correct for the concepts they contain. On the personal–level conceptual role theory, meaning is determined by a set of conditions from which the new principles are independent. Their correctness, let alone their often *a priori* character, is a mystery under this option. Yet a personal–level conceptual role theory must either exclude or include the new principles, and a pure theory has no other resources for explaining the rational acceptability of the new principles. We should draw the straightforward conclusion: for at least some of the concepts involved in the new principles, a pure personal–level conceptual role theory is not correct.

Conceptual Competence

James Higginbotham

1 Introduction

I have argued elsewhere (Higginbotham (1997)) that semantic theory should recognize a threefold distinction, between (i) merely possessing a word, or having it in one's repertoire, and so being able to use it with its meaning; (ii) knowing the meaning of the word; and (iii) having an adequate conscious view of its meaning. I thus distinguish between the meaning that a word actually has for a speaker and what I will call the speaker's *conception* of the meaning (which I allow to be tacit, even unconscious). The conception, if adequate and properly grounded, amounts to knowledge. And I distinguish both the meaning and the conception from the speaker's conscious opinion, or *view* of the meaning. These distinctions are advanced in the service of an understanding of linguistic theory that does justice to the normative and public dimensions of language, and at the same time allows full scope for the elaborations of semantic knowledge that appear to be required to characterize linguistic competence and language acquisition, and eventually to explain them.

Do the distinctions that seem to be called for in semantic theory arise also in the realm of concepts? If so, then there is such a thing as possessing a concept, so being able to deploy it, without having an accurate or full conception of it; and likewise such a thing as having an accurate or full conception, but lacking an adequate conscious view of the nature of the concept.

Consider the first alleged distinction, between concept–possession and one's conception of the concept possessed. By analogy to the notion of linguistic competence in the realm of semantics (that is, the state of mind that is attained when one knows the meanings of one's own words), I will say that *conceptual competence* is the state of mind of one who knows the nature of his own concepts. Just as there is a question whether one can use a word with its meaning while being less than competent, so there is a question whether one can deploy a concept in the absence of competence with that concept, or in the terminology I introduced above whether one's conception of a concept that one uses must be adequate to the concept. In my original abstract for this article I had stated that the view of Fodor (1996) may preclude a distinction between concept possession and conceptual competence; but I now think that, if anything, Fodor's view allows one to make the distinction plausible. In any case, I will explore the thesis that the distinction ought to be made, and that a view of concepts according to which their possession does not imply an adequate conception of them allows us to think about the development of knowledge in the individual and in collaborative, self–conscious inquiry in a way that clarifies both ordinary experience and those parts of developmental psychology, particularly developmental psycholinguistics, that construe the learner as engaged in theory construction.

My second distinction, between one's concept or one's conception of it and one's conscious view, I believe to be at least very close to a distinction Tyler Burge has argued is to be found in Frege, between the *sense* of an expression and a person's grasp of its sense. As I am using the term 'concept', a crucial feature of what Frege called the sense of an expression is shared by the concept: both have the property of being, or anyway determining, conditions on reference that something must meet, in the one case to be the reference of the expression, in the other to be something to which the concept truly applies.[1] Burge argues that if the distinction is made, so that one may deploy a sense that one does not grasp, then senses must be distinguished from linguistic meanings, precisely because in his view linguistic meanings do not show the gap between one's (considered) view of meaning and either one's conception of it, or the meaning itself (Burge 1990: p. 55, fn. 4).

---

[1]In this formulation I intend to include all of the usual referential apparatus of language: n–place concepts of objects, what is expressed by singular terms, quantifiers, higher–order or intensional operators if any, and so forth.

12. CONCEPTUAL COMPETENCE

In a similar vein, Christopher Peacocke has recently argued that thinkers should sometimes be credited with what he calls *implicit conceptions*, the use of which is responsible for some phenomena in the history of science, especially including mathematics and logic. For example, Peacocke notes that Leibniz appreciated the fact that the derivative $(fg)'(x)$ of $f(g(x))$ is the product $f'(g(x)) \cdot g'(x)$, despite not having a definition of the limit of a function at a point, on which the derivation of this fact is founded. Leibniz's insight may be said to depend upon his implicit conception. There are also things that all of us have experienced, such as recognizing a general principle as true without grounding the recognition in anything but reflection, which may be seen as realizing one's implicit conceptions. For example, when I first happened to come across 'Aristotle' in my parents' encyclopedia, I was told that Aristotle had enunciated a principle called the law of excluded middle, that every statement is either true or false. I recall that Aristotle's law struck me immediately as (a) true, and (b) something I had not realized before. Perhaps I had just been suckered into classical logic, but anyway my experience was of a common sort, in which I attained, or seemed to have attained, an explicit view of something that I "knew all along", involving in Peacocke's terms my implicit conceptions of truth, negation, and disjunction.

The distinctions suggested by Burge and by Peacocke, however, would serve to separate only one's conscious view of a concept, or conscious appreciation of principles in which it figures, from the cognitive powers involving the concept that allegedly lie behind and help to explain what appears in conscious thought. They would not separate concept–possession from what I am calling one's conception of a concept. Their distinctions are thus far compatible with the thesis that the concept is completely determined by the conception. They are also to this extent compatible with the thesis that, although we can certainly command a concept without having turned our thoughts to a conscious examination of its nature, we are at least potentially conscious of our own concepts, as it has been urged that we are potentially conscious of the meanings of our own words. That thesis itself may come in various grades of strength, depending upon what is allowed to count as bringing the content of a concept to consciousness. At one extreme, we would count only the ability to answer more or less offhand various questions about the concept, and our conception of a concept would be like other items of our implicit but accessible knowledge; i.e., items that we can perfectly well recognize as being correct if only we turn our attention to them. At another, noted by both Peacocke and Burge, we may allow the elaboration of theories involving the concept, over a long period of time and through the efforts of many people. Mathematical and logical examples, as they note, are paradigmatic here. Concepts such as that of the limit of a sequence, continuity of a function at a point, or logical truth, have received elucidations only through self–conscious research. But we were in touch with these concepts before the elucidation was achieved, and only because of that could we recognize the properties of particular instances, evaluate proposals concerning them, and recognize the elucidations as correct.

If Burge and Peacocke are right, then besides examples from mathematics and logic there should be compelling cases drawn from obviously empirical subject matter (as Peacocke notes). Indeed, I think that examples from the history of linguistics illustrate the theme of implicit conceptions at least equally well. For instance, you cannot speak a language unless you know what the words are, and what categories they belong to. But grasp of words and categories is normally tacit. Every documented discovery about the categories of words belongs to conscious critical inquiry; and it is certain that not all discoveries have yet been made.

If on anything like the grounds suggested the concept can be separated from one's conscious view of it, can we also separate concept possession from concept mastery? If, as might be suggested on the grounds of a broadly–based naturalism, a person's conceptual repertoire is simply constituted by that person's conceptions, then there is no possibility of the inadequacy of the conception to the concept: an inadequate conception of the concept CHAIR is at best a conception of some other concept. The distinction between the concept and the conception of it is thereby undermined.

Jerry Fodor in work from a few years ago, and more recently in his Locke lectures, has suggested that concept possession is a matter of having appropriate mental representations, and that a person's capacities stand in an evidential, but never a constitutive, relation to concept possession. His account is bound up with other features of his views, notably the representational theory of mind, a systematic skepticism about the definability of concepts, a conception of interpretation of language as translation into the language of thought, and the problem of articulating a view of what it is to acquire a concept on the basis of experience. Part of what I want to explore in what follows is the degree to which the general thesis, that a distinction can be made between having a concept and having an adequate conception of it, can be detached from these, or other, further doctrines. But it will also be important to consider what the distinction between concept possession and concept mastery is *for*, and for this purpose I begin further back, with the semantics of language.

2 Meanings and Concepts

The distinction between the meaning of a word for a person and the person's tacit conception of the meaning allows us to ascribe expressions of thoughts to that person, whose content she herself only partly understands, or even misconceives. It also allows us, in my view appropriately, to see the process of language acquisition as coming to know the meanings of words, where at a given stage the learner's conception is an hypothesis about the meaning. Likewise, if there is a distinction between the concept that a person possesses and her conception of it, it will be appropriate to ascribe to that person thoughts involving the concept that she only partly apprehends, or even misconceives; and the distinction allows us to view a person's increased sophistication with a concept as a consequence, not of progressive replacement in thought of one concept by another, but of acquiring a more adequate conception. After addressing some features of the semantic distinctions, I will consider what analogies and disanalogies there are between semantics and the realm of concepts.

I assume a version of semantic theory that identifies the meaning of a word with what is known when the meaning of that word is known. To illustrate the assumption, consider that a person who knows the meaning of a typical one–place predicate such as 'chair' knows something of the form

$$\text{'chair' is true of } x \text{ iff } C(x)$$

where C is some more or less complicated condition. The assumption is idealized in several respects. For one thing, there is no reason to assume that there is a single target necessary and sufficient condition C. There may be several, all of which are required to be known. For another, it may be unrealistic to demand a non–trivial condition that is both necessary and sufficient. The problem is not that there is a dearth of necessary conditions, but that the level of detail required even to approach sufficiency is hard to attain. The usual situation is well–exemplified by English (and other languages') transitive verbs with a causal component, such as 'persuade'. As remarked in recent linguistics literature (and in far earlier work) to persuade someone of something involves bringing about a change in the persuadees' state of belief, and to persuade someone to do something involves bringing about a change in the persuadees' intentions, pushing them in the direction of the thing of which the persuadee was persuaded. But there are many ways of changing a person's intentions that are not cases of persuasion; that is why it is a joke, for instance, to speak of persuading someone with a shotgun. Persuasion involves a change by what Judith Thomson has called a specific causal route. Roughly, the change in intention has to be brought about by the judgment, by the persuadees' own lights, that the thing the persuader recommends would be a good or reasonable thing to do, independently of external sanctions imposed by the persuader. At the same time, persuasion can involve deceit or seductive influence, as when your host persuades you to have one for the road. Persuading must be distinguished from convincing. And so it goes down the philological and philosophical road, from concrete examples and counterexamples to attempted definitions and revisions. In any case, it is I believe clearly a necessary condition of understanding 'persuade' that one appreciate that persuasion involves causation, as above.

Since the meanings of words are to be individuated by the conditions for knowing them, we allow the case where a person deploys a word with its meaning, but does not know what the meaning is. If meaning were constituted by an individual's conception of meaning, then there would no room for saying in all literalness that a person has a partial or mistaken understanding of a word. Similarly if meanings of words are individuated in terms of their functional roles or dispositions to use them, or any combination of these. Delete the distinction between knowledge and belief, or constitute meaning on grounds independent of a cognitive relation between the speaker and the theoretical statement that spells out the meaning, and the possibility of error, apart from being out of step with oneself, disappears. There can be error only when one's view of meaning misconstrues or only partially reveals one's conception (in fact, the usual case, but not relevant here). In particular, the possibility of error disappears if meanings of words are individuated by the conditions on having, or deploying, those words.

It is clear enough how an individual's conception of the meaning of a word can be partial or mistaken: the individual has picked up the word somehow, and is committed, and intends, or has no choice but, to mean by it what others mean; but the individual has got only partial information, possibly mixed in with various errors. It is far from clear how a whole population's most competent users can be partial or mistaken, for it is their activities that give the words what meaning they have, and their conceptions of meaning are canonically evidenced by those activities. Similarly, although it is clear how an individual or group can have a half-baked view of meaning, or simply have no reflective view at all, it is far from clear how, upon deliberate and careful reflection, they could fail to bring the meaning to light. The reason is that the activities in virtue of which words have the meanings that they do are not hidden, but intersubjective, and out in the open. I remarked above that, on Burge's interpretation of Frege, sense cannot be identified with linguistic meaning, just because meaning is ultimately transparent, if not to individuals, then to the most competent speakers, under appropriate conditions of reflection.

Supposing the above picture underlying the distinctions among meaning, one's conception of meaning, and one's conscious view of it, what analogy is there to concepts? In discussion at the Barcelona meeting, Steve Schiffer remarked that the threefold distinction at which this paper aims could be derived at least in some applications by assuming (a) that the verdict for cases of incomplete understanding in language is that the ignorant subject deploys the concept that a word expresses, but does not have an adequate conception of it, and (b) what is clear if tacit knowledge is admitted, that the same subject's conception of the concept may be distinct from her view of it. The illustration is not adequate establishing a general distinction, however, since it confines itself to the special case where the concept is exhausted by the interpretation of a linguistic expression (since otherwise it collapses into the linguistic case, contrary to the assumption that the concept is to be distinguished from the meaning). It would be possible, for example, to grant the threefold distinction as supported by (a) and (b) but to deny the illustration from linguistic theory given in section 3 below.

If there is a distinction between having a concept and having an adequate conception of it, then it cannot be both that concepts themselves are individuated in terms of the conditions for having them, and also that the conditions for having them amount to tacit knowledge of what they truly apply to. The general form for concept individuation will be

(i) the concept CHAIR is the concept F such that x has F iff $A(x, F)$

If we say that

(ii) x has an adequate conception of CHAIR iff x knows that for all y, CHAIR is true of y iff $C(y)$

and we put 'x knows that for all y, F is true of y iff $C(y)$' for '$A(x, F)$' above, then it becomes impossible to have a concept for which one lacks an adequate conception (although it is possible to have an adequate or an inadequate view of one's concepts).

I want to hold on to (ii), and more generally to the idea that one's conception of the concept CHAIR is constituted by what one takes to be the conditions on reference that apply to it. These conditions on reference will often purport to be (one might as well use the word) *analytic* to the concept; and in favorable cases they will be.

Small children know that chairs are seats, and they have backs. Their conception of the concept CHAIR has in part the content

CHAIR is true only of seats with backs

and they are in a cognitive state which has this content for its object. I have heard tell that small children sometimes refuse to apply common nouns, such as 'fork' and 'spoon', to any but the forks and spoons in their own households. They, and their family members, have forks and spoons; other people have at best pseudo–forks and pseudo–spoons. Supposing this story to be correct, these children's conceptions of the concept FORK would have in part the content

FORK is true only of tined utensils in my house

This content is not analytic to the concept FORK, since it is not even true of it. It does not follow that the children lack the concept FORK. On the contrary, they must have that concept, having as they do the concept TINED UTENSIL, which is exactly what a fork is.

If (ii) remains in force, and the distinction between concept possession and concept mastery is to be maintained, the concept as individuated by the conditions for having it must put something non–epistemic for '$A(x, F)$' in (i). Jerry Fodor's suggestion, as I understand it, is (iii):

(iii) the concept CHAIR is the concept F such that x has F iff x has a mental representation whose content is the property of being a chair[2]

On this view of matters, concepts are in one–to–one correspondence with properties. An alternative, which would take as its starting point what is achieved when one has an adequate conception of a concept, is to take the contents of representations as structured along the lines of the formulations that spell out the conditions on the reference of words (what Fodor refers to, I believe, as taking "concepts

---

[2]Fodor applies the word 'concept' to the mental representation itself, rather than to what it expresses; terminology aside, intend (iii) to reflect his views.

as definitions"). Properties, I take it, are not so structured. Either way, the conditions on having a concept are non–epistemic.

We may, I believe, retain the ideal of formulations like (ii) even if actual definitions are rare. The goal, as I see it, is to interrelate concepts, and to bring out how an adequate conception of one concept involves knowing its relations to others, a point to which I return below.

Suppose, then, that we have a non–epistemic criterion of concept individuation on one or another of the above lines, and retain (ii) as the formulation of having an adequate conception of a concept. We can now ask where the so far purely formal distinction will show up in cognitive explanation.

3 Examples

If a person's conception of the meaning of a word is partial or mistaken, then under the right circumstances the partiality or error will show up, either through a manifestation of ignorance or a mistake in application. Analogously, the inadequacy of a person's conception of a concept will show up in failures of knowledge or positive misapplication of the concept. Suppose that failures or errors come to light, and modifications are made. Then if the modifications are properly viewed as *corrections* to the original conception, the distinction between the concept and its conception is supported.

For example: when Euclidean geometry was first investigated using formal axiomatic methods, it was rapidly discovered that there were a number of tacit presuppositions in the system, including especially the axiom of Pasch, that if points a, b, and c are non-collinear, so that they form the vertices of a triangle abc, and L is a line crossing ac but not crossing it at a vertex of abc, then L crosses either ab or bc. Of course, the truth of the Pasch axiom was always known; but it was not taken as among the defining characteristics of the Euclidean plane. Pasch's axiom is independent of the other axioms of what Tarski called elementary geometry, and its omission from Euclid shows the partiality of earlier conceptions of what principles together were sufficient to characterize the Euclidean plane. When we bring the tacit presupposition to light, our conception of the concept BETWEEN(x, y, z) (on the Euclidean plane) has changed, but the concept has not been replaced; rather, since we regard the changing conception as a more adequate conception of the same concept, we underscore the distinction between the concept and the conception.

For another example: I said above that you have to have a conception of what a word is, and to what category it belongs, to know a language, or to learn one. When children first speak, they speak in words, despite the difficulty of determining in a stream of speech where one word leaves off and another begins.[3] But children's view of the concept WORD is known to be poor (Carey (1985): preschool children are apt to deny that 'ghost' is a word, because there are no ghosts, and they are often willing to call a word only an independent major part of speech, denying that status to closed–class items, which however they must know are words). Appreciating consciously as they do later on that these items are words, we may suggest that their conception of wordhood has become more adequate, whereas the concept has always been available.

4 Concept Inclusion

Above I cited what I understand to be Fodor's view of concept–individuation and concept–possession, noting that although there were two versions, depending upon whether one took concepts to correspond one–to–one with properties, or rather to be structured somewhat like the meanings of linguistic expressions, both allowed the distinction between the concept possessed and one's conception of it. But now, if one's conception of a concept becomes more adequate as one comes to know (tacitly) the conditions on its reference, then inclusions of concepts, either necessary conditions for the true application of a concept X, or sufficient conditions for the true application of some other concept Y, where X figures in having an adequate conception of Y, are going to be involved in any general account of their nature. I want now to consider whether such inclusions are to be admitted, in the face especially of the stern lesson owing, I believe, to Leonard Linsky: "Never try to give necessary and sufficient conditions for anything".

There has been much discussion over whether semantic equivalences or inclusions are linguistically represented, with a number of researchers, especially those engaged in constructing machines for what they refer to as "language understanding", affirming that they are, and with corresponding skepticism, and with intermediate views

---

[3]It has been suggested that information about word boundaries is present, in the form of transition probabilities between syllables: where all syllables are equally likely, there is likely to be a word boundary. In any case, there is no stage at which children speak in mixtures of words and non–words.

of various sorts. It is important to distinguish two questions here: (i) whether the input to the semantic component of a grammar is a syntactic representation of what is said, or whether on the contrary the representation is remote, typically in virtue of decomposing expressions into primitive parts; and (ii) whether the theorems of the semantic component, linking syntax with conditions on reference and truth, effectively reproduce, in the metalanguage, the structures that they interpret, or whether on the contrary they involve links between concepts. Both questions are open–ended, of course, but the distinction between them is nevertheless sharp. Consider, for instance, a grammar that decomposes the word 'kill' into 'cause to die under circumstances X', where X is whatever it is that, together with causing death, implies killing, but then interprets the resulting structure straightforwardly. The sentence 'John killed Bill', on this procedure, is first syntactically transformed, and then interpreted, resulting in the theorem

'John killed Bill' is true iff John caused Bill to die under circumstances X.

A very different view, issuing nevertheless in the same theorem, would be to put as an axiom for the semantics the statement

'kill' is true of x and y iff x causes y to die under circumstances X.

The first procedure answers 'yes' to (i) and 'no' to (ii) for the example chosen; the second answers 'no' to (i) and 'yes' to (ii). Evidently, a theory might answer 'yes' to both or 'no' to both.

For the questions (i) and (ii) to be distinguished, there must be a sharp distinction between syntax and semantics, and in particular the semantics must issue in genuine truth conditions, not translation into some formalism.

Now, Jerry Fodor and Steve Schiffer have suggested that perhaps all there is to interpreting a human language is translation into the language of thought. As Fodor puts it provocatively in (1996), "English has no semantics". I have argued elsewhere (Higginbotham (1995)) that this view changes nothing in linguistic theory, and specifically that the standard explanations of conscious knowledge of meaning in terms of implicit or even unconscious knowledge of a theory of meaning for words and construction, together with a procedure (about which nothing much is known) for deducing the consequences of the theory, survive completely intact even if, as on the scenario envisaged, it is through some translation from what strikes the ear to mental representations in one's language of thought that one understands speech. For, assume that explanations of understanding involve tacit or explicit knowledge of conditions on reference. Then, according to the representational theory advocated by Fodor, there will be a formula of the language of thought that expresses the knowledge, and I am supposing that it will be deployed in interpretation. The upshot of deploying it will, on the account envisaged by Fodor and Schiffer, be a formula in the "belief box" whose interpretation is that one just heard someone say that so–and–so. Thus the transition from the input signal to the formula whose reference is the reference of 'that so–and–so', its translation into the language of thought, is mediated by semantic knowledge. The notion of semantic knowledge is drawn, as it were, within linguistic theory and not outside it; so there must be room for it within any general account of the possibility of rational thought.

Returning to the issue of concept inclusion, the point in the present connection is that, since the only notion of interpretation thus far offered is syntactic, questions (i) and (ii) have not yet been distinguished. Similar remarks apply to work by Ray Jackendoff and others who allude to a hypothetical level of "conceptual structure", a layer of syntax that is said to be the "interface" to a "conceptual system". Although the latter notions are not clear to me, it seems safe to say that conceptual structure in this sense is a level of representation, a syntax. Now, conceptual structures, in the various proposals in the literature, are overflowing with representations that are remote from standard syntactic levels, and often involve lexical decomposition. Fodor and LePore have argued at length that these levels are unmotivated, and there have been rejoinders. All of this, however, is a debate only about question (i), and leaves question (ii) untouched.

I suggest, as in the example of the verb 'persuade' above, or lately of 'kill', that question (ii) should be answered in the negative; that is, the links between concepts must form a crucial set of the theorems of semantics. But that there should be such links, and that relations among concepts should form a crucial part of knowledge of meaning, is consistent with the difficulty (or impossibility) of explicit definition, and with taking the inputs to interpretation to have plain-vanilla phrase structures, with no lexical decomposition or syntactic markers for conceptual inclusion.

Fodor remarks that the analytic in a sense survives his "atomistic" view of concepts; roughly, the view that the best that can generally be done by way of definition is inadequate. I differ only in supposing that, since semantics is a matter of knowledge of conditions on reference, the characterization of the, really in many cases rather obvious and highly productive, relations of reference involved in having an adequate conception of meaning should take their rightful place in a theory of linguistic and conceptual competence.

5 Concluding Remarks

I have argued that there is support for a threefold distinction between the concept, the conception of the concept, and the conscious view of the concept; that the representational theory of mind is congenial to the distinction, but does not imply it; and also that the representational theory does not undermine the notion that one's conception involves tacit knowledge of conditions on reference. There are a number of issues, however, that have been held in abeyance here, and I will mention two of these in closing.

We certainly interact with concepts through our conceptions of them. Can we also interact with them in other ways? If one can have a concept either innately or through some form of "triggering", then the deployment of a concept is possible independently of the conception, if any. But how one should think about this question will depend upon whether the conception of a concept is a purely intellectual affair —a matter of knowledge— or whether the conception should be extended to include, for instance, recognitional capacities. Then we would need to inquire how closely these capacities are tied to concept possession.

Another issue, which arises prominently for concepts for natural kinds, is whether an adequate conception of concepts of kinds of things amounts to a grasp of what makes them the kinds of things they are, something that is generally known if at all only through self conscious empirical science. Hilary Putnam especially has promoted the view that reference can remain constant through changes in theory. To the extent that we take scientific advancement as issuing in more adequate conceptions of a concept, we have the consequence that the concept itself remains constant through changes in theory. Do we conclude that not only the reference of 'gold', but even the concept GOLD itself, is something of which we had no adequate conception until at least the nineteenth century? An affirmative answer to this question is not as radical as it might appear, however, if concept possession does not have an epistemic basis. The nature of some of our concepts may then be beyond the reach even of our most sophisticated conceptions.

If concepts are not epistemically individuated, there is an affinity between the concept and what, starting from a different point of view, would be called the essence of its reference. Concepts are not like meanings, not so much because, as in Burge, meanings are relatively transparent upon reflection, as because the nature of concepts can be completely opaque. In any case, the result is a rationalist picture of concepts not only of logic, mathematics, and language, but also of natural kinds. But this picture does not bring the promise that we have the resources to form adequate conceptions, let alone that we can, as the rationalist physicists tried to do, say in advance in terms of what sorts of essences natural kinds had to be constituted. It may be that our resources in this direction are very limited, and that we are in no position to say what the relation is between kinds of things, concepts for which we deploy, and the kinds of things that we are that makes it possible for us to have the concepts in the first place. Spinoza (1951: p. 9), discussing the various modes of knowledge, ranked as highest and most certain that which we have when a thing is known "solely through its essence, or through knowledge of its proximate cause". He goes on to observe, as we might, that "the things which I have been able to know by this kind of knowledge are as yet very few".

REFERENCES

Burge, Tyler (1990). "Frege on Sense and Linguistic Meaning". D. Bell and N. Cooper (eds.), *The Analytic Tradition*. Oxford: Blackwell. pp. 30-60.

Carey, Susan (1985). "Are Children Fundamentally Different Kinds of Thinkers and Learners Than Adults?" S. Chipman, J. Segal, and R. Glaser (eds.), *Thinking and Learning Skills, vol. 2*. Hillsdale, New Jersey: Erlbaum.

Fodor, Jerry (1997). *Concepts*. Locke Lectures, University of Oxford.

Higginbotham, James (1995). "The Place of Natural Language". P. Leonardi and M. Santambrogio (eds.), *On Quine*. Cambridge: Cambridge University Press. pp. 113-139.

———— (1997). "On Knowing One's Own Language". To appear in C. Wright and B. Smith (eds.), *Knowing One's Own Mind*. Oxford.

Peacocke, Christopher (1996). "Implicit Conceptions, Understanding, and Rationality". To appear in M. Hahn and B. Ramberg (eds.), *Festchrift for Tyler Burge*.

Spinoza, Benedict de (1951). "On the Improvement of the Understanding". R.H.M. Elwes (trans.), *The Chief Works of Benedict de Spinoza, vol. II*. New York: Dover Publications. pp. 1-41.

The Significance of the Distinction between Concept Mastery and Concept Possession

Genoveva Martí

In this paper, Prof. Higginbotham invites us to tear apart three notions. On the one hand, he observes, it is possible to master a concept, i.e, to have a conception of something in one's mind that is complete and accurate, without that conception being conscious. Thus, our *mastery* of concepts, to use traditional terminology, may involve an *implicit* conception or a *conscious* one. On the other hand, he argues, it is possible to possess a concept and yet lack a conception that is complete and accurate (which, I submit, means that it is possible to possess a concept and have a conception associated to the concept in question which is incomplete or inaccurate). Thus, we need to distinguish *possession* of concepts from *mastery*.

In these comments I will make a couple of essentially interpretive remarks and I will then move on to pose a question.

First, what I think is a purely terminological clarification. As I read the paper, Prof. Higginbotham is claiming that it is possible to possess a concept, say for instance the concept CHAIR without having an adequate conception of chairs, and likewise, that is possible to have an adequate conception of chairs (and thus master the concept CHAIR) without this conception being conscious or explicit. In Higginbotham's own terminology the distinctions are drawn in different terms: "there is such a thing as possessing a concept,.... without having an accurate or full conception *of it*" [p. 149. Emphasis added]. And later on: "the concept can be separated from one's conscious view *of it*" [p. 152. Emphasis added]. So, it would seem that, in order to be strictly accurate in portraying Higginbotham's argument, we should distinguish between, say, possessing the concept CHAIR and having an adequate conception *of the concept* CHAIR, and, likewise, between mastering the concept CHAIR, i.e., possessing an adequate conception of that concept, and that conception of the concept being conscious.

I hope that in interpreting the relevant notions in the former way I am not missing something crucial. I have chosen that interpretation because it seems to me that what is at issue in this paper, or, at least, one coherent way of interpreting what is at issue in this paper, is already captured by that formulation which avoids the suggestion that the core of the distinctions proposed by Higginbotham requires an appeal to concepts of concepts or conceptions of concepts.

I think it is clear that the distinction between concept possession and mastery does not require such an appeal to second–level concepts and conceptions. It may be argued, however, that the distinction between conscious and non–conscious adequate conception does require such an appeal. For, after all, consciousness does not just demand *having* a concept in one's mind, it demands the capacity to have the concept *before* one's mind, i.e., to be able to make it the object of one's thoughts, something, it is presumed, one can only do *via* a conception of the concept. Now, this way of arguing depends on the view that making something, in this case a concept, the object of one's thoughts means having a conception of it (not the thing itself) as part of the content of the thoughts about the thing. This is a view that I do not share. In any case, even when it comes to the distinction between conscious and tacit conception, I think that there is a significant way of interpreting Higginbotham's argument without appeal to conceptions *of* and concepts *of* concepts. So, to put what I take to be the main point of the paper in simple terms: it seems to me that Higginbotham is arguing that someone may possess a concept, for instance the concept of a model, even though she would fail to count among models, say, structures with finite domains, thus revealing that her conception of models

13. THE SIGNIFICANCE OF THE DISTINCTION... 165

(not her conception of the concept of a model) is not accurate, and therefore revealing that she does not master the concept of a model. Similarly she may master that concept and yet her conception of a model may not be conscious; she may not be in a position, even under ideal circumstances, to articulate or explicate fully what a model is.

Second, I think it is better to understand the structure of the argument not so much as proposing a distinction between three different notions, but rather as advancing two different distinctions: one is a distinction between tacit and explicit conceptions associated with concepts. The other distinction, which cuts orthogonally, separates mastery from possession of concepts. I am saying this because I gather that the inaccurate or incomplete conception associated with a concept possessed, but not mastered, can itself be either tacit or conscious, just as much as a fully acurate conception can be tacit or conscious.[1]

That it makes sense to distinguish between a tacit conception and a conscious one, and that mastering a concept does not necessarily require having an accurate conscious conception, is not something too difficult to accept, even from a rather traditional standpoint as regards concept acquisition. The bulk of Prof. Higginbotham's paper is devoted to motivate the need for the second distinction, for it may be more difficult to accept that there is a significant difference to be drawn between concept–possession and concept–mastery. For here Higginbotham is arguing that two different people may possess the same concept, say the concept of a model, and yet they may both have different conceptions (implicit or explicit) of what models are. And this goes against the, *prima facie*, plausible view that having a concept consists precisely in having a conception of a class of things — the things that fall under the concept. Thus, on the view Higginbotham is arguing against, the different conceptions of things one has in mind constitute the concepts one possesses —and masters. In short, on that view, there is no distinction to be drawn between a conception of a class of things and the concept under which those things fall.

---

[1] I am assuming here that whenever a concept is mastered or possessed there is a conception associated with the concept in question, i.e., that mastering or possessing a concept means, typically, acquiring a conception of the things that fall under the concept (be this conception complete or incomplete, accurate or inaccurate). I suppose that Higginbotham would not accept that it is possible to possess a concept in the total absence of *any* conception whatsoever, although I am not sure what his position is on this point.

As regards concept acquisition this view entails, for instance, that the person who would not count among models those structures with finite domains masters fully and completely a concept; it just happens not to be the concept MODEL. And when she learns that models can have finite domains she just acquires a new concept. If she made a mistake before, that mistake is only a matter of which labels go with which concepts. From this point of view one does not really learn that a concept one possesses applies to a thing one didn't think it applied to.

But if we think that acquiring conceptual competence is a gradual process in which the grasp of a concept one already possesses can be perfected, then it would seem we need some sort of distinction like the one Higginbotham is proposing between the concept itself and the conception of the things that fall under the concept; for as long as those two are not separated, changing one's conception of a class of things just *is* acquiring a new concept.

At this point, I think there are two interpretations of the significance of Higginbotham's claim that it is possible to possess a concept and yet have an inadequate conception associated with it. On the one hand, the claim can be interpreted as, essentially, a point about the graduality of the process of acquisition and mastery of concepts, the claim that conceptual competence is not a yes/no issue and that there are degrees of conceptual competence, in the same way in which there are degrees in language competence; there is a division of linguistic labor and some members of the community of speakers occupy higher ranks in the hierarchy. If Higginbotham is right, there is a separate hierarchy for conceptual competence —and this conceptual hierarchy does not collapse into a form of the linguistic one, i.e., the agents occupying the lower ranks should not be described as attaching labels to concepts wrongly. Indeed, some of the examples that Higginbotham presents in sections 2 and 3 of the paper to support his claim, specifically, the examples involving the concepts CHAIR, FORK and WORD, point towards this interpretation.

Nevertheless, I think that the remarks about natural kinds contained in the last section of the paper and the example on Pasch's axiom (from section 3) suggest a more radical interpretation of the significance of the distinction. For these examples suggest, I think, that there may be some concepts which are such that no one possessing them will ever be in a position to obtain an adequate conception of the kind of things the concept applies to. If I am right, and this is part of what Higginbotham means, his proposal to separate concept from conception involves an externalist view of concepts, for it makes concepts, some concepts at least, entities not fully accessible to an agent's mind.[2]

Now, I do not know whether the latter is an acceptable interpretation of the significance of Higginbotham's distinction. I am not sure either whether Higginbotham would accept or reject conceptual externalism. Some of his remarks seem, to say the least, sympathetic to it: "the nature of some of our concepts may then be beyond the reach of even our most sophisticated conceptions" (p. 161) and "... this picture does not bring the promise that we have the resources to form adequate conceptions" (p. 162). Moreover, Higginbotham points out that on his view "there is an affinity between the concept and what, starting from a different point of view, would be called the essence of its reference" (pp. 161-2); if one maintains the nature of some kinds may never become transparent to us, because their essence cannot be transparent to us, the possibility of attaining an adequate conception of the kind would be in the same boat. In any case, I think we cannot tell what his position on this issue is until he tells us more about how he views concepts of natural kinds and what he understands by *an adequate conception* associated to a natural kind concept. So, my query is an invitation to Prof. Higginbotham to elaborate on this subject.

---

[2]The issue of accessibility is the crucial one in determining whether the view is or is not externalist. As David Sosa has pointed out, the difference between externalist and internalist theories should not be thought as a difference in the location of the entities an agent is related to ("in" the mind *vs.* "outside") for if that were the crucial difference, Frege should be characterized as a staunch externalist.

Conceptual Competence and Inadequate Conceptions

Pierre Jacob

In his stimulating paper, Professor Higginbotham argues for a threefold distinction between (i) having a concept, (ii) having a (possibly tacit) conception involving that concept, and (iii) having a conscious view involving that concept. This threefold distinction in the theory of concepts is supposed to mirror a parallel threefold distinction in semantics between (i) having a word in one's lexicon and being able to use it with its meaning; (ii) knowing the meaning of the word; and (iii) having a conscious view of the meaning of the word.

In my brief remarks, I will concentrate on one of the distinctions recommended by Jim: I will restrict myself to the distinction between having a concept and having a (possibly tacit) conception involving that concept at the expense of the distinction between either having a concept or having an adequate conception and having a conscious view. As I understand it, Jim's distinction between having a concept and having an adequate conception involving that concept can serve what seem *prima facie* to be two quite different projects: one is to account for the possibility of partial or incomplete mastery of a concept; the other is to try to reconcile a non–epistemic account of concept individuation or concept possession with an account of how a person's concepts relate to one another. I will now say first why I think Jim's distinction between having a concept and having a (possibly tacit) conception involving that concept is important. And then I will ask Jim three related questions about what is an individual's conception involving a concept.

The main goal of Jim's paper is, I think, to provide a disciplined account for a variety of phenomena ranging from an individual's mainly non reflective conceptual development to the reflective development of scientific theories in the history of science. In the process of conceptual development, a child will learn new facts pertaining to some phenomenon or property F. Let's say that she thinks of F by means of concept F. At some earlier stage, she might have false beliefs about F. In other words, some of her thoughts involving F may well be false thoughts. In the process of learning, she will come to acquire new thoughts and revise some of her earlier thoughts. But in order to make sense of the learning process, we must assume that she is learning new facts about property or phenomenon F, not some other property or phenomenon. We must assume that some of her incorrect thoughts before the learning process were thoughts about F, not about some other property or phenomenon. And we must assume that thanks to the learning process, the new thoughts she comes to entertain are thoughts about F, not about some other property or phenomenon. So presumably, we must assume that both her former incorrect thoughts about F and her new thoughts about F involve F —her concept of property F— not some other concept.

Similarly, in the history of science, to make sense of a great many scientific changes in a single area of scientific research at different periods of time, we have to assume that scientists across different paradigms may refer to the same kinds of things although they may have different theories or conceptions of them. In other words, although scientists at different periods of time may have different conceptions of e.g., gold, their different conceptions may involve one and the same concept, GOLD.

What is common to the ontogenetic and the scientific historical phenomena is that we want to be able to say that a person may entertain thoughts involving a particular concept even though the person has a partial, incomplete, inaccurate or deficient command or mastery of the concept in question. A person may entertain thoughts involving some concept F. Some of her F–involving thoughts may be true; others may be false. The point here is that we want to be able to say of her thoughts —both her correct thoughts and her incorrect thoughts— that they involve F, not some other concept. So we want to be able to ascribe to her the concept F or to say that she

14. CONCEPTUAL COMPETENCE AND INADEQUATE... 171

possesses the concept F even though some of her thoughts involving that concept are incorrect. As pointed out by Putnam and Burge, even though I may have a partial mastery of what arthritis is, I may nonetheless entertain thoughts involving the concept of arthritis; my thoughts may nonetheless be about arthritis.

In order to account for the possibility that a person may entertain incorrect thoughts involving a given concept, Jim suggests first that we distinguish between a person's possession of concept F and a person's F-involving conceptions. And I think he is right to do so. In terms of Jim's analogy —to which I'll come back momentarily— between words and concepts, I quote, "if meaning were constituted by an individual's conception of meaning, then there would be no room for saying in all literalness that a person has a partial or mistaken understanding of a word. Similarly, if words are individuated in terms of their functional roles or dispositions to use them, or any combination of these" (p. 154). As he puts it, there must be a gap between what it takes for a person to have a concept and what it takes for her to have an adequate conception involving that concept.

His second suggestion is to move towards a non–epistemic account of concept possession or concept individuation. In fact, Jim seems attracted to the kind of purely informational account of concept possession or concept individuation lately advocated by Jerry Fodor. At least, I suspect that Jim's proclivity is to accept Fodor's non–epistemic pure correlational account of concept individuation for concepts of nomic properties (or concepts of natural kinds). I suspect that for concepts of either non–nomic properties or logical and mathematical concepts, Jim would not recommend a purely correlational account of concept individuation.

This move towards a non–epistemic account of concept individuation (or concept possession) allows one who, like Jim, wants to maintain a gap between having a concept and having an inadequate conception involving that concept to embrace an epistemic account of what it takes an individual to have an adequate conception involving that concept. Now, consider Jim's condition (ii) for having an adequate conception: x has an adequate conception of CHAIR iff x knows that for all y, CHAIR is true of y iff $C(y)$ (p. 155). As this condition makes clear, for a person to have an adequate conception of a concept is to know the conditions of reference for that concept, i.e., to know what something must satisfy for the concept to be true of it (or to apply to it). And this piece of knowledge will involve some of the person's other concepts —the concepts making up condition C. This is why as he puts it, the task of an account of what it takes a person to have an adequate conception involving a concept is to "interrelate" the person's concepts or "to bring out how an adequate conception of one concept involves knowing its relations to others".

I have purposefully characterized Jim's distinction as the distinction between having a given concept and having a (possibly tacit) conception involving that concept. But this is not Jim's own way of putting it. Rather, Jim draws a contrast between having a concept and having a (possibly tacit) conception of the concept. Unless I'm mistaken, the reason why Jim's contrast is drawn in this way is that Jim wants an individual's conception of concepts to stand to concepts as an individual's tacit knowledge of meanings of words stands to meanings. Now, from what Jim says in this paper, he seems to accept a view according to which meanings are public properties of words and what confers meaning onto a word are communal practices. As he puts it, "the activities in virtue of which words have the meanings that they do are not hidden, but intersubjective, and out in the open" (p. 155).

Supposing that what confers meanings onto words are communal practices, then, in the semantic domain, one may, I think, clearly distinguish the meaning of a word from a speaker's tacit knowledge of it, i.e., the meaning of the word. The latter is, the former is not a psychological state of the speaker. Now, consider my conception of arthritis. I take it this is what allows me to deploy the concept of arthritis in forming thoughts —both in forming correct thoughts and in forming incorrect thoughts. I take it that Jim wants to say that what it is in virtue of which I can entertain true and false thoughts about arthritis is not a conception of arthritis, the disease, but a conception of the concept ARTHRITIS. What it is in virtue of which I can entertain true and false thoughts about water is not a conception of water. What it is a conception of is not water —the liquid— but the concept of water.

The first question I want to ask Jim then is: What are the building blocks of what he calls an individual's conception of concepts? Another way to put the question is: How tacit is an individual's conception of concepts? I want to suggest that there are two lines of response to this question in Jim's paper and that these two kinds of response each correspond to one of the two constraints which, according to Jim, an account of what an individual's conception of a concept ought to be responsive to.

I assume that there is a difference between the thoughts entertained by an individual and the individual's subdoxastic information carrying states. I further assume that the former are built out of concepts which, as we might put it, the individual may grasp (more or less fully). An individual might be said to have a grasp of a concept

14. CONCEPTUAL COMPETENCE AND INADEQUATE... 173

if she is aware of being occasionally in psychological states with the content corresponding to the concept in question and if she is able to relate it to some of her other concepts, as in "if something is a dog, then it's an animal". I assume that an individual's subdoxastic information carrying state is not so built out of concepts of which the individual has a grasp. So an individual may have tacit knowledge of what linguists call "c–command relations" among grammatical constituents of her language without having a grasp of the c–command relation. The sense in which the individual has tacit knowledge but no grasp of the c–command relation is the sense in which she is unaware of being occasionally in a cognitive state with that content and she is unable to relate the concept of c–command to her other concepts. So the question is: Is an individual's conception of a concept more like the individual's tacit knowledge of c–command or more like one of the individual's thought or propositional attitude? It seems to me, there are two lines of response to this question in Jim's paper.

On the one hand, as I said above, the task of a theory of what it takes a person to have an adequate conception involving a concept is to "interrelate" the person's concepts. This is the first of the two constraints mentioned above. What this suggests —to me at least— is that a person's conception is a set of thoughts, where a person's thought may be one of his or her propositional attitudes whose building blocks are concepts of which the person has a grasp. This line of thought may seem corroborated by the following disanalogy between an individual's conception of a concept and the individual's knowledge of the meaning of a word. The building blocks of an individual's knowledge of the meaning of a word cannot be other meanings. By contrast, an individual's conception of a concept might have concepts as its building blocks.

On the other hand, according to Jim, an individual's conception of a concept ought to stand to the concept in question in the same relation as the relation which an individual's tacit knowledge of the meaning of a word stands to the meaning. In other words, an individual's conception of a concept is —like an individual's knowledge of meaning— a tacit subdoxastic cognitive state. This line of thought suggests therefore that an individual's conception of a concept too is a set of subdoxastic information carrying states of the individual. And this suggests —to me— that the building blocks of an individual's conception of a concept are not concepts of which the individual has a grasp in the above sense; or at least that they could be other things than concepts of which an individual has a grasp.

As I said above, Jim draws a contrast between having a concept and having a conception of a concept. So I want to ask Jim a second related question: Can an individual have some inadequate conception of a concept —e.g., the concept WATER without having the concept of a concept?

Finally, I want to ask Jim a third question (which could also be directed to Chris Peacocke, given his own notion of an implicit conception) which is this. How liberal is Jim's notion of a conception of a concept going to be? Could one and the same tacit conception of a concept underly two inconsistent explicit theories involving that concept? Did one and the same implicit (or tacit) conception of the concept PLANET underly both the Ancient Greeks' explicit Ptolemaic geocentric theory and the Copernican heliocentric theory of the Solar system?

On Concepts and Conceptions

Josep Macià

There are a number of important themes in professor Higginbotham's paper. I will focus here on what I take to be the main topic of the paper: whether there is a distinction to be drawn between what he calls "possessing a concept" and "having an adequate conception of a concept" and what this alleged distinction amounts to. I will claim that professor Higginbotham's paper certainly succeeds in showing that there is room for drawing some distinction of the kind he indicates. I will also argue, though, that the paper is less successful in making it clear what exactly the distinction it intends to draw is. My paper can be seen as a way of providing several specific requests for clarification of the distinction.

It is argued in Higginbotham (1987) that regarding the meaning of words there is a distinction between (1), (2) and (3)

(1) Having a word in one's repertoire

(2) Knowing the meaning of a word

(3) Having an explicit view about the meaning of a word

The idea, I believe, is roughly the following: I might not know, for instance, what "fortnight" means, but if I utter "I'll be back in a fortnight" with the right intentions, my utterance is an act of meaning with determinate truth conditions. In this case "fortnight" would be a word in my repertoire even if I do not (or do not fully) know its meaning. Regarding (3): I have an explicit view about the meaning of, for instance, the word "melt" if I explicitly know, say, that to melt is to become liquified by heat; I might know the meaning of the word "melt" even if I do not have an explicit view about its meaning (as for instance, if asked what "melt" means I am not immediately able to say that it means to become liquified by heat, but if questioned, I assent to statements such as: "ice melts when you take it out of the fridge and becomes water", "if an arctic explorer makes water out of a piece of ice using a grinder the piece of ice does not melt even if it becomes water", etc.).

Higginbotham's claim is that regarding concepts there is a threefold distinction analogous to (1)–(3). There is some variation in the terminology that Higginbotham uses to refer to each member in the threefold distinction he attempts to draw; we will here stick to the terminology in (1)', (2)' and (3)':

(1)' Possessing a concept

(2)' Having an adequate conception of a concept

(3)' Having an explicit view about a concept

It is fairly clear by analogy with (3) what (3)' is supposed to be. The main issue of the paper is whether there is a distinction between (1)' and (2)' and what the distinction is.

I believe we can distinguish three ways in which Higginbotham would show what the distinction he wants to draw between (1)' and (2)' is: (a) by analogy with (1)–(2), (b) by giving the general form of the possession conditions for concepts and the general form of possession conditions for adequate conceptions of a concept, (c) by giving examples. We will devote this paper to examine each one of these three ways of showing what the distinction between (1)' and (2)' is.

(a) The analogy between (1)–(3) and (1)'–(3)'

The first, introductory, way of showing what the distinction between (1)', (2)' and (3)' is is by assuming the distinction between (1), (2) and (3) (i.e. a distinction regarding knowledge of the meaning of words) and by claiming that we want to consider the analogous distinction with regard to possession of concepts.

As we have said the analogy seems to work well for (3) and (3)'. If we attempt to apply the distinction between (1) and (2) to the case of concept possession, though, all the analogy seems to yield is that we are looking for a distinction between two levels regarding the possession of concepts. Here is why:

Regarding (1) and (2) (i.e. having a word in one's repertoire and knowing the meaning of a word) we know that they are not the same because it is possible for someone to have a word in her repertoire while not knowing the meaning of the word. In one such situation even if one does not know the meaning of the word, one knows the word as a syntactic object. That is, one has the word as a syntactic object to start with; then, even if one cannot use the word with all the intentions that would be required if one were to understand the meaning of the word, one can use the word with the intention to refer to whatever the members of one's linguistic community refer to when using that word.

There is nothing directly analogous to this in the case of possession of concepts. So just knowing that (1)' and (2)' are to be 'the analogues' of (1) and (2) at the level of concept possession does not tell us much about what (1)' and (2)' are supposed to be. It is somewhat as if we are told that they are going to add a new rule to the game of baseball, and that this rule is going to be 'the analogue' of the basketball rule regarding 3-point field goals. If nothing else is added we would not really know what the new baseball rule is supposed to be.

(b) Possession conditions

The second, and I take it to be the most important, way of showing what the distinction between (1)' and (2)' is supposed to be is to provide the general form of the possession conditions for concepts and to provide the general form of the possession conditions for an adequate conception of a concept and to point to the fact that they are clearly different kinds of possession conditions. (iii) and (ii) below (which are taken and adapted from (iii) and (ii) in Higginbotham's paper [pp. 155-6]) give, respectively, the form of the possession conditions for a concept F, and the form of the possession conditions for an adequate conception of a concept F:

(iii) x has concept F iff
x has a mental representation whose content is the property of being an F

(ii) x has an adequate conception of concept F iff
x knows that for all y: F is true of y iff $C(y)$

Higginbotham claims that we might have a more adequate formulation of (iii) if in the right hand side of the biconditional we do not necessarily appeal to the property of being an F, but rather we allow the content of a representation to be structured "along the lines of the formulations that spell out the conditions on reference of words". The following instance of the possession conditions might seem to illustrate the idea:

(iii)' x has the concept MELTING iff
x has a mental representation whose content is the property of becoming liquified by heat

Higginbotham suggests, though, that appealing to properties in the right hand side of the biconditional will not allow us to appropriately deal with the structure that the content of representations can have. Examples like (iii)' may suggest otherwise (it all will depend, though, on what our assumptions regarding the identity conditions for properties are). Still if we wanted to avoid appealing to properties in the right hand side of the conditional, we might take the general form of the possession conditions for a concept to be such that (iii)'' would be one specific instance:

(iii)'' x has the concept MELTING iff
x has a mental representation whose content is: "becoming liquified by heat"

In any case, whether we take the general form of the possession conditions for a concept to be (iii) or to be some other kind of condition that has (iii)' or (iii)'' as instances, it seems obvious that the general form of the possession conditions for concepts is very different from the general form of the possession conditions for adequate conceptions of a concept.

Even if the two kinds of possession conditions are obviously different, though, their being different does not guarantee the falsity of (the universal closure of) the following:

(iv) x has concept F iff x has an adequate conception of F

The rather technical point is this: If one accepts (v) and (vi)

(v) (x has a mental representation whose content is the property of being an F) iff
(x knows that for all y: the property of being an F is true of y iff $C(y)$)

(vi) (x knows that for all y: the property of being an F is true of y iff $C(y)$) iff
(x knows that for all y: F is true of y iff $C(y)$)

then, given (iii) and (ii), one has to accept (iv), and so, one has to accept that there is no extensional distinction between (1)′ and (2)′.

One might accept (v) and (vi) but, of course, one does not have to accept them. In particular one does not have to accept (v) (it is probably harder not to accept (vi)). It seems clear that Higginbotham does not accept (v). Still, the rather technical point we have made (namely: the fact that (iii) and (ii) have different form does not guarantee by itself that there is a distinction between (1)′ and (2)′) shows the need to say more about the key notions appearing in (iii) and (ii). In particular: what is it for an individual to have a representation? What is it for a property to be the content of a representation (if nothing epistemic is to be involved)? What kind of knowledge is appealed to in (ii) —could we, for instance, analyze it in terms of dispositions to behaviour, or in functional terms? (if so, and if having a representation with certain content can also be analyzed in those same terms, then the door for the collapse of the distinction between (1)′ and (2)′ is open). What is it to have beliefs "about" certain concept (such as the ones appealed to in the right hand side of (ii))?

I believe these are not questions that can be put aside here and regarded as a matter for complementary or further inquiry. The answers to these questions completely affect what (iii) and (ii) tell us about what concepts and adequate conceptions of concepts are. Without knowing more about these questions, as we pointed out, we do not even know whether (iv) is the case. We need to know more about the key notions appearing in (iii) and (ii) both to be sure that possessing a concept and having an adequate conception are distinct properties and to know what exactly each of these two properties is.

It would seem, then, that (ii) and (iii) leave some questions open regarding how the distinction is to apply to specific examples. Higginbotham offers several examples and I take them to be an important part of his justification of the existence and relevance of the distinction he is drawing between (1)′ and (2)′.

(c) Examples

Higginbotham offers basically three examples to help clarify what the distinction between (1)′ and (2)′ is.

WORD example. In the introductory section Higginbotham has said: "...you cannot speak a language unless you know what the words are and what category they belong to" (p. 152). In a latter section he gives the following example:

[...] children's view of the concept WORD is known to be poor (Carey (1985): preschool children are apt to deny that 'ghost' is a word, because there are no ghosts, and they are often willing to call a word only an independent major part of speech, denying that status to closed-class items, which however they must know are words). Appreciating consciously as they do latter on that these items are words, we may suggest that their conception of wordhood has become more adequate, whereas the concept has always been available. (P. 158.)

If I interpret it correctly, the point of the example is this: since children are able to understand language, and so they are able to appropriately brake what they hear into words, they must have the concept WORD. That is, given that they behave in a way that shows that they are able to discriminate between a part of speech that is a word and a part of speech that is not, they must have the concept WORD. On the other hand, there are changes in their conception of wordhood (it becomes more adequate) without there being a change in the fact that they posses the concept WORD. This is supposed to show or at least to illustrate that possessing a concept is not the same as having an adequate conception of a concept.

Notice that in the way the example is described it does not strictly show that it is possible to possess a concept without having an adequate conception of it (and so that possessing a concept is not the same as having an adequate conception of the concept). The example would only show that a concept does not need to be the same as the conception that certain individual has of the concept (we have been offered a case where the concept possessed at two different times is the same, but the conception that an individual has of it is different). The specific wording used at some other places in the Examples section in Higginbotham's paper might also suggest that the primarily distinction being considered there is the one between concepts and conceptions, and not the one between concepts and adequate conceptions.

Nevertheless, it seems clear that the examples are relevant to show what the intended distinction between concepts and adequate conceptions (i.e. between (1)' and (2)') is. If we described, for instance, the WORD–example not just as a situation where the concept possessed remains the same while the conception changes by becoming more adequate, but rather as a situation where there is no change in

15. ON CONCEPTS AND CONCEPTIONS   181

the fact that the child possesses the concept WORD while the child goes from a stage where he has a non–adequate conception of the concept to a stage where she has an adequate conception of the concept, then we have certainly illustrated the distinction between (1)′ and (2)′: we would have presented a situation (the stage at which the child has a non–adequate conception of the concept WORD) that can plausibly be described as a situation where someone possesses a concept without having an adequate conception of the concept.

Regarding this WORD–example I would like to make three related observations:

1. If the fact that the children are able to understand language is what shows that they have the concept WORD, then they must also have many other syntactic concepts such as NOUN–PHRASE, VERB–PHRASE, etc. One must certainly be able to discriminate between the parts of speech that fall under these concepts and the parts that do not. Other concepts that anyone who understands language would have to possess are the concept of a node dominating another in a tree, or the concept of a node c–commanding another (this is the concept of a relation that holds between a node X and a node Y in a tree if every branching node that dominates [is an 'ancestor' of] X also dominates Y). The relation of c–commanding is involved in the formulation of the so called "Binding Principles", which are the ones that say, for instance, that we cannot interpret "Everybody loves him" as meaning that everybody loves himself. We are able to correctly apply the Binding Principles when we use language, and that means that we must be able to discriminate between nodes in a tree that are in the c–commanding relation from nodes which are not. Following the same reasoning that led us to conclude that young children must have the concept WORD we must conclude that all of us who understand language must have the concept C–COMMANDING.

If what I am saying correctly interprets Higginbotham's WORD example then it is possible to have a concept without having a conception (adequate or not) of the concept: since every reader of this paper is able to understand language and so to apply the Binding Principles, he or she must have the concept C–COMMANDING (and must actually have had it since he or she was a child). But those readers who had not previously heard about it did not have any conception of the concept C–COMMANDING.

2. Higginbotham's WORD example, and what we have said so far would seem to support (vii) and (viii):

(vii) x has concept F if x is capable of behaving in a way that discriminates between what falls under F and what fails to fall under F.

(viii) x has a conception of concept F only if x is able to have explicit thoughts involving the concept F.

If, according to (viii), being able to have explicit thoughts involving the concept is a necessary condition for having a conception of the concept, then this condition is certainly also necessary for having an adequate conception of the concept. This would seem require that (ii) be strengthen or at least that the appeal to 'knowledge' in (ii) be interpreted so that it guarantees that if a subject x knows the necessary and sufficient condition for the true application of a concept that figures in (ii) then x is able to have explicit thoughts involving the concept.

On the other hand, regarding the possibility of taking the sufficient condition in (vii) to be also a necessary condition: If we were willing to say, for instance, that some individual who were not able to discriminate between what is a word and what fails to be one does not have the concept WORD, then, as we pointed out at the end of section (b), the door for the collapse of the distinction between (1)' and (2)' would be open if we were also willing to analyze 'knowledge of A' in terms of the capability to discriminate between what is A and what is not A.

3. If I am correctly interpreting Higginbotham's WORD example, we might be forced to say that anyone who can see has the complicated mathematical concept of FOURIER TRANSFORMATION, given that it seems that we use Fourier transformations when calculating where the borders of the objects in our visual field are (we behave in a way that shows that we discriminate between points related in certain ways that involve Fourier transformations and points which are not related in those ways). If we do not want to reach this conclusion, it would be helpful to know what exactly the distinction between Higginbotham's WORD example and my C–COMMANDING and FOURIER TRANSFORMATION examples is.

(Incidentally, if my C–COMMANDING and FOURIER TRANSFORMATION examples are at all examples of the distinction that Higginbotham wants to draw between (1)' and (2)' then they, rather than the WORD example, would seem to be good candidates to be used against Steve Schiffer's objection: They are cases in which an individual has a concept without having any word in his repertoire expressing that concept; so possessing a concept cannot just be to have a word in one's repertoire which expresses that concept.)

Pasch's axiom example: The example is the following:

Pasch's axiom is independent of the other axioms of what Tarski called elementary geometry, and its omission from Euclid shows the partiality of earlier conceptions of what principles together were sufficient to characterize the Euclidean plane. When we bring the tacit presupposition to light, our conception of the concept BETWEEN(x, y, z) (on the Euclidian plane) has changed, but the concept has not been replaced; rather since we regard the changing conception as a more adequate conception of the same concept, we underscore the distinction between the concept and the conception. (P. 157.)

According to this example, the fact that we acquire a new belief involving the concept BETWEEN (on the Euclidean plane) —namely, the belief that there is certain logical relationship between different statements we already believed to be true— makes it the case that there is a change in our conception of the concept BETWEEN. The example would seem to suggest, then, that the following is true

(ix) x's conception of a concept F depends on (consists in?) all of x's beliefs that involve the concept F.

(ix) agrees with a pretty common use of the term 'conception' —I believe it is the one that Ruth Millikan assumed in her commentary to Fodor— according to which, for instance, everyone in Barcelona has the concept PHILOSOPHER but my conception of the concept might be pretty different from the one other people have; and presumably this would be so because those people's beliefs involving the concept PHILOSOPHER are pretty different from mine.

This Pasch's axiom example gives us some information about what conceptions are that is different from, though it seems that compatible with, what could be inferred from the previous example.

Notice also that if in (ix) we use only the expression "depends on" (and not "consists in"), then (ix) and also (ii) are compatible with letting the conception that an individual has of certain concept to depend also on some non–propositional elements, such as the emotions linked to the concept. My father used to tell me that I did not know what a war is. What he said should of course not be taken literally but rather as meaning that since, unlike him, I had been lucky enough not to live through a war my conception of it did not have some essentially emotional elements attached to it that he regarded as important (and I would not have them even if I gathered as much information as he had about the facts regarding the war).

FORK example: This example is given when discussing the possession conditions for concepts and adequate conceptions. I believe that even if it also points to a distinction between $(1)'$ and $(2)'$, it points towards a distinction of a different sort from the one suggested by the previous example. The example is the following:

> I have heard tell that small children sometimes refuse to apply common nouns, such as 'fork' and 'spoon' to any but the forks and spoons in their own households. They, and their family members, have forks and spoons; other people have at best pseudo-forks and pseudo-spoons. Supposing this story to be correct, these children's conceptions of the concept FORK would have in part the content
>
>   FORK is true only of tine utensils in my house
>
> [...] It does not follow that the children lack the concept FORK. On the contrary, they must have that concept, having as they do the concept TINED UTENSIL, which is exactly what a fork is. (P. 156.)

Regarding this example it seems that we would first want to say that there probably is some problem with the way the child would use the word 'fork' (on the one hand intending to refer to what other people refer, on the other intending to refer only to forks in his house). Leaving the issues regarding the child use of the word 'fork' aside, though, it would seem that there are two concepts involved (TINED UTENSIL, and TINED UTENSIL IN MY HOUSE) and that the child has both. Furthermore, TINED UTENSIL IN MY HOUSE is (or is part of) the child's conception of FORK (i.e. TINED UTENSIL).

What does allow us to say that TINED UTENSIL IN MY HOUSE is the child's conception of FORK? I believe the example would suggest that something like (x) should be true:

(x) We say that a person x has a conception G of concept F if x has concept G and usually uses it when we would use concept F.

or more generally

(x)′ A person x has a conception G of concept F with respect to community T, if x has concept G and usually uses it when people in community T would use concept F.

The child is described in the example as usually using the concept TINED UTENSIL IN MY HOUSE when adult people would be using the concept TINED UTENSIL. About the "usually" appearing in (x): the child only very rarely interacts with forks outside his home; the situations where he uses his conception of FORK with respect to forks not at home, are situations consisting in denying

15. On Concepts and Conceptions 185

the application of his conception to forks, and so are not situations where adults would use the concept FORK. These situations are assumed to be very rare, though. (If someone were to use the concept TINED UTENSIL IN MY HOUSE fairly often to deny that it applies to forks outside his house [i.e., he would often use it when most other people would not use the concept FORK], it would no longer be natural for us to say that his conception of FORK includes 'being a tined utensil in my house', but we would rather say that he is using a different concept.)

As we already pointed out, it does not seem that this distinction between possessing a concept and having a conception of a concept that is suggested by the FORK example is the same as the distinctions between concepts and conceptions suggested by the previous examples.

The Concept–Conception Distinction

Maite Ezcurdia

1. Higginbotham[1] argues in favour of a threefold distinction between possessing a *concept*, having a *conception* of the concept and having a conscious *view* of it. But in speaking of having a conception, one must take care to distinguish having a conception *of a concept* from having a conception *associated with* the concept which one takes to be *analytic to* or *constitutive of* that concept. In terms of Fodor's account of concepts: one thing is to have a conception of a mental representation M which is a concept and has as its content the property P, and another to have a conception of P which one takes to be *analytic* to or *constitutive* of the concept M.[2] In speaking of conceptions, I take Higginbotham to be meaning something like the latter. Similarly, in speaking of a view I take him to mean a view of P, not of the concept M or of a tacit conception of P. As I see it, the distinction between a view and what he calls 'a conception' is

---

[1] Higginbotham, J. (1997) "Conceptual Competence", present volume.
[2] One can have conceptions about what shape the concept of water takes as a mental representation, but not worry at all about what it represents. This would be a conception of the concept though not of its content. I want to thank Professor Jerry Fodor for explaining this to me during the Conference.

that whilst the former is always conscious, the latter is *always* tacit or unconscious.[3] Henceforth I use 'tacit conceptions' for the latter, leaving 'conceptions' for both views *and* tacit conceptions.

An advantage to drawing the concept–conception distinction lies in its allowing for accounts of (*a*) the *public* or *intersubjective* character of concepts and (*b*) a *certain normative* aspect involved in possessing a concept, viz. the possibility of misapplying a concept one possesses.[4] Higginbotham's (1997) example of the child who applies FORK to only tined utensils in her house serves to illustrate how the distinction between possessing a concept and having a *tacit* conception allows for explanations of (*a*) and (*b*). But the explanatory advantage also emerges in cases where a subject possess a concept and has an inadequate *conscious* conception.

(*a*) Suppose Sam believes a tiger is a striped animal but Paul doesn't. In the light of the concept–conception distinction, we say Sam and Paul possess the concept TIGER but disagree on their conscious conceptions of tigerhood. There being something shared by subjects with different conceptions vindicates the *public* character of concepts.

(*b*) The concept–conception distinction underwrites the *possession–mastery* distinction. One can possess a concept without having an appropriate conception, without mastering it. The gap between possessing a concept and having an appropriate conception allows for explanations of how a subject can possess a concept whilst misconceiving or only partially grasping it, and so of how she may misapply it and make improvements on the associated conception. Such a distinction, for example, helps explain what sort of cognitive state a subject takes herself to be and to have been in on uttering (1), avoiding reinterpreting it as (2).

(1) I used to believe that a fortnight was a period of ten days, but now I know that a fortnight is a period of fourteen days.

(2) I used to believe that 'fortnight' meant a period of ten days, but now I know that 'fortnight' means a period of fourteen days.

---

[3] Making the distinction in this way still allows for views to be out of sink with tacit conceptions. A child, for instance, may only be partially conscious of the tacit conception that guides her application of a concept.

[4] There is a normative aspect to concepts presupposed by the distinction: that present in the intentional relation between a concept and its content. This normative aspect is explained by Fodor as a causal–cum–nomological relation between a property which is the concept's content and the mental representation which is the concept.

The distinction helps explain in a *non–metalinguistic* fashion reports of past mistakes concerning a concept. Avoiding reinterpretations like (2) prevents false belief–reports in a language different from that of a monolingual believer. This suggests that the believer's mistake concerns not a word of a given language, but rather something that crosscuts (public) languages, viz. a concept.[5]

Although we *seem* to be on the right track for accounts of (*a*) and (*b*) on the basis of the distinction, whether we are requires a fleshing out of the concept–conception distinction. In what follows, I indicate ways of fleshing it out as well as lines of enquiry that must be pursued.

2. On Higginbotham's view, having a conception is (*i*) what purports to give a subject individuating knowledge of the content of concepts *and* (*ii*) what actually gives her cognitive causal powers with respect to them.

(*i*) Having a conception is a matter of being in certain conscious or tacit *epistemic* states, and perhaps having certain recognitional abilities. Ignoring recognitional abilities, we may say that not everything one thinks true of fortnights needs to figure in one's conception of a fortnight.[6] My thinking of it as a long vacation period or short work period doesn't feature in my conception of a fortnight. My conception is characterized by only those features which *I take* to be providing *identifying knowledge* of fortnights, knowledge about what distinguishes fortnights from other things. In Higginbotham's terms, a conception is constituted by what the subject takes to be the concept's conditions of application or reference, where those conditions are intended to be *analytic* to the concept. When the conception is adequate the subject has (conscious or tacit) knowledge of a fortnight, even if she still thinks some false things about fortnights. Thus, having full knowledge of a concept, being fully competent and mastering a concept, doesn't require a subject to have *only* true thoughts of the entities that fall under it.

On Higginbotham's view, unlike conception–possession conditions, conditions for concept–possession are non–epistemic. On Fodor's account to possess a concept is to have a representation of the language of thought which has as its content a certain property. However, the concept–conception distinction isn't supposed to be committed to Fodor's account of concepts. According to Higginbotham, the dis-

---

[5] For more on these kinds of cases see T. Burge (1978) "Belief and Synonymy", *Journal of Philosophy*, LXXV.

[6] I speak of thinkings or conceivings as the epistemic states involved in having (tacit or conscious) conceptions.

tinction should be made within other theories of concepts and their possession. Could senses, i.e. non–syntactic modes of presentation, uphold the distinction?

The usual test for identity and difference of senses is *epistemic*: if a subject who is rational and conceptually competent can take different epistemic attitudes towards the thought Fa from those towards the thought Fb despite a's being b, then the sense of a differs from that of b; if she can't, then the senses of a and b are the same.[7] This seems to suggest that senses are conceptions. But the epistemic nature of the test doesn't by itself suffice to claim that to possess a sense is to be in an epistemic state, for all it does is say how to identify sameness and difference in sense when it shows up in thought. Furthermore, the restriction that the ideal subject in question be conceptually competent, know her own concepts, suggests that the difference in attitudes amounts to a difference in concepts; hence that the test is for concepts, not conceptions. Whether senses could themselves be concepts under the distinction requires accounts of grasping a sense in a non–epistemic way and of the nature of senses and tacit and conscious conceptions.

For a subject to have a *conscious* conception (a view) is for her to have a belief. For a subject to have a *tacit* conception (even tacit knowledge) may involve having a subdoxastic contentful state, but it may simply be grounded in the way her cognitive system works. At least in the cases where beliefs or subdoxastic contentful states are involved, we may clearly distinguish a conception from the having of it: a conception just is the content of those states. But *prima facie* concepts are the ultimate constituents of contents, thus putting the concept–conception distinction under threat.[8] The threat, however, is easily dispelled. A content is constituted by concepts, but is a conception *relative to* another concept. A subject's conception of a fortnight as a ten day period involves concepts like PERIOD–OF–TIME, TEN and so on, which *relative to* the concept FORTNIGHT gives her a conception of a fortnight.

(*ii*) On Higginbotham's view, to have a (tacit) conception is to have cognitive powers regarding a concept which help explain what appears in (conscious) thought and intentional behaviour, and it is

---

[7]The test is usually framed in terms of *linguistic* competence. But for the present purposes it is best to frame it in terms of *conceptual* competence.

[8]This threat doesn't arise for tacit conceptions grounded only in the working ways of the system. For here it is the theorist who uses concepts in characterizing a subject's or system's conceptions. But it is not the conception possessed by the system what is constituted by concepts.

what (typically) gives one access to one's own concepts. A subject's behaviour is evidence of her conception because it is her conception what gives her cognitive powers regarding the use of a concept. Yet, if conceptions not only purport to provide the subject with individuating knowledge but *also* with causal powers, what use is there to possessing a concept without a conception?

Whether it is only via a conception that we have access to our own concepts and whether concept–possession on its own lacks causal powers are issues that need to be addressed.[9] Higginbotham (1997) leaves open the question of whether conceptions include recognitional abilities, implying that if they don't then concept–possession is causally responsible for recognitional behaviour, and if they do then concept–possession has no causal powers without an accompanying conception. But independently of whether conceptions involve recognitional abilities, one may, in a Fodorian spirit, distinguish causal powers associated only with concepts from those linked specifically to conceptions. Causal powers involved in *inferential* processes that explain *systematicity* and *productivity* of thoughts are linked solely to *concept*–possession, whilst causal powers that are involved in judging what sort of entities fall under a concept are linked to having a *conception*. Appeal to concepts' causal powers helps explain why on thinking that Paul killed Laura María is able to think that Laura killed Paul (systematicity), and why she is able to think, on thinking that John believed that Paul killed Laura, that Ian believed that John believed that Paul killed Laura, and so on (productivity). Appeal to conceptions' causal powers of helps explain why it is that a subject put a thought together, eg. the thought that tigers are striped animals. Although possessing a concept hooks me up with certain entities in the world via an intentional relation, it is the associated conception what determines the way in which I conceive that relation.

The relation (or rather interaction) between having a conception and possessing a concept needs more work in order to get a full account of the cognitive powers pertaining to each, work which addresses the questions of what a concept is, what it is to possess a

---

[9]It's an issue of some importance whether we require a conception in order to interact with the concepts we actually possess. Millikan ((1990) "The Myth of the Essential Indexical", *Noûs*, XXIV) argues that where the self–concept or representation is concerned, no conception is required. All that is needed is for it to hook up with the dispositions to act, think and perceive of the person *I know* how to move. Generalizing, it's a good question whether we need conceptions to interact or relate to our own concepts, or whether merely hooking up with the appropriate dispositions to act, think and perceive suffices.

concept and how that differs from having tacit and conscious conceptions. I have indicated lines of enquiry that still need to be pursued and ways in which the concept–conception distinction might be elaborated. Whether such elaborations are successful depends on the work that still needs to be done.

Response to Commentators

James Higginbotham

The generally sympathetic but appropriately critical comments by Maite Ezcurdia, Pierre Jacob, Josep Macià, and Genoveva Martí have helped me to clarify some of the issues that I confronted in my article. More than anything else, they have convinced me that some of the difficulties that I thought I saw were real difficulties for the position I endeavor to illustrate and defend, that there is a three-way distinction to be drawn between concept possession, (tacit) concept mastery (or what in the article I called an adequate conception of a concept), and one's conscious or explicit view of a concept.

One difficulty, emphasized by both Ezcurdia and Macià, is that of defending an appropriately non–epistemic view of concept possession. As one way of formulating such a view, I allude to Jerry Fodor's suggestion that possession of the concept F amounts to having mental representation whose content is the property F. But surely (it may be objected) the "having" of the representation must be linked in some way to capacities of the agent, and would not these in turn amount not only to ascribing a tacit conception, but even to exhausting it? If so, then the non–epistemic view would, as Macià notes, not after all serve the distinction between merely being able to deploy a concept and having a tacit conception of it. On the other hand, I think that Ezcurdia is right to note that even if the test for sameness and difference of concepts C_1 and C_2 is what she calls epistemic —amounting to the question whether one can rationally adopt different attitudes toward thoughts ...I_1...and ...C_2...— it does not follow that concept possession is itself an epistemic matter. In any case, I require that it be possible to sever, by Fodor's device or another, the question what concepts one possesses from the question what conceptions one has. Where I spoke in terms of a three–way distinction, Martí suggests instead a cross–classification: one's conception may be on the one hand either explicit or merely tacit, and on the other either adequate or not. In this framework, the question will be whether there can be such a thing as an inadequate tacit conception.

On some points, my choice of vocabulary was perhaps unfortunate. Thus I write of one's "conception of a concept", but did not intend that the conception have the concept as its target, or anything else of what Martí calls a "2nd–level" conception. Suppose I deploy a concept which I tacitly take to be true of an object x iff Fx; and in fact it is not. In this case I say that my conception of the concept diverges from the concept; but I need not have any thoughts at all about what my concept is (thoughts in which my concept is mentioned, rather than used). Anyway, I agree with her remark that if it is possible for the concept and the conception to diverge as stated, then a certain externalism is the consequence, independently of the question whether the concept is "within" or "outside" the mind (or neither). Such externalism might result in a kind of alienation of our concepts from our conceptions, where we are unable fully to bring to light the nature of the concepts we ourselves deploy.

If alienation is an extreme possibility, the illustrations that may reinforce the distinction between our concepts and our conceptions can very well come from our successes, including our successes in humanly accessible realms where talk of essences, at least in the sense associated with natural kinds, seems out of place; viz., the ethical and legal spheres. As Ronald Dworkin has emphasized, legal practice sees itself as determining the extension of terms such as 'contrast' and 'privacy' in cases not governed by precedent or antecedent agreement, not arbitrarily or on the basis of relationships of power and influence, but rather on the basis of the outcome of inquiry and debate as to what the *right* extension would be in such cases. Taken at face value, this practice is inconsistent with the thesis that the conception alone determines the concept.

Macià and Jacob raise questions about the tacit possession of technical concepts, the linguist's c–command in particular. Macià suggests that speakers of human languages must have this concept (which figures in the linguistic account of conscious judgements that they make) but do not have any conception of it. Jacob, following a standard terminology, distinguishes between subdoxastic informational states, individuated in part through concepts such as c–command, and tacit or implicit thoughts involving such concepts, and asks whether what I am calling one's conception belongs with one or the other. In the article I offered as one illustration the child's capacity to deploy the concept WORD, coupled with a documented inadequate conception of what a word is, as shown for instance by refusal to apply 'word' to humble items like 'of', or to items like 'ghost' that are not true of anything. But in this example (as in the example of the concept FORK) the child actually had the means of expressing the concept —the word 'word' itself— while for c–command, or other linguistic relations, such a means is often lacking. Professional linguists and hangers–on aside, does the concept C–COMMAND figure only in subdoxastic states? If so, then the question of a speaker's conception, on their view, does not arise; but that would restrict the domain of applicability of the distinctions that I wish to draw to the case where some explicit view exists; and that in turn would leave open how if at all the distinction between concept possession and the conception is to be drawn. To revert to Martí's way of putting it: it would leave open the question whether there can be inadequate conceptions as well as inadequate conscious views of a concept.

Now, it is critical to linguistic theory, conceived as a theory of tacit knowledge, that it provide intentional explanations of behavior and behavioral capacities in terms of the deployment of such knowledge; and that the deployment in question be by the agent herself. The latter clause distinguishes such explanation from, for example, the intentional explanation of the structures attributed to visual experience as the outcome of problem solving. To use Macià's example, we may say that the concept FOURIER TRANSFORM figures in the intentional explanation of the agent's attribution of an object–description to a visual scene, but this concept is not deployed by the agent (as opposed to, say, the agent's visual cortex). I assume, however, that the concept WORD is in fact deployed by the child learning a first language from scratch, and that it figures in, for example, her grasp of the distinction between affixes, which cannot occur in isolation, and true words, which can.

The concept C–COMMAND is, on the interpretation I am assuming, deployed by speakers and hearers in determining the possibilities for pronominal cross–reference, in English and other languages, with differences from language to language that are the subject of active research. Pathologies apart, speakers and hearers not only have the concept, but also have an adequate conception of it, even in the absence of any conscious view; or so I am supposing. It would be particularly interesting, from this point of view, to examine cases where the concept is only tacitly deployed, but where the conception, unlike that of C–COMMAND, is not adequate; and Macià, I think, is right to point out that cases of this kind would underscore the difference between the view I am exploring and the more accessible thesis that one's conscious or explicit view may be inadequate to the concept. The space of these comments does not permit an examination of the question here; but the commentators are right to discern a significant issue in the question of the status of subdoxastic states of the agent.

Finally, Jacob asks the engaging question whether a single tacit conception could underly each of two different explicit views (perhaps in the same individual, though he does not mention that possibility explicitly). Examples might, I think, include the entering conception we have of the area under a curve, and its development in mostly coinciding but sometimes different ways in different types of definite integration. But in this and similar examples, where the concept is originally exemplified to us only in a proper part of the cases to which the explicit theory applies, it will be a delicate matter to judge whether we are developing a fixed concept in divergent ways, or have replaced it with one or more others.

What the Externalist Can Know *A Priori**

Paul A. Boghossian

Even after much discussion, it continues to be controversial whether an externalism about mental content is compatible with a traditional doctrine of privileged self–knowledge. By an externalism about mental content, I mean the view that what concepts our thoughts involve may depend not only on facts that are internal to us, but on facts about our environment. It is worth emphasizing, if only because it is still occasionally misperceived, that this thesis is supposed to apply at the level of sense and not merely at that of reference: what *concepts* we think in terms of —and not just what they happen to pick out— is said by the externalist to depend upon environmental

---

*First appeared in *Proceedings of the Aristotelian Society*, pp. 161-175.
Earlier versions of the argument of this paper were presented to my seminar on "Self–Knowledge" at Princeton in the Spring of 1991, to my seminar on "Mental Content" at the University of Michigan in the Spring of 1992, and to the plenary session of the Conference on Self–Knowledge at the University of St. Andrews in August of 1995. I am grateful to those audiences for helpful comments and reactions. I am especially grateful to Anthony Brueckner and Stephen Schiffer for detailed comments on a previous draft and to John Gibbons and Christopher Peacocke for numerous helpful conversations on the general topic.

facts. By a traditional doctrine of privileged self–knowledge, I mean the view that we are able to know, without the benefit of empirical investigation, what our thoughts are in our own case. Suppose I entertain a thought that I would express with the sentence 'Water is wet'. According to the traditional doctrine, I can know without empirical investigation (a) that I am entertaining a thought; (b) that it has a particular conceptual content, and (c) that its content is <u>that water is wet</u>.

Let us call someone who combines an externalist view of mental content with a doctrine of privileged self–knowledge a *compatibilist*. In this paper, I will present a *reductio* of compatibilism; in particular, I propose to argue that, if compatibilism were true, we would be in a position to know certain facts about the world *a priori*, facts that no one can reasonably believe are knowable *a priori*. Whether this should be taken to cast doubt on externalism or on privileged self–knowledge is not an issue I will attempt to settle in this paper. Anti–compatibilist arguments with this general form have been attempted in the past, but I believe that those earlier efforts have misstated the case that needs to be made.[1] Before we get into the details, however, it will be useful to outline certain semantical preliminaries.

1 Semantical Preliminaries

In the case of a general term —for instance 'water'— I recognize a three–fold distinction between its extension, its referent, and its meaning. A term's extension is just the set of actual things to which it correctly applies. In the case of 'water,' it is all the bits of water existing anywhere in the universe. Since we know that those bits of water are just aggregates of H_2O molecules, we may also say that the extension of 'water' consists in the set of all aggregates of H_2O molecules that exist anywhere (including those aggregates that we may never encounter).

---

[1] See, for example, Michael McKinsey, "Anti–Individualism and Privileged Access", *Analysis* 51 (1991), pp. 9-16, and the effective response by Anthony Brueckner, "What an anti–individualist Knows A priori", *Analysis* 52 (1992). This style of anti–compatibilist argument is to be distinguished from the 'traveling case' arguments discussed in my "Content and Self–Knowledge", *Philosophical Topics* 17 (1989), pp. 5-26.

By a term's referent, I mean the property that it denotes. In the case of 'water' it will be natural to say that its referent is the property of being water. It is possible to wonder whether it would be equally correct to say that it is the property of being H_2O. That depends on whether the property of being water may be identified with the property of being H_2O, an example of an interesting question in the theory of properties, but not one that I need to settle for present purposes. What is important here is to be able to distinguish between a term's extension and its referent, so that we are able to say that a term may express a property that nothing actually has. I think of a sentence's *truth condition* as the proposition it expresses; and I think of the proposition it expresses as composed out of the referents denoted by its terms. Thus, the truth condition of the sentence 'Water is wet' is the proposition made up out of the property of being water and the property of being wet and that says that anything that has the one has the other.

I distinguish between the property that the term 'water' denotes and its meaning. The terms 'water' and 'H_2O' may have the same referent, but they do not have the same meaning. What do I mean by the meaning of a term? I wish to be as neutral about this as possible and not to presuppose any particular view. I will let the reader decide to what extent I have succeeded in my neutrality.

Finally, I identify a word's meaning with the concept it expresses, and so I take the meaning of the sentence 'Water is wet' to give the content of the belief that a literal assertoric use of the sentence would express. I use quotes to name words and underlining to name the concept those words express: thus, water is the concept expressed by 'water.' Now, for the argument.

2 Externalism and Twin Earth

Abstractly speaking, externalism is easily enough defined. It is simply the view that facts external to a thinker's skin are relevant to the individuation of (certain of) his mental contents. So stated, externalism does not commit one to any specific form of dependence of mental contents on external facts, just to some form of dependence or other.

However, philosophers who embrace externalism don't do so because they regard it as a self-evident truth. They embrace it, rather, because their intuitive responses to a certain kind of thought experiment —Putnamian Twin Earth fantasies— appear to leave them little choice.[2] And that sort of thought experiment motivates externalism only by motivating a specific form of dependence of mental contents on external facts. In particular, it underwrites the claim that, in the case of an atomic, natural kind concept C, the substance actually picked out by C enters into the individuation of C. To put the claim another way: the substances with which a person actually interacts help determine what atomic, natural kind concepts, if any, that person has.[3]

To see this, let us remind ourselves how the Putnam thought experiment is supposed to work. Whereas Oscar, an ordinary English speaker, lives on Earth, his molecular and functional duplicate, Toscar, lives on Twin Earth, a planet just like Earth except that the liquid that fills its lakes and oceans, while indistinguishable from Earthly water in all ordinary circumstances, is not H_2O but some other substance with a different chemical composition —call it XYZ. Going by whatever criteria are relevant to such matters, water and twin water are distinct kinds of substance, even though a chemically ignorant person would be unable to tell them apart. Now, widespread intuition appears to have it that, whereas Oscar's tokens of 'water' apply exclusively to H_2O, Toscar's tokens of 'water' apply exclusively to XYZ. Widespread intuition appears to have it, in other words, that Oscar's and Toscar's 'water' tokens have distinct extensions. If this intuition is sustained, then that implies either that their 'water' concepts are not individuated individualistically or that they are not individuated in terms of their referents. For Oscar and Toscar are molecular and functional duplicates of each other: they are alike in all internal respects (up to intentional description). Yet the referents of their concepts differ. Hence, either those concepts don't determine what they refer to in some context–independent way (they are not individuated in terms of their referents) or

---

[2] In this paper, I will be restricting myself to externalist theses that are motivated by Putnamian Twin Earth experiments concerning natural kind concepts. In particular, I want to put aside for present purposes externalist theses that are motivated by the influential Burge–style thought experiments involving deference to the usage of linguistic communities. I believe that an argument parallel to the one given in this paper can be mounted for those sorts of externalism as well, but will not argue for this here.

[3] By the schema 'x individuates y', I just mean that if the value of 'x' had been different, the value of 'y' would have been different, too. By itself, this doesn't tell us anything about what the value of 'y' is for any particular value of 'x'. More on this below.

they do determine what they refer to and so are not individuated individualistically.

It is worth emphasizing that a Twin Earth experiment by itself does not get you all the way to an externalism about concepts; it only gets you as far as this disjunction. It is possible to respond to the experiment, and to the intuitions it generates, by opting for the individualistic disjunct and abandoning the idea that concepts are individuated in terms of their referents. That is the response favored by so-called 'narrow content' theorists. To get an argument for concept externalism you need not only Twin Earth intuitions, you also need to insist that any notion of mental content deserving of the name has to be individuated in terms of its truth conditions, has to determine the conditions for its truth or satisfaction in some context-independent way. Given this further assumption, there is then no option but to say that Earthly and Twin Earthly tokens of 'water' express distinct concepts —water in the case of the former, and let us say, twater in the case of the latter.

Let us make explicit, then, the various presuppositions involved in using the TE thought experiment as a basis for concept externalism. First, and least controversially, water and twater have to be thought of as distinct substances, distinct natural kinds; otherwise, it won't be true that Oscar's word 'water' and Toscar's word 'water' have distinct extensions and referents. Second, the word 'water' —whether on Earth or on Twin Earth— must be thought of as aiming to express a natural kind concept; otherwise, the fact that water and twater are distinct natural kinds will not be semantically relevant. Third, Oscar and Toscar have to be thought of as chemically indifferent, as having no views about the chemical composition of the liquid kinds around them; otherwise, they won't end up as functional duplicates of each other in the way that the experiment requires. Fourth, the concepts expressed by the Earthly and Twearthly tokens of 'water' have to be thought of as atomic concepts, not compound concepts that are compositionally built up out of other concepts in well-defined ways. For example, the experiment presupposes that water can't be thought of as capable of being defined as: A tasteless, odorless liquid that flows in the rivers and faucets. For if it were a compositional concept of that sort, its extension would be determined by the extension of its ingredient parts. Hence, a conclusion to the effect that water and twater have different extensions would have to proceed differently than it does in Putnam's original experiment, by showing that one of the *ingredients* of water —the concept expressed by 'liquid', for example— has a different extension from that expressed by its Twin counterpart. Finally, and as I have recently noted, concepts must be thought of as individuated in terms of their referents.

3 The Argument

Now, let us suppose that Oscar —our prototypical Twin Earth subject— is a compatibilist. I claim that Oscar is in a position to argue, purely *a priori*, as follows:

1. If I have the concept water, then water exists.

2. I have the concept water.

Therefore,

3. Water exists.

Since the conclusion is clearly not knowable *a priori*, one of the premises in Oscar's evidently valid reasoning had better either be false or not knowable *a priori*. The question is: Can Oscar, qua compatibilist, safely count on one or the other claim? I shall argue that he cannot, that he is committed to both premises (1) and (2) and to their being knowable *a priori*. If I am right, then the compatibilist is committed to the manifestly absurd conclusion that we can know *a priori* that water exists.

Now, the *a priori* knowability of premise (2) just is the view that I have called the doctrine of privileged self-knowledge, so we don't have to spend any time debating its dispensability for compatibilism. The only real question concerns premise (1), to an extended discussion of which I now turn.

4 Perhaps: Water is not required for Water

Two possible objections need to be considered. On the one hand, an opponent might wish to reject the first premise out of hand, on the grounds that it isn't necessary, on an externalist view, that water exist for someone to have the concept water. On the other, he might wish to argue that, although it is true that water is required for water on an externalist view, that fact is not knowable *a priori*. Which, if any, of these two alternative strategies is available to the compatibilist? Let us begin with a discussion of the first.

How might Oscar have acquired the concept water without actually interacting with some water, according to a Twin Earth externalist? He couldn't have acquired it merely by virtue of the internal functional role of 'water', for his duplicate shares that functional role and yet is said not to have the concept water. And he couldn't have acquired it by theorizing that the liquid around him is H_2O, for it is stipulated that Oscar is no chemist and has no specific views about the microstructure of water.

An externalist could claim that Oscar might have acquired water from other speakers who have the concept. This suggestion harbors a number of difficulties which limitations of space prevent me from discussing here.[4] Even if it were ultimately sustained, however, its impact on the argument I'm pursuing would be minimal —it would simply force us to slightly complicate the absurd conclusion that I have claimed the compatibilist is in a position to derive *a priori*. Instead of (3), we would now have the equally unpalatable disjunction:

3'. Either water exists or other speakers who have the concept water exist.[5]

For now, however, I propose to set aside this complication and say, simply, that if Twin Earth externalism is true, then contact with water is required for possession of the concept water.

5 Water is required for water, but that fact is not *a priori*

The most important challenge to the line of argument I'm pursuing derives not from opposition to the truth of this claim, but from opposition to its alleged apriority. This opposition can be stated in

---

[4] Part of what I have in mind here is that not all speakers could reason in this way, for some of them must have acquired the concept without any help from others. But it would be a needless distraction to go into this now.

[5] It is interesting to note that here we are in agreement with Tyler Burge, if not on the apriority of the disjunction, then at least on its truth, as far as externalism is concerned:
What seems incredible is to suppose that [Oscar], in his relative ignorance and indifference about the nature of water, holds beliefs whose contents involve the notion, even though neither water nor communal cohorts exist.
See "Other Bodies", in Woodfield (ed.) *Thought and Object* (Oxford: OUP 1982), p. 116.

a number of related ways; I shall present the strongest version I can think of.

According to the externalist, we know that water is required for possession of the concept water because we know, roughly, that 'water' is one of those words on which a Twin Earth experiment can be run. But doesn't our knowledge that a given word is Twin Earth–eligible rest on empirical information? Compatibilists are very fond of saying that it does;[6] however, it is rare to find their reasons explicitly spelled out. Where exactly do empirical elements intrude into the TE experiment? Let us look at this in some detail. What conditions does a word have to meet if it is to be TE–eligible?

As we have seen, it has to be a word that expresses an atomic concept. It also has to aim to name a natural kind. Furthermore, the user of the word must be indifferent about the essence of the kind that his word aims to name, he must be chemically indifferent.

But aren't all these conditions available *a priori* to the user of the word? More to the point, wouldn't a compatibilist have to hold that they are?

The answer is perfectly straightforward, it seems to me, in the case of the latter two conditions. Whether or not a person has beliefs about the microstructure of the kinds around him, and whether or not he intends one of his words to name one of those kinds, are matters that not only seem intuitively *a priori*, but that a believer in privileged access would have to hold are *a priori*. Notice that we are not asking whether the word actually names a natural kind, but only whether its user intends it to do so. And according to the doctrine of privileged access, the contents of one's intentions and beliefs are available to one *a priori*.

It might be thought, however, that the question about atomicity is somewhat more delicate. For is it so clear that facts about compositionality are *a priori*? Haven't we, as philosophers, often been in the unhappy position of assuming that a concept was compositional, investing a lot of effort in seeking its definition, only to conclude that it has none, that it must be deemed atomic after all?

It is important not to conflate apriority with ease. A fact may be *a priori* but very difficult to uncover, as the example of any number of mathematical or logical theorems might illustrate. We need not claim that facts about atomicity are easy, only that they are not empirical. And in fact it is hard to see how they could be

---

[6]Tyler Burge has urged this in conversation; for a statement in print, see Brueckner, *op. cit.*

18. WHAT THE EXTERNALIST CAN KNOW A PRIORI   205

otherwise. What sense can we make of the idea that knowledge of whether a concept is internally structured might depend on empirical information about the external world?

So far, then, we have not come across a TE–eligibility criterion that could plausibly be claimed not to be available *a priori*. We are now about to consider another criterion, however, which, if it really were a criterion, would definitely make TE–eligibility an empirical matter. The criterion is this: In addition to *aiming* to express a natural kind, a word must *actually* name a natural kind, if it is to be Twin Earth–eligible. One cannot run a TE thought experiment on a word that aims, but fails, to name a kind.[7]

In support of this claim someone might offer the following. Putnam's original experiment is carried out on a term —'water'— in full knowledge that it does refer to a kind, namely, H_2O. That knowledge plays a central role in the experiment. Twin Earth by itself doesn't speak to what we should say about a term that doesn't name a natural kind. So, for all that Twin Earth overtly commits us to, actually naming a natural kind is a condition on TE–eligibility and that is certainly not a condition that is available *a priori*. True, Twin Earth teaches us that water is required for the word 'water' to name the concept water, such an objector would concede; but we only learn this because we know —empirically— that water is the kind actually named by 'water'. Hence, TE–eligibility is not *a priori*.

Now, I think that this objection, as stated, isn't very effective; buried within it, however, is another objection that is considerably more challenging. The reason this particular objection doesn't succeed is that it is quite clear that we *can* run a TE experiment on a word that doesn't actually name a natural kind. Suppose we had such a word, W, on Earth. Then, to get a successful TE experiment, all you need to do is describe a Twin situation in which, although the users of the word type W are functional and molecular duplicates of their counterparts on Earth, W does name a kind in the Twin situation. Provided intuition still has it that the extension of Earthly tokens of W are different from the extension of the Twin tokens of W —which of course they will be since the extension of the former will be empty and the extension of the latter won't be— the experiment will succeed.

Now, however, the objector would appear to be in a position to pose a more difficult challenge. For if this is in fact right, and we

---

[7] I am grateful to my colleague John Gibbons for helping me see the need to confront this objection and the general line of argument that it opens up.

can run TE experiments even on terms that fail to refer, then how do we know *a priori* that water is required for 'water' to express water? We can't infer that claim merely from the fact that 'water' is TE–eligible, for we have established that even empty terms are TE–eligible. Maybe water is the concept that 'water' expresses when it fails to name a natural kind, when there is no water for it to name. If we can be said to know that water is required for water, we know that only by virtue of our knowledge that 'water' does name a natural kind, namely, water. And that, of course, is something that we could only have come to know empirically. Hence, our knowledge that water is required for water is not *a priori*.

Here, finally, we come across the most important challenge to the line of argument I've been pursuing. It will be interesting to uncover the reason why it doesn't ultimately protect compatibilism from the charge of absurdity.

6 The Empty Case

I want to approach a response to this objection somewhat indirectly, by focusing on the following question: What should a Twin Earth externalist say about the case where a word aiming to name a natural kind fails to do so? Two sorts of scenario might lead to such an outcome. On the one hand, a word like 'water' may fail to name a natural kind because the liquids to which it is competently applied don't form a natural kind, but rather a heterogeneous motley. On the other hand, a term may fail to name a kind because there fails to be anything at all out there —motley or otherwise— to which it could correctly be said to apply. Here I want to concentrate on the second more extreme sort of case because it throws the issues of interest into sharper relief.

So let us imagine a planet just like ours in which, although it very much seems to its inhabitants that there is a clear, tasteless and colorless liquid flowing in their rivers and taps and to which they confidently take themselves to be applying the word 'water', these appearances are systematically false and constitute a sort of pervasive collective mirage. In point of actual fact, the lakes, rivers and taps on this particular Twin Earth run bone dry. All of this may seem very far-fetched, and no doubt it is. However, the scenario described is not substantially different —except in point of pervasiveness— from what has actually turned out to be true in the case of such terms as 'phlo-

18. WHAT THE EXTERNALIST CAN KNOW A PRIORI 207

giston' and 'caloric'; and, anyway, the point isn't to describe a genuine possibility. Rather, it is to inquire how a particular semantical theory proposes to treat cases of reference failure and whether it is committed to treating such cases in a particular way. What *concept*, if any, should a Twin Earth externalist say would be expressed by tokens of the word 'water' on Dry Earth?

Some may think the answer to be obvious. Since externalism is the view that the concept expressed by a word is individuated in part by the referent of that word, then it follows, does it not, that if the word has no referent that it expresses no concept?

This reasoning would be far too hasty. It confuses the claim that a concept is individuated in terms of its referent, with the claim that the existence of the concept depends on the existence of a referent. To put matters in terms of a familiar technical vocabulary, it confuses externalist individuation with object–dependence. All that Twin Earth externalism is committed to, strictly speaking, is the claim that, if the referent of a given word were different, the concept it would then express would be different, too. And that is consistent with the claim that the word would express a concept in a case where it fails to refer, provided that the concept it would there express is different from any it would express in a case where it does refer. To say it again, externalist individuation, in the sense in which Twin Earth externalism is committed to it, is just the view that, if two words differ in their referents, then they also differ in the concepts they express; strictly speaking, this is consistent with a word's expressing some concept or other even when it fails to have a referent.

But what concept should we say 'water' expresses under the conditions described, in which there fails to be any natural kind for it to refer to? We may consider options under two main headings: compound and atomic.

We could try saying that under the envisioned dry conditions, 'water' expresses a suitable compound concept made up in the familiar way out of other available concepts. Which compound concept? Most plausibly, I suppose, something like: <u>the clear, tasteless, colorless liquid that flows in the taps and the rivers around here and.</u>... It won't matter much for the purposes of this argument how precisely this proposal is fleshed out. On any such view, the word 'water' will contribute a complex property to the proposition expressed by whole sentences involving it, one which, as a matter of contingent fact, nothing in that environment possesses.

Intuitively, this seems to me to be a plausible view of the matter. When I think of a group of people just like us, applying the word 'water' confidently to something that appears to them to be a clear, colorless, tasteless liquid in their environment, when in fact there is no such liquid in their environment, I feel tempted by the sort of error theory of their linguistic behavior that the present proposal delivers. It seem plausible to me to say that what these people mean by the word 'water' is this clear, colorless, tasteless liquid etc., which, however and unfortunately, is not to be found in their environment.

The problem is that it is very difficult to see how such a view could be available to the Twin Earth externalist. Remember, the TE externalist is committed, for reasons detailed earlier, to holding that 'water' expresses an *atomic* concept under conditions where it has a non–empty extension, whether that extension be H_2O or XYZ or whatever. That is one of the presuppositions of the Twin Earth experiment. But, then, how can the very same word, with the very same functional role, express an atomic concept under one set of external conditions and a compound, decompositional concept under another set of external conditions? A concept's compositionality is exclusively a function its internal 'syntax' and can't be contingent upon external circumstances in the way that the present proposal would require.

Let me forestall a possible misunderstanding of this point. My argument here is not that, if the compatibilist were to embrace the compound notion, that would undermine his commitment to privileged access. For although it is true that embracing the compound option for 'water' on Dry Earth, while being committed to its atomicity on Earth, would have the effect of making facts about compositionality come out *a posteriori*, that would not flout any doctrine of privileged access that I have defined.

Nor is my argument here that the compound option is unacceptable because it runs into conflict with the independently plausible claim that facts about compositionality are *a priori*, although, as I noted above, that is something I believe and would be prepared to defend.

In fact, my argument here is not epistemic at all, but rather metaphysical. The compound option requires the externalist to say that one and the same word, with one and the same functional role, may express an atomic concept under one set of external circumstances and a compound decompositional concept under another set of external circumstances. But it is hard to see how the *compositionality* of a concept could be a function of its external circumstances in this

18. WHAT THE EXTERNALIST CAN KNOW A PRIORI 209

way. Compositionality, as I understand it, can only be a function of the internal syntax of a concept; it can't supervene on external circumstances in the way that the compound proposal would require. (This is especially clear on a 'language of thought' picture of mental representation, but is independent of it.)

How do things look with the other main class of available options, that according to which the empty tokens of 'water' express an atomic concept? On this branch, too, we need to answer the question: Which atomic concept will that be, according to the TE externalist?

The externalist will know quite a lot about which concepts it cannot be: in particular, he will know that it cannot be identical with any of the concepts that are expressed by non–empty tokens of 'water'. To suppose otherwise would contradict his overriding commitment to individuating a concept in terms of its referent. But can he tell us, in line with his overriding commitment, what concept is expressed by the empty tokens of 'water'?

Unfortunately, there would appear to be a compelling argument showing that the externalist will not be able to say what atomic concept is expressed by the non–referring tokens of 'water', because by his own lights there can't be such a concept. Let me explain.

We have seen that one of the assumptions that is needed to transform a TE experiment into an argument for externalism is the assumption that concepts have context–independent conditions of satisfaction, or, in the case of thought contents, context–independent conditions of truth. So let us ask this: What are the satisfaction conditions for 'water' on Dry Earth, to what sorts of liquid does it apply? By assumption, of course, the actual extension of 'water' is empty on Dry Earth, so there is no liquid in its actual environment to which it applies. But the question I am asking is consistent with the word's actual extension being empty, and consistent even with its extension being empty in all worlds. What I want to know is: What proposition —what truth condition— is expressed by sentences of the form, 'Water is wet', for example, as uttered on Dry Earth? What is it that gets said? Never mind if such sentences are ruled false in the actual world, or even in all worlds.

On the line we are currently investigating, the answer has to be that there is no fact of the matter what truth condition is expressed by sentences involving 'water' on Dry Earth, for there is no fact of the matter what property is denoted by those tokens of 'water'. Since there is no natural kind at the end of the relevant causal chain leading up to uses of 'water' on Dry Earth, there is no fact of the matter what the referent of 'water' is and so no fact of the matter what proposition is expressed by sentences involving it.

But on an externalist view, this admission is fatal to the claim that there is a concept there in the first place, for an externalism about concepts is fueled in part by the conviction that thought contents must possess context–invariant conditions of satisfaction or, as appropriate, of truth. If, in a given context, there is no fact of the matter what the referent of a given concept is, then to that extent there is also no fact of the matter what the concept is.

We have looked at two possible tacks that an externalist might take regarding empty tokens of 'water', and we have found them both to be irremediably problematic. Letting the empty tokens express a compound concept, while having the virtue of supplying the word with a property to refer to, runs directly into conflict with the externalist's commitment to the atomicity of 'water'. Evading this problem by letting the word express an atomic concept, on the other hand, runs into direct conflict with the externalist's commitment to the idea that concepts must possess determinate, context–independent, conditions of satisfaction.

What then is the externalist to say about the empty case? The answer would appear to be that he has to say just what the proponent of object–dependence said he should say all along —namely, that the empty tokens simply don't express a determinate concept. That turns out to be the right thing to say not because TE externalism is conceptually equivalent to object–dependence, but because TE externalism, in conjunction with its other commitments, entails object–dependence.

7 The Argument Completed

If this is right, then the compatibilist is in a position to conclude —via purely *a priori* reasoning— that if a term expresses a concept in the first place, that it must have a non–empty extension. Moreover, privileged access assures him that he will be able to tell *a priori* whether or not a given term does express a concept, and indeed, if it does, which one. In particular, our friend Oscar will be able to tell non–empirically that his term 'water' expresses a concept, and in particular that it expresses the concept water. Putting these two bits of information together, he is in a position to conclude, *a priori*,

18. WHAT THE EXTERNALIST CAN KNOW A PRIORI 211

that water must have existed at some time. And that, we are all agreed, is not something he ought to be able to do.[8]

---

[8]To generate our problem for the compatibilist we have had to assume that when Oscar reasons as we have described, his *a priori* warrant for the premises of his argument transmits, across the *a priori* known entailment, to the entailed conclusion. Recently, some philosophers have taken to questioning whether this principle is correct. Aren't there cases, they have asked, where although A is known *a priori*, and although A is known *a priori* to entail B, nevertheless B is not known *a priori*. See, for example, the interesting paper by Martin Davies, "Externalism, Architecturalism and Epistemic Warrant", in MacDonald, Smith and Wright, *Knowing Our Own Minds* (Oxford: Oxford University Press, 1997). I have to say that I would be very surprised if there turned out to be any such cases that survived scrutiny. However, defending this claim in full generality is something that deserves separate treatment and will have to be left for another occasion. Here, I will settle for discussing one such case that has been suggested to me (by Stephen Schiffer). Consider the following inference:
1. If I have toothache, then teeth exist.
2. I have toothache.
Therefore,
3. Teeth exist.

I have defined '*a priori* knowledge' as 'knowledge that is obtained without empirical investigation'. Relative to this (admittedly vague and informal) characterization, don't the premises of this argument come out *a priori*? Can't I know that I have toothache without empirical investigation? And, also, that if I have toothache then that I have teeth? However, the conclusion of this argument is clearly not *a priori*. Therefore, there must be something wrong with the transmission of warrant principle that we have been assuming.

My perhaps predictable reply is that it is not at all clear that the premises of the toothache argument are *a priori*, relative to the intended notion of '*a priori*'. That we are in pain, and even that we are in a particular kind of phenomenologically classifiable pain (a 'toothachey' pain) —these matters seem clearly *a priori*. But there is no intuitive reason to believe, it seems to me, that we can know *a priori* that we have toothache, if that is supposed to mean, as it evidently does in the objection under consideration, that we have an ache *in a tooth*. Imagine a toothless person insisting that he has toothache; would we have to defer to his alleged *a priori* access to that fact.

Is There a Good Epistemological Argument against Concept–Externalism?

Brian Loar

According to externalism about *reference*, the reference of externally directed concepts consists in externally determined (e.g. causal) relations between those concepts' possessors and objects, kinds, properties etc. According to externalism about *concepts*, concepts are constituted (in part) by their externally determined references, either their own references or those of semantically connected concepts. One externalist might hold that the concept expressed by 'water' must stand in a certain external relation to water or else it is not the concept *water* (or at least that it stands in a certain social relation to other people's concept H_2O). A more lenient externalist may hold that the concept expressed by 'water' needs only to be conceptually related to other concepts of the same person, e.g. the concept *liquid*, whose individuation itself consists in part in an externally determined relation to liquidity, i.e. to that mind–independent property.[1] In any case, all concept–externalists hold that no sense

---

[1] Such an externalist might for example hold that the concept water is a rigid designator of the form "that liquid in our vicinity which does A, B and C".

can be made of our concepts' being constituted entirely by internal factors. They deny that there are two equally legitimate ways of individuating concepts, one internalist and the other externalist; I take any such permissive position to conflict with what the serious concept–externalist wishes to assert.

Logical space has room for a reference–externalism that is not concept–externalist. And it is a rather central question whether such a position is viable, given that concepts must be individuated by "intentional" properties. I am rather inclined to think there is such a position.[2] But I am not so partisan as to think that concept–externalism can effectively be refuted *except* by the construction of an internalist theory. One familiar style of refutation is epistemological: concepts by their very nature must be accessible to their owners in a privileged way while externally determined concepts would not be so accessible. Some concept–externalists may be more vulnerable to this style of argument than others.

Externalists about *reference* face a puzzling question about the apparent privilege of self–interpretation: if reference is an externally determined relation, then my knowledge that my use of "Socrates" refers to Socrates is privileged only if my knowledge that I stand in a certain contingent externally determined relation to Socrates is privileged. And there are good reasons to be puzzled about how that might be so.[3] The externalist about concepts faces not only that puzzle about privileged access, but also the question of privileged access to the *existence* of her references. The externalist about reference can say: really what I have privileged access to is that *if* Socrates exists then my use of "Socrates" refers to Socrates. There is no intuitive reason for the externalist about reference to regard as privileged the knowledge that Socrates exists. But if the concept *water* is distinguished from other concepts by its relation to water then (putting aside social relations, as Paul Boghossian does in his paper), water must exist if the concept *water* exists. And some solutions to the problem of privileged knowledge of the relation[4] will not solve the problem of privileged knowledge of existence. What I will try to show is that the question of privileged knowledge of the existence of the references of concepts is answerable for *some* special concepts, and that that is enough to defend *some* forms of externalism about concepts, if not the sort that concern Paul Boghossian. I am rather inclined to think that certain concept–externalists should

---

[2] See Loar [forthcoming].
[3] See Loar 1994.
[4] Loar 1994.

19. IS THERE A GOOD EPISTEMOLOGICAL ARGUMENT... 215

not be worried by the (quite reasonable) demand for a person's privileged access to her concepts.

Let "twin–Earth externalism" be a strong externalist theory that entails that "water" expresses different concepts for me and my twin. It seems to me that Boghossian's argument is correct about twin–Earth externalism about concepts. He is quite persuasive that compatibilism is difficult to defend for such an externalist.

Early in the paper Boghossian characterizes externalism about mental content in a way that is on the face of it weaker than twin–Earth externalism: concept–externalism is "the view that what concepts our thoughts involve may depend not only on facts that are internal to us, but on facts about our environment" (p. 197). I take "environment" to mean nothing as specific as Earth *vs.* twin–Earth, but rather any facts about our environment, for example that we live in a spatial world of physical objects to which we are connected in certain basic ways. Now I don't think that externalism in this sense implies twin–Earth externalism, not even with certain reasonable assumptions Boghossian makes. I will try to do two things. (1) I will argue that a certain simple externalism can, *prima facie*, accept the compatibility thesis. (2) I will say why simple externalism may not imply twin–Earth externalism.

Here is an externalism that is *prima facie* weaker than twin–Earth externalism. It is an externalism about certain basic concepts, such as spatial concepts, concepts of physical objects and their parts and the like. (Think here of all concepts that satisfy this condition: you wouldn't be surprised if developmental psychologists found some evidence that such concepts are innate.) This is compatible with holding that more specific concepts, such as "water", do not depend on their own references, even though one accepts twin–Earth thought experiments for reference. They do however depend, indirectly, on the references of the basic concepts.

Can we defend compatibilism for the weaker form of externalism? I will say yes. The question is whether the compatibilist position can be defended for the basic concepts. Let *SP* be the proposition that our spatial predicates refer to the expected spatial properties etc. Then the representative question we face is this: might the judgment that *SP* be *a priori*?

I suspect that the notion of *a priority* is not definite enough to do effective philosophical work here. Perhaps on some very strong notion of *a priority* knowledge of contingent external existence can never be *a priori*. Still, that may not be enough to embarass an externalist who is inclined to accept compatibilism. Perhaps all he needs is a not terribly strong sense of *"a priori"* that is yet a well motivated sense. What does it mean to say that p is *a priori*? If it means that one is entitled to believe that p independently of empirical confirmation, then it seems fair to say that the judgment that *SP* is true is *a priori*. If it means that p is nondisconfirmable then I rather think that *SP* is *a priori* in that sense as well. For I take it to be a reasonable epistemology that allows that we cannot confirm all facts about the external world from scratch. And it is not unreasonable to suppose that certain basic assumptions —or states that issue in such assumptions when they are triggered— are more or less innate. These include the assumption that we live in a spatial world and that we are in referential contact with spatial properties etc.

Why should innateness imply *a priority*? The latter notion is normative —what it is reasonable to believe independently of empirical confirmation. And certain innate cognitive structures, it seems plausible to say, issue in beliefs which it is reasonable to take for granted. It could be replied that the belief that certain concepts track spatial properties requires some sort of inference to the best explanation. But perhaps certain beliefs must be presupposed if we are to confirm *anything* about the external world, e.g. beliefs that one's perceptions track spatial structures. The permissive externalist could then be comfortable in accepting compatibilism. For his beliefs that he possesses the relevant spatial concepts will be *a priori* in a well motivated sense. This seems to me a reasonable defense of privileged access to intentional mental content on a (weak) externalist theory of concepts, if that is, 'privileged access' can be defined in terms of '*a priori*'.

Might weak externalism imply twin–Earth externalism given Boghossian's further point about the concept 'water'? Let the proponent of weak externalism say that concepts are determined by their *wide* conceptual roles, in a special sense of that. Basic concepts must be anchored in reference to properties etc: these are the concepts whose references make the conceptual roles of other concepts wide. Basic concepts include not only spatial concepts, general concepts of physical objects, and other type–concepts but also singular demonstratives that pick out places, e.g. "here". A concept can be determined by wide conceptual role in this sense even if it is *syntactically atomic*. So syntactically atomic concepts can get their satisfaction conditions from the references of terms that they are conceptually connected with.

This form of weak externalism is compatible with my and my twin's concepts 'water' being the same, even though they pick out different substances and are atomic. This can be seen in two steps. a) Consider the thesis that 'water' abbreviates a description, say of the form "the stuff that in my vicinity is F, G, H" where the latter are concepts whose references are essential to what concepts they are. Boghossian will reject an 'indexical–description–theory' of 'water' on the ground that 'water' is a natural kind term and hence *atomic*. Let us agree. b) Now take the indexical–descriptive information and spread it among the conceptual connections of the atomic concept. We then have a syntactically atomic concept shared by me and my–twin and hence not individuated by its reference. The view is externalist because the conceptual roles are wide: basic concepts in my thought are individuated in part by their references, i.e. the basic spatial and other properties that they stand for. That is where the externalist grounding of concepts in general occurs according to this relaxed externalism.

As I see things, we get a form of externalism that is vulnerable to Boghossian's objection *only if* it implies that concepts that are not plausibly among the basic ones mentioned above depend in part for their individuation on their property–references, and hence on the existence or contingent instantiation of those references. I do not think the weak externalism sketched should yield on epistemological grounds.

REFERENCES

Loar 1984. "Self–interpretation and the Constitution of Reference", *Philosophical Perspectives 8*, February 1994, pp. 51-74.

―――― forthcoming. "Phenomenal Intentionality and the Basis of Mental Content". Forthcoming in a *festschrift* for Tyler Burge, ed. by Martin Hahn and Bjorn Ramberg, Oxford University Press.

Self–Knowledge & Semantic Luck

Stephen Yablo

1 Paul's Paradox

There is no prize in philosophy for the shortest *a priori* proof of an external world; longest would be more like it. If a prize were to be given, though, it would have to go to the argument just set out:

(1) If I have water–thoughts, then water exists.

(2) I have water–thoughts.

(3) So, water exists.

I mean, of course, that this argument would win the prize if it worked: if, in particular, its premises were *a priori* knowable. Paul maintains that it doesn't work. What we have is rather a *paradox* in which two enormously plausible hypotheses —one backed by privileged access, the other by externalism about content— are found to entail an incredible result, viz. the *a priori* knowability of there being such a thing as water.

2   Saul's Paradox

Before Paul's paradox, there was Saul's. Saul's paradox is in a way more the urgent of the two, because it casts doubt on the compatibility, not of calling (1) and (2) *a priori*, but of calling them (or statements very like them) *true*. Here is a passage from *Naming and Necessity*:

> [...] it is said that though we have all found out that there are no unicorns,... [u]nder certain circumstances there *would* have been unicorns. And this is an example of something I think is not the case... Perhaps according to me the truth should not be put in terms of saying that it is necessary there should be no unicorns, but just that we can't say under what circumstances there would have been unicorns.[1]

Notice that *two* things are "said": first, that there aren't any unicorns, and second, that under certain circumstances there would have been unicorns. It is only the second claim that Kripke disputes. He takes it for granted that unicorns don't exist; this indeed is why "unicorn"-sentences lack truth conditions, and why unicorn-thoughts —which presumably *need* truth conditions to exist— are ruled out entirely.

Now, suppose it is really true that for there to be X-thoughts, there have to be Xs.[2] Then what is to prevent a philosophically reflective 18th century thinker —what for that matter is to prevent you or I— from arguing like so:

(1') If I have caloric-thoughts, then there is caloric.

(2') I have caloric-thoughts.

(3') So, there is caloric.

Since the conclusion is false —there is no caloric— one of the premises must be false as well. Which one? I call this a paradox because one has, as Kripke likes to say, a considerable feeling that *both* premises properly understood are correct.

Having just asserted that there is no caloric, the second premise will be hard for me to deny; the thought that there is no caloric is a caloric-thought if anything is. And I have other caloric-thoughts

---

[1] *Naming and Necessity* (Cambridge, MA: Harvard University Press, 1980), 24.
[2] A restriction is obviously needed on "X"; I won't attempt to formulate it here.

as well: people used to believe in caloric; if there is caloric, then so much the worse for the atomic theory of heat.

But the first premise is hard to argue with too. A thought is something with truth conditions; it can be compared to a possible world and found to be either true of that world or false of it. And in the absence of any real caloric to set the standard, there seems to be just no saying which of the caloric-like substances in other possible worlds are relevant to the counterfactual truth-values of my caloric-thoughts.

3 Kripkean *vs.* Fregean Truth Conditions

The Kripke passage paints a picture of unicorn-thoughts as true without possessing truth conditions. How is this possible? A thought is true, it would seem, only if it puts conditions on reality, which conditions are in fact met. These conditions though could hardly be other than the thought's truth conditions. And wasn't it truth conditions that were supposed to be going missing on the Kripkean picture?

An analogy may help. Suppose I introduce H as a predicate that, no matter how the world may turn out, is to be true of all and only the hedgehogs. Now consider the statement, or thought, that there are Hs. Are you in a position to compute its truth conditions? Not in the sense at issue in the Kripke passage, for I haven't told you anything about what it takes for H to be true of a *counterfactual* object. (And I'm not going to; the whole meaning of H has now been explained.) And yet there would seem to be little doubt that the thought is true. Because whatever *there are Hs* says or doesn't say about other worlds, *this* world it describes as containing hedgehogs. Here then is a case of a truth that is lacking in truth conditions.

But wait a minute, you say. Of course the thought that there are Hs has truth conditions; it is true under the condition that hedgehogs exist.

There is clearly something to this. The thought has truth conditions *of a sort*: its (actual) truth-value depends on whether such and such conditions are (actually) met. It remains, though, apparently, that the thought lacks truth conditions of the kind intended by Kripke: conditions that determine whether a (possibly counterfactual) world is correctly *described* by the thought. To have some language for this unusual state of affairs, let's say that *there are Hs* has "Fregean" truth conditions, but little or nothing in the way of "Kripkean" ones.

4 Consequences for the Paradoxes

What does this tell us about Saul's paradox? If "having a thought to the effect that there is caloric" means "having a thought with the *Kripkean*, or modalized, truth conditions that there is caloric", then (1') looks true; without actual caloric to set the standard, how can there be a fact of the matter about caloric's counterfactual career?[3] But (2') is false. I am *not* thinking that there is caloric because my "thought" leaves it (more or less) wide open which worlds are caloric–worlds.

If on the other hand we are talking about "having a thought with the *Fregean*, or actualized, truth conditions that there is caloric", then matters are reversed. I am indeed thinking that there is caloric —so (2') is true— but, (1') to the contrary, my ability to do this is not hostage to the real existence of the stuff.

Will the same approach work with Paul's paradox? Take first Kripkean water–thoughts, or water–thoughts individuated by their Kripkean truth conditions. *A priori* reflection suggests that these require actual water, as stipulated in (1). But that I am thinking a Kripkean water–thought is, it may be argued, not something I can tell *a priori*. So (1) is *a priori* but (2) is not.

If we switch now to the Fregean truth conditions of my thought —the way its truth–value in the actual world depends on the actual facts— this does seem to be *a priori* detectable. Even the full Fregean *meaning* of my thought —the way its truth–value across *all* worlds[4] depends on the actual facts— is *a priori* knowable. But so what? Thoughts individuated by their Fregean truth conditions, or meanings, don't call *a priori* for actual water. This time then it is only (2) that's *a priori*.

5 Let's Be Kripkean

Terrific; except that all this time we have been walking into a neatly laid incompatibilist trap. Here is what the incompatibilist will say:

> I don't care if Fregean thoughts are *a priori* knowable, because Fregean thoughts are not *externalist* in my sense. Your view appears to be that externalism and privileged access can both be true, *but not of the same thoughts*. Why should I disagree?

---

[3] I'll take this back in a little while.
[4] Its Kripkean truth conditions, in other words.

This reply forces us to put the Fregean notions aside for a bit, and look again at Paul's claim that Kripkean truth conditions go missing on Dry Earth. (Truth conditions are henceforth Kripkean; the one Fregean notion that will recur is "meaning", and that not until the last section.)

One thing is clear: if this be Dry Earth, then the great majority of worlds are not classifiable either as containing water or lacking it. It's the next step that bothers me. Does it really follow that *there is water* is lacking in truth conditions?

That depends. It probably does follow, if truth conditions are seen as singular propositions made up *inter alia* of full–blooded properties; in the absence of water, there can be no full–blooded property of *being* water, which is curtains for the proposition.

But the singularist conception is a surprising one in a context where truth–conditionality is being treated as a condition of thought. After all, the capacity for water–thought is intuitively quite *independent* of ontological disputes about what sorts of properties there may be, including disputes about whether properties exist at all. I suppose one could say: let's have a pleonastic conception of properties on which the needed properties come for free. But they come for free only when the predicate is suitably meaningful, and the meaningfulness of "water" on Dry Earth is just what we are arguing about.

What sort of object should play the role of truth conditions, if not a full–blooded singular proposition? The answer is that any object will do that encodes the possibility of interrogating a world on such matters as whether it contains water; that's what it takes for water–thought, hence that's all that can be asked of truth conditions considered as a requirement of such thought.[5] For the sake of definiteness, let me suggest that the encoding role is most directly and efficiently played by (truth conditions conceived as) rules or recipes for classifying worlds. Singular propositions can serve in some cases as handy repositories of classificatory information. But if we're talking about truth conditions in the sense essential to thought, it's the rule that matters.

6 Degrees of Taxonomic Power

Now rules, as we know, are apt to have blind spots: sometimes big ones. It is not much remarked on, but the rules defining "true" leave

---

[5]Up to and including singular–proposition–like objects adapted to avoid Paul's worry about the lack of a property.

us hanging as often as they deliver a verdict; there are fully as many paradoxes as definite truths and falsehoods. (One can imagine alternative rules that would make the ratio still worse.) That thought about truth and falsity is somehow nevertheless possible suggests a conjecture: "there is water" *does* have truth conditions on Dry Earth,[6] but truth conditions with not much resolving power as between cases. A few utterly dry worlds are ruled out, but on most worlds they just fail to pronounce.[7]

The truth analogy has its limits, because the sniffing out of paradoxes has a significant *a priori* component. A better analogy is with Carnap's semantics for theoretical terms in *Testability & Meaning*.[8] Carnap lays it down that an object immersed in water is soluble iff it dissolves; and that chemical analogues of *solubilia* (*insolubilia*) are themselves soluble (insoluble); and that's it. As he is quick to point out, this leaves a great many cases completely undecided —for all we can tell *a priori*, it leaves *every* case undecided.

These empirical uncertainties notwithstanding, Carnap has, it seems, infused the word "soluble" with substance enough to allow for solubility–thoughts —and hence with substance enough for truth conditions, to the extent that solubility–thoughts require them. One does not feel the truth conditions of *this is soluble* to be dwindling away into nothing as the number of actual immersals declines. One feels rather that they are pronouncing on fewer and fewer cases, and to that extent falling short of their destiny as truth conditions. But thoughts with underperforming truth conditions are still thoughts.

7 Paradox Redux

You can guess where this is heading. If we are unlucky enough to be living on Dry Earth, then as Paul says, there is no (full–blooded) property of being water. That doesn't in itself make nonsense of the question "which actual and counterfactual stuffs deserve to be described as water?" It doesn't rule out that "there is water" puts a condition on worlds, albeit a condition with less taxonomical power

---

[6]E.g., a world contains water if there is a unique watery stuff on Dry Earth which it sufficiently resembles, and lacks water if it is thoroughly dry. (This is crude.)

[7]The similarly pathetic truth conditions of "there is caloric" rule out different worlds; this is enough to mark the two as distinct. (I assume the physics of heat on Dry Earth is exactly as here.) They are distinct too in being *poised* to rule different worlds *in*, given more favorable empirical conditions.

[8]*Philosophy of Science* (1936/7), Vol. 3, 419–471, and Vol. 4, 1–40.

than might ideally be wanted. (And it does have *some* taxonomical power, for it rules negatively on Dry Earth.)
The claim then is that the compatibilist can simply *deny* that water–thoughts *a priori* require water. But while this may be enough to counter the paradox as presented (specifically the first premise), what about the following variant, where "taxonomical" means "has a good deal of taxonomical or classificatory power":

(1*) If I have taxonomical water–thoughts, there is water.

(2*) I have taxonomical water–thoughts.

(3) There is water.

I want to say that the revamped paradox just reverses the problem with the original one. It may be true, and true according to externalism, that (1*) is *a priori*.[9] But privileged access ought *not* to be understood as making (2*) *a priori*. The hypothesis that I'm thinking *taxonomical* water–thoughts is too close to the hypothesis that there is water for one to be *a priori* and the other not.

8 Knowing What

At this point the original question —how am I to tell without empirical research *whether* I'm thinking?— begins to transmogrify itself into a more familiar one: how am I to tell without empirical research *what* I'm thinking?[10] To claim *a priori* knowledge of my thoughts, in particular of their truth conditions, I should at a minimum be able to tell whether these conditions possess any genuine bite.

Such an argument may seem only common sense. But it trades on a very particular conception of "knowing what" —a conception that may itself seem only common sense, but that requires scrutiny. I call it *absolutism* about knowing what:

---

[9] I have doubts about the *a priority* of (1*) too, because I suspect that "water" could stand on Dry Earth for a superficial phenomenological kind. "Natural kind" terms stand for the most natural kind available; they rise to their own level, in Kripke's phrase. That some of "air", "earth", "fire", and "water" strike us now as more natural-kindy than the others reflects no preexisting semantic commitments, but just that they are the ones that got lucky. (I grant that there *could* be terms that denote natural kinds or nothing, and so I am not pressing the point.)

[10] This is of course the "other" externalist threat to privileged access.

knowing what X is is knowing inherently important facts about what X is, that is, X's identity or essence or nature.

If the truth conditions of my thought are not terribly taxonomical, then that would seem to be an important fact about their nature —the kind of fact that, according to absolutism, someone who knows what the truth conditions are ought to be cognizant of. Since I can't attest *a priori* to their resolving power, it seems that I don't know *a priori* what the truth conditions of *there is water* really are.

Is absolutism correct? A look at a few of its consequences will help us decide. Absolutism entails that (i) facts about X's nature are crucial to knowing what it is; (ii) facts not about X's nature are irrelevant to knowing what it is; and (iii) the same facts are relevant to knowing what X is regardless of how it is described.

I hope I'm not the only one who finds all of this highly debatable. As against (ii), to know what magenta is, you have to know how it makes things look, *even if* magenta is an intrinsic property of external objects with no essential relation to human experience. Similar remarks apply to the north pole (it's on top of the world), LSD (it gets you high), dirt (it's cheap), and the Earth (it's the planet we live on). To go by (i), only a philosopher can tell you what the least prime number is; the mathematicians talk a good game, but they aren't even decided whether two is a set. As for (iii), squareness and diamond–shapedness are the same property, but different recognitional abilities are required to know what they are. Whoever doesn't know what salt is must have been living under a rock, but sodium chloride is a different story. The anhedonic physiologist knows what p–fiber firings are but not pleasure, even if pleasure and p–fiber firings are one and the same.

Of course, the application that interests us is to knowledge of truth conditions. But absolutism seems wrong here too. I know what the truth conditions of Goldbach's conjecture are and yet I am ignorant of as basic a fact as this about them: whether they are necessary or impossible.[11] (Think too of theoretical identities in science, genealogical conjectures, etc.) If I can get by without *a priori* knowledge of one "basic metaphysical fact" about truth conditions, their satisfiability, why not another, the fact of how taxonomical they are?

---

[11]Suppose some mathematician tells me they are impossible. It is far from clear that this in itself helps me to understand the conjecture any better.

9 A Non–Absolutist Alternative?

After all this shirking of epistemic obligations, someone might ask: what *do* I have to know to know the truth conditions of my thought? As an alternative to the "metaphysical" conception just scouted, suppose we try the following:

(*) I know *a priori* what the truth conditions of my thought are iff I know *a priori* that it has the truth conditions that P —for P an appropriate (?!?) sentence of my language.[12]

This leaves the incompatibilist one final opening. To know *a priori* that my thought has the truth conditions that P, I need to know *a priori* that it *doesn't* have the (alternative) truth conditions that Q. And if externalism is correct, then for some values of Q, I don't. E.g., for all I can tell *a priori*, the thought I express with the words "there is water" might be true under the condition that there is XYZ.[13]

Here is how I would *like* to respond; the details are still under construction. *A priori* knowledge resembles ordinary knowledge in an important respect: it requires us to rule out some counterpossibilities but not all the counterpossibilities there are. This is clear from consideration of simple examples. I know *a priori* that my location is here, but I *don't* know *a priori* that my location is not Kinshasa, despite the fact that being here (in Ann Arbor) is strictly incompatible with being in Kinshasa. I know *a priori* that Kabila is Kabila, but I don't know *a priori* that Kabila isn't Mugabe, despite the fact that being Kabila is incompatible with being Mugabe.

And now a speculation, offered in the spirit of something that would be neat if true: the alternatives I have to rule out *a priori*, to know *a priori* that I am thinking the Kripkean thought that there is water, are ones that I *can* rule out *a priori* just by virtue of my *a priori* grasp of Fregean meanings (as described at the end of section IV).

To see why this is not completely insane, suppose we ask why I *don't* have to know *a priori* about not being in Kinshasa to know *a priori* about being here.

Answer: for all I can tell *a priori*, "I am here" and "I am in Kinshasa" have identical Kripkean truth conditions; whence for all

---

[12] This is ignoring expressibility worries, which are legitimate but not to the present point.

[13] This could be questioned, since "XYZ" is explicitly introduced as standing for a substance distinct from the actual watery stuff, viz. water. But let that pass.

I can tell *a priori*, "my thought has the truth conditions that I am here" and "my thought has the truth conditions that I am in Kinshasa" have *compatible* Kripkean truth conditions.

Obviously, though, I cannot be required to rule out *a priori* scenarios that are, for all I can tell *a priori*, *compatible* with what I think, as a condition of that thought's constituting *a priori* knowledge. This would empty the category of *a priori* knowledge altogether; even logical truths like *Kabila* = *Kabila* would lose their *a priori* status, since I cannot rule out *a priori* that Kabila = Mugabe. I conclude that

(**) To know *a priori* that A, I have to know *a priori* that not B —but only in cases where B is *a priori* incompatible with A.

Applied to knowledge of truth conditions, this means that

(***) To know *a priori* that my thought has the truth conditions that P, I have to know *a priori* that it does not have the truth conditions that Q— except in cases where it is *a priori* possible (i.e., not *a priori* false) that P and Q have the *same* truth conditions.

The connection between (**) and (***) is simply this. The cases where it is *a priori* possible that P and Q agree in their truth conditions are all and only the ones where B = "my thought has the truth conditions that Q" fails to be *a priori* incompatible with A = "it has the truth conditions that P".

Now, do I have the *a priori* knowledge that (***) requires of me? I see no reason to doubt it. If P and Q are *a priori* different in their truth conditions, it will be *a priori* too that no P–thought has the truth conditions that Q. To infer *a priori* that *my* thought doesn't have the truth conditions that Q, I will need to know *a priori* that my thought is a P–thought. But that is the commonsense view; it is the incompatibilist's job to undermine it, not mine to shore it up.

As a matter of fact, though, it can be shored up, if we allow ourselves an assumption to which incompatibilists are not *per se* opposed. The assumption is that I have *a priori* knowledge of *Fregean meaning*: of how the truth conditions of my thoughts and sentences depend on the actual–world facts.[14] Why should incompatibilists deny this? Fregean meaning is intrinsic and their problem is about *extrinsic* content.

---

[14] See the end of section IV.

Suppose then that I am granted a complete *a priori* grasp of the Fregean meanings of my thoughts, and of relevant sentences of my language. This tells me, for each Q meeting the proviso of (***), that however the actual world comes out, my thought never acquires the truth conditions that Q. From this I conclude *a priori* that I am not thinking that Q. Any block raised by (***) to my knowing *a priori* that I am thinking that P is thus removed.

So much is to defend against an objection. But it seems possible to make a *positive a priori* case that I am thinking that P by the same method: "noticing" that my thought comes out with the truth conditions that P on every hypothesis about actuality. By (*), nothing more is required for *a priori* knowledge of what it is that I am thinking. The apparent result is that a "complete" *a priori* grasp of my Fregean thoughts[15] provides me with "ordinary" *a priori* knowledge of my Kripkean ones.

---

[15] And the Fregean meanings of relevant sentences.

A Challenge to Boghossian's Incompatibilist Argument

Josep E. Corbí

1. Let me rehearse, to begin, the core of Boghossian's incompatibilist argument. From premises

(1) If I have the concept of water, then water exists.

(2) I have the concept of water,

it follows that

(3) Water exists.

The paradox arises as we realize that (3) is clearly not knowable *a priori*, but (1) and (2) are. (2) holds '*a priori*' because, according to Boghossian, it "just is the view that I have called the doctrine of privileged self–knowledge" (p. 202). The core of the paper is devoted, though, to argue that an externalist (i.e., someone who holds the view that "...facts external to a thinker's skin are relevant to the individuation of (certain of) his mental contents" (p. 199). is bound to concede that (1) is knowable '*a priori*'. It would follow that, contrary to intuition, (3) can be known *a priori* since is the conclusion of an inference that relies on two premises that are, in turn, knowable *a priori*. All this is envisaged by Boghossian as an argument for incompatibilism, that is, for the claim that Externalism and Privileged Access are inconsistent because their combination leads to utterly absurd consequences.

In the present comment, however, I will advocate for compatibilism. My challenge to Boghossian's incompatibilist argument divides into two steps. At a first stage, I will focus on premise (2), and explore to what extent the privileged access that a subject has to her own mental contents may ensure the '*a priori*' knowability of premise (2). To this purpose I will compare my access to the truth of the claim 'I have the concept of water' with my access to the truth of claims like 'I know how to ride a bike', 'I master the concept of checkmate', 'I think I have a checkmate in two moves', and 'I think there is some water in the fridge'. The upshot will be that, contrary to what premise (2) indicates, I cannot know '*a priori*' that I master a certain concept, since it seems clear that it could occur that I would wrongly believe that I master a certain concept. This does not amount to denying, as we shall see, a privileged or special access to one's own concepts, but not so privileged as to exclude the possibility that certain facts of the world may come to challenge one's beliefs in this respect.

At second stage, I will shift to premise (1). I will then insist that the externalist only needs to grant this premise on the assumption that *water* is a natural kind concept, and not merely on the assumption that 'water' is aimed at expressing a natural kind concept. To reach this conclusion, I will certainly have to rebut Boghossian's remarks to the contrary. But, if I would succeed, then it would follow that the externalist, even if she should grant the '*a priori*' knowability of premise (2), would not have to concede that the fact that water exists is also knowable '*a priori*'. For her knowledge of premise (1) would rest on an assumption (i.e., that *water* is a natural kind concept) whose truth can only be known '*a posteriori*'. As a result, Boghossian's incompatibilist argument would be under some pressure.

2. Let us consider premise (2). At the outset, the Privileged Access doctrine is presented like this: "I can know without empirical investigation (a) that I am entertaining a thought; (b) that it has a particular conceptual content, and (c) that its content is that water is wet" (p. 198). This is referred to as the traditional doctrine. And, strictly speaking, Boghossian is supposed to explore to what extent this doctrine is consistent with Externalism. I must confess that, faced with this rather general characterization of Privileged Access,

I feel uncertain as to how much this doctrine should comprise and, relatedly, how plausible it may finally be. In an attempt to elaborate this perplexity, let me consider a few cases that may help us to determine in a slightly more precise way the content of a plausible Privileged Access doctrine, and see whether, on such a doctrine, I could know '*a priori*' premise (2).

2.1. Undoubtedly, I know that I know how to ride a bike. How does I get to know about this ability of mine? There is a trivial sense in which I needn't carry out any empirical investigation to have this valuable piece of knowledge. But, indeed, none would deny that my knowing that I possess that ability depends on my knowledge of certain facts of the world that involve my previous performances on a bike.

Take the mental content 'I know how to ride a bike'. Adult people are rarely wrong in this respect, but, of course, one would not be surprised if a child may mistakenly believe that she knows how to ride a bike or how to swim and, more typically, if a child would unwarrantedly have that kind of belief. Thus, I once heard of someone who, being otherwise more or less a normal person, decided that he had learned how to swim by studying how other people were performing and, after this conscientious study, dived into the swimming pool. Fortunately, there was someone around to rescue him. What strikes me about this case is not that this person had the false belief that he knew how to swim, but rather that he could have acquired that belief by such manifestly inadequate means. Watching other people's performance is not a means (at least, ordinarily) to learn swimming. For a certain practice in that art seems indispensable. In general, we assume that, typically, a human being can only justifiedly belief that she knows how to swim if she has gone through a certain process of training.

A consequence of this is that certain public facts about me must be true, for me to justifiedly believe that I know how to swim and, thereby, for me to know that I know how to swim. It does not sound then reasonable to claim that I can know '*a priori*' that I have this ability. It is true that, in a trivial sense, in order to have this kind of knowledge I needn't carry out any empirical investigation. But in this trivial sense I also know without empirical investigation that water exists.

The second moral I want to draw from this example goes like this. It is not accidental that, in order to describe a situation where someone unjustifiedly believes that he knows how to swim, I have shifted to the attitudes of children or the case of a relatively weird person. In fact, we tend to assume that, among normal adult people, this kind of thing does not happen but very rarely. But how is it? Does this reveal a special access to one's abilities on the side of normal adult people? Notice that I say 'special', not '*a priori*' or 'independent of one's knowledge of some particular facts of the world'. Yes, special, but not mysterious: it has to do with the way 'normal adult people' and their beliefs about their own abilities are individuated. X is a normal adult human being only if beliefs about her abilities are typically acquired by means that justify her in having those beliefs. It follows from this metaphysical principle, that a human being that does not satisfy this condition is weird or childish or, at least, temporarily weird or childish.

2.2. What is the relevance of these stories about swimming pools and bikes to the knowledge of one's mental contents? To answer this question, let us see how our remarks above apply to cases where beliefs about one's mental contents are involved. I am playing chess with my friend Michael. I know that I believe that I have a checkmate in two moves unless Michael protects his king with a certain improbable move. I try hard to hide my excitement so that my friend should not suspect and engage in any extraexploration of the available moves.

I have a special access to my belief, an access that is alien to my behavior and expressions at that particular moment. That is why the hiding maneuver is at all possible. Yet, my having such a belief presupposes a certain mastery of the rules of chess and, more specifically, of the concept of checkmate.

It sounds clear, however, that someone may wrongly believe that she masters the concept of checkmate or that she masters the rules of chess. This is, of course, quite common during the process of training. Moreover, it is quite strange that someone would believe that he has a mastery of those rules and concepts without having engaged in certain practice with chess or related games. Once again, it seems that the means by which ordinary people acquire the belief that they master a certain concept are also means that justify their having such a belief. There is room, indeed, for an ordinary person exceptionally acquiring that belief in an inappropriate way, or for weird people to unjustifiedly believe that they master a certain concept. This sort of disadjustment has a limit beyond which it would be unclear that the subject at stake is actually having a belief about her mastery of a certain concept.

So, it seems that my justifiedly believing that I master the concept of checkmate is not independent of the correctness of some past (and, for similar reasons, future) performances of mine. Moreover, the idea of '*a priori*' knowledge seems to comprise an internalist element:

knowing that p 'a priori' involves my being able to provide certain reasons to justify my believing that p —reasons that, indeed, should not mention any particular facts of the world. So, if I should know 'a priori' that I master the concept of checkmate, I should be able to provide some sort of evidence that is independent of what occurs in the world. But it seems that this cannot be done, that I should ultimately include within that evidence the reasons why I believe that I performed correctly in the past or, alternatively, supply some further examples of my current capacities. It sounds then that my knowledge of the concepts I master is not 'a priori', even if it is special. And the source of this specialness, like in the riding of a bike, derives from some metaphysical principles of individuation. These principles ensure that when a normal adult person claims 'I master the concept of checkmate', she typically needn't provide any justification. The problem for Boghossian's argument arises as we realize that, in those situations where that person would need to justify the truth of her belief, the kind of evidence that may supply could hardly be gathered 'a priori'.

2.3. All this has quite direct implications for the epistemic status of premise (2), namely: 'I have the concept of water'. It is quite clear, and follows from my previous remarks, that someone (typically, a child) may mistakenly believe that she has the required mastery of the concept of water and, also, that any attempt that this person may undertake to justify her belief that she has the mastery at stake will require that this person should mention her knowledge of certain facts of the world. So, once again, the knowledge that an adult person may have of premise (2) is special —since she needn't provide any justification of it but in exceptional circumstances: there are some metaphysical individuation principles that ensure that adult persons can't be but exceptionally wrong in this respect— but not a priori.[1]

2.4. To sum up this first step of my discussion, I could say that I have tried to make room for the specialness of a subject's access to her own concepts without being committed to the implausible claim that they are known 'a priori', that is, independently of our knowl-

---

[1] In these remarks, I have focused on a subject's beliefs about the mastery of a certain concept, since that is the nature of the belief stated in premise (2). Yet, it is clear that the traditional doctrine about Privileged Access tends to target a different kind of belief, namely: beliefs about a certain mental content like 'I think I have a checkmate in two moves'. The special access that a subject may have to her own mental contents differs in some important respects from the special access to the concepts that she may master. This is, however, a point on which I cannot dwell now.

edge of particular facts of the world. The intuition is that, in those scenarios were the subject is recognized as having privileged access to her concepts, the conditions under which a subject acquires a belief about her concepts typically coincide with those that justify that belief. All this casts doubt on Boghossian's argument insofar as those conditions involve particular facts of the world whose instantiation cannot be known 'a priori'.[2]

3. Let us now shift to premise (1). At first sight, it sounds that an externalist would only concede its truth on the assumption that

(A) *water* is a natural kind concept.

Moreover, an externalist will have reason to deny that (A) could be known 'a priori', since the truth of (A) would depend, on her account, on some environmental facts.[3] This contention does not

---

[2]My approach surely exploits some aspects of the treatment of self–knowledge that Donald Davidson and Tyler Burge have suggested in some of their writings (cf. Davidson (1987) and Burge (1989)). They tend to insist that self–knowledge is not a mystery because the conditions for the individuation of mental content coincide with the conditions for believing that one has such contents. So, there is little (or no) room for a gap between having a certain thought and believing that one has that thought, and this vigorous metaphysical connection seems to ensure the transition from believing that one has a certain thought to knowing that one has it. Relatedly, I have been pointing out that the conditions for the individuation of the mastery of concepts (and mental contents) typically coincide with the conditions for justifiedly believing that one masters that concept (or possesses a certain mental content).

Yet, I have tried to belabor this intuition by highlighting, firstly, that such a coincidence has partly to do with the fact that normal adult human beings are individuated in such a way that the means by which they may acquire the mastery of a concept are also the means by which they acquire the belief that she masters that concept. Secondly, I have insisted that it is compatible with this metaphysical principle that, occasionally, a subject should unjustifiedly believe that she masters a certain concept C and, consequently, that one must leave some room for disadjustment between believing that one masters a concept and mastering it. My main point has, in any case, been that the combination of all these elements allows us to explain why a subject's knowledge about the concepts that she masters may be special, but not 'a priori', since the kind of reason she may mention to justify her belief would necessarily comprise her knowledge of some particular facts of the world.

[3]This is a point that Jessica Brown (cf. Brown (1995, p. 154)) seems to concede. She seeks, however, to neutralize the impact of assumption (A) by stressing that there is still some kind of 'a priori' knowledge of the world that the externalist is bound to recognize. Thus, Burge would have to accept that, "for example, from the fact that he [Oscar] knows *a priori* that he has a thought involving the concept of water, he could come to know *a priori* that (either his environment

necessarily conflict with the Privileged Access doctrine or even with the '*a priori*' knowability of premise (2). For one could reasonably claim that my knowing that I have the concept of water does not entail that I know that *water* is a natural kind concept. This is, in fact, a point that Boghossian seems to grant and, therefore, I will save you the rationale.[4] In any event, if all this turned out to be true, then premise (1) could not be known '*a priori*' since it relies on

---

contains water and the concept of water is a natural kind concept, or he is part of a community which has the concept of water)" (Brown (1995, p. 155)). In my view, this line of reply significantly debilitates the initial argument, whose strength derives from the neat conviction that one cannot know *a priori* that water exists or any other particular fact of the world. For, on Brown's disjunctive proposal, it sounds now quite natural to grant that, if a subject can know '*a priori*' that she has a certain concept, she can also know '*a priori*' that the world must be such as to enable her to possess that concept. Furthermore, assuming —as Boghossian's argument does— that the externalist doctrine is knowable '*a priori*' seems almost equivalent to assuming the '*a priori*' knowability of the fact that the disjunctive condition is part of those enabling circumstances.(Cf. Miller (1997) for a discussion of this point, and Burge (1993) for the notion of '*a priori*' that may be involved). Hence, if one would be inclined to disapprove of the '*a priori*' knowability of the latter, one would have to dismiss the '*a priori*' knowability of externalism and, as a result, the incompatibilist argument would be damned.

In any event, Brown's line of defense is not only quite inadequate, but unavailable to Boghossian because Brown's strategy presupposes that *water* would be atomic or compound depending on some external circumstances and, as we shall soon see, this is something that Boghossian cannot accept.

[4]In any event, it is not hard to motivate the claim that someone may know that she has the concept of water without knowing that *water* is a natural kind concept; specially, if one assumes the '*a priori*' knowability of premise (2).

It seems clear that different individuals may have the same concept C despite variations in their respective degree of mastery of it. This seems a precondition for several individuals to have the same thought, the same desire or belief, since identity of thoughts presupposes identity of concepts. Yet, a consequence of this fact is that the possession of concept C is consistent with a limited access on the side of the subject to the elements involved in that concept. This limited access seems to be a sequel of the identity of concepts across individuals.

If this were true, then I could claim that someone may possess the concept of water without having a complete mastery of that concept. And, more interestingly, that someone may know that she possesses the concept of water without knowing every element involved in the concept of water. Still, we should need to motivate a more particular claim, namely: that someone may know that she possesses the concept of water without knowing a particularly central feature of it, that is, that it is a natural kind concept. Let us see how this could be done.

Consider now two well-known cases of concepts that aimed at designating a natural kind: *phlogiston* and *caloric*. It sounds plausible to describe the situation as follows: at a certain stage in the history of science, scientist justifiedly believed that *phlogiston* and *caloric* were two natural kind concepts, but in time they discovered that they were wrong, that there is no natural kind that they may

an assumption to which we have only an '*a posteriori*' access and, consequently, Boghossian's incompatibilist argument would fail.

4. But, indeed, Boghossian is quite reluctant to grant that an externalist could only be forced to accept premise (1) on assumption (A). For, as he points out, a Twin–Earth argument can be run even if 'water' does not actually express a natural kind concept, but only aims at being so:

> The reason this particular objection doesn't succeed is that it is quite clear that we can run a TE experiment on a word that doesn't actually name a natural kind. Suppose we had such a word, W, on Earth. Then, to get a successful TE experiment, all you need to do is describe a Twin situation in which, although the users of the word type W are functional and molecular duplicates of their counterparts on Earth, W does name a kind in the Twin situation. Provided intuition still has it that the extension of Earthly tokens of W are different from the extension of the Twin tokens of W —which of course they will be since the extension of the former will be empty and the extension of the latter won't be— the experiment will succeed. (P. 205).

---

designate. Nothing like that has occurred with the concept of *water* precisely because there is empirical evidence that there is a single substance that plays a certain causal role R. This is a contingent fact.

It seems to me that a similar intuition lies behind David Lewis' and Jaegwon Kim's (Cf. Lewis (1970, 1994) and Kim (1992))remarks about how multiple realization may pose a problem as to the causal efficacy of functional properties. The fact that 'human pain' designates a property depends on the rather contingent fact that the functional role that is proper to pain has the same realization in every member of the human species. It is perfectly intelligible that we could discover, for instance, that 'human pain' is multirealized and, in that case, one would have to claim that such phrase does not pick up a property but only a functional role. I guess that what goes for 'human pain', holds for 'water' as well: it is intelligible that we could have discovered that 'water' does not designate a property, but simply picks up a functional role. This is not something that we know '*a priori*'.

To see the relevance of this discussion to our present point, I could firstly say that it follows from the previous remarks that people that master the concepts of *human pain, water, caloric,* or *phlogiston* may discover, after empirical investigation, that some of such concepts do (or don't) have a referent, do (or don't) designate a property. So, if one is supposed to have '*a priori*' access to one's concepts, then the fact that a term has a referent, that it designates a property, it is not something that one knows by the mere fact of knowing that one possesses the concept that such a term expresses. It seems then that, at least those who acknowledge the '*a priori*' knowability of premise (2), must recognize that someone may know that she has the concept of water without knowing that *water* is a natural kind concept.

I suspect, however, that this sort of consideration may be both wrong and irrelevant.

a) Let me indicate firstly why I think it may be irrelevant. Suppose I concede that a Twin–Earth experiment can be run on a word W which on Earth does not express a natural kind concept, my question is: why should this affect my claim that an externalist only needs to concede premise (1) on assumption (A)? It is true that, if Boghossian is right, a term may be TE–eligible even if, on Earth, the corresponding (A)-premise does not hold with respect to it. But my previous line of reasoning is not merely saying that "in addition to aiming to express a natural kind, a word must actually name a natural kind, if it is to be Twin Earth–eligible" (p. 205), which is the explicit target of Boghossian's reply. What I am insisting is that an externalist only needs to concede (1) if (A) is true and, in this respect, it seems clear that the fact that a term is TE–eligible does not guarantee that an externalist should concede that the corresponding (1)-premise is true with regard to the concept that word W expresses on Earth, since, as Boghossian himself insists, a word W may be TE–eligible even if the corresponding (1)-premise is false on Earth. It sounds then that in order to admit (1), the externalist needs more than TE–eligibility, she needs (A).

b) Let us now see why I suspect that Boghossian's considerations in the quote above are wrong or, in other words, the reasons why I doubt that a Twin–Earth experiment could be run on a word W which does not express a natural kind concept on Earth. The reason is this. Putnam's Twin–Earth argument relies on the assumption that natural kind terms contain a tacit indexical element, that their extension and referent is irreducibly fixed by means of an ostensive definition like, for instance: *"'water' is stuff that bears a certain similarity relation to the water around here"*.[5] Or, in other words, 'water' designates a liquid like this. Boghossian takes it that for a given word W, even if it is not a natural kind term on Earth, it could be so on Twin–Earth. My question is, though: how could the extension and reference of W on Twin–Earth be determined? What sort of ostensive definition could one employ to that purpose? Let us consider a pair of possibilities:

---

[5] Putnam (1975, p. 234). By saying this, I am not committing myself to the claim that 'water' is an indexical term, that is, that 'water' behaves like indexicals in every crucial respect. To put it in Burge's terms, what I am claiming is that having beliefs about water "requires that one be in not–purely–context–free conceptual relations to the relevant entities. That is, one must be in the sort of relation to the entities that someone who indexically refers to them would be". (Burge (1982), p. 106).

i) One might treat Twin–Earth as if it were another planet with real people, trees, and rivers on it. In such a case, we can make sense of someone providing an ostensive definition of word W on Twin–Earth. But, no wonder, this won't serve to the purposes of Boghossian's incompatibilist argument. For, in that case, it would be an empirical question whether W is a natural kind term on Twin–Earth and, hence, TE–eligibility would still depend on some empirical facts.

ii) Suppose, on the contrary and most reasonably, that Twin–Earth refers to a counterfactual situation. How do we produce ostensive definitions in counterfactual situations? How do we point to a certain region in the counterfactual space? It sounds that the individuation of those situations is essentially parasitic upon some actual indexicalizations: it would be like this pointing but differing in that and that respect. Now, Boghossian's scenario is such that we could not actually point to any natural kind in defining the word W, since there is no such natural kind. So, how could we define a natural kind term in the Twin–Earth counterfactual situation? At first sight, it may sound that we have quite a simple procedure, namely:

(P) 'W' designates the natural kind that on Twin–Earth accomplishes such and such functional role.

Yet, this procedure clearly falls short of what a natural kind term requires. It is essential to a natural kind term that one could discover that some aspects of the functional role initially employed to individuate that natural kind do not belong to it, are not properties of such natural kind. But this kind of discovery is trivially excluded by procedure P. This epistemic circumstance is not alien to the semantics of natural kind terms, since one of its crucial functions is to allow speakers to refer to the same stuff despite variations in their knowledge of its functional role. Hence, a term whose extension is fixed by that procedure P is not a natural kind term. But, how else could the reference and extension of word W in the Twin–Earth counterfactual situation be fixed so that it could operate as a natural kind term? This is, perhaps, the form that my second question to Boghossian may adopt. In any event, it is obvious that Putnam's Twin–Earth experiment is not at all prey to this kind of objection: Twater is the stuff that has on Earth the same functional role as water on Earth, and this holds stable across variations in our knowledge of that functional role.

5. I conjecture, to close, that Boghossian would be dissatisfied with my line of reasoning on point (a). For, he would argue, I am assuming that word W would not only express a different concept on

Earth and Twin–Earth, but also a concept of a different nature: one would be a natural kind concept, but not the other. And, faced with this situation, the externalist would have to acknowledge that W on Earth would be a compound concept and on Twin–Earth an atomic one. And Boghossian is quite reluctant, in virtue of some metaphysical reasons, to accept that the atomicity or compositionality of a concept should depend on external circumstances such as those that the externalist mentions:

> A concept's compositionality is exclusively function of its internal 'syntax' and can't be contingent upon external circumstances in the way the present proposal would require. (P. 208).

In the face of this, I would like firstly ask for some remarks as to the kind of metaphysical reasons that Boghossian may have in mind, since his contribution is quite hermetic in this respect.

Secondly, I would also welcome any comments as to how I should interpret the distinction between atomic *vs.* compound concepts. In the light of the rather scarce remarks that figure in the paper, I am inclined to say that, according to Boghossian:

> A concept is compound if it is solely individuated in terms of a functional role

while, given that the distinction is assumed to be exhaustive:

> A concept is atomic if and only it is not solely individuated in terms of a functional role.

It follows that, by definition, natural kind terms are atomic, and general terms that fail to be natural kind are equally by definition compound. It seems, then, that according to the externalist, the syntax of a concept should depend on certain external circumstances. But, according to Boghossian, this cannot be. Yet, insisting on this point, without providing any further motivation, sounds like begging the question against the externalist. For the externalist, in claiming "that facts external to the thinker's skin are relevant to the individuation of (certain of) his mental states" (p. 199), seems to be assuming that the individuation of the nature (as natural kind concepts and, by definition, as atomic) of some of the concepts involved in such mental states also depends on facts external to the thinker's skin.

6. With this I close my exposition of the reasons why I think that an externalist needn't concede that she can know (1) '*a priori*'. Moreover, in my revision of premise (2), I concluded that a reasonable

account of privileged access does not supply 'a priori' knowledge about whether one masters a certain concept. So, if I am right, there is no reason why the combination of externalism and the privileged access doctrine should lead to 'a priori' knowability of the fact that water exists.[6]

REFERENCES

Boghossian, P. (this volume), "What the Externalist can know A Priori".
Brown, J. (1995), "The Incompatibility of Anti–Individualism and Privileged Access", in Analysis, 55, pp. 149–156.
Burge, T. (1982), "Other Bodies", in A. Woodfield (ed.), Thought and Object. Essays on Intentionality, Oxford, Clarendon Press, pp. 97–120.
―――― (1988), "Individualism and Self–Knowledge", in Journal of Philosophy, 85/11, pp. 649–63.
―――― (1993), "Content Preservation", in The Philosophical Review, vol. 102, no. 4, pp. 457–488.
Davidson, D. (1987), "Knowing One's Own Mind", in The Proceedings and Addresses of the American Philosophical Association, 60, pp. 441–58.
Kim, J. (1992), "Multiple Realization and the Metaphysics of Reduction", in Philosophy and Phenomenological Research, 52, pp. 1–26.
Lewis, D. (1970), "How to Define Theoretical Terms", in Journal of Philosophy, 67, pp. 427–46.
Lewis, D. (1994), "Lewis, David: Reduction of Mind", in S. Guttenplan (ed.), A Companion to the Philosophy of Mind, Oxford, Basil Blackwell, pp. 412–431.
Miller, R.W. (1997), "Externalist Self–Knowledge and The Scope of The A Priori", in Analysis, 57, pp. 67–75.
Putnam, H. (1975), "The Meaning of 'Meaning'", in H. Putnam, Philosophical Papers v. 2: Mind, Language and Reality, Cambridge, Cambridge University Press, pp. 215–271.

---

[6]Earlier drafts of this text have significantly benefited from comments by Carlos Moya, Tobies Grimaltos, Josep L. Prades, and Marcelo Sabatés. Research for this paper have been funded by the Spanish Government's DGICYT as part of the projects PS–03–0178 and PB93–1049–C03–02. My thanks to this institution for its generous help and encouragement.

Boghossian's *Reductio* of Compatibilism*

Carlos J. Moya

In a number of papers,[1] Paul Boghossian has argued against the compatibility between content externalism and self-knowledge by trying to show that, if externalism is correct, then there are possible situations in which a subject would be systematically wrong about the identity and difference of his thought contents. These possible situations involve the subject's being unwittingly switched between, say, Earth and Twin Earth. In this case, he would judge that two of his thoughts are of the same type when, on an externalist individuation, they are not. In Boghossian's terms, externalism is incompatible with transparency of mental content. This line of

---

*Research for this paper has been funded by the Spanish Government DGI-CYT as part of the projects PB93-1049-C03-02 and PB93-0683. My thanks to this institution for its generous help and encouragement. I also thank Josep Corbí and Tobies Grimaltos for comments on previous drafts.

[1] Especially in 'Content and Self–Knowledge', *Philosophical Topics* 17 (1989), pp. 5-26; 'Externalism and Inference', in E. Villanueva (ed.), *Rationality in Epistemology*, Philosophical Issues 2, Ridgeview Publishing Company, Atascadero (California), 1992, pp. 11-28; and 'The Transparency of Mental Content', *Philosophical Perspectives* 8 (1994), pp. 33-50.

argument has received considerable attention and been the object of a wide and subtle discussion in recent times.[2]

In the present paper, however, Boghossian has turned to a different line of attack to compatibility between self-knowledge and externalism. He now tries to elaborate a *reductio ad absurdum* of compatibilism by trying to show that this position is committed to the claim that a subject can come to know, purely *a priori*, substantial truths about the world which every reasonable person would agree can only be known *a posteriori*.

There are some antecedents to this line of argument, as well as some criticisms to it, and I shall eventually refer to them while discussing this paper.[3]

According to Boghossian, Oscar, a compatibilist, is in a position to argue, purely *a priori*, as follows:

1. If I have the concept water, then water exists.

2. I have the concept water.

Therefore,

3. Water exists.

---

[2]Participants in this discussion include Ted A. Warfield, 'Privileged Self–Knowledge and Externalism Are Compatible', *Analysis* 52 (1992), pp. 232-237 and 'Knowing the World and Knowing Our Minds', *Philosophy and Phenomenological Research* 55 (1995), pp. 525-545; Stephen Schiffer, 'Boghossian on Externalism and Inference', in E. Villanueva (ed.), *op. cit.*, pp. 29-37; K. Falvey and J. Owens, 'Externalism, Self–Knowledge and Skepticism', *The Philosophical Review* 103 (1994), pp. 107-137; J. Owens, 'Pierre and the Fundamental Assumption', *Mind and Language* 10 (1995), pp. 250-273; P. Ludlow, 'Externalism, Self–Knowledge, and the Prevalence of Slow Switching', *Analysis* 55 (1995), pp. 45-49; T. Burge, 'Our Entitlement to Self–Knowledge', *Proceedings of the Aristotelian Society* 91 (1996), pp. 91-116; C. Peacocke, 'Our Entitlement to Self–Knowledge. Entitlement, Self–Knowledge and Conceptual Redeployment', *Proceedings of the Aristotelian Society* 91 (1996), pp. 117-158, among others. I myself have contributed a paper on this subject, 'Externalism and Self–Knowledge', to the VIII Inter–University Seminar on Philosophy and Cognitive Science, University of Granada, 23-25 May 1996.

[3]See M. McKinsey, 'Anti–Individualism and Privileged Access', *Analysis* 51 (1991), pp. 9-16; A. Brueckner, 'What an Anti–Individualist Knows *A Priori*', *Analysis* 52 (1992), pp. 111-118; M. McKinsey, 'Accepting the Consequences of Anti–Individualism', *Analysis* 54 (1994), pp. 124-128; A. Brueckner, 'The Characteristic Thesis of Anti–Individualism', *Analysis* 55 (1995), pp. 146-148; J. Brown, 'The Incompatibility of Anti–Individualism and Privileged Access', *Analysis* 55 (1995), pp. 149-156. See also note 7.

Clearly, that water exists is something that cannot be known *a priori*. The form of the argument is valid. So, at least one of the premises will be either false or not knowable *a priori*. Boghossian, however, holds that Oscar is bound to accept that both premises are true and knowable *a priori*. Therefore, he is bound to accept that the existence of water can be known *a priori*. Since this is absurd and is implied by compatibilism, compatibilism must be false.

I would like to resist being forced to choose between externalism and self–knowledge. I think we can have both. I am, then, a compatibilist. My aim in this comment is going to be mainly negative: I will try to show that Boghossian's incompatibilist argument does not succeed. But I will also say something positive in defence of compatibilism, by giving some indications about how a plausible compatibilist externalism might be construed.

Premise 1 of Oscar's argument is based on the externalist thesis that there is a dependence relation between thought content and external individuation conditions. Premise 2 rests on the assumption of self–knowledge. Though Boghossian takes this premise to be obviously acceptable, I find the way it is stated rather controversial. Normally, self–knowledge is held to extend to thought contents, rather than to the concepts one possesses in thinking those contents. In fact, it is hard to accept that one enjoys privileged access to the concepts one has, at least if this means the concepts one *masters*, in having a certain thought. Normal adults, I would say, know directly, non–inferentially, what they are currently thinking, in that they can give true reports of these thoughts, but I am pretty sure that they are quite often wrong about their mastery of the concepts that make up those thoughts. Burge's social externalism might have some bearing on this claim. So, if premise 2 is to be plausible, 'having a concept' has to be understood in a weak sense. One has a concept, in this weak sense, just in case one is able to have and to express, with a sufficient degree of competence, according to normal standards, thoughts involving the concept. So understood, premise 2 is certainly acceptable, given self–knowledge.

Premise 2 and the antecedent of premise 1 in Boghossian's argument are stated under the assumption that the concept had by Oscar the compatibilist, namely the concept water, fulfills a number of conditions, related to presuppositions involved in Twin Earth experiments. First, water and twater (that is, any other substance macroscopically indistinguishable, but microscopically, chemically distinct from water) 'have to be thought of as distinct substances, distinct natural kinds'. Second, the word 'water' is intended by Oscar to express a natural kind concept. Third, Oscar has no views about the chemical composition of water. Fourth, Oscar's concept water is atomic, not compositional. Finally, the concept is to be thought of by Oscar as individuated in terms of its referent. If Oscar is to know premise 1 *a priori*, it is essential that these conditions are known by him *a priori* and that they, together with his possession of the concept, logically imply the consequent, namely that water exists.

Is a Twin Earth externalist committed to hold that premise 1 is true and knowable *a priori*? A natural and powerful response (which Boghossian considers and finally rejects) by an externalist would be to say that the second condition is too weak for this premise to be accepted. For imagine Peter, a compatibilist and a defender of the phlogiston theory. He intends his term 'phlogiston' to express a natural kind concept, as does Oscar with his term 'water'. Following Oscar's example, he reasons as follows:

A. If I have the concept phlogiston, then phlogiston exists.

B. I have the concept phlogiston.

Therefore,

C. Phlogiston exists.

An externalist will contend that what leads Peter to a false conclusion is that 'phlogiston' does not actually name a natural kind, so that the concept it expresses is not the concept of a natural kind. What is implied by externalism is not premise 1, but, at most, premise 1′, which should replace the former:

1′. If I have the concept water and the concept water is the concept of a natural kind, then water exists.

Now, however, conclusion 3 cannot be deduced from premises 1′ and 2. Besides, and more importantly, the antecedent of 1′ cannot be known *a priori*. Whether a term actually names a natural kind and so expresses the concept of a natural kind can only be known *a posteriori*. If this is correct, premise 1′ becomes a triviality. Nothing substantial about the natural world can be obtained from externalism together with self-knowledge *a priori*.

Boghossian's strategy is to block this natural externalist move by denying that an externalist can allow for the existence of atomic concepts expressed by terms with an empty extension, such as 'phlogiston' in our world or 'water' on his extraordinary Dry Earth. On the other hand, taking such terms to express compound concepts makes questions about compositionality or atomicity of concepts depend on contingent external circumstances, such as the existence or non–existence of a natural kind, and this he deems unacceptable. Compositionality and atomicity are internal, non–relational properties of a concept; these properties supervene on the molecular and functional structure of the concept's possessor and are not contingent on what there can be in the outer world. If all this is correct, an externalist must concede that if a term expresses an atomic concept, then it has a non–empty extension. Now Boghossian is in a position to establish his *reductio* of compatibilism against objections. He can now reject premises of the form of our premise 1'. The antecedent of the conditional need not include that the concept Oscar has is the concept of a natural kind, which could only be known *a posteriori*. It suffices that Oscar intends to use it as a natural kind concept and that the concept is atomic (together with the rest of conditions stated above). And all this can be known by Oscar *a priori*. So, Oscar, the compatibilist, knows *a priori* that the concept he expresses with his term 'water' is the concept water and that this concept is atomic. So his term 'water' has a non–empty extension. Since this term expresses the concept water, and he knows it does, he knows that the term's referent is the property of being water and that its extension is everything that has this property, namely all bits of water. He can conclude, then, purely *a priori*, that water exists o has existed at some time. But to think that this can be known *a priori* is absurd. Therefore, compatibilism is false.

Let me try to assess Boghossian's incompatibilist argument. A crucial question is the role that empirical information, e.g. that water is H_2O, that water is a natural kind, or that the term 'water' names a natural kind, plays in externalism as a philosophical theory of meaning and content. This question is controversial, but is essential in discussing incompatibilist arguments. Once the role played by empirical information is rightly understood, it can be seen that no substantial truths about the external world can be obtained from externalism together with self–knowledge *a priori*. Externalism is the view that our thought contents, including our concepts, are individuated, in part, by external conditions. But there are several possible ways of developing this basic insight. Twin Earth experiments are supposed to show that tokens of 'water' do not mean the same on Earth as on Twin Earth. But why is this so? The most common answer is: because Earthians and Twin Earthians causally interact with different substances, water and twater respectively. This answer corresponds to a widely held version of externalism. 'Causal externalism' might this version be called. This simple version faces, in my opinion, serious, maybe insurmountable difficulties.[4] But it is not the only possible version. On the version I would favour, the answer to the above question would be: because Earthians and Twin Earthians learn and teach the meaning of 'water' in connection with samples of what are in fact different substances. On this version, our words' meaning depends on external conditions because certain bits of the external world are used to *define* those words, to give those words its meaning. If, in order to define 'water', I say to someone 'water is *this*', then the ostended bit itself gets into the meaning of the word and into the concept it expresses. This external bit becomes a norm for a correct use of the word. It is part of the structure of the concept this word expresses. This construal of externalism, inspired in some Wittgensteinian reflections,[5] might be called 'normative externalism'. Normative externalism includes causal externalism, but not conversely. Normative externalism is not really far from Putnam's conception. Remarks about paradigmatic samples, with a clear Wittgensteinian flavour, can also be found in Putnam's "The meaning of 'meaning'". But these remarks are often forgotten in favour of cruder causal versions. On the normative construal, when I point to a sample of water to define the word 'water', I need not know what its chemical composition is, nor do I need to be able to distinguish it from, say, twater if I were confronted with it. But the actual essence of the sample, whether we know it or not, helps giving the word its meaning, and this meaning is different from that it would be given to the word on Twin Earth. If this is on the right lines, it might reconcile Boghossian's view that compositionality and atomicity are internal to concepts with dependence of these properties on external conditions, as far as these conditions are an aspect of the concept itself. Let us see how.

On this construal of externalism, the real essence of a certain substance, which is only discoverable *a posteriori*, is given a constitutive role in individuating content and concepts. It is plausible to think that our present conviction that water is an atomic concept is not independent of the empirical discovery that water is a natural kind,

---

[4]I do not know whether this causal version of externalism can meet Boghossian's objection of *reductio* we are dealing with. But I am pretty sure that it cannot meet objections based on 'switching cases', which I referred to in the first paragraph of this paper. It also faces the 'disjunction problem' that Fodor discovered in causal theories of meaning and content.

[5]See especially Wittgenstein, L., *Philosophical Remarks*, Blackwell, Oxford, 1975, I, 6, and *Philosophical Investigations*, Blackwell, Oxford, 1963, I, 50. Remarks about paradigmatic samples, with a clear Wittgensteinian flavour, can also be found in Putnam's 'The meaning of "meaning"'.

namely H_2O. Before this discovery, human beings might well be agnostic about atomicity or compositionality of their concept water. We would not say that the liquid on Twin Earth is not water if we did not know that water is H_2O, and this is only knowable *a posteriori*. However, the constitutive relevance of this *a posteriori* information in determining our concept water and its difference from Twin Earthians' concept twater depends on our prior commitment to define terms like 'water' by means of external samples.[6] It might be objected that our acceptance of the difference between the concepts water and twater shows that our concept water was atomic in the first place, prior to the empirical discovery that water is a natural kind, so that atomicity does not really depend on *a posteriori* information. My answer would run as follows. For some concepts, such as water, gold, or tiger, we may hold an assumption that there is a hidden unitary essence lying behind the items that fall under the concept. But this assumption, which we may know *a priori*, is not enough to make those concepts atomic, for, on the normative version of externalism, the assumption is defeasible, in so far as we leave the last word about atomicity or compositionality of those concepts to the real nature of paradigmatic samples. Therefore, we do not have, *a priori*, a sufficient amount of data to decide the issue. In saying 'water is *this*', the ostended bit becomes an aspect of the concept, so that, if we discover that no common unitary essence underlies the different samples, we cancel the atomicity assumption, and compositional aspects become decisive. If atomicity of such concepts as water was settled in advance, then, were we to discover that there is no common essence to water, we would say 'so, there is no water' or 'water does not exist'; but we would not say this; what we would say, instead, is that water was, in fact, a collection of different substances.

Counterfactuals such as 'if there were no H_2O in our environment, our term "water" would express a different concept from the one it now expresses' rest, I contend, on our decision to understand by 'water' *this*, where the ostended bit is a sample. In this frame, the empirical discovery that paradigmatic samples of water are H_2O confirm the (defeasible) assumption that water is an atomic concept. If this is correct, we cannot know *a priori* that the concept water is atomic. Therefore, an externalist cannot conclude, purely *a priori*,

---

[6]This commitment might not be optional. Meaning might need, as a condition of its existence, such external, objective samples, at least is something like Wittgenstein's private language argument is accepted as cogent. The indispensability of external samples is a plausible way of reading this argument.

that water exists. He *might* conclude that, since he has the concept water, there have to be external possibility conditions for that concept, but this transcendental reasoning to the effect that there are some external conditions or other, controversial as it may be, is not absurd.[7] If all this is correct, an externalist may plausibly hold that tokens of the same word–type can express an atomic concept in one world and a compositional concept in another, even if their inhabitants are molecular and functional duplicates. Thereby, he can vindicate premise 1' and avoid *reductio*.

Suppose, however, that Boghossian is right and that atomicity or compositionality of concepts supervenes on molecular and functional structure of their possessors, independently of what there is in the outer world. If so, the concept expressed by 'water' on Dry Earth would be atomic. Could an externalist accept, against Boghossian's contention, that a term with an empty extension expresses nonetheless an atomic concept? I think he could.[8] What are the truth conditions of 'water is wet' on Dry Earth? We can start with the following statement:

> 'Water is wet' is true on Dry Earth if, and only if, Dry Earth's water is wet.

But 'Dry Earth's water' has no referent. Before this, an externalist could opt, couldn't he, for saying that the right part of the biconditional is false or for saying that it has no truth value. Only in this latter case might he be forced to say that 'water is wet' has no meaning on Dry Earth. If he opts for saying that lack of reference of a component makes the sentence false, he can say that 'water is wet' is false on Dry Earth, but has meaning. But then, in what conditions would it be true? Well, it would be true if there were in fact a substance, a natural kind, in the extension of 'water' and this substance were wet. Why an externalist may not say this? He could then say what is the concept expressed by tokens of 'water' on Dry Earth: it is the concept Dry Earthians would have if there were in fact a natural kind, with the right external appearance, denoted there by tokens of 'water'. It must be conceded, however, that in order to be more precise about the concept an externalist should

---

[7]This is something that Brueckner points out against McKinsey's incompatibilism. See note 3.

[8]I have been led to think of this by Peter Carruthers' treatment of empty demonstrative thoughts in his article 'Russellian Thoughts', *Mind* 96 (1987), pp. 18-35.

22. BOGHOSSIAN'S REDUCTIO OF COMPATIBILISM

know *what* natural kind would be denoted. But the above description of the concept seems precise enough to counter Boghossian's claim that an externalist cannot allow for atomic concepts in empty cases. If all this works, it could again support premise 1' in Oscar's argument, which, to recall, included in the antecedent the condition that the concept had by Oscar has to be the concept of a natural kind, instead of just being intended by him to be so.

These possible replies to Boghossian's incompatibilist argument may not be compossible. But if at least one of them is successful, this would suffice for compatibilists to elude *reductio*.

Replies to Commentators

Paul A. Boghossian

1 Reply to Loar

In "What the Externalist Can Know *A Priori*" (hereafter, EAP), I argued that combining an externalism about concepts with a traditional doctrine of privileged access to the contents of one's own thoughts leads to absurd results. For, I argued, such a compatibilist combination would allow us to argue purely *a priori* as follows:

(1) If I have the concept water, then water exists.

(2) I have the concept water.

Therefore,

(3) Water exists.

Strictly speaking, Brian Loar does not dispute this central claim. He says:

> Let "twin–Earth" externalism be a strong externalist theory that entails that "water" expresses different concepts for me and my twin. It seems to me that Boghossian's argument is correct about twin–Earth externalism about concepts. He is quite persuasive that compatibilism is difficult to defend for such an externalist. (p. 215)

What Loar wishes to argue, however, is that a compatibilist position may not be so implausible for a weaker form of externalism, one that applies only to certain very basic concepts, such as spatial concepts, concepts of physical objects and their parts and the like.

I am not averse to the idea that there might be *a priori* routes to the truth of certain very basic propositions —for example, that there is an external world, that it contains things that occupy space. To that extent, I have nothing to say against a view, or cluster of views, that issues in *a priori* knowledge of such very basic propositions. The sort of anti–compatibilist argument I offered in EAP works only to the extent that the knowledge yielded by the compatibilism at issue is clearly and manifestly not knowable *a priori* —for example, that water exists. If I am right, then this style of argument works against a compatibilism that seeks to combine self-knowledge with a *generalized* externalism about concepts, the sort of externalism that would be yielded by twin–Earth experiments. If the compatibilism at issue is restricted to cases where the results are not embarrassingly strong —for example, to the sorts of results that have always been envisioned by proponents of transcendental arguments for the existence of an external world— then, to that extent, the argument of EAP has nothing against it.

2 Reply to Yablo

Steve Yablo has a lot of interesting things to say in his comment, but his main counterclaim is that it is none too clear that sentences involving the word 'water' have no determinate truth conditions on Dry Earth. He says:

> One thing is clear: if this be Dry Earth, then the great majority of worlds are not classifiable either as containing water or lacking it. It's the next step that bothers me. Can we really conclude that *"there is water"* is lacking in truth conditions?
> That depends. It probably does follow, if truth conditions are seen as singular propositions made up *inter alia* of full–blooded properties; in the absence of water there can be no full–blooded property of *being water*, which is curtains for the proposition.
> But the singularist approach is surprising in a context where truth–conditionality is being treated as a condition of thought. After all, the capacity for water–thought is intuitively quite independent of ontological disputes about what sorts properties there may be. (p. 223)

23. REPLIES TO COMMENTATORS

If we are not to think of satisfaction conditions and truth conditions in terms of full-blooded properties, how should we think of them?

> The answer is that any object will do that encodes the possibility of interrogating a world on such matters as whether it contains water; that's what it takes to have water-thought, hence that's all that can be asked of truth conditions as a requirement of such thought. It seems to me that the encoding role is most directly and efficiently played by (truth conditions conceived as) rules or recipes for classifying worlds. Singular propositions can serve in some cases as handy repositories of classificatory information... [but] it's the rule that matters... (p. 223)
>
> If we are unlucky enough to be living on Dry Earth, then as Paul says, there is no (full-blooded) property of being water. That doesn't in and of itself make nonsense of the question "which actual and counterfactual stuffs deserve to be described as water?" It doesn't rule out that "there is water" puts a condition on worlds, albeit a condition with less taxonomical power than might ideally be wanted. (And it does have *some* taxonomical power, for it rules negatively on Dry Earth.) (Pp. 224-5)

Now, it is true that in EAP, I did identify the truth condition of a sentence with the singular proposition, if any, that it expresses. But I don't really see that that is essential to my argument. I could equally well put it in terms of *kinds*, for example; and that, I take it, no one could object to: talk about kinds is presumably not controversial in the context of a discussion of the semantics of natural kind words.

So my idea was this. If there is no kind denoted by a given natural kind term —say, 'water'— then no satisfaction conditions for that term will have been pinned down. The actual kind of stuff at the end of the relevant causal chain is supposed to fix the kind of stuff that is denoted by 'water'. If there's nothing there, then, it would seem, there is no fact of the matter what kind of stuff there would have to be for the extension of the term not to be empty.

Steve wants to deny this. But I wish he had explained at somewhat greater length why he thinks he is entitled to deny it. What his remarks suggest is this: There are conditions laid up in the meaning of 'water' that are sufficient to rule out certain things' counting as 'water', even if there isn't enough information there to rule anything in. In particular, the concept rules that there is no water on Dry Earth. So we can say that there is something thinkable there, even if it has "less taxonomical power than might ideally be wanted".

If this is what Steve has in mind, then I wish he had filled it out a little more, because in the way that I understand his proposal, it flies in the face of what most externalists believe about natural kind terms. Let me explain.

What considerations drive someone to be a concept externalist in response to the Twin Earth experiments? Why not be a narrow content theorist?

One of the principal considerations has to do with how *thin* the narrow concept associated with a natural kind term would have to be, if we removed the information associated with its extension. For let us ask this: What can we plausibly insist upon up front is packed into the concept of a natural kind, say, to use Putnam's famous example, the concept cat? Furriness? Having four legs? Meowing? Not even the concept animal, Putnam argued, could be thought of as built into the concept cat (cats might turn out to be robots). Similarly for gold (not required that it be yellow or a metal or precious) and water (not required that it be a liquid or odorless or tasteless) and so on. If we insisted that narrow contents *are* thinkable contents, then we would have to conclude that most of our thoughts about natural kinds are virtually blank and so don't determine, in and of themselves, any sort of determinate truth conditions for themselves.

To avoid this unacceptable construal of content, the externalist reasons, we should think of the truth conditions as determined by the causal facts and then let them individuate the thinkable contents, the concepts. That way we have a notion of content that is rich enough to distinguish between cat and cat–robot, water and twin water, elm and beech, and which determines the right satisfaction conditions for them. The price is letting the externally determined reference fix the thinkable concept.

If I understand Steve correctly, however, he is basically saying that if we happen to be living on Dry Earth, then we should think of the thinkable contents associated with 'water' as given by whatever *narrow contents* are associated with 'water'. But this proposal is problematic for two reasons. One is that there may be nothing in the narrow concept except the bare idea of some kind of stuff or other, which by virtue of its blankness would rule nothing out. And the other is that, if this is an acceptable reaction to Dry Earth, why is it not an acceptable reaction to Twin Earth? If there is nothing inherently wrong with thinking of virtually blank narrow contents as thinkable contents, how do we get an *argument* for concept externalism on the basis of the Twin Earth experiments?

But even if we were to set aside all of these objections and accept Steve's proposal, how does it help vindicate the compatibility of privileged self–knowledge and concept externalism? If the only sense in which I know my thoughts *a priori* doesn't enable me to tell whether I have a virtually blank concept of 'water' that doesn't have anything to say about whether most actual and possible substances are or are not water, or a concept that's so rich that it distinguishes between water and twin water, then I, for one, will have lost my grip on what this vindicated knowledge is supposed to amount to.

3 Reply to Corbí

Corbí essentially makes two claims. First, he argues that a reasonable account of privileged access would not yield the *a priori* knowability of premise (2), so compatibilism as I conceive it isn't what needs arguing about. Second, he contends that the externalist is not committed to the *a priori* knowability of (1) in any event, so my argument against the misconceived target misfires anyway. I shall take these points in turn.

To claim that I can know that I have the concept water *a priori* is to claim that I can know without empirical investigation that I have thoughts that involve the concept water. Since for me, as for Frege and lots of others, concepts just are what thought contents are composed of, this is just another way of saying that I can know without empirical investigation what my thought contents are.

This claim I take to be, along with the principal compatibilists involved in this debate —for example, Tyler Burge and Donald Davidson— the minimal core of a doctrine of privileged access. It is this claim, as I understand them, that they insist can be reconciled with externalism. My argument is designed to show that this is not true. Claiming, as Corbí does, that no one should construe the doctrine of privileged self-knowledge in this way, does not engage the point of my argument, which is that *this* doctrine, as all parties to the debate agree in construing it, is not compatible with externalism.

If (2) isn't the way we should construe privileged access, then how, according to Corbí, should we construe it? Corbí's view appears to be that we know what our thought contents are in the same way that we know that we have certain abilities, for example, that we know that we know how to ride a bike. He says:

> How do I know about this ability of mine? There is a trivial sense in which I needn't carry out any empirical investigation to have this valuable piece of knowledge. But, indeed, no one would deny that my knowing that I possess that ability depends on my knowledge of certain facts of the world that involve my previous performances on a bike. (p. 233)

But this is like saying that there is "a trivial sense" in which I needn't conduct an empirical investigation to know that the next time I sit on this chair it will support me, although no one would deny that my knowing this depends on my previous experiences with this and other chairs. The point is that the knowledge in these cases is through and through empirical: it's based on induction on past experience. There is no useful sense in which my knowledge of the content of my oc-current thoughts is based on induction. Indeed, the suggestion is probably not just wrong but incoherent. In any event, when Tyler Burge seeks to vindicate compatibilism with his deployment of the idea of a logically self–verifying second–order thought, he is evidently not trying to reconcile inductively based knowledge of thought content with externalism.

Corbí's second claim is that an externalist is committed to (1) only if water, in addition to aiming to name a natural kind, actually does name a kind. Since, however, it is not *a priori* knowable whether a concept does name an actual kind, (1) is not *a priori*.

I confess to not fully understanding Corbí's remarks here. To support his claim he spends some time rebutting a passage of mine, a passage which is used merely to pave the way for the Dry Earth argument. That's the crucial argument that needs rebutting. Corbí does eventually come around to discussing this argument. His idea, if I understand him, is that on Dry Earth 'water' will express a complex concept that turns out not to name any kind. He rightly notes that I would object that this has 'water' expressing a compound concept in one person and an atomic concept in another functionally identical person, with the two differing only in respect of the external circumstances that they happen to be in. But he expresses puzzlement as to what would be problematic about this.

He thinks that on my view a concept is compound if it's individuated solely in terms of its functional role (p. 241). But this is a bad misunderstanding. I understand what it is for a concept to be compound in that way that I take it it is commonly understood —i.e., as saying that a concept is literally composed, typically by Boolean means, out of other concepts. Thus, bachelor is compound because it *is* the concept unmarried and male. Clearly, this notion of compoundness has nothing to do with being individuated solely in terms of functional role. If the constituent concepts of a compound concept are themselves externalistically individuated, then, naturally, the compound concept won't be individuated solely in terms of its functional role.

Now, having clarified what we mean by the compoundness or compositionality of a concept, it is easy to see why it couldn't supervene on external circumstances. The point to bear in mind is that having a compound concept requires one to have all the ingredient concepts that compose that concept, including the concepts of conjunction or disjunction. Suppose 'water' expresses an atomic concept $\underline{A}$ on Earth, and that on Twin Earth it expresses the compound concept $\underline{B \text{ and } C \text{ and } D \text{ and } E}$. Then we would have to say that external circumstances determine not only *which* concept a given word expresses, but also *how many* concepts a person has. Without any change in one's cognitive or functional capacities, and just by being in one environment as opposed to another, one might have either one concept or five. I don't see how this could happen and that is my basis for saying that the compositionality of a concept does not supervene on external circumstances.

4 Reply to Moya

Moya echoes Corbí's misgivings about whether the apriority of (2) correctly expresses the doctrine of privileged self–knowledge. He says:

> Though Boghossian takes this premise to be obviously acceptable, I find the way it is stated rather controversial. Normally, self–knowledge is held to extend to thought contents, rather than to the concepts one possesses in thinking those contents. In fact, it is hard to accept that one enjoys privileged access to the concepts one has, at least if this means the concepts one *masters* in having a certain thought. Normal adults, I would say, know directly, non–inferentially, what they are currently thinking in that they can give true reports of these thoughts, but I am pretty sure that they are often quite wrong about their mastery of the concepts that make up those thoughts. (p. 245)

This confuses knowing what concept one has with knowing how to explicate or analyze that concept. On behalf of the doctrine of privileged access, I claimed the former but not the latter. I never assume, merely on the basis of the doctrine, that we know that arthritis can't be a disease of the thigh, but only that if we know that we have arthritis thoughts then we know that we have the concept arthritis. Trivially, the one item of knowledge entails the other. If I know that I am thinking that arthritis is wet (or whatever) I know that my thought involves the concept arthritis.

More importantly, Moya claims that, *pace* what I say, an externalist could accept that a term with an empty extension expresses an atomic concept. He gives the truth conditions of 'Water is wet' on Dry Earth as follows:

'Water is wet' on Dry Earth iff Dry Earth's water is wet.

He claims that we could say that because "Dry Earth's water" lacks reference, the right hand side of the biconditional is false and hence that its left hand side is false as well. Since something can't be false without being meaningful, that vindicates the existence of a 'water' concept on Dry Earth. But then in what conditions would 'Water is wet' as used on Dry Earth be true? He answers as follows:

> Well, it would be true if there were in fact a substance, a natural kind, in the extension of 'water' and this substance were wet... [An externalist could then say] what is the concept expressed by tokens of 'water' on Dry Earth: it is the concept Dry Earthians would have if there were in fact a natural kind with the right appearance denoted by tokens of 'water'. (p. 250)

I take it that neither 'mimsy' nor 'borogrove' has meaning, so that someone uttering 'All mimsies are borogroves' doesn't say anything and his statement has no truth conditions. Mimicking Moya's suggestion, however, we seem to be able to say that it is meaningful after all. For consider:

Mimsies are borogroves' is true iff mimsies are borogroves.

Since neither 'mimsy' nor 'borogrove' refers to anything, we can take the view that 'Mimsies are borogroves' is false. What are its truth conditions? It would be true if there were some things in the extension of 'mimsy' and some things in the extension of 'borogrove' and if all the former were instances of the latter. And the concept we do express by 'mimsy' is the concept that we would express if there were in fact things in the extension of 'mimsy'.

A Theory of Concepts and Concept Possession

George Bealer

A theory of concepts should answer three questions: (1) Do concepts exist and, if so, what is their modal status (*post rem, in rebus, ante rem*)? (2) What are concepts (assuming that they exist)? (3) What is it to possess a concept? My starting point is the truism that *the concept of being F* is a concept. This canonical gerundive form identifies the primary sense of the term 'concept' in ordinary English and serves to anchor usage in philosophical discussions. I hold that concepts, in this primary sense, are *sui generis* irreducible entities comprising the ontological category in terms of which propositions (thoughts, in Frege's sense) are to be analyzed. Some people believe that one must invoke psychology to justify the ontology of concepts. Even if this style of justification succeeds, I believe that the existence of concepts and propositions is more convincingly established by certain considerations in logic —specifically, modal logic and the logic of logical truth— where one deals with 'that'-clauses, gerundives, and other canonical intensional terms. Moreover, unlike the psychological approach, the logical approach is able to settle the question of *modal status*; specifically, it implies the *ante rem* view of propositions and concepts (i.e., the view that they are mind-independent entities which would exist whether or not they apply to anything). But what is it to possess a concept? Continuing a theme of several past papers, I hold that concept possession is to be analyzed in terms of a certain kind of reliable pattern in one's intuitions. The challenge is to find an analysis that is at once noncircular and fully general. Environmentalism, anti-individualism, holism, analyticity, etc. provide special obstacles. If correct, the analysis forms the basis of an account of *a priori* knowledge, which in turn implies a qualified autonomy and authority for logic, mathematics, and philosophy *vis-à-vis* empirical science. Other implications concern the Benacerraf problem about mathematical truth and the Wittgenstein–Kripke puzzle about rule-following.

Concept possession is a central philosophical notion which calls out for analysis. The primary goal of this paper is to venture one. No doubt the analysis is in need of further refinement, but I hope that it at least points the way to a successful analysis.

Part I. A Realist Framework

The appropriate starting points for a theory of concept possession are realism about the modalities (possibility, necessity, contingency), realism about concepts and propositions, and realism about the propositional attitudes —including, in particular, intuition. In this part I will discuss some of these starting points in more detail.

1 The Modalities, Concepts, and Propositions

Although I will simply assume realism about the modalities, realism about concepts and propositions requires elaboration, especially in connection with their modal status. The way I propose to approach concepts is to extrapolate from certain arguments concerning propositions: since concepts are of the same general ontological type as propositions, most ontological conclusions about the propositions — e.g., about their modal status— hold for concepts as well. In the tradition of Frege's critique of psychologism, my view is that propositions (and the concepts in terms of which they are analyzable) are ontologically independent of the mind. Propositions are independently required for the purposes of logical theory, and they have the modal status one would expect logical objects to have. Thus, I disagree with Jerry Fodor when he says, "[P]ropositions exist to

24. A THEORY OF CONCEPTS AND CONCEPT POSSESSION

be what beliefs and desires are attitudes *toward*".[1] It would more correct to say that propositions exist to be the primary bearers of truth, possibility, necessity, impossibility, logical truth, etc. This is the view I defend in "Universals" (1993). The following provides some of the flavor of the argument.

Considerations of logical form and truth conditions lead us to the following preliminary conclusions. Expressions such as 'is true', 'is possible', 'is necessary', 'is impossible', 'is logically true', 'is probable', etc. are one–place predicates; 'that'–clauses are singular terms; and sentences of the form ⌜It is F that A⌝ have referential truth conditions: ⌜It is F that A⌝ is true iff there is something which the 'that'–clause ⌜that A⌝ designates and to which the predicate ⌜F⌝ applies.

Consider the type of entities designated by 'that'–clause. (We will allow for the possibility that some of entities of this general ontological type are not designated by any 'that'–clause, due to the expressive deficiencies of natural languages.) For terminological convenience, let us call entities of this general type *propositions*. This will not be question–begging, for it does not prejudge the question of what these entities *are*. Are they linguistic entities, psychological entities, extensional complexes (e.g., ordered sets or sequences), possible–worlds constructs, etc.; or are they *sui generis* and irreducible? Nor does it prejudge the question of the modal status of propositions. Are they *post rem, in rebus, ante rem*? (Advocates of the *in rebus* view hold the following: for all x, necessarily, the proposition that ...x... exists only if x exists; and, necessarily, for all y, the proposition that ...y... is actual only if y is actual.[2] Advocates of the *ante rem* theory of propositions deny this.)

As I have said, I believe that logical theory makes commitment to propositions prior to any consideration in psychological theory. The following truisms illustrate the point:

It is logically true that triangles are triangles.

It is *not* logically true that triangles are trilaterals.

The explanation of this plus kindred phenomena require, not only a commitment to propositions, but to a commitment to types of

---

[1] J. Fodor, *Psychosemantics*, P. 11.
[2] In contemporary logical theory, the most familiar example of an *in rebus* theory identifies propositions with extensional complexes —ordered sets or sequences.

propositions having all the richness as those required for psychological theory. Important as this conclusion is, however, it does not settle the modal status of propositions.

I will now proceed to sketch my defense of the *ante rem* view. (In this defense, we will assume actualism. In the present context, we should feel free to do this. The reason is that possibilism leads to a view of propositions that is similar to an actualist *ante rem* theory of propositions. For, according to possibilism, all possible worlds exist, and all possible propositions exist. In this way, propositions have a kind of prior existence, just as they do on an actualist *ante rem* theory. This is the underlying point I am trying to establish.)

My defense will focus on a family of intuitively true sentences which I call *transmodal* sentences. Here is an illustration:

> Every x is such that, necessarily, for every y, the proposition that $x = y$ is either possible or impossible.[3]

We may symbolize this sentence thus:

(i) $(\forall x)\Box(\forall y)$ (Possible $[x = y]$ ∨ Impossible $[x = y]$).

How is the embedded 'that'-clause to be treated? If it has narrow scope, (i) would imply:

(ii) $(\forall x)\Box(\forall y) (\exists v)v = [x = y]$.[4]

That is, every x is such that, necessarily, for every y, the proposition that $x = y$ exists. Therefore, on the *in rebus* view, this implies:

$(\forall x)\Box(\exists v)v = x$.

That is, everything necessarily exists. A false conclusion, for surely there exist contingent objects.[5] On the other hand, consider the wide scope reading of (i). On it, (i) entails that every x is such that, necessarily, for all y, there exists an *actual* proposition that $x = y$. In symbols:

---

[3] One could replace '$x = y$' with 'if x and y exist, $x = y$'.

[4] On an extensional–complex theory, (ii) might be represented thus:

$(\forall x)\Box(\forall y) (\exists v)\ v = \langle x, \text{'identity'}, y\rangle$.

Yet, necessarily, a set exists only if its elements exist. So (ii) would imply:

$(\forall x)\Box(\exists v)v = x$.

I.e., everything necessarily exists. This is the implausible consequence we are in the midst of deriving in the text in a more general setting.

[5] At least according to actualism, which I am assuming here. Certain possibilists might accept the conclusion of the *reductio* in the text. But these possibilists would already be willing to accept (something like) the *ante rem* view of propositions, so I need not discuss their view in the present context.

24. A Theory of Concepts and Concept Possession 265

(iii) $(\forall x)\Box(\forall y)\, (\exists_{\text{actual}} v)\, v = [x = y]$.[6]

But, on the *in rebus* view, this implies:

$\Box(\exists y)\, y$ is actual.

That is, necessarily, everything (including everything that might have existed) is among the things that actually exist. Again, a false conclusion: clearly it is possible that there should have existed something which is not among the things that actually exist.[7] So, on both of its readings, the intuitively true sentence (i) entails falsehoods if the *in rebus* view is correct. So the *in rebus* view is incorrect. Of course, the underlying error is to think that things are literally *in* propositions. As Frege says (in "The Thought"): "[W]e really talk figuratively when we transfer the relation of whole and part to thoughts".

Now much the same sort of argument carries over *mutatis mutandis* to *post rem* theories of propositions, according to which propositions are some sort of mind–dependent psychological entity. This leaves the *ante rem* theory.[8]

---

[6]On an extensional–complex theory, (iii) might be represented thus:

$(\forall x)\Box(\forall y)\, (\exists_{\text{actual}} v)v = \langle x, \text{`identity'}, y\rangle$.

But, necessarily, a set is actual only if its elements are actual. So (iii) would imply:

$\Box(\forall y)\, y$ is actual.

I.e., necessarily, everything (including everything that might have existed) is among the things that actually exist. The same implausible consequence we are deriving in the text in a more general setting.

[7]Notice that the above argument is entirely consistent with actualism: I am not supposing that there are things which are not actual; I am only supposing that it is *possible* that there should have existed things which are not among the things that actually exist. Nowhere in the argument am I committed to the existence of nonactual possibilia, for the relevant quantifiers always occur within *intensional* contexts, viz., 'it is possible that', 'necessarily', etc. As such, these quantifiers have *no* range of values. E.g., that it is possible that there should have been more planets than there actually are does not entail that there are possible planets.

[8]The above transmodal considerations allow us to reach an even stronger conclusion: necessarily, if a proposition could exist, it actually exists; furthermore, every actual proposition exists necessarily. The argument goes as follows. Suppose that (ii) is true iff (iii) is true. Recall that either (ii) or (iii) or both must be true. Since one must true, both are true. But (iii) tells us that the relevant transmodal propositions are already actual, and (ii) tells us that they exist necessarily. If this holds for propositions of the sort relevant to (ii) and (iii), uniformity supports the conclusion that it holds for all propositions.

As for reductionism, most reductionist theories of propositions are either *in rebus* or *post rem* theories —for example, those which identify propositions with linguistic entities (in a natural language or a "language-of-thought") or with mental entities (mind–dependent conceptual entities) or with entities constructed from linguistic and/ or mental entities. So the foregoing argument leads to the conclusion that those reductionistic theories of propositions fail. (The foregoing does not count against the possible–worlds reduction of propositions, for possible–worlds reductionists may hold that the variables 'x' and 'y' in the argument range over possibilia. Although I believe that there are convincing objections to this sort of reduction, I do not have the space to give them here. But as far as the issue of modal status of propositions is concerned, possibilism leads to a view is similar to our actualist *ante rem* view. For according to possibilism, possible worlds and, in turn, propositions have a kind of prior existence resembling that asserted by the actualist *ante rem* view.)

Now, as I have said, propositions and concepts intuitively belong to the same general ontological type. So, absent an argument to the contrary, we are led to the conclusion that concepts, too, are *ante rem* entities. This conclusion is supported further by a theoretical consideration which emerges in the next section. According to the approach taken there, even though propositions are irreducible entities, they nevertheless have logical analyses. In those analyses, concepts play the role of *predicate entities*. Since these analyses give the *essence* of the propositions, concepts ought to have the same modal status as propositions.

So it remains to establish the supposition: (ii) is true iff (iii) is true. Here is the argument. First we show (iii) implies that, for all x, it is necessary that, for each y that is not now actual, the proposition that $x = y$ is already actual. If in our actual situation such transmodal propositions already exist, it would be odd in the extreme if in other possible situations analogous transmodal propositions did not exist as well. But (ii) implies that each contingent object x is such that, in every possible situation in which x does not exist, it is nevertheless the case that, for all y, the transmodal proposition that $x = y$ exists in that situation. But if this holds, (ii) would hold in its full generality: for any x (contingent or necessary), it is necessary that, for all y, the proposition that $x = y$ exists. The conclusion is that, if (iii) is true, it would be odd in the extreme if (ii) were not true as well. Analogous considerations show that the converse implication holds as well: that is, if (ii) is true, so is (iii). Note that this argument is given in the setting of actualism.

Although possibilists might not agree with the conclusion, they would accept something similar, for they grant to propositions a kind of prior existence.

2 The Nonreductionist Approach to Concepts and Propositions

Consider some truisms. The proposition that A & B is a conjunction of the proposition that A and the proposition that B. The proposition that not A is a negation of the proposition that A. The proposition that Fx is a predication of the concept of being F of x. The proposition that there exists an F is an existential generalization on the concept of being F. The proposition that everything is F is a universal generalization on the concept of being F. And so on. These truisms tell us what these propositions are essentially: they are by nature conjunctions, negations, predications, existential generalizations, universal generalizations, etc. These are rudimental facts which require no further explanation and for which no further explanation is possible.

It turns out that this nonreductionist point of view can be developed systematically by adapting algebraic logic to an intensional setting. To do this, one assumes that examples can serve to isolate fundamental logical operations —conjunction, negation, singular predication, existential generalization, and so forth— and one takes concepts and propositions as *sui generis ante rem* entities. The primary aim is then to analyze their behavior with respect to these fundamental logical operations. This may be done by studying what I call *intensional algebras*.[9] Within this setting, propositions have *logical analyses* (in terms of the inverses of the logical operations). On the picture that emerges, concepts may be defined as those noncontingent entities which play the role of predicate entities in the logical analysis of predicative and general fine-grained propositions.[10]

---

[9] This method was presented in "Theories of Properties, Relations, and Propositions" (1979), *Quality and Concept* (1982), and "Completeness in the Theory of Properties, Relations, and Propositions" (1983). Special issues of hyper–fine-grainedness are dealt with in "A Solution to Frege's Puzzle" (1993) and "Propositions" (1997). The main ideas of the nonreductionist algebraic approach were developed in my dissertation *A Theory of Qualities*, University of California at Berkeley, 1973.

[10] Can properties also play this role? The characterization in the text supposes that they cannot. Some philosophers, however, believe they can. On certain versions of their view, the characterization in the text would need to be refined. On one such version, for example, concepts are always distinct from properties even though properties can play the role indicated in the text. On this view, the characterization in the text should be modified thus: from the logical point of view, what distinguishes concepts from properties is that, whereas properties can

The algebraic approach can be extended to a more complex setting in which concepts and propositions, on the one hand, and properties, relations, and states of affairs (or conditions), on the other hand, are treated concurrently. In such a setting, moreover, a relation of correspondence between the two types of entities can be characterized in terms of the fundamental logical operations.[11] Concepts and propositions function as bearers of truth, logical truth, necessity, etc. and also as cognitive and linguistic contents. Properties, relations, and states of affairs (or conditions) play a fundamental constitutive role in the structure of the world.

Some philosophers (for example, Jerry Fodor and Robert Stalnaker) believe that, when theorizing about propositions, one is forced to make a hard choice between sentence–like hyper–fine–grained propositions, on the one hand, and bead–like hyper–coarse–grained propositions, on the other hand. This is a false dilemma, which is evidently engendered by the debate between those who would reduce propositions to functions on (or sets of) possible worlds and those who would use hypothetical languages–of–thought as the guide to propositional identity. No such choice must made. The right view is that there can be a whole spectrum of types of propositions, ranging from hyper–coarse–grained to hyper–fine–grained.[12] The algebraic approach was designed to be able to capture this sort of spectrum, that is, to be able to deal concurrently with such a spectrum of diverse granularities. These different granularities would be suited to various different roles they might play in logical theory, metaphysics, and psychological theory. In psychological theory, for example, hyper–coarse–grainedness might be relevant when belief acquisition and revision are treated as just (probabilistic) information flow; hyper–fine–grainedness might be relevant when belief acquisition and revision are treated as proof–like.

---

play a predicative role in the analysis of both propositions and states of affairs, concepts play such a role only in the analysis of propositions.

I should also note that there is a view on which certain concepts are no different from their corresponding properties. On this view, for example, simple concepts (i.e., those which have no logical form) are like this; e.g., in the case of a particular phenomenal shade, there is no difference between the concept and the property. The thing is presented directly to the mind under no aspect. If this view were correct, the characterization in the text would still be right but should be taken in this light.

[11] This two–tier picture was the picture developed in *Quality and Concept*.

[12] Propositions of an intermediate granularity, for example, would include those which, while sensitive to individual contents, are insensitive to various distinctions of form in the associated 'that'–clauses as long as those 'that'–clauses always yield necessarily equivalent outputs for the same content inputs.

Against this background we can characterize the notion of the *conceptual content* of a proposition:[13] If x belongs to every analysis of z (under the inverses of the logical operations whose values are of the same granularity as z), then x belongs to the conceptual content of z; and if x belongs to the conceptual content of y and y belongs to the conceptual content of z, then x belongs to the conceptual content of x.[14]

Everything I will say about concept possession is consistent with the view that there is a spectrum of diverse granularities. For heuristic purposes, however, let us adopt the assumption that there is only one type of proposition, namely, hyper–fine–grained propositions —or that there are only two types of proposition, namely, hyper–fine–grained propositions and hyper–coarse–grained propositions. Doing so will simplify our discussion at certain places.

3 The Propositional Attitudes

I come now to the propositional attitudes. Again, I will assume a traditional realism. First, with respect to the question of what propositional–attitude states *are*, I will assume the classical analysis: a subject is in the state of believing that P iff the subject stands in the relation of believing to the proposition that P; likewise, for other propositional–attitude states (states of desiring, remembering, etc.). This classical analysis of course doubles as an analysis of mental content: a mental state has the proposition that P as its content iff it consists of a subject standing in a propositional–attitude relation to the proposition that P.

How does this traditional realism bear on the analysis of concept possession? Although I personally adopt a nonreductionism about the attitudes,[15] my positive analysis of concept possession does not

---

[13]This notion of conceptual content is the natural generalization of the notion of the "intension" —or "comprehension"— of a concept, which was prominent in traditional logic. See my "Intensional Entities" (1998).

[14]Unlike hyper–fine–grained propositions, hyper–coarse–grained propositions can be analyzed infinitely many different ways (under the inverses of the relevant logical operations, i.e., the logical operations whose values are hyper–coarse–grained intensions). For every concept which appears in one of these analyses, there is always another analysis in which the concept does not appear. That is, no concept appears in every logical analysis of the proposition. This leads to the view that hyper–coarse–grained propositions do not have any specific conceptual content; from that point of view they are just "marbles" from which no specific conceptual content can be recovered.

[15]See "Mental Properties" (1994) and "Self–Consciousness" (1997).

presuppose this position. Nearly everything I have to say should be consistent with reductionism. What is crucial is this. Whether or not one accepts the nonreductionist point of view, one should feel free to adopt the traditional realist framework I have been sketching —specifically, realism about the modalities, concepts, propositions, and the standard propositional–attitude relations (believing, remembering, etc.). In the case of the most important kind of concept possession —what I will call *determinate concept possession*, or in common parlance, *understanding a concept*— analyses which do not take the attitudes as starting points (whether or not reducible) are doomed in my opinion. In this connection, the propositional attitude that will be most central to our analysis will be *intuiting*. (See below.) A related point is that, in an analysis of concept possession, one should feel free to admit other psychological notions such as those pertaining to the quality of the cognitive conditions —intelligence, attentiveness, memory, constancy, and so forth. Again, there will be nothing circular about this, and failure to admit them all but ensures that the analysis will fail. Remember that our goal will be to give a conceptual clarification of what it is to possess concepts in the various ways we do, not to give an ontological reduction of concept possession. In this connection, I will adopt a further thesis about the propositional–attitude relations, namely, that they are "natural" (*vs.* "Cambridge") relations.[16] Given the acceptability of this thesis, it should also be acceptable to take as a starting point an analogous thesis concerning the various ways in which we standardly possess concepts, namely, that they are "natural" modes of possession (*vs.* "Cambridge" modes). I will adopt this thesis as well. Given it, we may think of our project as follows: to locate, within the space of "natural" modes, various prominent ways in which we standardly possess concepts.

Incidentally, if reductionism fails (as I personally believe it does), adopting the proposed realist framework does not mean abandoning naturalism. After all, naturalism is not primarily a doctrine about reduction but rather *explanation* —that all occurrences[17] have explanations wholly within nature, that all causes are natural causes. There is no violation of naturalism if, in one's analysis of the various kinds of concept possession, one takes the modalities, concepts,

---

[16] I defend this thesis in "Self–consciousness". The distinction between "natural" and "Cambridge" properties and relations is defended at length in *Quality and Concept*.

[17] This might need to be qualified for the following reason: individual quantum occurrences might have no explanation, but presumably this would not refute naturalism.

propositions, the attitudes and other psychological notions as starting points, accepting that they may well be irreducible. For it is entirely consistent with naturalism to view mental occurrences as belonging to nature, as being real causes and effects in nature even if mental properties and relations are not reducible. On a related note, many philosophers think that, if reductionism fails, understanding concepts must amount to some kind of mystical "grasping". This is not so. Indeed, if (something like) my analysis proves successful, it will actually show by example that understanding concepts is not mystical at all.

4 Intuition

Our final preliminary point concerns intuition. It is uncontroversial to say that intuitions are frequently invoked in our standard justificatory practices. What do we mean by intuitions in this context? We do not mean a magical power or inner voice or a mysterious "faculty" or anything of the sort. For you to have an intuition that A is just for it to *seem* to you that A. Here 'seems' is understood, not as a cautionary or "hedging" term, but in its use as a term for a genuine kind of conscious episode. For example, when you first consider one of de Morgan's laws, often it neither seems to be true nor seems to be false; after a moment's reflection, however, something new happens: suddenly it *seems* true. Of course, this kind of seeming is *intellectual*, not sensory or introspective (or imaginative).

Intuition must be distinguished from belief: belief is not a seeming; intuition is. For example, there are many mathematical theorems that I believe (because I have seen the proofs) but that do not *seem* to me to be true and that do not *seem* to me to be false; I do not have intuitions about them either way. Conversely, I have an intuition —it still *seems* to me— that the naive truth schema holds; this is so despite the fact that I do not believe that it holds (because I know of the Liar paradox).[18] There is a rather similar phenomenon in sensory (*vs.* intellectual) seeming. In the Müller–Lyer illusion, it still *seems* to me that one of the arrows is longer than the other; this is so despite the fact that I do not believe that it is (because I have

---

[18] I am indebted to George Myro, in conversation in 1986, for a kindred example (the comprehension principle of naive set theory) and for the point it illustrates, namely, that it is possible to have an intuition without having the corresponding belief.

measured them). In each case, the seeming (intellectual or sensory) persists in spite of the countervailing belief.

Similar phenomenological considerations make it clear that intuitions are likewise distinct from judgments, guesses, hunches, and common sense. The final starting point I will adopt is the thesis that, like sensory seeming, intellectual seeming (intuition) is just one more *sui generis* propositional attitude. Incidentally, it is worth noting that the existence of the logical and semantical paradoxes shows that the classical modern infallibilist theory of intuition is incorrect. We shall be mindful of this fact in what follows.

Part II. Concept Possession

There are at least two different but related senses in which a subject can be said to possess (or have) a concept. The first is a nominal sense; the second is the full, strong sense. The first may be analyzed thus:

> A subject possesses a given concept at least nominally iff the subject has natural propositional attitudes (belief, desire, etc.) toward propositions which have that concept as a conceptual content.[19]

Possessing a concept in this nominal sense is compatible with what Tyler Burge calls misunderstanding and incomplete understanding of the concept. For example, in Burge's arthritis case, the subject misunderstands the concept of arthritis, taking it to be possible to have arthritis in the thigh. In Burge's verbal contract case, the subject incompletely understands the concept of a contract, not knowing whether contracts must be written. (Hereafter I will use 'misunderstanding' for cases where there are errors in the subject's understanding of the concept and 'incomplete' understanding for cases where there are gaps —"don't knows"— in the subject's understanding of the concept.) Possessing a concept in the nominal sense is also compatible with having propositional attitudes merely by virtue of

---

[19] If you question whether there really is this weak, nominal sense of possessing a concept, you may treat this as a stipulative definition of a technical term. Doing so makes no difference to my larger project. Incidentally, in the simplified setting in which all propositions are hyper–fine–grained we would have the following: x possesses a given concept *at least nominally* iff x has natural propositional attitudes (belief, desire, etc.) toward propositions in whose logical analysis the concept appears.

24. A Theory of Concepts and Concept Possession 273

attributions on the part of third-person interpreters. For example, we commonly attribute to animals, children, and members of other cultures various beliefs involving concepts which loom large in our own thought. And we do so without thereby committing ourselves to there being a causally efficacious psychological state having the attributed content which plays a role in "methodological solipsistic" psychological explanation. Our standard attribution practices, nonetheless, would have us deem such attributions to be correct. Advocates of this point of view hold that these attribution practices reveal to us essential features of our concept of belief (and, indeed, might even be constitutive of it). Everyone would at least agree that we could have a word 'believe' which expresses a concept having these features. In what follows, the theory I will propose is designed to be compatible with this practice-based view but will not presuppose it. These then are some weak ways in which a person can possess a concept. And there might be others belonging to a natural similarity class. This, too, is something which our theory will be designed to accommodate but not to presuppose.

With these various weak ways of possessing a concept in mind, we are in a position to give an informal characterization of possessing a concept in the full, strong sense:

> A subject possesses a concept in the full sense iff (i) the subject at least nominally possesses the concept and (ii) the subject does *not* do this with misunderstanding or incomplete understanding or just by virtue of satisfying our attribution practices or in any other weak such way.

In ordinary language, when we speak of "understanding a concept", what we mean is possessing the concept in the full sense. In what follows, this ordinary-language idiom will help to anchor our inquiry, and I will use it wherever convenient.[20] It will also be convenient

---

[20] It is not essential to our inquiry that the ordinary-language idiom fit exactly the informally characterized notion of possessing a concept in the full sense. If it does not, my eventual proposal should be viewed an analysis of the informally characterized notion. There is a long tradition of isolating a theoretically important notion informally by means examples and then turning to the theoretical project of giving a positive general analysis of it. Indeed, there is a tradition of doing this even when there is no ordinary-language idiom which exactly fits the notion in question. We see this kind of project in Aristotle in connection with the notions of substance, eudaimonia, etc.; in St. Augustine and Russell in connection with the notion of acquaintance; in Kripke in connection with his notion of epistemic possibility; and so forth. If need be, my project should be viewed in the same way. Having made this qualification, however, I will assume

to have available the technical term 'possessing a concept determinately', which is just another way of expressing the notion of understanding a concept (i.e., possessing a concept in the full sense).

Now just as a person can be said to understand a concept (that is, to possess it in the full sense, i.e., possess it determinately), a person can be said to misunderstand a concept and can be said to understand a concept incompletely and so on. Similarly, a person can be said to understand a proposition, to misunderstand a proposition, to understand a proposition incompletely, and so forth. For example, the person in Burge's arthritis case, not only misunderstands the concept of arthritis, but also misunderstands the proposition that he has arthritis in his thigh. Likewise, the person in Burge's contract example, not only understands incompletely the concept of a contract, but also understands incompletely the proposition that he has entered into a contract. And so forth. This suggests the following necessary condition: a subject *understands a proposition* only if the subject understands the concepts belonging to its conceptual content. And a sufficient condition: a subject *understands a proposition* if the subject knows a logical analysis of the proposition and understands the concepts appearing in that analysis. A jointly necessary and sufficient condition is much harder to come by. Now just as a subject can understand a proposition, a subject can misunderstand it, understand it incompletely, and so forth. As a terminological convenience, we will extend our earlier use of 'determinate' to the case of propositions. In this connection, we will allow associated adverbial forms. Accordingly, we will say that a subject understands a proposition determinately iff the subject does indeed understand the proposition; and we will say that a subject understands a proposition indeterminately iff the subject misunderstands it, understands it incompletely, or understands it just by virtue of satisfying our attribution practices or in some other weak such way.[21]

I have characterized determinate possession characterized informally —negatively and by means of examples. And we seem to have a fairly well established ordinary-language idiom for this notion. We readily see what it, and it seems clear that it is important theoret-

---

that the ordinary-language idiom does fit the notion of possessing a concept in the full sense, and I will proceed to use this idiom whenever convenient.

[21] Note that we will make an analogous use of the adverbials 'determinately' and 'indeterminately' in connection with the understanding of concepts: a subject understands a concept determinately iff the subject does indeed understand the concept; and a subject understands a concept indeterminately iff the subject misunderstands it, understands it incompletely, or understands it just by virtue of satisfying our attribution practices or in some other weak such way.

ically. It is therefore a legitimate philosophical project to try to give a positive general analysis of this notion. Indeed, it cries out for one. But there is no satisfactory general positive analysis in the philosophical (or psychological) literature. There are attempts to characterize what is, in effect, determinate possession of a particular concept (e.g., conjunction) or families of concepts (e.g., concepts of midsized perceptible physical natural kinds). We see such efforts in the work of Christopher Peacocke and Jerry Fodor, for example. But setting aside the question of whether such analyses are satisfactory as far as they go (I do not think that they are), we can see that they do not promise *generality*. What in general is it for someone to possess an arbitrary concept determinately —to understand it? Evidently, no extant approach suggests an answer. In what follows I will attempt to give one, at least in outline.

5 Examples

The purpose of this section is to consider a series of examples which serve to isolate some ideas which will play a role in the eventual analysis. To begin with, however, it is helpful to ask what general factors might be relevant to possessing concepts determinately. (1) Some theories feature the *functional* or *conceptual role* of the concept. On the usual versions, a person's concepts are uniquely fixed (or even implicitly defined) by the pattern they display in the beliefs which the person has or would have. (2) Some theories feature *causal* relations to relevant objects in the subject's immediate environment or in the environment of the subject's biological ancestors. (3) Other theories feature social or socio–linguistic relations; for example, the role the concept (or linguistic expression of the concept) plays in the beliefs (belief dispositions) and/or speech (speech dispositions) of the subject's whole community. (4) Other theories feature the naturalness (or salience) of the concept —either the inherent naturalness (salience) or its naturalness relative to the relevant environment or community. Each of these factors is relevant to a finished analysis. What I want to do now is to examine some examples in which a certain kind of conceptual role is prominent. One of the many ways in which this sort of conceptual role differs from that which is usually discussed is that it focuses on *intuitions* as opposed to beliefs. This difference will play a significant role in our eventual analysis.

The Platonist logician. This example is designed so that neither features of other people nor of the larger social, linguistic context are relevant. Nor are features of the environment. Nor are features such as salience, naturalness, metaphysical basicness.[22] Consider a Platonist logician whose practice is to jot down notes in a journal in the notation of the first-order predicate calculus. Through use, this man introduces a property-abstraction operator: if ⌜Ax⌝ is a formula with one free variable, ⌜$x(Ax)$⌝ is a singular term which denotes the property of being an x such that A. At no time, however, does he enrich his notation with an operation of propositional-abstraction, i.e., an operation that when applied to a sentence yields a singular term which denotes the proposition expressed by the sentence. Now, through use, our logician begins to write expressions of the form ⌜$[x(Ax)]$⌝. His patterns of use indicate that ⌜$[x(Ax)]$⌝ is a sentence, and his inferential patterns show that it is necessarily equivalent to the existential proposition that there exists an x such that Ax —and so, of course, that it is necessrily equivalent to the singular predicative proposition that the property of being an x such that A is manifest. But his uses do not settle what proposition ⌜$[x(Ax)]$⌝ expresses. Let us suppose that things are narrowed down to are two candidates: on the one hand, ⌜$[x(Ax)]$⌝ might be an existential generalization. Accordingly, ⌜$[x(\ )]$⌝ would be an existential quantifier —equivalent to ⌜$\exists x(\ )$⌝— which when applied to a formula ⌜Ax⌝ yields a sentence ⌜$[x(Ax)]$⌝, and, like ⌜$[\exists x(Ax)]$⌝, this sentence would express the proposition that there exists an x such that Ax. On the other hand, '[ ]' might function as a kind of predicative device. When applied to the property abstract ⌜$x(Ax)$⌝, '[ ]' yields a sentence ⌜$[x(Ax)]$⌝ which is a singular predication, not an existential generalization; accordingly, ⌜$[x(Ax)]$⌝ would express the proposition that the property of being A is manifested. Although this proposition is necessarily equivalent to the proposition that there exists an x such that Ax, they are not identical. Suppose that the person determinately understands the proposition that $[x(Ax)]$ and that this proposition is one of the two candidates just characterized. Now suppose the person were to consider the question of whether the proposition

---

[22] I expressly chose an example in which, at least in the context, the options were equally salient, equally natural, equally basic, equally useful, etc. The person already has available a notation for existential generalization ⌜$[\exists x(Ax)]$⌝, but it would not be unnatural to have a notational variant of it. At the same time, the person already has a notation for property abstraction, and it would be natural to have a notation for predicating a certain salient property which some of these properties have —namely, being manifested. I also chose this example so that I would avoid the debate over the possibility of "alternate conceptual schemes": the "conceptual scheme" associated with the envisaged notation is the same as ours; in the example, the "alternatives" are natural choices each of which is already available within our own conceptual scheme.

24. A THEORY OF CONCEPTS AND CONCEPT POSSESSION 277

that $[x(Ax)]$ is an existential generalization; or whether the proposition that $[x(Ax)]$ is a singular predication; or whether $\ulcorner[x(Ax)]\urcorner$ means that $\exists x(Ax)$; or whether $\ulcorner[x(Ax)]\urcorner$ means that the property of being A is manifested. Suppose that the person determinately understands all the test questions. Suppose that all the person's cognitive conditions (intelligence, attentiveness, memory, constancy, etc.) are wholly normal. Then, the person would intuit that the proposition that $[x(Ax)]$ is an existential generalization if and only if it is *true* that it is an existential generalization. Likewise, the person would intuit that the proposition that $[x(Ax)]$ is a singular predication if and only if it is *true* that it is a singular predication. And so forth. That is, the person's intuitions would be truth–tracking *vis-à-vis* such questions.

The cognitively and conceptually fit tribe. Consider a social variant on the above example, a tribe of beings whose (sole) language is syntactically just like the notation of our Platonist logician —that is, the first–order predicate calculus supplemented with property abstracts $\ulcorner x(A)\urcorner$ and sentences of the form $\ulcorner[x(Ax)]\urcorner$. As in the earlier example, a sentence of this form expresses the proposition that there exists an x such that A, or it expresses the proposition that the property of being A is manifested. Let us agree that just which proposition is expressed is a definite fact, and suppose that everyone in the tribe determinately understands this proposition. Suppose that in all relevant respects the tribe members are in cognitive conditions at least as good as the Platonist logician's. Suppose that they determinately understand all the test questions and that they consider the test questions attentively. Then, just as in the case of the logician, their intuitions would track the truth *vis-à-vis* these questions. That is, they would intuit that the proposition that $[x(Ax)]$ is an existential generalization if and only if it is *true* that it is an existential generalization. And so forth.

The conceptually deficient tribe. Suppose that we vary the example slightly. Suppose the cognitive conditions of the tribe (intelligence, attentiveness, memory, constancy, etc.) are as good as before. But suppose that the tribe members presently lack the conceptual resources to pose the indicated test questions. Whether the proposition that $[x(Ax)]$ is an existential proposition, or alternatively a predicative proposition, is nonetheless a definite objective fact. This is not the sort of distinction over which a language would be indeterminate; its semantic force is built into the elementary syntactic structure of the language. Suppose now that the tribe members eventually come to possess the relevant test concepts determinately (e.g., the concept of being an existential proposition, the concept of being a singular predicative proposition, etc.). Then, as in the previous example, the tribe members would have truth–tracking intuitions vis-à-vis the test questions, supposing that the quality of their cognitive cognitions remain consistently high and that throughout they continue to understand determinately the proposition that $[x(Ax)]$ and all the various test concepts.

The cognitively and conceptually deficient tribe. Let us modify the example slightly. Suppose that everything is as before except that this time the tribe members are cognitively limited: they are unable to acquire the test concepts, or if they do, they are unable to consider the specific test questions. When appropriate efforts are made to impart the concepts or to get them to entertain the test questions, they simply fall asleep. It turns out, however, that there are ways to improve their cognitive conditions (drugs, neurosurgery, or whatever). Suppose that this is done and that their cognitive conditions become exactly as good as those of the cognitively fit tribe. Suppose that they thereafter come to possess the test concepts determinately. Throughout the process they understand the proposition $[x(Ax)]$ determinately. Accordingly, they are able to understand the test questions determinately. Suppose, finally, that they consider the test questions. Then, just as in the previous case, they would have truth–tracking intuitions *vis-à-vis* these questions.

Nomologically necessary deficiencies. Let us modify the example one last time. Suppose that everything is as before except that the tribe members are irreversibly cognitively limited: it is not nomologically possible for the tribe members to consider any of the relevant test questions. It is nomologically necessary that, whenever modifications occur (e.g., drugs, neurosurgery, "brain meld", "body transfer", etc.) which might enable them to get into the relevant states, they slip into irreversible coma and die. Moreover, this limitation holds as a matter of nomological necessity for any (contingent) being inhabiting the world under consideration. Still, the semantic force —existential or predicative— of sentences of the form $\ulcorner[x(Ax)]\urcorner$ could be a definite objective fact for the tribe's language; as before, the semantic force of these sentences is built into the very syntax of the language. And the tribe members determinately understand what is meant when they write $\ulcorner[x(Ax)]\urcorner$.[23] Consistent with

---

[23] Some people believe that there must be a difference in the "hidden "syntactic processing" which would signal whether the proposition $[x(Ax)]$ is an existential generalization or, instead, a singular predication. That is, when the tribe members think this proposition, perhaps there must be an associated tokening of Mentalese sentences in their Thinking Boxes, where the "hidden syntactic forma-

24. A THEORY OF CONCEPTS AND CONCEPT POSSESSION 279

all of this, however, there is another metaphysical possibility: the tribe —or some tribe whose epistemic situation is qualitatively identical to that of the tribe— could thereupon be in improved cognitive conditions without there being any shift in the qualitative character of their epistemic situation. In particular, this improvement could happen without there being any (immediate) shift in the way they understand any of their concepts or the propositions involving them. In this situation, there would then be no barrier to the tribe coming to understand and to consider the test questions determinately. Intuitively, all this could happen. And, intuitively, if it did , just as in the foregoing examples, the tribe members would have truth-tracking intuitions *vis-à-vis* regarding these questions.

We have been considering a tribe for whom certain improved cognitive conditions are metaphysically possible even though they are not nomologically possible. For this particular example, we can be sure that the envisaged cognitive conditions are metaphysically possible, for *we* are beings in such cognitive conditions. However, this is only an artifact of the example. When we generalize on the above set-up, facts about actual human beings drop out. Thinking otherwise would be a preposterous form of anthropocentrism.

The moral is that, even though there might be a nomological barrier to there being intuitions of the sort we have been discussing, there is no metaphysically necessary barrier. (Remember: these intuitions need not be in the original tribe; they may be in population of beings whose epistemic situation is qualitatively identical to that of the original tribe.) This leads to the thought that determinate concept possession might be explicated (at least in part) in terms of the metaphysical possibility of truth-tracking intuitions in appropriately good cognitive conditions. The idea is that determinateness is that mode of possession which constitutes the categorical base of this possibility. When a subject's mode of concept possession shifts to determinateness there is an associated shift in the possible intuitions accessible to the subject. In fact, there is a shift in both quantity and quality. The quantity grows because incomplete understanding is replaced with complete understanding, eliminating "don't knows". The quality improves because incorrect understanding is replaced with correct understanding.

Before we proceed, a cautionary remark is in order. Our goal is to give an analysis of determinate possession. Our eventual analysis

---

tion history" of this token somehow reveals whether the sentence is existential or predicative and, in turn, whether the proposition is existential or predicative. But it is easy to construct counterexamples to this general proposal.

will be compatible with the idea that determinateness might come in degrees, achieved to a greater or lesser extent. What the analysis is aimed at is the notion of completely determinate possession. If you find yourself disagreeing with the analysis on some point or other, perhaps the explanation is that you have in mind cases involving something less than completely determinate possession.

6 Working Toward an Analysis

Al though we have isolated an idea on which we might base an analysis, we are still a great distance from having a finished proposal. The following are some of the problems we must first overcome: circularity, reliance on subjunctives (counterfactuals), possible absence of elementary cases, possible absence of decisive cases, radical holism, environmentalism, anti–individualism (including reliance on experts), the role of naturalness and salience, etc. In this section, I will propose a progression of analyses, each beset with a problem which its successor is designed to overcome —converging, one hopes, on a successful analysis.

Before I begin, a general remark about strategy is in order. I believe that the problems facing a general analysis of determinate concept possession are so difficult that any attempt to overcome them piecemeal (as some philosophers have tried to do) is beyond us. What are needed at least in some cases are philosophically neutral analytical devices which, when inserted into the analysis in the right ways, automatically provide the benefit of solutions without our actually having to produce the solutions explicitly. If we did not adopt this strategy, I believe that the analysis of concept possession would simply be too difficult at the current stage of our intellectual history.

a. Subjunctive analyses. I will begin with a final example. This time it will be a real–life example featuring the concept of being a polygon. Suppose x's possession of the concept of being a polygon is determinate in all respects expect perhaps those regarding whether or not triangles and rectangles are polygons. Suppose that *either* the property of being a polygon = the property of being a closed plane figure, *or* the property of being a polygon = the property of being a closed plane figure with five or more sides. Suppose x determinately possesses all relevant test concepts (the concept of being a triangle, the concept of being a rectangle, etc.). Suppose x is considering the test question of whether it is possible for a triangle or a rectangle to be a polygon.. Suppose x's cognitive conditions (intelligence, at-

24. A THEORY OF CONCEPTS AND CONCEPT POSSESSION   281

tentiveness, etc.) are entirely normal. Then, on analogy with our earlier considerations, we are led to the following:

x determinately possesses the concept of being a polygon iff:

x would have the intuition that it is possible for a triangle or a rectangle to be a polygon iff it is *true* that it is possible for a triangle or a rectangle to be a polygon.

In turn, this suggests the following:

x determinately possesses the concept of being a polygon iff:

x would have intuitions which *imply* that the property of being a polygon = the property of being a closed plane figure iff it is *true* that the property of being a polygon = the property of being a closed plane figure.

x determinately possesses the concept of being a polygon iff:

x would have intuitions which *imply* that the property of being a polygon ? the property of being a closed plane figure iff it is *true* that the property of being a polygon ? the property of being a closed plane figure.

x determinately possesses the concept of being a polygon iff:

x would have intuitions which *imply* that the property of being a polygon = the property of being a closed plane figure with five or more sides iff it is *true* that the property of being a polygon = the property of being a closed plane figure with five or more sides.

x determinately possesses the concept of being a polygon iff:

x would have intuitions which *imply* that the property of being a polygon ? the property of being a closed plane figure with five or more sides iff it is *true* that the property of being a polygon ? the property of being a closed plane figure with five or more sides.

These are all alike except that the right–hand sides run through the positive and negative forms of each of the relevant test property–identities.

In a context where we already know that x possess the target concept determinately in all respects except perhaps those which would decide these test property–identities and nonidentities, each is equally good; any one of them suffices. Suppose, however, that we remove the background supposition that x determinately possesses the target concept in all respects except perhaps those which would decide just these property–identities and nonidentities. We would then want to generalize on the above pattern. The natural generalization the following:

x determinately possesses the concept of being f iff, for arbitrary test property–identities $p(f)$:

x would have intuitions which imply $\pm p(f)$ iff $\pm p(f)$ is true.

Here '$p(f)$' is a "complex variable" intended to range over arbitrary property–identity propositions of following sort: the proposition that the property of being $f =$ the property of being A. And '$\pm p(f)$' has two functions —first, to pick out the positive form of $p(f)$ and, then, to pick out the negative form. Accordingly, the formula 'x would have intuitions which imply $\pm p(f)$ iff $\pm p(f)$ is true' should be read as follows: x would have intuitions which imply $p(f)$ iff $p(f)$ is true, and x would have intuitions which imply $\neg p(f)$ iff $\neg p(f)$ is true'.[24]

Suppose that we transform this proposal into a direct definition of *determinateness*, the mode of understanding involved when one understands determinately. We obtain the following:

determinateness = the mode m of understanding such that, necessarily, for all x and property–identities p which x understands m–ly,

$\pm p$ is true iff x would have intuitions which imply $\pm p$.

---

[24]Thus, x determinately possesses the concept of being f iff, for every test proposition to the effect that the property of being $f =$ the property of being A, x would have intuitions which imply this proposition iff this proposition is true, and x would have intuitions which imply the negation of this proposition iff the negation of this proposition is true.

In a fully finished presentation '$\pm p$' should be replaced with '$\pm_0 p$'. The effect of '0' is to allow for the prospect that p might fail to be truth–evaluable. In the framework of realism about propositions, concepts, and properties, this prospect might seem odd. But we should not dismiss the prospect of non–truth–evaluability in connection with certain kinds of vagueness (e.g., boundary questions concerning color concepts). When we allow for this, contraposition and the importation and exportation of negation do not behave classically. With these prospects in the offing, I will not in this paper attempt any simplifications in the clauses containing '$\pm p$'.

This, by the way, indicates how in general I want to deal with vagueness here: x's intuitions (suitably processed) should track the "contour of vagueness" as long as there is a definite fact of the matter at some order and as long as x's understanding is determinate.

24. A THEORY OF CONCEPTS AND CONCEPT POSSESSION 283

Notice that in this formulation we have shifted focus to determinate understanding of *propositions*. Determinate understanding of concepts will follow along automatically. I will return to that point at the close.

The purpose of transforming the analysis is tied to the problem of radical holism and the worry that an analysis of determinate understanding of a given concept might wrongly require determinate understanding of all concepts. To avoid this trap, we do not try to say directly what it takes to possess determinately a given concept f. Rather, we try to isolate a general feature of determinateness, namely, how it behaves with respect to arbitrary test property–identities. The proposal tells us that determinateness is that mode m of understanding that has a certain kind of truth–tracking stability *vis-à-vis* arbitrary m–understood test property–identities p. The idea is that it should be possible for a person to use intuitions to evaluate these test propositions in a truth–tracking fashion as long as the person continues to understand the test propositions m–ly (i.e., determinately). If too much misunderstanding or too much incomplete understanding of background concepts were to arise, however, that fact would flip the person out of his m–understanding (i.e., determinate understanding) of the test propositions. Thereupon, the truth–tracking character of the intuitions *vis-à-vis* the test propositions would lapse. How much is too much misunderstanding? How much is too much incomplete understanding? Radical holism threatens at this point because we do not know of a principled way to draw the line expressly and perhaps we never will. The proposed formulation —in terms of modes m— does the job automatically without our having to draw the line expressly. After all, given the truth of realism, there is a fact of the matter: too much misunderstanding of background concepts and/or too much incomplete understanding of background concepts —*whatever that amount turns to be* (we do not need to know)— would force x's understanding of p out of mode m. By quantifying over modes m of understanding we are able, without circularity, to invoke such facts of the matter in the analysis. And we can do so without invoking the analytic/synthetic distinction.[25] This is the first of our automatic labor–saving devices.

b. *A priori stability*. There is, however, an obvious objection to this analysis, namely, that it relies unacceptably on the subjunctive 'would'. The problems that result resemble those which often arise when one uses counterfactuals in a philosophical analysis. First, the

---

[25] I believe that the analytic/synthetic distinction would not, in any case, serve to draw the line in the right way. See my "Analyticity" (1998).

analysis directs us toward the intuitions x would have which *imply* an answer to p. What intuitions are these? Well, they are intuitions which x would have in response to specific question he might put to himself. But exactly what questions are those? The analysis is silent about this. Second, x's cognitive conditions (intelligence, attentiveness, memory, constancy) will greatly affect the intuitions x would have (in response to the questions he puts to himself). Indeed, if the questions are difficult and the level of the cognitive conditions low relative to them, x's intuitions could be prone to error, or x just might have no intuitions at all regarding them. Third, the value of subjunctive statements can shift relative to "possible worlds". One reason is that the laws (e.g., psychological laws) can vary from "world" to "world". But we are venturing an analysis, something that should be "world–neutral". For all these reasons, our use of subjunctive is unsatisfactory.

The solution is to retreat to a certain ordinary modal notion free of subjunctives. I will call this modal notion "*a priori* stability". I represent it thus: $\diamond x \vdash_m \pm p$. Read $\diamond x \vdash_m \pm p$ as follows:

it is possible for x (or a counterpart of x in a qualitatively equivalent epistemic situation[26] to go through an intuition–driven process in which x stably settles $\pm p$ understood m–ly.

When this purely modal notion is substituted for the offending subjunctive in the earlier analysis, we arrive at the following:

determinateness = the mode m of understanding such that, necessarily, for all x and property–identities p which x understands m–ly,

$\pm p$ is true iff $\diamond x \vdash_m \pm p$.

The next step is to get clear about the notion of *a priori* stability.

The best way to understand this notion is to begin with an informal characterization of the indicated intuition–driven process. At every point in this process, x is to understand the test proposition

---

[26] More precisely, this notion of qualitative epistemic counterpart is to be understood anti–individualistically: x and y are qualitative epistemic counterparts iff, for some whole population C and some whole population C', there is a one–one map f from C onto C' such that, for all u in C, u and $f(u)$ are in qualitatively the same epistemic situation and $y = f(x)$. Thus, arthritis–guy and tharthritis–guy are not qualitative epistemic counterparts. But water–guy on earth and twater–guy on twin–earth are. It is understood here, and elsewhere, that the populations C and C' are to be entire populations, not local groups such as those supporting dialects.

24. A THEORY OF CONCEPTS AND CONCEPT POSSESSION 285

p m–ly. At the outset of the process, x gathers intuitions regarding examples (actual and hypothetical) and *prima facie* plausible principles which seem to x to be relevant to whether p is true. Then, x seeks the best theoretical systematization of these intuitions. Next, x tests the resulting systematization —and its consequences ("theorems")— against further intuitions. The entire process is then repeated. Throughout, x seeks to expunge the potentially corrupting influence of *doxa*. At each stage (the best theoretical systematization of) x's previous intuitions might suggest new families of cases which might shed further light. In the course of this, x's intuitions might be "educated". It might also be that the acquisition of new concepts (recall the conceptually deficient tribe in our earlier example) would lead to significant new results. This kind of growth in x's conceptual repertory is to be pursued repeatedly.[27] At any given stage, x's best theoretical systematization of elicited intuitions might purport to settle, one way or the other, whether p is true.[28] At some later stage, however, the best theoretical systematization of x's intuitions might settle this question the other way. But, eventually, the process might stabilize on a single answer. That is, no matter how the process is continued after that —for example, no matter how x's conceptual repertory is enlarged and no matter what new cases are considered— the same answer is always reached. Suppose this kind of stability is reached.[29] Despite this initial stability, there might be another way to destabilize the answer. Suppose that throughout the process x's cognitive conditions (intelligence, attentiveness, memory, constancy, etc.) were of a certain quality. But surely it is at least metaphysically possible that x's cognitive conditions be better (recall the cognitively deficient tribe in our earlier example).[30] Conceivably, if x's cognitive conditions are better, however, the process does not

---

[27] Perhaps, as a nomological necessity, one's conceptual repertory cannot increase beyond a certain point. No matter, we are talking about metaphysical possibility. Moreover, it does not matter that it be the very same individual who carries on the process. Anyone would do as long as the person is a qualitative epistemic counterpart of x.

[28] Or it might deem the question to have no a definite answer; see note 24.

[29] It is not required that the theoretical systematization be a recursively specified (or specifiable) theory. It might instead be a body of beliefs such that the associated body of intuitions would serve to justify those beliefs.

[30] Perhaps, as a nomological necessity, one's cognitive conditions cannot increase beyond a certain level. No matter, we are talking about metaphysical possibility here. Moreover, it does not matter that it be the very same individual whose cognitive conditions improve. It could be anyone as long as that person is a qualitative epistemic counterpart of x.

stabilize, or if it does, it stabilizes on a different answer.[31] Even so, perhaps there is a still higher level of cognitive conditions such that, once that level is reached, the process always stabilizes, and it always stabilizes on the same answer. That is, no further improvement in the cognitive conditions produces an instability.[32] In this event, the indicated answer is *a priori stable*.[33]

Strictly speaking, the entire informal characterization of the intuition-driven process plays only a heuristic role. The strictly correct, and most neutral, way to characterize *a priori* stability is simply to quantify over the processes x might go through in an attempt to settle p using intuitions as the evidential base. At some level of cognitive conditions (which ensures x's rationality) and equipped with some appropriate conceptual repertory (which ensures that x is able to think of the right things to do —e.g., gather evidence, form theories, etc.), x will eventually do the right thing. For heuristic purposes, however, it will be helpful to continue to think in terms of the informal characterization.

With remarks in mind I offer the following definition:

$$x \vdash_m \pm p \text{ iff}_{\text{def}} (\exists l)(\exists c)(x\, l\, c \models_m \pm p \ \& \ \Box(\forall l' > l)(\forall c' > c) \ x\, l'\, c' \models_m \pm p).$$

Using the informal characterization, we would read the right-hand side as follows: for cognitive conditions of some level l and some conceptual repertory c, (1) x has cognitive conditions of level l and conceptual repertory c and x attempts to elicit intuitions bearing on p and x seeks a theoretical systematization based on those intuitions and that systematization affirms that p is true (or p is not true) and all the while x understands p m–ly, and (2) necessarily, for cognitive conditions of any level l' greater than l and any conceptual

---

[31] An analogy will help. Maybe, to begin with, x has a mistaken intuition regarding the Barber Paradox: maybe has an intuition that there could be someone who shaves everyone who does not shave himself and who shaves no one else. But, if x's intelligence were to increase, x might be able to intuit straight off that such a barber is impossible.

[32] We do not take a stand on the question of the possibility of infinitary intelligence on the part of x (or counterparts of x). If this were possible, so be it. In that case, however, we would have to adjust our understanding of what would be the best theoretical systematization of x's intuitions. For example, it almost certainly would not be recursive. But it would presumably need to have various other standard theoretical virtues —consistency, explanatoriness, ontological economy, etc.

[33] For a sufficiently elementary test proposition p (e.g., red = red), *a priori* stability might be easy to achieve. We need not judge this question.

24. A THEORY OF CONCEPTS AND CONCEPT POSSESSION 287

repertory c' which properly includes c, if x has cognitive conditions of level l' and conceptual repertory c' and x attempts to elicit intuitions bearing on p and seeks a theoretical systematization based on those intuitions and all the while x understands p m–ly, then that systematization affirms that p is true (or p is not true).[34]

A diagram can be helpful here.

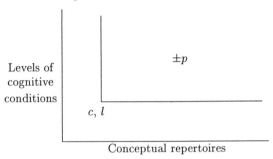

The idea is that, after x achieves c, l, the theoretical systematizations of x's intuitions always yield the same verdict on p as long as p is m–understood throughout. That is, as long as p is m–understood, p always gets settled the same way throughout the region to the northeast of c, l.

Return now to the analysis:

determinateness = the mode m of understanding such that, necessarily, for all x and property–identities p which x understands m–ly,

True $\pm p$ iff $\diamond x \vdash_m \pm p$.

The biconditional divides into two parts:

True $\pm p \rightarrow \diamond x \vdash_m \pm p$

and

True $\pm p \leftarrow \diamond x \vdash_m \pm p$.

The former is a *completeness* property: for every m–understood property–identity p, if $\pm p$ is true, it is possible for x to settle with *a priori* stability that $\pm p$ is true, all the while understanding p m–ly.

---

[34] When I speak of higher level cognitive conditions, I do not presuppose that there is always commensurability. In order for the proposal to succeed, I need only consider levels of cognitive conditions l' and l such that, with respect to every relevant dimension, l' is definitely greater than l.

The latter is a *correctness* (or soundness) property: if it is possible for x to settle with *a priori* stability that $\pm p$ is true, all the while understanding p m–ly, then $\pm p$ is true. The completeness property tells us about the potential *quantity* of x's intuitions, given that x m–understands p: it is possible for x to have enough intuitions to reach *a priori* stability regarding the question of p's truth, given that x m–understands p. And the correctness property tells us about the potential *quality* of x's intuitions, given that x m–understands p: it is possible for x to get into a situation such that from then on x's intuitions yield only the truth regarding p, given that x m–understands p. According to the analysis, determinateness is that mode of understanding which constitutes the categorical base for the possibility of intuitions of this quantity and quality.

The notion of *a priori* stability is another example of the sort of automatic labor–saving device mentioned at the outset. Many property–identity questions are significant philosophical questions in their own right. On several approaches to the problem of concept possession, those questions must be answered *before* the analysis can be formulated. For this reason, these approaches put success out of our reach, perhaps indefinitely. By contrast, on our approach we include, in the analysis itself, quantification over those very intuition–driven processes whereby such questions might eventually be answered (if only by persons in cognitive conditions superior to ours). The idea is that, by speaking in a general way about *a priori* stable answers, we obtain the *benefit* of having answers without actually having to obtain the answers ourselves. Short of some such automatic labor-saving device, I am afraid that the analysis of determinate concept possession would have to await another era.

There is a residual question regarding the restriction to property-identities p. Concerning this restriction, the formulation might be exactly right just as it stands. On a certain view of properties, however, an additional qualification would be needed. I have in mind the view according to which (1) all necessarily equivalent properties are identical and (2) for absolutely any formula ⌜A⌝, all expressions of the form ⌜the property of being an x such that A⌝ denote properties no matter how *ad hoc* and irrelevant ⌜A⌝'s subclauses might be. On this view, for example, the following would be true if God exists:

(i) The property of being a tomato = the property of being a tomato and such that God exists.

And the following would be true if God does not exist:

(ii) The property of being a tomato = the property of being a tomato and such that God does not exist.

Thus, if both (1) and (2) hold and the above analysis contains no further qualification on test propositions p, the completeness clause in the analysis would require that it be possible to settle *a priori* whether God exists or not. Although there is a tradition supporting this possibility —namely, *a priori* existence proofs and *a priori* nonexistence proofs— such proofs are controversial, to say the least. Of course, if God does exist, the possibility of someone (i.e., God) settling the question *a priori* would be realized. In fact, God would presumably know this intuitively. But, if God does not exist, the question could well be open as far as *a priori* considerations are concerned. It is this prospect that is disturbing. Because of it, it is desirable to have a way to restrict the property–identities p. There are four cogent ways to do this. The first is to invoke a logical theory on which conditions (1) or (2) or both fail and on which (i) and (ii) can therefore be denied without taking a stand on God's existence. There are some interesting arguments supporting certain logical theories of this variety. The second way is to accept (1) and (2) but to adopt an enriched logical theory which is able to mark the distinction between property–identities which are *ad hoc* in the indicated way and those which are not. There are already at least two elegant examples of this sort of theory in the literature —Michael Dunn's application of relevance logic and Kit Fine's logic for the notion of essence.[35] The third way is to formulate an analysis, in terms already available to us, of the indicated notion of *ad hoc*–ness. After all, nearly every philosopher, at some point or other, has a need for marking a distinction quite like the one we need to solve the current problem. The fourth way is simply to take the indicated notion of *ad-hoc*–ness as primitive, at least provisionally. There would be no threat of circularity in doing so: this notion does not presuppose the notion of determinate understanding, which we are trying to analyze. Surely, one of these four ways is successful.

 c. *Accommodating scientific essentialism*. There is, nonetheless, a serious problem with the completeness clause in the above analysis of determinateness —namely, scientific essentialism (SE). This is the doctrine that there are necessary truths that are essentially *a posteriori*. For example, the property of being water = the property of being H_2O. The argument consists of two steps. First, pro–SE intuitions supporting the property–identity are elicited. (In all known cases, these intuitions either are or can be reworked into twin–earth style intuitions.) Second, it is shown that there is a cer-

---

[35] Michael Dunn, "Relevant Predication 2: Intrinsic Properties and Internal Relations" (1990). Kit Fine, "Essence and Modality" (1994).

tain rephrasal strategy that can be used to deflate the force of our anti–SE intuitions but not our pro–SE intuitions and, in addition, that there is no rephrasal strategy which has the opposite effect. If both steps succeed (as I believe they do), we have a straightforward counterexample to the analysis.

Plainly, the completeness clause in the analysis goes too far. Something weaker is needed. To see what it is, let us begin informally. Consider the following truisms: two is a number; qualities are properties; a gram is a quantity; water is a stuff; etc. These truisms serve to identify the general categories of the relevant items. For the moment I will take the liberty of using the part/whole metaphor in connection with concepts. Let us separate the "parts" (i.e., entailments) of a concept into two classes —the categorial "parts" and the non–categorial "parts". These "parts" are just certain properties which are entailed by the property corresponding to the concept. For example, the property that corresponds to the *concept* of being water is the *property* of being water. The property of being water entails the property of being a stuff (i.e., necessarily, whatever has the former property has the latter). I will say that the latter property is a categorial "part" of the concept of being water. (I believe that there are many others.) Similarly, the property of being water entails the property of containing hydrogen. I will say that the latter property is a noncategorial "part" of the concept of being water. (Again, there are others.)

The fact that the property of being a stuff is a categorial "part" of the concept of being water is manifested in two ways (corresponding to the two steps in SE arguments). First, in a standard twin–earth set–up, the property of being water$_{\text{twin earth}}$ is the property on twin–earth which is the counterpart of the property of being water on earth. Like the latter, the former also entails the property of being a stuff. That is, necessarily, water$_{\text{twin earth}}$ is a stuff. Second, consider the proposition that water is a stuff. In the mental life of twin–earthlings, the proposition that water$_{\text{twin earth}}$ is a stuff is the counterpart of this proposition. Thus, the indicated categorial "part" of the concept of being water shows up in the thought of twin–earthlings in the same way it does in our thought. My view is that, when the notion of a categorial "part" of a concept is suitably defined, truths about the categorial "parts" of a concept are immune to scientific essentialism and, instead, are open to *a priori* discovery. By contrast, consider a noncategorial "part" of the concept of being water, say, the property of containing hydrogen. It is guaranteed to have none of these features. It certainly is subject to SE and off–limits to *a priori* discovery.

24. A Theory of Concepts and Concept Possession

How does this bear on the analysis of determinateness? The idea is that the completeness clause should be weakened so that it does not require that it be possible to settle with *a priori* stability every m–understood property–identity p. Instead, the completeness clause should only require that it be possible to settle with *a priori* stability those property entailments which are categorial "parts" of the associated concepts.[36]

I believe that the appropriate notion of the categorial "parts" will have to be far more robust than the above simple examples indicate. (See below for the reasons.) You might disagree; you might even think that the notion should be less robust. How robust does it in fact need to be? Well, it must include everything that needs to be available to determinate possessors of the target concept. How much is that? We could try to spell out an answer by studying various families of representative cases and, then, looking for a generalization. But this path threatens to be another one of those huge philosophical projects which we cannot hope to finish in the foreseeable future. What is needed, therefore, is one of our automatic labor–saving devices that achieves the benefit of having the answer without our actually having to produce it. I know of two such devices that do the job. The one I will present here has the advantage of being readily applicable; that is, the resulting class of test propositions p will be immediately identifiable. So, when *we* are in the role of x, we will know what sort of thing would need to be done *vis-à-vis* trying to establish our own determinate understanding.[37]

---

[36] One worry is that this proposal might have to presuppose the possibility of infinitary intelligence. This would be so if it turned out that there is no clear way to draw the line between those entailed properties over which a determinate possessor should have a possible *a priori* command and other entailed properties. Plausibly, this worry could be met in a way akin to the way the analogous problem is dealt with in the case of property identities. See the closing paragraph of the previous subsection.

[37] The second method (discussed in *Philosophical Limits of Science*) is to implement a notion which I call *modal stability*: a proposition p is modally stable iff, necessarily, for any proposition p' and any pair of populations C and C' whose epistemic situations are qualitatively identical, if p' in C' is the qualitative epistemic counterpart of p in C, then p and p' have the same modal value (necessary, impossible, contingent). The idea is to restrict the test propositions p in the analysis to modally stable propositions of the following sort: the property of being F entails the property of being A. It is required further that, associated with this sort of property-entailment proposition p, there must be a non-*ad-hoc* property–identity proposition q of the following sort: for some B, the property of being F = the property of being A & B. The intention is that q is to be the sort of non-*ad-hoc* test property-identity proposition discussed at the close of

The idea is to build the analysis so that the following holds for arbitrary test property–identities p. It should be possible that any determinate possessor be able to settle with *a priori* stability whether there is some property–identity p' which is an *epistemic counterpart* of p which is true (false, or neither) —whichever is in fact the case for p itself. For example, the following are epistemic counterparts: (1) the proposition that the property of being water = the property of being a stuff constituted of H_2O and (2) the proposition that the property of being water$_{\text{twin earth}}$ = the property of being a stuff constituted of $H_{\text{twin earth}} 2_{\text{twin earth}} O_{\text{twin earth}}$. Of course, this example deals with just one relevant property–identity p. Determinate possession requires the analogous possibility for every m–understood property–identity concerning the property of being water. Taken together, these possibilities serve to ensure the sort of command of the categorial "parts" of the target concepts that are necessary for possessing it determinately.

We thus arrive at the following revised analysis:

determinateness = the mode m of understanding such that, necessarily, for all x and property–identities p m–understood by x,

(a) True $\pm p \leftarrow \diamond x \vdash_m \pm p$

(b) True $\pm p \rightarrow \diamond x \vdash_m (\exists p' \in CP(p))$ True $\pm p'$.

The restricted quantifier '$(\exists p' \in CP(p))$' is to be read as follows: for some p' which is a qualitative epistemic counterpart of p. And the notion of a qualitative epistemic counterpart is defined thus:

p' is a qualitative epistemic counterpart of p iff$_{\text{def}}$ it is possible that, for some population C, it is possible that, for some population C', C' is in qualitatively the same epistemic situation as C and p' in C' is the counterpart of p in C.

In symbols:

$p' \in CP(p)$ iff$_{\text{def}}$ $\diamond(\exists C) \diamond (\exists C')C'$ is in qualitatively the same epistemic situation as C and p' in C' is the counterpart of p in C.

---

the previous section; if it is, p then inherits from q an associated non–*ad–hoc*-ness. In our metaphorical vocabulary, the property of being A plays the role of a test categorial "part" of the concept of being F, and the property of being B tags along either in the role of a noncategorial "part" or in the role of an additional categorial "part".

24. A Theory of Concepts and Concept Possession

This revised analysis solves the problem associated with the categorial "parts" of our concepts.

Before proceeding, note that there is an important family of test propositions p which are entirely immune to scientific essentialism, namely, those which I call *semantically stable*: p is semantically stable iff, necessarily, for any proposition p' and any pair of populations C and C' whose epistemic situations are qualitatively identical, if p' in C' is the qualitative epistemic counterpart of p in C, then $p = p'$.[38] (There is of course an analogous notion of a *semantically stable concept*. These notions were isolated in "Mental Properties" and examined further in "*A Priori* Knowledge and the Scope of Philosophy" and "On the Possibility of Philosophical Knowledge".) Thus, if p is a semantically stable proposition, the qualified completeness clause (b) in the revised analysis entails the unqualified completeness clause (b) from the earlier analysis:

(b) True $\pm p \rightarrow \Diamond x \vdash_m \pm p$ (for property–identity p).

This fact is significant philosophically. For most of the central propositions in the *a priori* disciplines —logic, mathematics, and philosophy— are semantically stable and, therefore, are immune to scientific essentialism. (This theme is explored further in the paper just mentioned and in *Philosophical Limits of Science*.)

Return now to the question, posed above, of how robust the categorial "parts" of our concepts must be. In the case of our semantically stable concepts, the answer is now clear —very robust. What about our semantically unstable concepts? These are the concepts for which scientific essentialism holds: for example, natural–kind concepts such as the concept of being water, the concept of being gold, etc. Semantic instability has to do with the effects of the external environment. An expression is semantically unstable iff the external environment makes some contribution to its meaning. Some people think that the categorial "parts" of such concepts are quite anemic, perhaps even vacuous. But there is good reason to think that this view is mistaken.

The reason is that there are patterns in our twin–earth intuitions that would defy explanation if the categorial "parts" of our semantically unstable concepts were not quite robust. Here is an example taken from "Philosophical Limits of Scientific Essentialism" (a range of others are given there as well). You and I have a vivid twin–earth

---

[38] Semantically stable propositions form a proper subclass of the modally stable propositions (just characterized).

intuition for water: if all and only water here on earth is composed of H_2O, then on a twin earth a stuff which has all the macroscopic properties of water (drinkable, thirst–quenching, etc.) but which is composed of XYZ ($\neq H_2O$) would *not* qualify as water. But you and I lack the corresponding twin–earth intuition for drink; indeed, we have the contrary intuition: even if all and only drink on earth is composed of certain specific hydrocarbons ABC, on a twin earth a stuff which has all the macroscopic properties of drink (potable, thirst–quenching, etc.) but which is composed of UVW ($\neq$ ABC) *would* nonetheless qualify as drink. What accounts for the difference?

No doubt the answer begins with the fact that water is a compositional stuff whereas drink is a functional stuff (drink is *for* drinking and quenching thirst).[39] But how does the compositional/functional distinction help to explain the curious asymmetry in our intuitions? The answer is that the associated properties *somehow* figure in the categorial "parts" of the respective concepts, the concept of being water and the concept of being drink. The simplest way would be that the property of being a compositional stuff is straight–away a categorial "part" of the concept of being water and, as such, could be known *a priori* (via our intuitions) to be the ontological category of water. But this would be too hasty.

To see why, notice that we have a wealth of other twin–earth intuitions which go against this idea. Here are a few illustrative examples. If [like jade] all and only water here on earth falls into two (or twenty) distinct kinds whose instances, respectively, are samples of UVW and XYZ, then on a twin earth a stuff whose instances are composed of XYZ *would* qualify as a *kind* of water. If [like live coral or caviar] all and only water here on earth is composed entirely of certain micro–organisms, then on a twin earth a stuff which contains no micro–organisms whatsoever but which nevertheless contains the same chemicals as those found in samples of water on earth would *not* qualify as water.[40] If every disjoint pair of samples of water here on earth have different microstructural compositions but they nevertheless have uniform macroscopic properties, then on a twin earth a stuff which has those same macroscopic properties *would* qualify as water. And so on.

---

[39] I introduced this puzzle and the compositional–stuff/functional–stuff distinction in "Philosophical Limits of Scientific Essentialism".

[40] Analogy: Suppose that you kill the live coral, crush the result, and reconfigure the remaining powder into a rock–like "reefs". Now synthesize a chemically equivalent rock–like material and configure it into "reefs" on twin earth. Is it coral? So what about "live water"?

24. A Theory of Concepts and Concept Possession

Further interesting phenomena emerge when we explore twin–earth intuitions involving other semantically unstable concepts. For example, twin–earth intuitions concerning drink have a pattern of their own, which is distinctively different from that of these various twin–earth intuitions concerning water. (Like the concept of arthritis, I take it that the concept of drink has some semantic instability.)

If we continue this sort of survey, it emerges that our concepts fall into types, members of which display similar sorts of patterns. The explanation of this typology is that the respective concepts share something robust —namely, substantive categorial "parts". (Should we be worried that we cannot, within our current philosophical theories, readily say exactly what these categorial "parts" are? Not at all. For we know that they are needed to explain a robust phenomenon.[41] We are thus led to the following conclusion: categorial mastery is a necessary condition for the determinate possession of our concepts, and from one type of concept to another there are robust differences in what the requisite categorial mastery consists in.

d. Accommodating anti–individualism. By weakening the completeness clause (b) to avoid clashing with scientific essentialism, we have created a predictable problem having to do with the non–categorial "parts" of our concepts. Suppose x is in command of nothing but the categorial "parts" of a certain pair of concepts, say, the concept of being a beech and the concept of being an elm. He would then be in a position resembling that of Hilary Putnam, who was entirely unable to distinguish beeches from elms. In this case, x would certainly not possess these concepts determinately. A symptom of his incomplete mastery would be his complete inability —*without relying on the expertise of others*— even to begin to do the science of beeches and elms. What is missing, of course, is that x's "web of belief" is too sparse. An analogous problem would arise if x were too often to classify beeches as elms —and/or conversely.

---

[41]Personally, I believe that in the case of concepts like the concept of being water the underlying categorial property is equivalent to a conjunction of default conditionals. The property of being a compositional stuff figures prominently in some of those conditionals, but other categorial properties figure with equal prominence in others. The categorial is conditional.

Even if vagueness and other pathologies infects these conjunctions of default conditionals, that does not undermine the prospect of a neat general typology for the indicated categorial "parts". After all, various semantically stable properties (maybe even justice or knowledge) can be like this, too; that should not lead us to think that they are not Forms.

What is needed for determinate possession is that x's web of belief be improved in appropriate ways. But what in what ways? The problem is that a huge (perhaps infinite) variety of quite different sorts of improvements would suffice. Can we say what is common to them? Once again, we are confronted with a challenge pretty much as difficult as the challenge of analyzing determinate concept possession itself. Indeed, there might be no stateable *direct* characterization of the sort of web of belief needed for determinateness. To solve our problem, we need another one of our automatic labor–saving devices which provides the benefit of a solution without our actually having to produce one. The idea of *truth–absorption* does the job.

Here is the idea. People who determinately possess their concepts can absorb ever more true beliefs without switching out of their determinate possession. Consider, by contrast, people who while having a categorial mastery of their concepts are nonetheless suffering from some form of indeterminateness. They cannot absorb ever more truths without switching out of their deficient modes of understanding, coming thereby to possess their concepts determinately.

Thus, we arrive at the following:

determinateness = the mode m of understanding such that, necessarily, for all x and all p m–understood by x,

(a) True $\pm p \leftarrow \diamond x \vdash_m \pm p$

(b.i) True $\pm p \rightarrow \diamond x \vdash_m (\exists p' \in CP(p))$ True $\pm p'$ (for property–identity p)

(b.ii) True $\pm p \rightarrow \diamond x$ believes $\pm p$ m–ly (for p believable by x).[42]

(Incidentally, maybe 'believes' should be strengthened to 'rationally believes' and p restricted to propositions which x can rationally believe. Remember: rational belief can be based on the testimony of a trusted informant —an "empirical oracle", if you will.)

In this analysis the completeness property divides into two components —(b.i) which deals with the categorial "parts" and (b.ii) which deals with the noncategorial "parts". So the analysis has this form:

determinateness = the mode m of understanding with the following properties:

(a) correctness

---

[42]Because there is no evident problem with the correctness clause but only the completeness clauses, we impose the restrictions on test propositions only there.

24. A THEORY OF CONCEPTS AND CONCEPT POSSESSION 297

(b) completeness
  (i) categorial mastery
  (ii) noncategorial mastery.

But this raises a question. Once (b.ii) is added, is (b.i) really needed? That is, given the truth–absorption clause, is a separate categorial-mastery clause really needed?

Suppose, on the one hand, that the truth–absorption clause does not entail the categorial–mastery clause. Then, it must be possible that x should absorb any number of relevant truths involving a certain concept (e.g., the concept of being water) and yet not be able (even as metaphysical possibility) to settle with *a priori* stability relevant test questions (e.g., whether there is a true epistemic counterpart of the proposition that the property of being water = the property of being a compositional stuff whose instances are composed of H_2O). That is, it must be possible that x should come to believe any number of relevant truths concerning water and yet not be able (even as metaphysical possibility) to have the twin–earth style water intuitions of the sort that would settle the question. If it really were metaphysically *impossible* for x^{43} to have such intuitions about water, would you want to say that x determinately possesses the concept of being water? Certainly not. So, on the assumption that the truth–absorption clause does not entail the categorial–mastery clause, we have no choice but to include the categorial–mastery clause in the analysis.

Suppose, on the other hand, that the truth–absorption clause does entail the categorial–mastery clause. Then the latter is not needed to make the analysis *acceptable*. But the analysis would still have the *implications* it would have if the completeness clause had been explicitly included. This is the conclusion I will need for the closing section. I suspect, however, that there are counterexamples to this entailment. My reason derives from a point raised in section 1, namely, the relative independence of intuition and belief. The idea is that x might acquire rote beliefs (based on texts he trusts) without those beliefs finding their way into his intuitions.[44] We already know that (from the Liar–Paradox case) that belief and intuition can be independent. The idea is that x's rote beliefs might co–exist with gaps or mistakes in x's categorial intuitions. In this case, we would

---

[43] And every counterpart of x in a qualitatively identical epistemic situation.

[44] To get a tight match–up with intuitions, beliefs need to be of a very special sort. What sort? Well, the sort that are based evidentially on (suitably processed) intuitions!

not want to say that x determinately possesses the relevant concepts; rather, he incompletely understands or misunderstands one or more of them. So we have an example in which x would have truth-absorption without categorial mastery (for m = incomplete understanding or m = misunderstanding).

Why, then, do improvements in the web of belief suffice to eliminate indeterminateness in the usual beech/elm cases? The reason is that (given the truth of scientific essentialism) there can be nothing else in which determinateness could consist in cases like this; the question of whether this is a beech or an elm is simply beyond the ken of *a priori* intuition. Absent intuition, web of belief is the default position on which determinateness rides. But when there are *a priori* intuitions, they prevail.

e. Determinateness as the genus of jointly correct and complete modes. There remains a refinement which might need to be made in our analysis. We have identified determinateness as *the* mode m of understanding that has both the completeness and correctness properties. I believe that there is not just one mode m like this. Here is an easy example (though I am not committed to it): if there is a relation of acquaintance like that posited in traditional epistemology, there is presumably an associated mode of understanding (i.e., x understands y acquaintedly or through acquaintance). If there are such modes of understanding, they would be species of a genus, and that genus would be the general mode of understanding, determinateness.

To accommodate this possibility, we should revise the analysis one last time:

determinateness = the genus of modes m of understanding such that, necessarily, for all x and all p m–understood by x,

(a) True $\pm p \leftarrow \diamond x \vdash_m \pm p$

(b.i) True $\pm p \rightarrow \diamond x \vdash_m (\exists p' \in CP(p))$ True $\pm p'$ (for property–identity p)

(b.ii) True $\pm p \rightarrow \diamond x$ believes $\pm p$ m–ly (for p believable by x).

Should it turn out that there are no species of determinateness, this analysis would still be acceptable assuming that it is taken the right way.[45]

---

[45] I.e., determinateness $=_{\text{def}}$ the mode m of understanding such that, for each mode m' of understanding which entails m, m' satisfies the rest of the analysis. Of course, these modes m' need to be "natural" modes of understanding.

A final point. In the course of our discussion, we found it convenient to shift from our focus from determinate understanding of concepts to determinate understanding of propositions. The analysis of the former notion, however, has always been only a step away:

x determinately possesses a given concept iff$_{\text{def}}$ x determinately understands a proposition which has that concept as a conceptual content.

We have ventured an analysis of determinate understanding. As noted at the end of section 5, the analysis is compatible with the idea that determinateness might come in degrees, achieved to a greater or lesser extent. What the analysis is aimed at is the notion of completely determinate understanding. If you find yourself questioning the analysis on some point or other, perhaps the explanation is that you have in mind examples involving something less than completely determinate understanding.

The following is an illustration. Suppose you question whether it is metaphysically possible to reach *a priori* stable answers to certain difficult mathematical property–identities. The analysis does not take a stand on whether you are right. Rather the analysis tells us what we should say *if* you are right. Namely, *if* it is metaphysically *impossible* to reach *a priori* stable answers to such mathematical questions, the right thing to say is that the questions themselves are not determinately understood. Conceivably, such a thing might arise in connection with the continuum hypothesis, for example. If *a priori* stable answers are really metaphysically impossible, the right thing to say is that the concept of being a set or the concept of set–membership is not determinately understood, not completely. Perhaps the understanding is always dancing around a cloud of relevant concepts, never permanently coming to rest on any one of them. Although such a thing would be intellectually disturbing, it would not be intolerable.

At this point it would be useful to show how various candidate counterexamples are handled by the analysis and to show how the analysis might be simplified if certain background theses about the completeness and correctness properties hold. I plan to do these things on another occasion.

7 Conclusion

I will close with a brief word about the three applications of the analysis of concept possession which I mentioned at the outset. First, the analysis promises to provide the basis for an account of *a priori* knowledge. Specifically, the correctness property provides the basis of an explanation of the reliability of our *a priori* intuitions and, in turn, our *a priori* knowledge itself. And the completeness property provides the basis of an explanation of the scope of our *a priori* intuitions and, in turn, our *a priori* knowledge. Furthermore, I believe that, taken together, these properties imply a qualified autonomy and authority for logic, mathematics, and philosophy *vis-à-vis* empirical science.

Second, recall Benacerraf's question concerning mathematical truth: What explains the reliability of our mathematical knowledge given that causal explanations (modeled on sense perception) are unsuccessful? Again, the correctness property promises to provide the basis for an answer.

Third, the completeness property, together with the correctness property, promises to provide the basis for a solution to the Wittgenstein–Kripke puzzle concerning rule–following. Rule–following is an intuition–driven activity. The completeness property ensures that people who understand the question at issue (e.g., What is 1000+2?) and whose cognitive conditions are relevantly good cannot fail to have intuitions bearing on the question. And the correctness property ensures that those intuitions (at least when processed) must settle the question correctly.

This holds for quite novel questions beyond our present conceptual repertory, as in case of the conceptually deficient tribe discussed earlier. Of course, we are not always in fact able to "keep on going". Just as certain questions were beyond the present cognitive level of the cognitively deficient tribe in our example, so certain hard questions which would amount to following a rule are beyond our own present cognitive level. But this should not lead us to think that we do not *understand* them.

REFERENCES

Bealer, George (1979) "Theories of Properties, Relations, and Propositions", *The Journal of Philosophy* 76, pp. 634-48.

───── (1982) *Quality and Concept*, Oxford: Clarendon.

───── (1983) "Completeness in the Theory of Properties, Relations, and Propositions", *The Journal of Symbolic Logic* 48, pp. 415-26.

───── (1987) "Philosophical Limits of Scientific Essentialism", *Philosophical Perspectives* 1, pp. 289-365.

───── (1992) "The Incoherence of Empiricism", *The Aristotelian Society, Supplementary Volume* 66, pp. 99-138.

―――― (1992) "A Solution to Frege's Puzzle", *Philosophical Perspectives* 7, pp. 17-61.
―――― (1993) "Universals, *The Journal of Philosophy* 90, pp. 5-32.
―――― (1994) "Mental Properties", *The Journal of Philosophy* 91, pp. 185-208.
―――― (1996) "*A Priori* Knowledge and the Scope of Philosophy", *Philosophical Studies* 81, pp. 121-142.
―――― (1996) "On the Possibility of Philosophical Knowledge", *Philosophical Perspectives* 10, pp. 1-34.
―――― (1997) "Self-Consciousness", *The Philosophical Review*, in press.
―――― (1997) "Propositions", *Mind*, in press.
―――― (1998) "Analyticity", *Encyclopedia of Philosophy*, London: Routledge, in press.
―――― (1998) "Intensional Entities", *Encyclopedia of Philosophy*, London: Routledge, in press.
―――― (1998) *Philosophical Limits of Science*, New York: Oxford, forthcoming.
Burge, Tyler (1979) "Individualism and the Mental", *Midwest Studies in Philosophy* 4, 73-122.
Dunn, Michael (1990) "Relevant Predication 2: Intrinsic Properties and Internal Relations", *Philosophical Studies* 60, pp. 177-206.
Fine, Kit (1994) "Essence and Modality", *Philosophical Perspectives* 8, pp. 1-16.
Fodor, Jerry (1987) *Psychosemantics*, Cambridge, Mass.: MIT Press.
Kripke, Saul (1972) "Naming and Necessity", in Davidson and Harman (eds.), *Semantics of Natural Language*, Dordrecht: Reidel, pp. 253-355 and 763-769. Reprinted as *Naming and Necessity*, Cambridge, Mass, 1980.
Peacocke, Christopher (1992) *A Study of Concepts*, Cambridge, Mass.: MIT Press.
Putnam, Hilary (1975) "The Meaning of 'Meaning'", in *Language, Mind, and Knowledge* (Minnesota Studies in the Philosophy of Science 8), Minneapolis: University of Minnesota Press, pp. 131-191.
Stalnaker, Robert (1984) *Inquiry*, Cambridge, Mass.: MIT Press.

Bealer's Intuitions on Concept Possession

Jaegwon Kim

Over the past two decades or so, George Bealer has produced an impressively systematic body of work on some of the central issues of metaphysics and philosophy of mind. His approach, which has remained admirably consistent over the years, has been characterized by a strong commitment to platonism, realism, and rationalism (or at least the rejection of hyper–empiricism). Further, in tune with current philosophical sentiments, Bealer has professed his allegiance to naturalism, although his conception of just what constraints naturalism places on philosophy probably differs in some significant respects from the prevailing conception.

In any case, Bealer's present topic is concept possession —what it is for a subject to possess a concept. As I said, Bealer's approach is highly systematic, and the paper in this volume is no exception. It builds on his earlier work on concept, property, proposition, modality, and the rest. While this undoubtedly helps to integrate it within Bealer's larger framework, it can make for some difficulties for his commentators, and readers, who happen not to be familiar with the details of the general setting in which Bealer's present proposals are formulated, and within which their success must be evaluated.

Unfortunately, I am one of those who are less than fully au courant with Bealer's general metaphysical/semantic framework, and I apologize for not being able to present to you an informed and full-fledged critical commentary on this very interesting and undoubtedly important paper. In what follows, I will concentrate my remarks on a few selected issues that lie at the foundations of Bealer's approach and some of the leading ideas that seem to guide his execution of it. This means that I will leave largely untouched the details of his formal/technical developments —in particular, the progressive refinements of his initial definition of concept possession to accommodate difficulties and objections. My thought is that many members of this audience may well be in the same boat, and that what I am going to say will hopefully encourage Bealer to provide clarifications that will help make his fundamental ideas better accessible to us. I doubt very much that my comments will be of any real use to Bealer himself.

Bealer's central idea on concept possession is that this is to be analyzed in terms of "a certain kind of reliable pattern in [the subject's] intuitions regarding the behavior of the concept" (p. 264). He seeks a fully general account that is noncircular, and that can meet the challenges of content/concept externalism, various forms of concept holism, questions about analyticity, and the rest. The benefits of his approach, Bealer tells us, are many: an account of a priori knowledge, a satisfying response to the Wittgenstein–Kripke puzzle about rule–following, and Paul Benacerraf's problem about mathematical truth. As you can see, the project on offer here is one of impressive scope, and what we get from Bealer on the present occasion is not a fully worked–out package dealing with all aspects of these issues. But from what he says about the core project, namely an account of concept and concept possession, we can, I think, get a glimpse of how these further problems might be approached within Bealer's general scheme. I myself find all this quite fascinating and of great possible significance.

Let us now turn to some of the specifics. First, a general remark about the realist aspect of Bealer's framework. He begins by saying: "The appropriate starting points for a theory of concept possession are realism about modalities (possibility, necessity, contingency), realism about concepts and propositions, and realism about propositional attitudes" (p. 264). I am not quite sure that I understand exactly what he means by saying that these realisms are "the appropriate" starting points, but I find the remark puzzling. Is Bealer saying that if one of us were to choose to be an irrealist about one of these items, say modalities, one is thereby precluded from developing a satisfactory account of concept possession —satisfactory from her point of view? This I find unconvincing (I am not saying that that's necessarily what Bealer meant to say); it doesn't even strike me as necessary to be a realist about concepts (whatever that exactly amounts to) to allow for concept possession and to give an account of it (you may recall what Quine said about meanings and having the same meaning). Shouldn't the question be rather this: If you are, as Bealer surely is, already committed to these realisms, what sort of account of concept possession would best fit with your scheme? Or, more generally, what sort of metaphysical/semantic scheme could yield the most satisfying account of concept possession? If the answer is that the Bealer–style realism is best fit for this purpose, that would be a recommendation in its favor. But, at least within the space of the present paper, we are left in the dark as to why the rejection of one or another of Bealer's many realisms should necessarily impede one's search for a theory of concept possession. Moreover, the way Bealer starts out here, by calling these by no means uncontroversial realisms "the appropriate starting points", does not seem like a wise philosophical strategy. For at the very outset it excludes any and all irrealists, about any of the items Bealer mentions, from participating in his project. If I were to undertake to develop an account of concept possession, or of anything else for that matter, I would try to cast my net as wide as possible, to make my account maximally accessible and acceptable, by keeping it neutral with respect to controversial philosophical doctrines and positions. Why should I want my account to carry any unnecessary metaphysical baggage?

The cornerstone of Bealer's account of concept possession is "intuition" or "intellectual seeming". According to him, intuition is a primitive propositional attitude, distinct in particular from believing. To quote: "For you to have an intuition that A is just for it to seem to you that A" (p. 271).

Roderick Chisholm, Roderick Firth, and others, around the mid–century, distinguished between two kinds of seeming or appearing: the epistemic/evidential and the phenomenal. When we say "It appears that the Republicans will win the Senate again", the appearing is epistemic/evidential; when we say "The dinner plate, although round, seems elliptical when viewed at an angle", the appearing is phenomenal. Bealer's intellectual seeming is neither, although it appears to resemble the second in some crucial respects. The epistemic seeming has to do with belief; it is what Bealer calls the "hedging" use of "seem". But intellectual seeming diverges from believing, just as phenomenal seeming diverges from believing. Bealer gives an example of perceptual illusion, the Mueller–Lyer illusion, in which, although you know, or believe, that the two arrows are of equal length, one of them still seems longer than the other.

To illustrate how intellectual seeming differs from belief, Bealer gives two examples: the simple truth schema and the unrestricted comprehension axiom of set existence. In these cases, we believe the propositions to be false —in fact, we know them to be so— and yet, Bealer tells us, they still seem to us to be true. That is, we have the intuition, though not the belief, that the comprehension axiom is true. One wonders whether there are simpler and more straightforward cases involving familiar empirical/contingent matters.

A general difference between belief and intuition has to do with their plasticity: belief is highly plastic —it can be manipulated in various ways, by feeding new (real or feigned) evidence to the subject, for example. But, according to Bealer, intellectual intuitions resist, or show stronger resistance to, such manipulations, being largely impervious to changes in evidence.

Are there intellectual intuitions in Bealer's sense? If there are, are they on a firm enough ground, and do they have the right sorts of properties, for Bealer's purposes —that is, serve as the foundation for a theory of concept possession?

On the question of plasticity, I believe Bealer is right about perceptual cases. The two arrows in the Mueller–Lyer illusion do look to have different lengths, no matter how firmly we believe that's not so. In fact, our visual system would not be working properly if the arrows, after we measured their lengths, began looking to be of the same length. Fred Dretske has stressed this point in his recent book on consciousness:[1] qualia, or sensory contents of perceptual experiences, are not plastic, whereas their conceptual contents are. The traffic lights are red. The visual quale of our experience is fixed, and is essentially immune to influences from the rest of our cognitive system. Our visual experience of the traffic lights also carries the content "Stop!". This conceptual content is highly plastic and is open to "recalibration" —we can make it say "Go!" instead, by suitably modifying portions of our cognitive system.

Are there cases involving nonsensory conceptual contents that behave like the qualia cases? I am not sure —at least, I am not persuaded that there are. The case of the truth schema (and the like) may only be a case in which we have a strong initial inclination to believe —in some sense, it is natural to believe— and there may well be a psychological/cognitive explanation for this. But this inclination

---

[1] Fred Dretske, *Naturalizing the Mind* (Cambridge: MIT Press, 1995).

is strongly —and decisively— counteracted by a deeper, theoretical understanding of the concepts and principles involved. After we have gone over the derivation of a contradiction from the truth schema, is there still a residual "seeming-true" that I experience with the truth schema? Well, looking inward in my own mind (perhaps not unlike Hume when he was trying to find a self), I don't find such experiences. What I do find is an appreciation of how the truth schema might have looked (epistemically) true to the uninitiated.

But we may remain open-minded on this point, and turn to the question how the concept of intuition is used by Bealer in building a theory of concept possession. Bealer distinguishes between two modes of concept possession: the weaker sense and the full, stronger sense. In the weaker sense, Tyler Burge's famous patient, who incorrectly believes that he has arthritis in his thigh possesses the concept arthritis, and the dog that barks up the wrong tree has the concept cat. This, however, is not the sense that interests Bealer. He wants a concept of concept possession that involves what he calls determinate possession and full understanding. This stronger notion excludes Burge–like cases involving misunderstandings or incomplete understandings. For a subject to possess a concept C fully, the subject must have a "full, determinate understanding" of C (p. 274). But what is it for a person to have a grasp of a concept in this strong sense?

Here is, as I take it, where the concept of intuition comes into play. The central idea, as Bealer explains it, is this: subject S possesses (in the strong sense) the concept of being f just in case S's intuitions about concept identities involving being f track truth of these identities. That is, S has correct intuitions regarding whether or not the concept of being f is the same concept as concept A, for all concepts A (anyway this is the way I read Bealer). In the polygon case, Bealer discusses only one specific identity, whether the concept polygon = the concept of a closed figure with more than four sides. But presumably for a full and determinate possession of this concept, the subject must have correct intuitions regarding all possible identities. For where could we draw the line? At least, so it seems, given Bealer's general approach.

I find Bealer's basic approach intuitive in many ways, and I think I see its motivation. But I have a few questions —points that it is possible that Bealer has already addressed in the more detailed developments later in his paper.

In any case, the first worry that occurs to me is whether, given the kind of full generality involving all possible concept identities, we are able to possess, in the sense that is of interest to Bealer, very many concepts —or any concept. In order to possess the concept C the subject must, on Bealer's account, have intuitions about the identity $C = A$, for each and every concept A. What is the range of "each and every" here? Presumably we cannot limit As to concepts already possessed by the subject; that would not yield a "full and determinate understanding" of C. A realist like Bealer would, I think, have to say As must include all the concepts that there are in the Platonic heaven. Now, this seems too much. In order to have intuitions about the identity $C = A$, it would seem —at least for the concept realist— that one must have some knowledge of C and A —some sort of cognitive contact with C and A, perhaps some "intuitions" about them. Or else why is it that the intuition is about $C = A$ rather than about $B = D$? As I take it, it is possible to have intuitions about a concept without fully possessing it —or otherwise, Bealer's account would have the consequence that in order to possess one concept one must possess all the concepts.

But is that really possible? Can one have intuitions about C without possessing C? How about Burge's patient? Bealer's story has to be that he has incorrect intuitions about the concept arthritis, and therefore does not fully possess this concept (although he possesses it in a weak sense). But if he doesn't possess C, how do we know he has intuitions about C rather than some other concept? Consider Burge's patient again: Why doesn't he have correct intuitions about the concept tharthritis (and hence fully and determinately possess this concept), not incorrect ones about the concept arthritis? Is there a matter of right or wrong here —except in relation to a specific linguistic context (which a realist like Bealer would presumably wish to avoid)?

Second, I have a problem with the role played by intuition in Bealer's approach. He talks of the subject's having a "vivid intuition" that a triangle can be a polygon. I fail to see why intuitions must be invoked here. Why isn't it enough to refer to strong belief, unreserved and spontaneous judgment, and the like? Exactly what would be lost if we did? Take concepts like desk, mortgage, democracy, curved spacetime,... Do I have intuitions, Bealer's intellectual seemings, about such concepts? All I seem to be able to find is something like linguistic disposition to apply these expressions to certain cases and withhold them from others (and probably lots of cases in between).

Bealer's approach requires our intuitions about concept identities to track the truth about them. These truths, for Bealer, are mind–independent realist truths about mind–independent abstract entities. As I take it, that's the heart of his realist, antipsychologistic, rationalist program. What isn't clear, however, is why the basic idea in Bealer's theory of concept possession cannot be implemented outside the realist scheme. What I find intuitive and plausible in Bealer's approach is something like this: a subject's cognitive responses to concept identities involving C are determinative of that subject's possession of C. It seems to me that this basic idea can be developed, largely by mimicking Bealer's own development in his paper, by those who don't accept his (some will say, extremely strong) realist framework. In fact, I have a feeling that Bealer's commitment to all those realisms may turn out to be a hindrance; consider, for example, the problem I mentioned earlier that, on Bealer's account, in order to fully possess a single concept the subject must have intuitions about all concepts, or at least all concept identities.

There are many other points in Bealer's paper that deserve serious discussion. I have to admit that I have not fully and determinately grasped all aspects of Bealer's theory; I won't be at all surprised if at least some of my complaints are due to misunderstandings or incomplete understandings of the intricacies of Bealer's account. If so, I can only say that my comments are the reactions of a novice who has run up against a highly systematic and sophisticated theory about a topic he knows little about. But I would like to make it clear that Bealer's paper has made me think about lots of things I haven't thought about before, and that I am happy to have had a chance to think about them.

Concepts and Ontology: A Query for Bealer

James E. Tomberlin

George Bealer's "A Theory of Concepts and Concept Possession"[1] is an extraordinarily rich contribution to the philosophical study of concepts and related matters. There is much that I admire in Bealer's important work. I endorse his realist account of propositions, concepts, and properties as abstract, objective, mind and language–independent entities. I agree that concepts and propositions are properly seen as irreducible *ante rem* items, and propositions, in particular, are not to be identified with linguistic items (in a natural language or a "language–of–thought"), mental entities (mind–dependent conceptual entities) or set–theoretical items such as functions from possible worlds to truth values. Additionally, I find his intensional algebraic treatment of concepts and propositions theoretically attractive, and I especially applaud the theoretically elegant manner in which this account handles the notorious cases of fine–grainedness: Kripke's Pierre, Mates–like puzzles, Salmon's catsup/ketchup, and Schiffer's dog/schmog. And finally I surmise that his positive

---

[1]Bealer (this volume). For important companion studies see Bealer (1982, 1987, 1993, 1996a and 1996b).

account of the perplexing matter of concept–possession is at least on the right track.

So much for admiration and/or agreement. A critic, after all, ought to be critical. In the study before us and elsewhere,[2] Bealer adheres to *actualism*: there are no objects that do not actually exist, and there are no philosophical problems whose solution calls for or requires an ontological commitment to non–actual entities.[3] As I understand it, Bealer accepts actualism across the entire ontological board —there are no possible but non–actual concrete objects, propositions, properties or concepts. Now I harbor a genuine skepticism as regards this ontological stance. In what follows, accordingly, I extend and sharpen the skeptical concerns previously voiced in my (1993, 1996, forthcoming) and Tomberlin and McGuinness (1994).

A central working assumption of the present essay is that actualism as regards concepts demands actualism concerning properties. According to the latter, of course, there are to be no genuine properties besides the actual ones. Let b be the collection of all and only those properties that actually exist. Then for the actualist, 'the unique non–member of b that is Al's favorite property' fails to pick out a property. Even so, I take it, statements like (1) may perfectly well be true:

(1) Bob wanted to study the unique non–member of b that is Al's favorite property.

Additionally, it is plausible to theorize that (1) should be treated on a par with (2):

(2) Ponce de Leon searched for the fountain of youth.

After all, in both (1) and (2) the definite description following the intentional verb does not refer to any actually existing entity. Since actualism requires that no person ever stands in genuine *de re* relations to non–actual objects or properties, the actualist seems forced

---

[2]See Bealer (1982, 1993).
[3]There are in fact *grades* of actualism. Alvin Plantinga (1985), for example, endorses actualism as the view that there neither are nor could have been objects that do not actually exist. But Nathan Salmon (1987) accepts actualism only by affirming the first half of Plantinga's characterization while explicitly rejecting the second (and modal) half. In addition, there are more technical characterizations of actualism in Menzel (1990) and Fitch (1996). As the reader may verify, my discussion here applies to all of the above. For extensive references on actualism, see the bibliographies of Tomberlin and McGuinness (1994) and Tomberlin (1996).

to one of these alternatives: (a) deny the truth of (1) and (2); or (b) interpret (1) and (2) in such a way that their truth does not stand actual individuals in genuine *de re* relations to non–actual ones.

How exactly should the actualist respond? Right here it will prove instructive to consider an actualistic treatment of (2) advanced independently by David Kaplan (1975) and Roderick M. Chisholm (1986). In effect Chisholm and Kaplan propose that the intentional verb in (2) be taken as expressing a dyadic *searched for* relation holding Ponce de Leon and an *attribute*. That is, they invite us to parse (2) as follows:

(2a) Ponce de Leon searched for the attribute of being a unique site of a unique fountain of youth.

Because there *is* such an actual attribute even though it fails to be exemplified (2) —so construed— does not stand Ponce de Leon in a *de re* relation to the nonexistent fountain of youth. To my mind, there are ample reasons for rejecting the Chisholm–Kaplan model for items such as (2). And I have so argued at length elsewhere, with the critique successively refined in Tomberlin (1988, 1994, 1996a, and forthcoming). Still, *whether or not* the Chisholm–Kaplan model is deemed theoretically attractive for (2), this model cannot accommodate (1). For if (1) is treated as (2) before, (1) becomes

(1a) Bob wanted to study the attribute of being a unique non–member of *b* that is Al's favorite property.

But then, contra property actualism, the truth of (1) requires that there *is* such a property as the attribute of being a unique non–member of *b* that is Al's favorite property.

So, how else might actualism come to grip with (1) and (2)? In what follows, I take up one additional suggestion. By the present view, when confronted with troublesome cases like (1) and (2), the actualist should "go adverbial".[4] Roughly, the proposal is to parse (2) as, say:

(2b) Ponce de Leon searched–for–a–unique–fountain–of–youthly.

Here 'a–unique–fountain–of–youthly' behaves as an *adverbial modifier* of the now *monadic* predicate 'searched for'. According to this adverbial model, (2) —so construed— does not ascribe a relation between Ponce de Leon and the non–actual fountain of youth. Indeed, thus understood, (2) does not ascribe a relation between Ponce de

---

[4]See Fitch (1996).

Leon and anything. Quite the contrary, unlike the Chisholm–Kaplan model, (2) is now seen to ascribe a complex but non–relational property to the single individual, Ponce de Leon. As such, we are told, the truth of (2) in no manner requires an actual object to bear a *de re* relation to some non–actual one.

Without worrying over the so far missing semantics for this adverbial account of (2), there appear to be telling objections to any such view. Just consider:

(μ) x searched for y.

Now if the singular terms replacing 'x' and 'y' should both refer to actual concrete objects, let us assume, then even under the adverbial proposal the resulting instance of (μ) ascribes a dyadic relation between those very individuals. (When, for example, Bob searched for his missing daughter last night, he really did bear the *searched for* relation to his missing daughter.) Suppose, however, that whereas the term replacing 'x' picks out an actual individual, the one replacing 'y' does not, as in (2):

(2) Ponce de Leon searched for the fountain of youth.

By the adverbial model, we are to believe that 'the fountain of youth' as it occurs in (2) does not behave as a singular term. (After all, (2) is parsed as (2b).) Under the present interpretation of the adverbial account, therefore, instances of schema (μ) come in (at least) two diverse sorts: when 'y' is replaced by a term denoting a concrete individual, the instance in question ascribes a dyadic relation; and yet, should the term that replaces 'y' fail to pick out an actual individual, the instance at issue ascribes a non–relational property to a single actual object.

This alleged shift in semantical behavior of the various instances of (μ) seems incredulous on two counts: first, outside of a prior commitment to actualism, the semantical shift at stake appears impossible to motivate or support independently; and second, any such view requires intolerably that *logical form* turns on matters of contingent fact —to know what sort of proposition is expressed by an instance of (μ) I must already know whether the singular terms involved do or do not refer to actual but contingent objects.

Our objection to an adverbial treatment of (1) or (2) has so far centered around the pivotal assumption that even under an adverbial account instances of (μ) ascribe a dyadic relation when the terms replacing 'x' and 'y' both refer to actual objects. What happens if this assumption is abandoned? Why not, that is, interpret adverbialism here in such a way that *every* instance of (μ) receives the sort of treatment accorded to (2), even when the singular term replacing 'y' refers to a concrete individual? There is a fatal objection to any such view. For even if the *searched for* relation never holds between actual concrete individuals, the same cannot be properly maintained for the *loves* relation —Bob genuinely bears the latter relation to his missing daughter, Jane. If so, however, the adverbial account, under the current interpretation, cannot do justice to true statements like

(3) Bob searched for Jane, his missing daughter he deeply loves.

After all, I gather in true (3) 'his missing daughter he deeply loves' incontestably ascribes the love relation between Bob and Jane. Accordingly, (3) won't be true unless 'Jane', as it occurs in 'Bob searched for Jane', refers to Bob's missing daughter. But 'Jane' does no such thing under the present interpretation of an adverbial treatment of (2).

This is no way to preserve actualism. And consequently, with the demise of both the Chisholm–Kaplan model and adverbialism, I now pose the following test for Bealer:

Challenge. Tender a credible treatment of (1) and (2) satisfying this theoretical constraint: (1) and (2) are both true, and yet their truth does not requires actual individuals to bear *de re* relations to non–actual ones.

REFERENCES

Bealer, George, 1982, *Quality and Concept*, Oxford: Clarendon.
———, 1987, "Philosophical Limits of Scientific Essentialism", *Philosophical Perspectives* 1: 289-365.
———, 1993, "A Solution to Frege's Puzzle", *Philosophical Perspectives* 7: 17-61.
———, 1996a, "On the Possibility of Philosophical Knowledge", *Philosophical Perspectives* 10: 1-34.
———, 1996b, "*A Priori* Knowledge and the Scope of Philosophy", *Philosophical Studies* 81: 121-142.
———, this volume, "A Theory of Concepts and Concept Possession".
Chisholm, Roderick M., 1986, "Self–Profile", in R. Bogdan, ed., *Roderick M. Chisholm*, Profiles, Dordrecht, D. Reidel.
Fitch, G.W., 1996, "In Defense of Aristotelian Actualism", *Philosophical Perspectives* 10: 53-72.
Kaplan, David, 1975, "How to Russell a Frege–Church", *Journal of Philosophy* 72: 716-729.

Menzel, Christopher, 1990, Actualism and Possible Worlds", *Synthese* 85: 355-389.

Plantinga, Alvin, 1985, "Self–Profile", in J.E. Tomberlin, and P. van Inwagen, eds., *Alvin Plantinga*, Profiles, Dordrecht, D. Reidel.

Salmon, Nathan, 1987, "Existence", *Philosophical Perspectives* 1: 49-108.

Tomberlin, James E., 1988, "Semantics, Psychological Attitudes, and Conceptual Role", *Philosophical Studies* 53: 205-226.

———, 1993, "Singular Terms, Quantification, and Ontology", in E. Villanueva, ed., *Philosophical Issues* 4, Atascadero, Ridgeview.

———, 1996, "Actualism or Possibilism?", *Philosophical Studies* 84: 263-281.

———, forthcoming, "Naturalism, Actualism, and Ontology", *Philosophical Perspectives* 12.

——— and McGuinness, Frank, 1994, "Troubles with Actualism", *Philosophical Perspectives* 8: 459-466.

Getting Clear on the Concept

David Sosa

George Bealer's "Theory of Concepts and Concept Possession" is a subtle and serious effort systematically to understand concepts and concept possession. Bealer holds that concepts are "*sui generis* irreducible entities comprising the ontological category in terms of which propositions (thoughts, in Frege's sense) are to be analyzed" (p. 261). His primary goal is an analysis of concept possession, a *general* analysis, not one that characterizes the possession of a particular concept or of a family of concepts (p. 275). And his starting point is realism: realism about the modalities, about concepts and propositions, and about the propositional attitudes. In what follows, I will articulate several reactions to Bealer's paper. Some of these amount basically to questions. But they will at least indicate where I myself was a bit unclear on the concept.

Before proceeding, let's consider the contours of Bealer's program. He wants to analyze what it is for an agent to be in possession of a concept, to *understand* a concept. His method is to attempt a series of approximations. He begins with an analysis of *nominal* concept possession, which requires only that a subject have a natural propositional attitude toward a proposition which has the concept as content. Such a weak variety of concept possession permits the subject to misunderstand the concepts she possesses and, Bealer claims, permits her to be in possession of a concept simply in virtue of the truth of certain third-party attributions. This gives rise to a negative, informal characterization of *determinate* concept possession: nominal concept possession without misunderstanding. And this in turn suggests that the key to the project is to find the weakest necessary condition that would rule out misunderstanding. What kind of understanding has features necessary and minimally sufficient to rule out *mis*understanding —*i.e.* to guarantee determinateness?

Generally, Bealer proposes "a certain kind of reliable pattern in one's intuitions" (p. 262). He considers a series of examples in which the question of determinate concept possession seems to hinge precisely on whether the relevant agents, or else agents "whose epistemic situation is qualitatively identical" to those of the agents in question, have "truth–tracking intuitions *vis-à-vis* [various] questions" (pp. 277–279). As to what *that* might be, he proposes a kind of modal covariation between certain distinguished "test" propositions and intuitions whose contents yield those propositions. Ultimately he is led "to the thought that determinate concept possession might be explicated (at least in part) in terms of the metaphysical possibility of truth–tracking intuitions in appropriately good cognitive conditions" (p. 279).

This very rough picture of Bealer's program so far leaves out many of the important details. But it may suffice as the background here for what is perhaps the central notion in Bealer's theory —*a priori* stability. That relation is borne by a subject x to a proposition p just in case it is possible for x (or a counterpart of x's in a qualitatively equivalent epistemic state) to go through an "intuition–driven process" by which x stably settles on a truth value for p —given that p is understood determinately (p. 284).

Bealer's analysis of *a priori* stability is later amended; but the current version will provide a peg on which to hang interesting issues that are not affected by the later amendments. The notion of *a priori* stability eventually plays such a central role in Bealer's theory of concept possession that it is important to consider it carefully and critically.

One significant feature of Bealer's analysis of *a priori* stability is its use of the idea of an "intuition–driven process." Bealer himself emphasizes the centrality of intuition in his analysis. And he is at pains to distinguish intuition from other propositional attitudes such as belief: "belief is not a seeming, intuition is" (p. 271). Accordingly, *a priori* stability is a modal relationship between intellectual *seemings* and certain propositions. It is in terms of this relation that determinate concept possession is ultimately defined. But why *in-*

27. GETTING CLEAR ON THE CONCEPT 319

tuition? Suppose someone does *not* have the defined correlation between his intuitions and the truth values of the relevant propositions. He can't help (and he couldn't help, and no epistemic counterpart of his could help) its still seeming to him as if *p* when in fact it's not the case that *p*. Suppose however that all of his other propositional attitudes *do* track *p* appropriately: he does not believe that *p*, his intentions never require that *p* be true, *etc*. Can't the agent understand the proposition determinately? I am suspicious of the negative response to which Bealer's analysis appears committed.

Consider an example of Bealer's own. Bealer does not believe that the naïve truth schema holds. But he has the intuition that it does. Now, suppose the schema in fact does not hold. Suppose, just for the sake of argument, that the liar paradox is a *reductio* of the schema (an idea by which I'm tempted) and that the schema fails. It may be, nevertheless, that though we might eventually, for various complex philosophical reasons, come to *believe* that the schema is false, that can never be *intuitive* to us. The intuition that the schema holds may be in a sense *epistemically pathological*. What I don't understand is why an agent could not still attain a determinate understanding of the proposition in virtue of the suitability of her *beliefs*.

Bealer might respond that even if we cannot intuit directly that the schema is false, our coming to believe that it is false would be a process *driven* by intuition. That there could be cognitive conditions and a conceptual repertory such that, having elicited all intuitions bearing on a proposition, the best systematization of those intuitions yields the verdict that *p*, and no improvement of cognitive condition or increase in conceptual repertory alters that verdict —that's all he intends by his talk of an intuition–driven process. Intuitions are *driving* the process that settles on a proposition in the sense that they serve as data for the systematization that yields the proposition as a verdict. So he could argue that in the example the agent *could* go through an intuition–driven process that stably settles on the falsity of *p*; she just wouldn't have a direct intuition of the falsity of *p*.

In the case of the truth schema in particular, philosophical intuitions, about the validity of arguments concerning the liar paradox for example, are likely to be importantly relevant to the beliefs we come to have. Propositions like the truth schema are to be believed or doubted ultimately on the basis of intuitions —though not necessarily intuitions about the very proposition in question. But what if the agent were in the same situation —wrong intuition, right belief— with respect to very many or even all of the relevant propositions? Bealer's situation with respect to the truth schema might generalize.

Where intuition and belief are at odds over test–propositions, it is apparently belief that matters. If an agent had all the right beliefs with respect to a concept, but very few of the right intuitions (acquiring the beliefs through other means), there still seems good reason to ascribe determinate understanding. That intuition is one way to acquire the beliefs that might constitute determinate understanding does not preclude there being other ways.

Bealer highlights the distinction between belief and intuition in terms of the possibility of believing what you don't intuit and intuiting what you don't believe. It turns out that the crucial attitudes may be beliefs after all. In some instances, perhaps, these beliefs will be based on the data of intuition: But why should this be required?

The reaction just canvassed leads naturally to another. Notice that Bealer places a limitation on *which* propositions are relevant to the determination of full–fledged concept possession. In the situation discussed above, for example, the truth schema would not qualify as a test proposition in Bealer's sense. Test propositions are supposed to be "property–identities" —propositions of the following sort: the property of being f = the property of being A (p. 282). My earlier question was why it should be *intuitions* rather than, say, beliefs or considered opinions or judgments or some combination thereof, that determine concept–possession. My second reaction is to ask why it should be stability with respect to property–*identities* that are dispositive.

It may be difficult to imagine a case that would test for the issue I'm attempting to raise, but why shouldn't determinate understanding depend, at least in some cases, on our considered beliefs about propositions that are not property identities? Bealer does not make clear why property–identities, in particular, should be the only test propositions. If an agent's intuitions (or beliefs, or other propositional attitudes) did not especially closely track property–identities (some errors, some 'don't knows') but tracked other aspects of the relevant property perfectly, then I think we might still correctly credit the agent with a relatively determinate understanding of the concept in question. On Bealer's view, it seems, the agent could have only nominal understanding of that concept.

So far I have worried about two features of *a priori* stability: why should it be *intuitions* that count rather than, say, beliefs; and, why should it be only property–*identities* that serve as test propositions. Here is a perhaps broader reaction to Bealer's project. Recall that Bealer is attempting to give a *general* analysis of determinate concept possession. But should we expect that such a general analysis is even possible? Some considerations may make us suspicious. Compare, for example the concepts of being a polygon, of being gold, and of being red; and then compare those with the concepts that one masters when one excels in, for example, a sport.

The concept of being a polygon, like other concepts from *a priori* disciplines such as logic, mathematics, and philosophy, is what Bealer calls "semantically stable." Such a concept contains no "noncategorial parts," in more of Bealer's terminology. The gist is that all property–identities with respect to these concepts can be decided *a priori*. The concept of being gold, on the other hand, is different. It has both categorial and noncategorial parts. A determinate possessor need master only those properties which are its *categorial parts*. For our purposes, what is distinctive is that the *kind* of categorial mastery required for full understanding varies significantly as between the concepts of being a polygon and that of being gold.

Thus far Bealer just agrees. His analysis abstracts away from this type of difference. And he is sensitive to the problem of scientific essentialism that may arise with respect to natural kind concepts. But consider now the concept of being red. The full understanding of that concept seems to involve a different variety of condition altogether. Beside categorial mastery, of whatever kind, there seems to be a *phenomenological* condition. You must have the right sort of experience in the presence of the property of being red (assuming the right conditions obtain) in order for you fully to understand the concept —think of Frank Jackson's Mary. She seems to many to be unable to have a full understanding of the concept *red* if she is unable to have the right kind of experience. Such a condition seems to be independent of any of the *judgments* an agent might make in response to any test property identities.

Perhaps more controversially, there are certain types of "know–how" or skills that involve the possession of concepts. Full possession of these concepts seems to have an essential connection to *behavior*. You don't fully possess the relevant concepts unless you are able to behave in certain ways under certain conditions. At the very least, better and better possession of these concepts seems sometimes to depend on behavioral manifestations. Michael Jordan's deep understanding of a fast break is manifest in his movements —no amount of proper epistemic reactions to test–propositions, actual or counterfactual, can suffice for that. No matter how much understanding of associated propositions you might have, unless you *react* to certain situations in the right way, you cannot be said to understand the concept in question as fully.

Another way to put this third reaction begins by characterizing Bealer's position as a kind of *coherentism*: you have determinate understanding just in case your *epistemic* situation has a certain coherence (tested across counterfactual space, as it were). But this does not include what we might call "entry" and "exit" conditions —conditions that involve ties to *experience* and to *behavior*. If these can be constitutive of concept possession, and it does seem that in some cases they are, then Bealer's position may yet be insufficient. Concept possession may be a fundamentally motley or variegated phenomenon.

Some Critical Remarks on an Explanation of Concept Possession

Eleonora Orlando

There are three aspects of George Bealer's theory of concept possession that I want to focus on in my paper: the role played by intuition, the relation between intuition and *a priori* knowledge and the problem of holism. Although, these three aspects are closely interrelated in the theory under consideration, I'll examine them separately, for the sake of clarity.

1 The Role of Intuition

As is obvious, intuition plays a central role in Bealer's theory. Simplifying his definition, we may say that understanding a concept amounts to having a truth–tracking ability based on intuition. The capacity for intuition that is at stake is understood in terms of intellectual seeming. Besides, it is worth pointing out that the theory is not presented as a theory of concepts but as a theory of concept possession. In my view, this is based on Bealer's metaphysical assumptions, according to which concepts, as well as thoughts or propositions, are conceived of as entities that exist objectively (*ante rem*); concepts are not thus psychological or linguistic entities but parts of objective thoughts; in other words, Bealer considers himself to belong to the Fregean tradition. Consistently, he is interested in explaining not the nature of concepts themselves, which should be taken to be whatever it is for Platonic kind of entities, but the nature of our epistemic relation to concepts. It is to play the last role that the above mentioned intuitive capacity is brought into the picture.

With regard to this, my critical strategy will be the following one. First of all, I will question the relation between intuition and truth. Secondly, I will point to the fact that Bealer does not give us any argument for the thesis that it is intuition rather than belief that plays a truth–tracking role. Finally, I will argue that he does not give us reasons either to think that his intuition–based theory is to be preferred to those ones based on causal relations.

First things first. According to what is suggested by Bealer himself, the theory may be interpreted as a special kind of conceptual-role theory: the state of possessing a certain concept is determined not by its role in the belief network but by its role in the intuition network. However, there is an important difference between the theory at stake and the more typical conceptual–role theories: on the one hand, the latter are conceived of not only as theories of concept possession but mainly as theories of concepts themselves; on the other hand, whereas in the latter belief and truth come definitely apart (they serve to characterize two different aspects of conceptual content), in Bealer's theory intuition is considered a truth–tracking epistemic capacity. Now, my point is that there is no explanation of why this is the case; in other words, there is no explanation of why a person's intuitions should be taken to track the truth about the content of the concepts she/he determinately possesses. In virtue of what does determinate possession of certain concepts ensure an intuitive correlation between a person and certain true propositions that serve to delimit the concepts in question? In simpler words, why trusting our intuitions, when we are not supposed to trust any of our epistemic capacities? Why giving this truth–tracking, central role to intuitions? There does not seem to be any justification for this, specially in the light of Bealer's definition of "intuition" in terms of intellectual *seemings*. Moreover, it should be taken into account that the assimilation of an epistemic capacity such as intuition to truth has usually characterized the so–called "epistemic" conceptions of truth, which are far away from the above mentioned Fregean tradition that Bealer takes himself to represent.[1]

As far as the case against belief is concerned, it seems to me that the central role is denied to belief by fiat or stipulation. In terms of Bealer's own example, intuitions are taken to be about thoughts like "The concept of water is the concept of a stuff", namely, those which predicate a categorial part of a concept; whereas, beliefs are taken to be about thoughts like "The concept of water is the concept of H_2O", namely, those which predicate a noncategorial part of it.

With regard to this, I would like to say, first, that I do not see the basis for this sort of division of labor between intuitions and beliefs: why are certain thoughts supposed to be the object of intuition and certain others the object of belief? In particular, why can't beliefs play the role of intuitions? Or, in other words, what is peculiar to categorial parts of concepts that make them the object of intuition —rather than belief? In general, beliefs are more likely to bear truth than intuitions: they are more plastic and capable of change, under the influence of experience or argument (as acknowledged by Bealer himself). (Consider, for instance, the naïve truth schema T mentioned by Bealer in his paper: "I intuit the naive truth schema T but don't believe it" (p. 271); we may add, "because it is not true".) If the purpose is the one of tracking truth, belief seems to be the obvious candidate for the job.

Secondly, and more importantly, if we grant Bealer's point, namely, that intuitions have a truth-tracking role only with regard

---

[1] Moreover, something similar may be said with regard to his replacement of an indefinite set of intuitions by an intuition–driven process leading to an *a priori* stable answer (to whether p is true or not):

(a) Why supposing that by repeatedly systematizing different levels of intuitions we will arrive to a single answer (to whether p is true or not)? The notion of a single, *a priori* stable answer seems to me to be a complete idealization.

(b) To keep its intuitive character, the intuition–driven process should avoid, at every step, analysis and deduction. I am not sure that this is what Bealer has in mind when talking of systematization.

(c) Suppose that a certain x does not have any intuition to begin with, how can she get into the whole process? There is nothing for her to systematize! And we may think that no cognitive improvement would change the initial situation as far as the presence of intuitions is concerned: there is no reason to think that a cognitive improvement has to be accompanied by an intuitive one.

to categorial parts of concepts, it is not clear to me why they are to be considered to play an essential role in a *general* theory of concept possession: given the empirical character of most of our concepts (like the above mentioned concept of water), noncategorial mastery seems to be essential. In general, for most concepts, *a priori* intuitions of the concept–identities alluded to by Bealer do not seem to serve to explain what possessing a certain concept amounts to, except in the meager way of contributing the information that possessing that concept implies possessing some others referred to its categorial parts —whose possession is in turn left centrally unexplained. In other words, *scientific essentialism* should be regarded not as an aspect to be accommodated at a late stage but as part of the main phenomenon to be explained. If this is so, it is not clear why belief should be taken to have a secondary role with respect to intuition.

Now, I will examine Bealer's supposed case against causal relations. At this point, I would like to address the following question: is it possible to consider that Bealer's metaphysical assumptions provide him with an implicit argument against causal accounts? At first sight, it may be thought that they do, because they afford the theory the *status* of a theory of concept possession while causal accounts are in general the core part of theories not only of concept possession but mainly of concepts themselves. However, on second thought, it may be objected that a theory of concept possession that says very little on the nature of concepts themselves does not go far enough. In other words, it may be considered that any epistemological explanation of how we are related to concepts has to be supplemented with an ontological explanation of what those concepts are. From this perspective, Bealer may be thought to say way too little on the last question, namely, just that concepts are objective entities.[2] More specifically, he may be considered to owe us an explanation of what concepts themselves are *made of* (representational properties? inferential relations?) on pain of depriving them of content. In other words, even if we grant him his metaphysics of concepts and his consequent claim that we are *intuitively* related to them, an account is needed of how, in so being, we are able to think about something. As Bealer himself would agree, intuitions can be granted to play an

---

[2] In support of this, it is worth mentioning that even Frege has said something not only about the relation between words and senses but also about the relation between senses and referents; in better words, the Fregean theory of understanding that is usually associated with the (properly) Fregean theory of meaning explains not only how we grasp senses but also how by grasping senses we come to refer to objects —by saying that senses determine referents—.

evidential or epistemic role but not a constitutive or ontological one; so, it may seem that a major part of the problem cannot be handled by the theory. It is exactly at this point where, given the truth of scientific essentialism, causal relations are usually thought to play a relevant role in the account of the representational factors of conceptual content.[3] Consequently, Bealer does not seem to be offering any argument against causal accounts; however, he does point to a phenomenon (scientific essentialism) that seems, at least in part, to require them.

2 Intuition and Aprioricity

According to Bealer, on the one hand, we intuit propositions that are true *a priori*, such as "The concept of water is the concept of a stuff"; on the other hand, we believe propositions that are true *a posteriori*, such as "The concept of water is the concept of H_2O".

Now, if Bealer wants to be considered a representative of the Fregean tradition, he should say that *a priori* true propositions are analytic. But if they are analytic, namely, true by virtue of an analysis of the meanings of their component parts, what do we need intuition for? This seems to suggest two different objections to Bealer's claims: first, that our understanding of the propositional conceptual components is prior to our grasping the proposition as true; second, that there is no need for intuition unless some reasons are offered in support of the thesis that the capacity for analysis is an intuitive capacity.

Moreover, his bringing intuition into the picture may make us think of Bealer as belonging not to the Fregean tradition but to the Kantian tradition, according to which *a priori* true propositions based on intuition are not analytic but synthetic. As is known, Kant's point is that the truth of such propositions cannot be stated on the pure basis of analysis: we need an external element, namely, intuition, which counts on a very precise definition in the Kantian system (i.e., a structure of the sensibility of the transcendental subject). However, none of this can be found in Bealer's paper. Furthermore, I think that none of this can be expected to be found

---

[3]At this point, it must be said that even the typical, belief–based conceptual role theories are, in principle, more explanatory than Bealer's atypical, intuition–based theory, since the former are meant to account not only for our epistemic relation to concepts but also for concepts themselves. How well they fare in comparison with causal accounts is another question.

there, since I seriously doubt that conceptual realism can be made compatible with an *a priori* synthesis; it seems to me that the last one can only make sense in relation to subjective capacities (which are not part of the realistic landscape).

Summarizing, my point is that Bealer's tie of intuition to *a priori* knowledge of truth is obscure; more specifically, there seems to be no point in bringing in intuitions to account for *a priori* knowledge of truth within the theoretical framework of the Fregean tradition; aside from that, it may lead us to think that he is obscurely talking of intuition in the more substantive sense of the Kantian tradition.

3 The Holism Threat

In this final section, I want to briefly address the problem of holism, which could be introduced by means of the following question: how many other concepts do we have to possess in order to possess a certain concept? As is known, the holistic answer is *all* of them, since the content of a particular concept is thought to be determined by its relations to any other concept in a system. The atomistic answer is *none*, since the content of a particular concept is regarded as independent of its relations to the rest. In between, we have the spectrum of molecularistic answers, according to which *some* other concepts are needed, in relation to which the content of a particular concept is defined.

Bealer's theory seems to belong to the third category, since he claims that determinate possession of a concept requires having truth–tracking intuitions with regard to *certain* concept–identities (and, if it is an empirical concept, truth–tracking beliefs with regard to *certain* others). Insofar, it involves a problem that is typical of all molecularistic positions: how to delimit the required knowledge? Exactly how many concept–identities must be epistemically accessed for the subject to be taken to possess the concept in question? In other words, which is the line that keeps the theory away from holism?

Bealer acknowledges the problem and proposes a labor–saving device. From my point of view, this does not solve the molecularist's problem: what is needed is a general criterion that allows us to distinguish, in each particular case, constitutive from non–constitutive concepts. (It is worth noticing that an alternative path would be arguing that no criterion is needed, as in Devitt 1996.[4]) To put it in

---

[4]Cf. Devitt, Michael. *Coming to Our Senses: A Program for Semantic Localism* (Cambridge: Cambridge University Press, 1996), specially ch. 3.

terms of Bealer's theory, we need a way of delimiting which propositions we need to have the truth–tracking ability for in order for us to possess a certain concept. (Given Bealer's explicit desire to avoid the analytic–synthetic distinction, I take it that his categorial–non categorial one cannot be considered to do the job; setting this aside, it must be pointed out that the distinctions in question look very similar to each other.[5]) Until we state that criterion —or we somehow justify the idea that no criterion is needed—, we'll be under the holism threat: all concepts may be relevant to the understanding of any particular one. I am not saying that this is true —I think it is not even plausible— or unanswerable: my claim is that Bealer has proposed a nonatomistic theory without giving us a clue as to how this nonatomism is to be distinguished from holism. Nonatomism need not be holism; as we have seen, it may be just molecularism; however, if we are worried about holism, the molecularist character of the theory has to be justified. Far from doing that, the way Bealer has chosen to deal with the problem in offering the above mentioned labor–saving device seems to be only a way of stating it.

In connection with this, I would like to discuss a certain aspect of Bealer's molecularism that makes me doubt. It is not implausible to think that there are some concepts for which Kripke's objections based on the arguments from ignorance and error do hold. According to this, it may be thought that understanding certain concepts is compatible with the existence of some gaps and errors as to which objects they apply to (even if not with total ignorance or complete error, to soften up Kripke's original thesis).[6,7] In the light of this,

---

[5]To take one of Bealer's own examples, exactly how many true concept–identities —such as "The concept of being a triangle is the concept of being a polygon" and "The concept of being a cylinder is not the concept of being a polygon"— do we need to be able to track so as to be considered to determinately possess or understand the concept of being a polygon? Bealer's proposal suggests that quite a lot, since, according to him, we need to be able to recognize all the objects to which the term "polygon" applies (no gaps) and just them (no errors). What is not at all clear is which ones those concept–identities are or what criterion is used to pick them out.

[6]To take a simple example, it may be thought that understanding the concept of water is compatible with not knowing that water is translucent (because the person may not have the concept of translucency) and with thinking that vapor is water (which would be false if we assumed that water is a liquid stuff). To take another example, a person could be in the following situation: (a) she/he understands the target concept, namely, the concept of fish; (b) she/he understands the test concept, namely, the concept of whale; but (c) she/he cannot answer the question whether whales are fishes or she/he gives a wrong answer.

[7]With regard to the thesis that attributions on the part of third–person inter-

Bealer's equation of understanding with full possession seems to be too restrictive: understanding a concept may not necessarily involve knowledge (either intuitive or credential) of all the characteristics of the entity to which the concept applies (no gaps) and no mistakes about it (no errors). If we allow for Kripke's objections, understanding seems to be perfectly compatible with what Bealer calls "weak" or "nominal" possession.

In accordance with the previous considerations, I would say that I am not sure whether it is legitimate to pose a general question and to look for a general answer with regard to the phenomenon of concept understanding. I tend to think that the explanation of what understanding a concept consists of will vary from certain kinds of concepts to others —just as, in certain theories of reference, the explanation of reference varies from, let's say, proper names to general and artifactual terms. To put an example, I do not see any reason to expect that (the state of) understanding the concept of red and (the one of) understanding the concept of sloop should have the same underlying structure: it may well be the case that an atomistic account applies to the first case while the second requires a molecularistic one. Likewise, the restrictions that Bealer imposes on full possession (no gaps and no errors) may be plausibly taken to hold just for mathematical and logical concepts.

---

preters do not involve understanding (or full possession), it must be said that it sounds strange in a realist's mouth. Why should there be an asymmetry as far as the ontological commitment is concerned between third-person attributions and first-person ones?

Concept Possession

George Bealer

I have proposed the following analysis of what it is for an *individual* x to possess a concept determinately, to understand it:

x determinately possesses a given concept iff$_{\text{def}}$ x determinately understands some proposition which has that concept as a conceptual content.

This analysis invokes the notion of determinately understanding a *proposition*. To understand a proposition determinately is to understand it in a certain *mode* —namely, determinately. The hard problem is to say what distinguishes this mode from other natural modes of understanding. My strategy for answering this question is to quantify over natural modes of understanding, including determinateness itself (much as in Ramsified functional definitions of mental properties one quantifies over properties, including the mental properties being defined). The goal in this setting is to isolate general properties which determinateness has and which other natural modes of understanding lack. My proposal is the following:

determinateness = the mode m of understanding with the following properties:

(a) correctness

(b.i) categorial completeness

(b.ii) noncategorial completeness.

(a) A mode m has the correctness property iff, necessarily, for all individuals x and all propositions p which x understands in mode m, p is true *if* it is possible for x (or someone initially in qualitatively the same sort of epistemic situation as x) to settle with *a priori* stability that p is true, all the while understanding p in mode m. (b.i) A mode m has the categorial completeness property iff, necessarily, for all individuals x and all true (positive or negative) property identities p which x understands in mode m, it is possible for x (or someone initially in qualitatively the same sort of epistemic situation) to settle with *a priori* stability that there is some true twin–earth style counterpart of p, all the while understanding p in mode m. (b.ii) A mode m has the noncategorial completeness property iff, necessarily, for all individuals x and all true propositions p which x understands in mode m and which x could believe, it is possible for x to believe p while still understanding it in mode m.[1]

Regarding this analysis, Kim says, "What I find intuitive and plausible in Bealer's approach is something like this: a subject's cognitive responses to concept identities involving C are determinative of that subject's possession of C" (p. 309). The question is whether the proposed analysis works out in its details. Now an analysis may be faulted (A) because it is subject to counterexamples or (B) because it is flawed methodologically. I will divide my comments with this division in mind.

(A) *Candidate Counterexamples.* To be successful, a counterexample would need to show that determinateness does not have one or more of the three indicated properties (this would show that the analysis does not provide a necessary condition), or it would need to show that there are modes of understanding other than determinateness which have the three properties (this would show that the analysis does not provide a sufficient condition).

Many commentators fail to understand that the three properties —correctness, categorial completeness, noncategorial completeness— are properties of determinateness, a general mode m of understanding. They instead treat them as properties of a particular subject's understanding of a particular concept C. This gives rise to

---

[1] I will suppress the question of whether there are species of determinateness which also have the three properties. If there are, determinateness is then to be identified with the genus of natural modes of understanding which have the properties.

the first sort of candidate counterexample, which questions whether the categorial completeness property is a necessary condition. Kim, for example, says, "In order to possess the concept C the subject must, on Bealer's account, have intuitions about the identity $C = A$, for each and every concept A" (p. 308). (See also Orlando p. 329, note 5.) But, of course, subjects can determinately possess a concept C without having intuitions concerning its relation to every concept A. This counterexample arises from a simple scope error. What the analysis implies is something far, far weaker —namely, that for every A, *if x already* determinately understands *the whole proposition* that $C = A$, then it would be possible for x (or someone initially in qualitatively the same sort of epistemic situation) to settle *a priori* whether (some twin–earth counterpart of) the proposition that $C = A$ is true. (It is understood that, to do this, x's cognitive conditions —intelligence, attentiveness, etc.— might need to improve or x's conceptual repertory might need to be enlarged.)

Next, a candidate counterexample to the sufficiency condition. David Sosa suggests (p. 321) that, for some mode m which has the three properties, there might be someone —e.g., Frank Jackson's Mary— who understands a phenomenal concept in mode m but who does not have a "full understanding" of the concept. For his counterexample Sosa seems to have in mind that m = determinate–in–all respects–except–phenomological–recognitional–abilities. To see that this m is not a counterexample to the sufficiency condition, let p be the following proposition: the property of being what it is like to experience red = the property of being like *this* (where *this* is what it is like to experience red). Then, as long as Mary continues to understand p in this indicated mode m, it is not possible that she settles p and necessarily always settles it the same way (as is required by the definition of *a priori* stability). Therefore, m lacks categorial completeness and so is not a counterexample.[2]

---

[2]Incidentally, not only does m fail to satisfy (b.i), but for much the same reason it also appears not to satisfy (b.ii).

Considerations like those in the text also show that we do not have a counterexample if m = incomplete understanding. For a third type of candidate counterexample to the sufficiency condition, suppose that Mary *misunderstands* what it is like to experience red, wrongly taking experiences of red to be like experiences of blue. In this case the associated modes of understanding m would not, however, be genuine counterexamples, for in her efforts to settle p *a priori* Mary would inevitably arrive at some *incorrect* answers, thereby showing that m does not satisfy the correctness condition.

As for Sosa's basketball example, basketball coaches presumably know *what* a fast break is, and they might even know what it would be *like* to execute one.

Finally, another candidate counterexample to the necessity condition. The claim is that someone x might determinately understand a property identity p (e.g., that $C = A$) even though it is not possible for x (or someone in qualitatively the same sort of epistemic situation) to settle whether there is a true twin–earth counterpart of p. Why? Because x might not have intuitions leading to answer this question. (See Kim, pp. 308-309; Sosa, pp. 318-320; Orlando, p. 325 note 1.) But this fails to appreciate the fact that, when I say that it should be possible for x (or surrogate of x) to settle this question correctly, the intention is that x (or surrogate of x) may have cognitive conditions of any quality, no matter how high the level as long as it is metaphysically possible. In particular, the *intelligence* level may be as high as would be relevant as long as it is metaphysically possible. Kim and Orlando, however, entertain the idea that the subject might continue to lack intuitions. But when one's intelligence increases, so does the scope of one's intuitions. If, no matter how great one's intelligence were, one still lacked intuitions, the right thing to say is that the subject does not determinately possess the relevant concepts. What else could account for the fact that the subject is drawing a blank? What is the relevant difference between the envisaged example and the examples (the Platonist logician, etc.) considered in the paper? Absent an answer, we would have an unexplained mystery. Why believe in such a thing?

(B) *Methodological Questions.* The preceding points about intuition leads naturally to a methodological question. Kim (pp. 308-309), Sosa (pp. 318-320), and Orlando (p. 325) each question whether the analysis of concept possession should invoke both intuition and belief —rather than just belief.[3] Three points are in order. First, presumably advocates of a purely belief–based analysis would want to take advantage of the various "labor–saving devices" developed for the proposed intuition–*cum*–belief analysis; without them, a belief–based analysis would be open to easy counterexamples. Second, the proposed analysis is evidently free of counterexamples. If there is also a counterexample–free analysis based solely on belief, that

---

But, despite this, many coaches (unlike a player such as Michael Jordan) are unable to execute fast breaks because they are too uncoordinated. Are such coaches *conceptually* deficient? It hardly seems so.

[3] Kim also suggests that intuitions can in some cases be identified with "a strong initial inclination to believe". For a critique of this sort of reductive treatment of intuitions, see my "*A Priori* Knowledge: Replies to Lycan and Sosa", *Philosophical Studies* 81, 1996, pp. 163-174; and "Intuition and the Autonomy of Philosophy", in *Intuition*, Michael DePaul and William Ramsey (eds.), Rowman and Littlefield, in press.

would not fault the proposed analysis. Nothing in principle prevents a notion from having two correct (and, hence, necessarily equivalent) analyses. Third, a reason to prefer the proposed analysis over a purely belief–based analysis is that it reflects the underlying psychological and epistemological reality, namely, that for a great many relevant cases intuition guides rational belief formation, not the other way around. In such cases, prior to considering the question at issue a person often has no beliefs one way or the other about it. Upon considering the question, however, the person forthwith has an intuition, and on that basis forms the associated belief.[4] If the envisaged purely belief–based analysis turned out to be correct, the explanation would be that, as one's cognitive conditions improve and one's conceptual repertory increases, one's beliefs on *a priori* matters are increasingly constrained by one's *a priori* intuitions. The reason, of course, is that intuitions are *evidence*, and as one's cognitive conditions improve, belief formation is ever–more rational and, accordingly, is ever–more under the control of the evidence.

The last point leads to a general point about explanatory order. In other papers,[5] I have given independent arguments in support the thesis that intuitions are evidence and that the only acceptable explanation of this fact is provided by a kind of reliabilism: intuitions are evidence because, in suitably good cognitive conditions, they have an appropriate tie to the truth. So far so good, but this account gives rise to the question of *why* intuitions should have such a tie to the truth.[6] The analysis of concept possession (which is based on a variety of examples such as the Platonist logician example) provides the answer: it is constitutive of determinate concept possession that

---

[4] Here is an example. Consider average twenty–year old college students with no background in logic, linguistics, or philosophy. *At least according to our standard belief ascription practices*, we would not say that they right now believe that there are two readings of 'Necessarily, the number of planets is greater than seven', one on which it is false and one on which it is true (assuming that there are nine planets). Nor would we say that they have the contrary belief. They have no belief one way or the other regarding this question. When they come to your lecture on this topic, they are going to acquire *new* beliefs. This at least is what our standard belief ascription practice dictates. Now suppose we confront the students with the above question. After some reflection, the good students come to see both readings; they have the intuitions. And therewith, not before, they come to have the associated beliefs.

[5] "*A Priori* Knowledge and the Scope of Philosophy", *Philosophical Studies* 81, 1996, pp. 121-142. "On the Possibility of Philosophical Knowledge", *Philosophical Perspectives* 10, 1996, pp. 1-34.

[6] Orlando (p. 324) raises this question but without knowing the larger explanatory structure developed in these other papers.

a person's intuitions should have the indicated sort of a tie to the truth; if there were not such a tie to the truth, the right thing to say is that the person simply fails to understand one of the concepts. Evidently, the only alternative explanation of intuition's truth-tie is one which (as in Gödel's theory of mathematical intuition[7]) identifies intuition with a kind of non-sensory perception. Many people find this explanation mysterious; but, even setting that worry aside, our explanation in terms of concept possession is superior just on grounds of simplicity.

The next methodological issue concerns a doubt that a general account of concept possession is possible. (Sosa, p. 321; Orlando, p. 330 raise this doubt.) But given that we do have a general notion of concept possession, it would be mysterious indeed if there were no account of what it amounts to, if it were an unexplainable primitive. Of course, the best response to the doubt is simply to produce an account. If it is free of defects, the doubt is erased.

The final methodological point concerns the matter of realism. I have said that the proposed analysis presupposes realism about concepts, properties, and propositions; realism about the modalities; and realism about the propositional attitudes and modes of possessing (or understanding) concepts and propositions. Kim (pp. 304-305) questions what I mean when I say this and whether it is a wise strategy. For our immediate purposes, a minimalist understanding suffices: I may be taken to mean that, in an analysis, use may be made of our ordinary modal idioms and of variables whose intended range of values include the indicated entities. I am convinced that no analysis of concept possession is feasible unless one takes advantage of such a framework; one must only look at the literature to see that efforts based on weaker resources have failed.

Of course, someone might approve the use of the indicated framework for the purpose of formulating an analysis but at the same time attempt some kind of nonrealist interpretation of it. (See Kim p. 307.) I need not take a stand on this as long as truth values of statements made in the framework would still conform to our intuitive assessments. This is all that is needed for the proposed analysis of concept possession to succeed.

Can something stronger be said in favor of realism? Well, there are convincing intuitive arguments that various positive existential

---

[7]Kurt Gödel, "What Is Cantor's Continuum Problem?", *Collected Works*, vol. II, Solomon Feferman et al. (eds.), New York: Oxford, 1990, pp. 254-270; "Some Basic Theorems on the Foundations of Mathematics and Their Implications", *Collected Works*, vol. III, 1995, pp. 304-323.

statements made in the above framework are true —for example, statements that concepts, properties, and propositions exist.[8] But by themselves such arguments do not rule out all nonrealist interpretations. (Something additional is needed; see below.) To see why such intuitive arguments do not by themselves suffice, let us turn to Tomberlin's comments on possibilism.

Tomberlin offers intuitive arguments that various positive existential statements made in a possibilist framework are true —for example, statements that there exist nonactual possibilia. (Of course, whether or not his arguments are sound does not affect the correctness of the proposed analysis of concept possession; that is an independent question.) The point I want to make is this. There is a way in which one can accept the possibilist framework without being a realist about nonactual possibilia, without admitting such entities into one's philosophical ontology. But the corresponding point does not hold for concepts, properties, and propositions. Let me explain.

The main idea is that in one's philosophical ontology *singular identity concepts* may fulfill theoretical functions similar to those of nonactual possibilia. (x is a singular identity concept iff it is possible for there to exist something y such that $x =$ the concept of being identical to y.) Although many of these concepts do not have instances, they *could*; and, if they were to have instances, they would serve to individuate those instances. At the same time, singular identity concepts —including those which do not have instances— are all actual, thus permitting one's philosophical ontology to be fully actualist. Now consider a superficially possibilist language, that is, a language with sentences such as 'There is a possible move which I coud have made but did not'. Suppose the above actualist philosophical ontology is enriched with a new logical operation corresponding to 'there is a possible'. In this setting, one could then identify the propositions which are meant by superficially possibilist sentences; and, by using singular identity concepts, one could give general truth conditions for these propositions, all the while invoking only actual objects in the account. Suppose that, knowing of this prospect, we decided to make positive assertions in the superficially possibilist language. Would we thereby be making ontological commitment to things beyond the actual? Would our philosophical ontology no longer be actualist? It hardly seems so.

---

[8]See, for example, my "Universals", *The Journal of Philosophy* 90, 1993, pp. 5-32, and my "Universals and Properties", *Contemporary Readings in the Foundations of Metaphysics*, S. Laurence and C. Macdonald (eds.), Basil Blackwell, 1998.

Can the tables be turned on our preferred actualist framework of concepts and propositions? No, for two transcendental reasons. First, an analogous nonrealist treatment of the language of concepts and propositions cannot be given, for this style of treatment requires the framework of concepts and propositions for its very implementation. Second, there is a fundamental epistemological difference between the framework of concepts and propositions and the framework of nonactual possibilia. The former is required for a satisfactory general account of what justified belief is, so denying these entities pushes us into an epistemically self-defeating situation. Such a framework has, therefore, the highest epistemic credentials a philosophical ontology can have. Not so for the conceptual framework of nonactual possibilia: it is not required for an account of what justified belief is; abandoning it does not lead to epistemic self-defeat.

What Might Nonconceptual Content Be?

Robert Stalnaker

I start with a bit of philosophical jargon, first introduced by Gareth Evans, but used since by many others who cite Evans, including Christopher Peacocke, John McDowell, and Michael Tye. My initial question was, what do these philosophers mean by "nonconceptual content", and its contrast, "conceptual content"? What kinds of objects are these different types of content, and how are they used to characterize perception and thought? It is controversial among those who talk of nonconceptual content whether there is such a thing, and whether perceptual states have a kind of content that is different from the kind that characterizes belief states and speech acts. But Evans gives us no direct and explicit characterization of the notion of nonconceptual content that he introduces —at least none that I can find. And it is not clear to me that the different philosophers using this term mean the same thing by it. Without some account of what nonconceptual and conceptual contents might be, it is difficult to have more than a general impression of what this controversy is about.

Some things Evans says suggest that it is mental states, rather than their contents, that are conceptual or non–conceptual, and sometimes he substitutes "non-conceptualized" for non-conceptual, but it is clear that he thinks there are two kinds of content, and not just two kinds of states that content is used to characterize, or two ways in which content might be expressed. "The process of conceptualization or judgement", he says, takes the subject from one kind of state (with a content of a certain kind, namely non-conceptual content) to his being in another kind of cognitive state (with a content of a different kind, namely, conceptual content)".[1] John McDowell, on the other hand, argues that the process of judgment does not introduce a new kind of content, but "simply endorses the conceptual content, or some of it, that is already possessed by the experience on which it is grounded".[2] It is issue behind this dispute that I want to try to get a little clearer about.

Let me confess at the beginning that I will not propose answers to my questions about how these philosophers should be understood. I am puzzled by much of what they say —I have the impression that their arguments are being guided, on both sides, by conceptions of content and its role in the explanation of perception and thought that have underlying presuppositions that I don't share, and don't fully understand. So my strategy will be indirect: rather than trying to ferret out those presuppositions by detailed examination of the texts, I will spell out my own assumptions about representational content, and ask how, given the way I understand this notion, a distinction between conceptual and nonconceptual might be drawn, and what role it might play in the explanation of the relation between perception and thought. I will begin with what I take to be some platitudes about content, assumptions that I would expect to be disputed only by a philosopher who rejected the whole idea of representational or intentional content. After a while, more controversial assumptions may emerge, but I hope we will be able to identify the point at which disagreement begins.

The notion of propositional content begins with the idea that *what is said* in a speech act —the proposition expressed— can be abstracted from two different aspects of the way it is said: first from the means used to express it, second from the force with which it is expressed. The same proposition can be expressed by different sentences of the same or different languages, and the same proposition can be the content of an assertion in one context, and of a supposition, a component of a disjunctive assertion, or a request in

---

[1] Gareth Evans, *Varieties of Reference*, p. 227. All page references to Evans are to this book.
[2] John McDowell, *Mind and World*, p. 49.

other contexts. Furthermore, the contents expressed in speech acts with different force are the same kinds of things as the contents of mental states of different kinds, such as belief, desire, intention, hope and fear. Just as *what is said* can be separated from how it is said, so *what is thought* can be separated both from the means of mental representation and from the kind of mental state (belief, wish, tacit presupposition, hope or fear) that the proposition is used to specify. Just as you and I might say the same thing, even though you say it in French and I say it in English, so you and I might believe the same thing even though the systems of mental representation in which the information is encoded in our respective minds is different. And just as I may assert what you merely suppose, so I might believe what you doubt, but hope for. And it seems at least *prima facie* reasonable to say that when something merely looks to me to be a certain way, even though I don't really believe that it is that way, then there is perceptual state with a certain content that might have been, but is not the content of any of my beliefs.

So what might these things be —things that are the contents of speech acts and mental states of various kinds? There are many different theories about what propositional content is, but two things seem common to all theories that take content seriously at all: first, a content is an abstract object of some kind (as contrasted, for example, with a sentence token, or a mental representation); second, it is essential to propositional contents that they have truth conditions. Perhaps they *are* truth conditions, perhaps something more fine-grained that allows for the possibility that different propositional contents may have the same truth conditions. Either way, what is assumed is that for any state, act or object with propositional content, one can ask whether or not things are as the state represents things to be, and this is to ask whether the truth conditions of the propositional content are satisfied.

What are truth conditions? Different things might be meant by this expression; here is one: think of the meaning of a sentence as a recipe for determining a truth value as a function of the facts. The recursive semantic structure of the sentence encodes such a procedure. One might identify the recipe with the truth conditions, since it spells out the procedure, or conditions, for determining whether the sentence is true. Here is a contrasting explanation: one might instead identify the truth conditions of a statement simply with the circumstances (the way things must be) for the proposition expressed to be true —the conditions under which the statement is true. Different recipes determined by statements with different constituent structure might end in the same place, no matter what the facts (as, for example, with statements of the forms $\neg(P \vee Q)$ and $(\neg P \wedge \neg Q)$). Such statements will have different truth conditions in one sense, but the same truth conditions in the other. I will make only the weaker assumption that propositional contents have truth conditions in the second sense.

Now there are many kinds of abstract objects that have, or determine, truth conditions in this sense —different candidates for a kind of representational content. Some of them may be appropriately called "conceptual" in some sense; others might appropriately be called "nonconceptual". For example, one might define complex objects, nested ordered sequences that reflect the recursive semantic structure of the sentences with which the structure is associated. The ultimate constituents of such structures might consist wholly of senses or concepts. Maybe *conceptual* content is an object of this kind, though it remains to be said what senses or concepts are. Alternatively, one might take the ultimate constituents of such structures to be individual objects and properties and relations (the referents of names and the properties and relations expressed by the predicates in the relevant sentences). Perhaps this is a kind of *nonconceptual* content. And there might be mixed cases —structures that contain concepts or senses (associated with predicates) and individuals (associated with names).

These different candidates for a kind of content are not independent; there will be correspondences between contents of the different kinds. In some cases there will be straightforward ways of determining a content of one kind as a function of a content of one of the other kinds. In particular, whatever senses are, they determine referents; whatever concepts are, it seems reasonable to say that concepts of the appropriate kind determine properties. (A concept of cat determines, I assume, the property of being a cat.) If this is right, then a structure that is made up of senses or concepts will determine a unique structure of the kind made up of individuals, properties and relations, though the reverse will not be true. So there is a clear sense in which structures made of senses or concepts are more fine-grained than those made of individuals and properties and relations, with the mixed cases falling between the two.

All of the candidates considered so far build into the content a recipe for determining truth conditions. One might instead take the recipe determined by some sentence as part of the means by which content is determined, rather than as essential to the content itself. One might, that is, identify the content with the truth conditions themselves —the possible circumstances that must be realized in order for some expression or thought with that content to be true.

30. WHAT MIGHT NONCONCEPTUAL CONTENT BE? 343

This is the most coarse-grained conception of content —the outer limit on a conception of content that meets the minimal conditions that we are requiring that any conception of representational content meet. Any conception of representational content meeting these conditions will determine a unique content of this most coarse-grained kind, so this is a kind of content that everyone should agree can be used to characterize mental and linguistic states, acts and events that can be said to have representational content of any kind. I will use the label "informational content" for content as truth conditions, propositions as functions from possible circumstances to truth values, or equivalently, as sets of possible situations. I suppose that if this is a kind of content, it is a kind of nonconceptual content, although since it can be used to characterize any kind of representational act or state, its use says nothing one way or another about whether any kind of act or state essentially involves the exercise of conceptual capacities (whatever this might mean).

Thus far I have been talking about the kinds of abstract objects that might be thought to be the representational contents of acts and states that have representational content, but I have said nothing about the states themselves, or about what it is about a cognitive, perceptual, or motivational state, or a speech act or act of judgment in virtue of which it has some particular representational content. Recall that part of the initial motivation for developing a conception of content at all was the idea that content could be abstracted from the force with which it is expressed and from the attitudes that are characterized in terms of content —a conception that might be used to describe states and acts of different kinds, and that was intelligible independently of its use to describe any representational states or acts. But of course the interest of these abstract objects will derive from their use for describing in a revealing way the phenomena they are used to describe, and for bringing out the relationships between different acts and states that are involved in representation. So I turn now to questions about the role of content in characterizing representational events and properties, beginning, again, with some platitudes.

Statements involving sentential complements (for example, statements of the form x believes that P, *it appears to x that P, x asserted that P*), state that a certain relation holds or held between x and something denoted by the term "*that P*". Sometimes the problem of intentionality is posed as the problem of how it is possible for a person to be related, as a matter of contingent fact, to the kind of abstract object denoted by a that-clause. The puzzlement is exacerbated by the causal metaphors philosophers often use to describe the ways we are related to propositions: they seem to be things we can get our hands around: we grasp propositions, we gather information, process it, and send it. Content travels in vehicles. Information saturates our thoughts, [Evans, p. 122] seeping into them like some kind of spiritual fluid. But the sober reality behind the metaphors need not be so mysterious. To be related to an abstract object is just to have a property that can be determined as a function of such an object, in the way that (to use a now familiar analogy) the property of weighing 75 kilograms can be determined as a function of the number 75. One way to get at the question, what is content? is to ask how whatever it is that is denoted by such sentential complements as "that the cat is on the mat" determines the properties that are ascribed in predicates like "believes that the cat is on the mat".

Consider a simple and straightforward example borrowed from Evans [p. 122]. I am thinking about something I can see: a black and white cat sleeping on a mat. I see that the cat is sleeping. Perhaps I suspect or speculate that the cat is a favorite of Queen Elizabeth. I entertain the possibility that the cat is ginger, rather than black and white, and judge that it is not (or in Evans's terms, I "grasp [the thought that the cat is ginger] as false."). Various properties are ascribed to me with the help of reference to some kind of abstract object that has truth conditions. Whatever is going on in me when I entertain the possibility that this cat is a favorite of Queen Elizabeth, we can describe it by attributing to me a relation to the proposition *that the cat is a favorite of Queen Elizabeth* (a proposition that is true in possible worlds in which that cat is one of her favorites and false in possible worlds in which it is not). The problem is to say what the world must be like for me to be related in the right kind of way to such an abstract object.

The thought episodes and belief states in such cases are, Evans notes, based on some *information* that the subject receives. "People are", he says, "in short and among other things, gatherers, transmitters and storers of information. These platitudes locate perception, communication, and memory in a system —the informational system— which constitutes the substratum of our cognitive lives" [p. 122]. Evans says little about what information is, or what informational states are, but here is a simple minded and crude version of a familiar story: one thing contains information about another if there are causal and counterfactual dependencies between the states of one and the states of the other. An object contains information about its environment if the object is in some state that it wouldn't be in if the environment weren't a certain way. x carries the infor-

[handwritten note: Too stringent. Different types of causes can have the same type of effect.]

mation that P if the object would not be in the state it is in if it were not the case that P. Some objects are sensitive to a range of alternative states of the environment in a way that makes them apt for transmitting or storing detailed information about some aspect of the environment. The pattern of light and dark on the ground on a sunny day, for example, carries information about the shape of the tree since there are systematic counterfactual dependencies between a range of alternative possible shapes of the tree and a corresponding range of alternative patterns on the ground. Obviously, artifacts such as thermometers and cameras are designed to be sensitive to the environment in just this way, and they are naturally described as devices designed to carry information. Equally obviously, animals have evolved a diverse range of systems —perceptual systems as well as internal monitoring systems of various kinds— that carry and use information in this sense. For a philosopher looking for a naturalistic account of intentionality, this conception of information and informational states provides a natural starting point.

Of things that carry information, we can say *what* information they carry. Information itself is something described with that–clauses —the information that a black and white cat is sleeping on a mat, or that *this* black and white cat is sleeping on a mat, or the information that the tree trunk is shaped roughly like a Y, that the temperature is seventeen degrees centigrade. Informational states have content —presumably (at least in some cases) a kind of content that is in some sense nonconceptual, since it would not be reasonable to attribute conceptual capacities to the patterns of light on the ground in virtue of the counterfactual dependencies that make it the case that those patterns have informational content.

Of course things that lack conceptual capacities (such as books) still might carry conceptualized information, and so might be correctly describable in terms of some notion of conceptual content. But whatever conceptual content turns out to be, it seem reasonable to think that for anything that *has* conceptual content, the fact that it does must have its origin in something with conceptual capacities, as the information contained in books has its origin in the thoughts and intentions of the members of the community in which they are written. (Pace George Washington, who is alleged to have said that all knowledge has its origin in the knowledge in books.) If the notion of an informational system is, as Evans suggests, to "constitute the substratum of our cognitive lives", and if the notion of information is to contribute to an explanation of the source and nature of the content of full blooded intentional states —acts of judgment, states of belief— then it is important that our account of what constitutes the carrying of information not presuppose, or be derivative from, states of mind.

Artifacts that are designed to record, display or store information (fuel gauges, thermometers, cameras, compact disks) are among the best examples of information carrying systems, and are often used to illustrate the strategy for explaining intentionality in terms of systems that function to carry information. Since the design of such things is explained in terms of the intentions of the designers, their information carrying capacities are in a sense dependent on the intentional states of persons. But it would be a mistake to think that the information such artifacts carry is derivative in the same way as the capacity of a book to carry the information expressed by the sentences written in it. Thermometers and cameras are designed with an information carrying purpose in mind, but facts about the way such devices happened to come by their informational capacities are inessential to the explanation of what it is that constitutes those capacities. A natural thermometer or camera brought into being by some fortuitous process (Swamp–thermometer, or Swamp–camera) would carry the same information in the same way as actual thermometers and cameras. The word–like marks in Swamp-book, on the other hand, don't mean anything, and they don't carry information that has anything to do with what such marks usually mean. I don't know whether Evans is making this mistake when he says "what gives a photograph its content is, of course, something quite different from what gives states of our brain their content. (The former is parasitic on the latter)" [p. 125, n. 8], but I think this claim is at least misleading in that it ignores the distinction between the inessential way in which the capacities of cameras are parasitic on those of our brains, and the important way that the capacities of books are parasitic on ours, but the capacities of cameras are not.

Information is by definition veridical. According to the simple story I have sketched, x cannot carry the information that P unless it is true that P. If this concept is to provide a basis for an account of representational content, we need to complicate the story, but the strategy for doing so is straightforward. As Fred Dretske has emphasized, even in the simple story, any characterization of the information carried by some object will presuppose a distinction between the facts that form the background conditions (or channel conditions) for the causal structure in virtue of which the object carries information and the facts that constitute the information carried. The correctness of the characterization of the content of the information carried will be relative to such presuppositions. So we say that the thermometer (which is in fact functioning normally, and which registers 17) carries the information that the temperature is 17 degrees centigrade, even though if, contrary to fact, the temperature were 27 degrees, and certain particular anomalous conditions also obtained, the thermometer would still be in the state it is in. The presupposed background conditions must obtain for information to be carried in the strict sense, but one can use the same content ascriptions, and the same distinction, without making the assumption that relevant conditions in fact obtain. One can say, that is, that x *indicates* that P if it is in a state that *would* carry the information that P if the appropriate background conditions obtained. If the conditions do not obtain, then what is indicated may be misinformation rather than information. But the essentials of the story remain the same.

Perceptual systems are paradigm cases of systems apt for receiving information, and statements about perceptual achievements are cases of content attribution that most straightforwardly fit the information theoretic picture. To say that O'Leary sees that the zebra is striped is to say, at least, that O'Leary receives via the visual system, the information that the zebra is striped. In this kind of straightforward perceptual statement there is no question of misinformation or misperception: the zebra must be striped for the statement to be true. Furthermore, if it is true that O'Leary sees that the zebra is striped, he must also come to believe —in fact, to come to *know*— that the zebra is striped. Suppose O'Leary thinks this: "That animal sure looks striped, but who ever heard of a striped horse. It is probably just the way the sunlight is filtering through the trees that makes it look that way". O'Leary is wrong to doubt his senses, let us assume. It really is a striped zebra that he sees; lighting is normal, and things are just as they appear to be. I assume that in such a case it would be wrong to say that O'Leary sees that the zebra is striped, though it might still be right to say in such a case that O'Leary received the information, through the visual system, that the zebra is striped. Despite the fact that O'Leary withholds judgment, it is still true that had the zebra not been striped, it would not have looked the way it does.

In the normal case —the one that is correctly describable by the statement, "O'Leary sees that the zebra is striped"— the information that the zebra is striped is received through the visual system and results in the knowledge that the zebra is striped. A case might be abnormal in at least two independent ways. First, the "information" might be misinformation: to use the terminology suggested above, it might be that the state of the visual system merely *indi-*

cates that the zebra is striped, meaning that it is in a state that, under normal conditions, would constitute receiving the information that the zebra is striped. Second (as in our example), it might be that the information (or misinformation) did not result in belief, and so not in knowledge. O'Leary's case deviates from the norm in the second way, but not in the first. It is also true that in this case, O'Leary falsely believes that it deviates from the normal one in the first way.

To describe what happens in a way that does not exclude either kind of deviation from the normal case, one might say that it looks to O'Leary as if the zebra were striped, or that it appears visually to O'Leary that the zebra is striped. (Though this is not how O'Leary would put it, since he doesn't realize that what appears to him to be striped is a zebra.) But how exactly are such statements about how things appear to be analyzed?

One idea, considered and rejected by Evans, is this: statements about the way things seem should be understood as dispositions to believe, or as something like defeasible or *prima facie* beliefs. For it to seem to you that P is for you to be in a state that would, except for some intervening factor, result in the belief that P, or perhaps for you to be in a state that produces an inclination to believe that P. More specific seeming or appearing states such as its *looking* to the you that P, would, on this strategy, identify a particular source for the inclination: something seems to be so as a result of the way things look. But on this proposal, one would still derive the content of the state from the content of the belief states that it would produce under normal conditions. Evans argues that this gets things backwards. Belief states are sophisticated cognitive states, while "the operations of the informational system are more primitive" [p. 124]. But I think the main problem Evans has with this attempt to explain the content of seeming states is not that the perceptual systems are intrinsically more primitive, but that they are earlier links in an informational chain. The informational content of a state should be explained in terms of the causal source of the state, and not its normal result. Consider the analogy between testimony and the senses, an analogy Evans alludes to and takes seriously [p. 123, n. 5]. The senses are like witnesses who tell us things that we may accept or reject. Just as in the normal case, when it looks to be that P, one comes to know that P, so in the normal case, when one is told that P, one comes to know that P. This implies that to be in the state of having been told that P is to be in a state that would under normal conditions result in the knowledge that P. But it would obviously be absurd to try to explain the content of the witness's testimony in terms of

30. WHAT MIGHT NONCONCEPTUAL CONTENT BE? 349

the content of the knowledge state in which it would normally result. Similarly, it gets things backwards to try to explain the way things look in terms of what one would come to believe if one judged that things are as they look.

This seems persuasive, but the way the contents of the components of some informational system are determined, and the way such contents are related to the way things seem, may be more tangled than this analogy suggests. Consider another kind of situation in which information received by the visual system fails to result in knowledge, this time a case where the explanation for the failure is that the subject lacks the conceptual resources to form the relevant belief. Eucalyptus trees, let us suppose, have a quite distinctive look. If the tree in the garden were of any other kind, then things would look differently to O'Leary than they do, so we might say that O'Leary's visual system receives the information that there is a Eucalyptus tree in the garden. But O'Leary doesn't come to know, or believe, that there is a Eucalyptus tree in the garden, since he doesn't have a concept of a Eucalyptus tree (by that name, or any other). While O'Leary's visual system succeeds in discriminating Eucalyptus trees from other kinds, O'Leary himself does not. Now it does not seem to me that this situation is correctly described as a case in which it appears to O'Leary that there is a Eucalyptus tree in the garden. Why not? One might think that it cannot be right that things seem to someone to be a certain way unless the person has the capacity to endorse the appearance —to judge that things really are that way. If this is right, then the knowledge and beliefs that normally result from perceptual states may constrain the content properly attributed to the kinds of states that are ascribed when one says how things look, appear or seem to be.

But whether this is right or not, it is clear that one cannot, in all cases, identify the way things seem, or look, with the information received or delivered by some component of the informational system, some link in a chain of information transmission that in normal cases results in knowledge. It is surely essential to seeming that the way things seem be accessible to consciousness, but this need not be true of information bearing states that are part of a process that normally results in knowledge. Consider a very early stage of the visual processing system such as the retina. Suppose the image of a tree is on our subject's retina: it is in a state that it would normally be in when, and only when, the subject is confronted by a tree (as we may suppose he is). So the subject's retina indicates, and carries the information, that there is a tree before him. But suppose a distortion is introduced very early in the process, so that the subject is under the impression that he is looking at something that bears no resemblance to a tree. There is no sense in which it would be correct to say, in this case, that it seems to him (retinally speaking?) that there is a tree before him. But the retina surely does carry information, and is in a state that has representational content. The retina is part of the informational system that "constitutes the substratum of our cognitive lives". In the normal case when the information on the retina is successfully transmitted up the line, it contributes to determining the content of the subject's states of knowledge and belief, and to the way things appear to be to him. And since I assume that it will be agreed that the retina does not have conceptual capacities, I assume that it is safe to conclude that states of the retina have only nonconceptual content.

Evans regards it as important to identify information-bearing states of perceptual system with states of seeming since he is anxious to avoid the traditional epistemologist's picture according to which the subject receives, through the perceptual systems, sensory data that is "intrinsically without objective content", but which forms the basis for inferences about the world that causes them. "The only events that can conceivably be regarded as data for a conscious, reasoning subject are *seemings* —events, that is, already imbued with (apparent) objective significance" [p. 123]. But information-bearing states of all kinds, even those of things that are too primitive for anything to seem to be some way to them, are imbued with objective significance. This will be true whether one is talking about the rational judgments of an articulate and conceptually sophisticated person, or about the way things look to such a person, or to an animal, or about the image of a tree on a retina, or about that of the moon on the surface of a pond. To attribute informational content to the state of someone or something is to make a claim about a relation between that person or thing and its environment, and so is to make a claim that is in part about the environment —about the kinds of things that are found in the environment, and about the way the states of the person or thing are disposed to reflect the properties of those things. So, for example, if it is true that it appears to O'Leary that the zebra is striped, then there must be zebra that O'Leary is looking at. The claim that O'Leary's retina indicates that the zebra is striped has the same consequence. Of course O'Leary's visual system might be in an intrinsically indistinguishable state even if there were no zebra present, even if he were seeing nothing, but was hallucinating. In that case it couldn't be true, or even intelligible, to say that it appears to O'Leary that the zebra is striped. We would have to say that it looks to O'Leary like there is a stripped zebra in front of him, and this would be to attribute a different property to him —to make a different claim, one that relates his visual system to a different piece of information— a different informational content.

One might be tempted to think that the *real* content of O'Leary's state of seeming is one that abstracts away from the environmental dependence. The zebra can't be part of the real content of the way things look to O'Leary, since things could look just as they do even if it weren't the zebra that looked that way, or even if nothing looked that way. But it would be a mistake to yield to this temptation, since one cannot eliminate the environmental dependence without getting rid of informational content altogether. (Suppose O'Leary were in an intrinsically similar state in a world in which pigs looked exactly like zebras in fact look, and vice versa. Then it would look to O'Leary like there was a striped pig before him. This counterfactual possibility should not incline us to say that it is compatible with the way things look to O'Leary that there is a striped pig before him.) If one succeeded in purging the content of perceptual states of their environmental dependence, what would be left is sensory data, "intrinsically without objective content". One would be left with the dreaded myth of the given.

Ascriptions of informational content are external in that the concepts used to ascribe them are not thereby attributed to the subject. When I make a claim about the informational states of some subject, I use my concepts to describe the way her environment is disposed to affect her, but the concepts I use may or may not be ones that she shares with me. That is why it does not matter very much whether the parts of the informational system to which we attribute content and that we take to be the proximate sources of the information that is the content of our beliefs and knowledge are themselves accessible to introspection —are properly described as states of seeming. We use conceptual resources to refer to the contents of states of seeming, and also of more primitive informational states, but we do not thereby refer to some kind of content that has the concepts we express as constituents. We can give a reasonably clear account of a kind of abstract object that satisfies our conditions for being a kind of representational content, and that is apt for describing both primitive states of informational systems and the states of belief and acts of judgment of sophisticated reasoners.

My concluding question is this: why shouldn't one take the contents of belief and judgment to be the same kind of content as the kind used to characterize the more primitive information carrying states? Let us grant (without looking too hard at what this means) that states of belief and judgment are essentially conceptual —states and acts that require the capacity to deploy concepts, and that manifest the exercise of this capacity. That does not by itself imply that the concepts that subjects deploy and are disposed to deploy when they are in such states or perform such acts are thereby constitutive of the contents that are used to describe the states and acts. Even if both I and the subject to whom I attribute beliefs must be assumed to have conceptual capacities, it might be that my concepts and hers are different —that we cut the world up in somewhat different ways. If your concepts are different from mine, then I would be unable to use my concepts to attribute beliefs to you if in doing so I were saying that you had beliefs with those concepts as constituents. But we might think of concepts as part of the means used to refer to informational contents, in the way we do when we ascribe content to more primitive informational states that do not involve the deployment of concepts at all. In general, we might say, to attribute content is to characterize various kinds of internal states of others by describing how they tend to vary with certain alternative states of the environment (or more generally, the world). We use our own conceptual resources to distinguish the alternative states of the world, but do not thereby imply that the subject uses the same means to distinguish the alternatives. We might say this even about information–bearing states that belong to what I refuse to call the space of reasons, or the realm of spontaneity.

Gareth Evans proposed that we distinguish different kinds of informational states, that are characterized by different kinds of content. John McDowell argued, in his criticism of Evans, that both kinds of states had the same kind of content: content is conceptual all the way down. I am inclined to agree with McDowell that the different kinds of states have the same kind of content, but I am suggesting that it is nonconceptual all the way up.

Grain and Content

Stephen Neale

It is widely held that entertaining a belief or forming a judgement involves the exercise of conceptual capacities; and to this extent the representational content of a belief or judgement is said to be "conceptual". According to Gareth Evans (1980), not all psychological states have conceptual content in this sense. In particular, perceptual states have non-conceptual content; it is not until one forms a judgement on the basis of a perceptual experience that one touches the realm of conceptual content:

> The informational states which a subject acquires through perception are *non-conceptual*, or *non-conceptualized*. Judgements *based upon* such states necessarily involve conceptualization: in moving from a perceptual experience to a judgement about the world (usually expressible in some verbal form), one will be exercising basic conceptual skills.... The process of conceptualization or judgement takes the subject from his being in one kind of state (with a content of a certain kind, namely non-conceptual content) to his being in another kind of cognitive state (with a content of a different kind, namely, conceptual content). (1980, p. 227)

Evans's argumentation for the non-conceptual content of perceptual experience draws upon two facts he takes to be undeniable. First, the operations of the informational system of which perceptual capacities are parts are "more primitive" than the conceptual operations that, amongst other things, play a role in mapping perceptual states into judgements and beliefs. Second, perceptual states may be more fine-grained than what we can call "central" states such as judgements and beliefs. For example, Evans claims that we do not have as many colour concepts as there are shades of colour that we can discriminate and that consequently perceptual experience involving colour discrimination cannot be conceptual.

Christopher Peacocke (1992) acknowledges the mismatch Evans postulates and concludes that perceptual experience is at least *partly* non-conceptual; John McDowell (1994) argues that both central and perceptual content are conceptual. Whatever the relative standings of the positions of Evans, Peacocke, and McDowell, the debate in which they are engaged is clear, and their disagreements take place against a background of shared assumptions and goals, inspired largely by Frege (and to some extent also by Strawson). Robert Stalnaker's (1997) recent entry into the debate is hard to assess: the argumentation seems to be set against fundamentally different background assumptions about what suffices for psychological content at all and what suffices for individuating particular candidate contents. Indeed, Stalnaker's professed unhappiness with the terms of the conceptual–nonconceptual debate and his overt claim that all content is nonconceptual, incline one to read his paper as exclusively an attempt to defend his own influential coarse-grained account of content from objections that might be engendered by taking a distinction between conceptual and nonconceptual content seriously enough to debate. Stalnaker suggests there is something quite puzzling about the debate, that it involves slippage between talk of mental states as conceptual (nonconceptual) and talk of the contents of such states as conceptual (nonconceptual). If I am correct in my interpretation of Evans, Peacocke, and McDowell, Stalnaker has not fully appreciated the antecedently Fregean nature of the conceptual–nonconceptual debate in which they are engaged: an overarching disagreement between those of a neo–Fregean persuasion as far as semantics and psychology are concerned and those persuaded of the mere semantic sufficiency of Russellian propositions or truth–conditions (in the standard sense) makes it necessary for the non–Fregean semanticist to explain, at least in a rudimentary way, the relationship between semantics and psychology in order to obtain admission to the conceptual–nonconceptual debate —bald appeals to "dual aspects", to distinctions between "wide" and "narrow" contents, to distinctions between characters/roles and objects referred to "directly", and so on are of little help. At times Stalnaker appears to be proposing a different position on the same field, for example when he suggests that McDowell is right in thinking that perceptual and central psychological states have the same kind of content but wrong to think it is conceptual. Representational content is, Stalnaker suggests "nonconceptual all the way up". But the way Stalnaker goes about promoting this position indicates that he thinks the invocation of a distinction between conceptual and nonconceptual representational states is based on some sort of confusion. He begins by asking what it is people want when they seek to contrast conceptual and nonconceptual states, a question which he believes can best be answered by reflecting on what kinds of objects can serve as these different types of content, and on how such entities can be used to characterize perception and thought. The objects in question are taken to be propositions, and Stalnaker's own position on the individuation of such entities has remained stable for many years: a strict truth-conditional account will suffice.

For common reasons, Stalnaker takes the contents of perceptual states to be environmentally dependent. Additionally, he takes our ascriptions of content to be external in the following sense: the concepts we employ in such ascriptions are not necessarily attributed to the ascribee by the sincere ascriber simply by virtue of making the ascription in question. We use our own concepts to describe the way the ascribee's external circumstances are disposed to impinge upon him or her; however, the concepts we employ need not be ones that the ascribee shares with us. We use our conceptual resources to denote the contents of the ascribee's central states, states of seeming, and primitive informational states; but we do not thereby refer to a kind of content that has the concepts we express as components.

On this account, there will be no important difference between ascriptions of central and perceptual content. Representational content is unitary, appropriate for descriptions of central or perceptual states —at least as long as we can provide a clear account of some sort of abstract entity that satisfies a set of conditions for being a kind of representational content. That it is correct to think of central and perceptual states as having the same type of content —whether conceptual or nonconceptual— is meant to be supported by the following consideration:

> [W]hen something merely looks to me to be a certain way, even though I do not believe it is that way, then there is a perceptual state with a certain content that might have been but is not the content of any of my beliefs (p. 341).

I do not want to quarrel with this. But there is a feature of Stalnaker's proposal that I find problematic. Stalnaker wants to pull the rug out from under those who would view talk of the contents of any psychological states as involving a commitment to conceptual content. As if by default, we are meant to be left with nonconceptual content as the sole type of content because our ascriptions are external in the sense noted above: the concepts we employ in such ascriptions are not thereby attributed to the ascribee. Of course, we can saddle the ascribee with our concepts, it's just that in our standard psychological ascriptions we do not, so we need a notion of informational content that does not presuppose the employment of our conceptual abilities, but whose use in the attribution of psychological states does. And according to Stalnaker, if we retreat to a minimal truth–conditional account of content, steered by considerations of causal and counterfactual dependencies, we get exactly what we want.

I have two main points to make here. First, we do not seem to get exactly what we want. Second, if we do not get what we want, the assault on conceptual content fails.

Stalnaker points out that contents must have three important features: (i) they must be abstract, (ii) they must transcend particular languages; and (iii) they must have truth conditions. Broadly speaking, there are three approaches to content. In descending order of fineness of grain: the Fregean, the Russellian, and the (merely) truth–conditional. In short, contents must be propositions, under some construal.

According to the Fregean conception that Stalnaker sketches, a proposition takes the form of a structured object composed wholly of (sequences of) senses or "concepts". (Assuming a theory of sense–compositionality that mirrors Fregean theories of reference–compositionality and respects Fregean accounts of the relationship between sense and reference, I suspect we will not be in a position to view the sense of a sentence as a structured sequence of senses, but let us put this aside.) Stalnaker suggests that it makes sense to view this sort of content as conceptual. But this is not the sense of "conceptual" that is meant to be at issue: the representational content of a belief or judgement is said to be "conceptual", according to Evans, in the sense that entertaining a belief or forming a judgement involves the exercise of conceptual capacities. This claim is logically distinct from the claim that contents are modes of presentation and the claim that they have senses as components (if they do).

According to the Russellian conception, a content takes the form of a structured object composed wholly of (sequences of) objects.

Famously, Russellian propositions are more coarse-grained than Fregean propositions. (Utterances of 'Hesperus is a planet' and 'Phosphorus is a planet' express the same Russellian proposition but distinct Fregean propositions.) According to Stalnaker, the Russellian picture is "nonconceptual" because objects rather than senses (or "concepts" as Stalnaker sometimes puts it) are the building blocks. Again, it seems to me that Stalnaker has misconstrued the nature of the conceptual–nonconceptual debate.

Stalnaker's preferred account of content is straightforwardly truth-conditional; he calls such content "informational". On such an account, a proposition can be viewed as a function from possible worlds to truth-values (or possible circumstances to truth-values, if this is helpful), and of course Stalnaker has done as much as anyone to explain the merits of this idea in the context of his pioneering work on the semantics of natural language and on modality. In the present context, Stalnaker suggests the advantage of injecting this notion of content into the debate is that it is

> [...] a kind of content that everyone should agree can be used to characterize mental and linguistic states, acts and events that can be said to have representational content of any kind (p. 343).

On the intended construal, this is correct: the Fregean and the Russellian agree that a proposition has truth conditions (and some, but by no means all, might even be prepared to view a function from possible worlds to truth values as an elegant way of capturing this fact). Truth-conditional ("informational") content is nonconceptual for Stalnaker because

> [...] although it can be used to characterize any kind of representational act or state, its use says nothing one way or the other about whether any kind of act or state essentially involves the exercise of conceptual capacities (whatever this might mean) (p. 343).

Has Stalnaker simply sidestepped the issue of the contents of mental states themselves? No. It is part of his picture that there is no more to be said about the contents of psychological states than is given by the truth-conditional contents of our ascriptive clauses, as long as these are not articulated in ways that display an obvious insensitivity to environmental dependence. We can get at the question "What is content?" Stalnaker believes, by asking how the abstract object referred to —or as I would prefer to put it *described by*— a complement clause of the form 'that p' determines the property ascribed by (e.g.) the verb phrase 'believes that p'. We provide an account of the abstract objects to which agents are relevantly related in terms of causal and counterfactual dependence, and we provide an account of the relation to the abstract object in terms of a property that can be determined as a function of the object, in much the same way that the property of weighing 75 kg can be determined as a function of the number 75.

One problem, of course, is that causal and counterfactual dependence is not enough to distinguish the belief that two plus two is four from, the belief that ten squared is a hundred, the belief that there is no largest prime, and so on. Similarly, one would like to be able to distinguish the belief that Hesperus is a planet and the belief that Phosphorus is a planet and thereby distinguish *in respect of truth conditions* utterances of 'John believes that Hesperus is a planet' and 'John believes that Phosphorus is a planet' whilst holding onto the truth that the embedded clauses do not differ truth-conditionally. And, of course, it is exactly this type of problem that the neo–Fregean armed with conceptual content claims to be able to solve. But without some systematic treatment of these old logical and psychological substitution issues, there is no reason to think the coarse-grained truth-conditional account of content that Stalnaker favours will do justice to the richness of propositional content, and so no reason to accept that we can make do with, or are left only with, nonconceptual content. All of this reinforces the familiar point that one's picture of psychological content and one's semantics cannot be entirely divorced (though of course, the possibility of a systematic semantics in no way compels us to posit entities for complement clauses of the form 'that p' to refer to or describe). Neo–Fregeans about semantic content are simply out of range of the type of argument Stalnaker is mounting against the conceptual content and thereby against the conceptual–nonconceptual debate in which they are engaged.

References

Evans, G., *The Varieties of Reference*. Oxford: Clarendon, 1980.
McDowell, J., *Mind and World*. Cambridge, Mass.: Harvard University Press, 1994.
Peacocke, C., *A Study of Concepts*. Cambridge, Mass.: MIT Press, 1992.
Stalnaker, R. "What Might Nonconceptual Content Be?" This volume.

Non–Conceptual Content, Subject–Centered Information and the Naturalistic Demand*

Juan José Acero

Professor Stalnaker begins his interesting paper[1] by wondering what non–conceptual content —NCC in what follows— might be. And he ends by suggesting, first, that every informational state, no matter whether perceptual or not, possesses the same kind of content; and second, that content is always non–conceptual in nature. Thus, Stalnaker not only rejects that we should distinguish two kinds of content, but also that content be conceptual. As discrepancies between Stalnaker and the advocate of NCC seem to be so acute, it is not wholly unreasonable to have the impression that this is a debate in which the parties involved do not share the same battlefield, and that the true object of contention lies somewhere else. In this note, I will insist on this conclusion by taking into account the relationship of NCC to its possessors; then I will refer to a feature of NCC, its

---

*The research put forward in this note has been made possible by a grant of the Spanish Ministerio de Educación y Cultura's DGICYT, No. PB93–1049–C03–03.

[1] "What Might Nonconceptual Content Be?", this volume.

subject–centered character, to point out that Stalnaker owes us an explanation of how to accomodate it in his view of content, and I will finally argue that this task shows that the project of naturalizing content must state precisely what its aims are.

Content: phenomenology versus causal dependency. The question about what the content of a speech act, i.e. an assertion, is has been answered by following one of these two main tracks. On the one hand, we may try setting up whether the assertion that p by a subject S is the same as the assertion that q by considering whether asserting that p at a certain moment of time necessarily amounts to asserting that q by S at that very moment. (An parallel criterion can be put forward that sets up when two thoughts are one and the same.) Determining such an equivalence (or lack of it) can be an exercise in what Dennett has called *hetero–phenomenology*, when it is not S, but someone else, who has to judge in what way S reacts to asserting that p, i.e. whether his behavior *vis–à–vis* this speech act betrays any feature that does not manifests itself in NCC behavior *vis–à–vis* the assertion that q. Alternatively, he should identify whether there is any circumstance in which the subject asserts that p but does not assert that q. The differences and equivalences I am alluding to have not to be inferred from the linguistic and non–linguistic behavior of only one subject; the research can be take into consideration any number of members of a linguistic community. On the other hand, the quest for content can be an exercise in *self–phenomenology* —or simply, *phenomenology*—, when it is each of us who must tell whether p and q are the same content. (And there are a number of paths that could be followed to do that.) If at a certain moment of time we can accept that p without accepting that q, then these two thoughts are not the same. In both variants of this approach though for historical and systematic reasons the second qualifies higher—, Frege's concept of cognitive significance sets up the pattern to articulate the notion of a speech act and thought content. (Given this requirement as to when two thoughts are the same originates with Frege, I will refer to it as Frege's principle.)

Part of the recent vindication of a non–conceptual kind of content, specially that advocated by philosophers such as Peacocke, Cussins or Chrisley,[2] has this sort of phenomenological nature. For them,

---

[2] C. Peacocke, "Analogue Content", *Proceedings of the Aristotelian Society*, Supplementary volume LX (1986) 1-17; *A Study of Concepts* (Cambridge, MA: The M.I.T. Press, 1992), chap. 3 ("Perceptual Content"), reprinted as "Scenarios, Concepts and Perception" in T. Crane (ed.), *The Contents of Experience*,

the content of a subject's perceptual state is conceived as a way the world presents itself to the subject, specifically as a way of filling out the space around the perceiver at the time of his experience. Differences between two ways of filling out that space in consecutive moments not only can be recognized by the subject herself, but can be detected by someone else and emerge in the subject's behavior as well:

> Suppose you are in a field in the early autumn in England and see mist in a certain region. Can a theorist specify part of the representational content of your visual experience by means of the proposition that the region has the property of being misty? [...] Suppose the region in question is to your north. Someone for whom the region is in a northeasterly direction may also see it to be misty [...]. But the region is clearly presented in perception in different ways to you and to the other person. Each of you sees it as being in a different direction relative to yourself, and your actions may differ as a result. Any description of the contents of your two experiences that omits this difference is incomplete.[3]

Perceptual content is to be taken into account within the thought-forms catalogue, as Peacocke emphasizes, on pain of falling short of a complete description of our experience.

Stalnaker's concerns are clearly in another orbit. For him, content is an abstract entity —a truth condition, a set of possible worlds— whose interest for us originates in a view of speech and thought acts as consisting of two ingredients: the proposition expressed, i.e. what is asserted, asked, commanded, and so on, and the force with which it is expressed, i.e. the assertion, the question, the command and so on. It is when we are pressed to explain how it is possible for anyone to be related to an abstract object that Stalnaker shows how far is he from the NCC advocate and how foreign to his worries is what Frege's principle requires from a theory of content. The abstract objects with whose help he characterizes speech acts and mental states and processes are, according to Stalnaker, convenient ways of describing informational relationships between the subject's environment states and his own inner states. (We invoke these abstract objects because the determination of what the subject's mental or linguistic property

---

Cambridge University Press, 1992; A. Cussins, "The Connectionist Construction of Concepts", in M. Boden (ed.), *The Philosophy of Artificial Intelligence*, Oxford University Press, 1990; T. Crane, "The Nonceptual Contents of Experience", in T. Crane (ed.), *op. cit.*; D. Chrisley, *Non-conceptual Psychological Explanation: Content and Computation*, PhD Dissertation, Oxford University, 1996.

[3] C. Peacocke, *A Study of Concepts*, p. 70.

is like, i.e. that S believes that p or that S asserts that q, is a function of those abstract entities.) These relations are causal and counterfactual: it is the subject's sensitivity to a range of states of the environment that qualifies him to process information on it. Mental and linguistic content is then a matter of causal etiology and counterfactuality, of what environment states are in the origin of the subject's mental states and of what counterfactual links relate both kinds of states to each other. A brain state B carries the information that p, if the brain would not be in B if the environment to which it is attuned were not in the state that p.

Now, it is clearly rather difficult to reconcile these two approaches. While Stalnaker's is openly naturalistic in spirit, Peacocke has admitted not to feeling attracted to such a doctrine when developing a theory of content.[4] While content is for Stalnaker an abstract object as a function of which content bearers can be attributed intentional properties, because of their causal and counterfactual links to their environment, for Peacocke the adscription of those properties to people has mainly to answer both phenomenological and hetero–phenomenological constraints. This is why I am inclined to think that Stalnaker's reluctance to admit that there are two kinds of content is a symptom of further and deeper differences with some of NCC advocates. Though I agree with a substantial portion of Stalnaker's theory of content, I miss this further significance in his contribution.

The subject–centeredness of information. A suggestion that it might be useful to consider at this point is that, due to the difficulty of finding a shared battlefield on which to work out his differences with the NCC advocate, Stalnaker has chosen Evans as his interlocutor. Evans' introduction of the idea of NCC occurs within a theoretical framework that can properly considered naturalistic. People, he says, are gatherers, storers and transmitters of information: perception, communication and memory constitute what Evans calls the informational system. Through such a system information can be carried in a number of ways. In communicating a piece of information, the propositional, conceptual, format is mandatory. However, for Evans the perceptual subsystem is isolated in the sense that it identifies its objects in a more primitive way —a way that does not not involve concept mediation and that serves as the input to a number of higher modules of the information system: to the thinking,

---

[4] See his recent "Can Possession Conditions Individuate Concepts?", *Philosophy and Phenomenological Research*, LVI (1996) 433-460. See specially pp. 438 ff.

concept–applying, reasoning subsystems. If this were the whole story about Evans' view of content, it would be most natural to identify content with the information about the world the information system gathers, processes and serves. To Stalnaker's surprise —a feeling I share with him—, Evans does not take this step. He does not do it because in giving the content of a thought Evans requires that we must not only specify the thought's target, the object it gives information about; we have also to do this "in a way which mirrors the mode of identification which the subject employs".[5] And Evans believes that there are modes of identification specific to sensory modalities. Therefore, perceptual states thus have a kind of information content, a NCC, of their own. This explains why Evans thinks that he has won the right to say that whereas the senses yield non–conceptual content, the information language embodies is conceptual.

Now, I repeat, Evans' idea of the information system lends itself nicely to a kind a view of information content close to Stalnaker's, in addition to answering the naturalist demands. Why then does Evans require from a theory of content more than causal links and worldly targets? Because he accepts Russell's principle as well, that is to say, the constraint that a subject cannot have any thought about an individual unless he has discriminative knowledge of such an individual, i.e. the capacity to distinguish it from all other individuals. In allowing for the possibility that this capacity might not be conceptually exercised, the gates are open to perceptual, demonstrative, non–conceptual ways of identification: to NCC. Thus, the real obstacle to Stalnaker's notion of content is either Russell's principle —as for Evans— or Frege's principle -as for Peacocke, Cussins or Crane; and what he needs is to neutralize them. Since he does not do so, he is open to the following kind of objection:

Imagine I am sitting at my table, looking at what there is on it and seeing my dictionary to the left of my computer. Someone enters my office and also sees my English dictionary and my computer, but she sees the former as being to the right of the latter. (My office door is in front of my table desk.) Would it be wrong to say that the information we obtain is the same? What counts as the same information and what as different information in a case like this? Should the set of possible worlds that qualify as the infor-

---

[5]G. Evans, *The Varieties of Reference* (Oxford: Clarendon Press, 1982), p. 139. According to the *Varieties*'s editor, this requirement follows from Russell's Principle, the principle that "a subject cannot make a judgement about something unless he knows which object his judgement is about" (*op. cit.*, p. 89).

mation content of my perceptual state be thought of in terms that answer what is common to my visitor's and my own mental states? Or should we rather say that, being involved in the same state of affairs, our mental states' information contents differ? Questions like these may have led Peacocke to put forward scenarios —ways of filling in the space around a subject— as a kind of (non–conceptual) content; and may have pushed Cussins to conceive of NCCs as essentially indexical or demonstrative ways of registering the world. In both cases, a reference to the subject's location in space time and his access to information from this very location seem to be unavoidable.[6] As information gatherers, our body defines the axes that determine what we perceive, tingeing the information we manage to obtain with its subject–centered tones: what we see, hear, touch from the perspective determined by our body's position. This is a metaphor, of course, but I do believe it conveys a relevant point, namely, that third–person view of information in terms of causal and counterfactual dependencies, though conforming to the naturalism rule, should be supplemented with an account of the information's subject–centered character, if it has to appeal against the NCC advocate's demands. Most of the information we gain and use wears a first–person dress.

Normal conditions and the extent of Stalnaker's naturalism. It seems reasonable to me to demand from a causal view of information that it should leave room for such a subject–centered feature, thus explaining everything that differences either in scenarios or in demonstrative ways of registering the world help to explain. However, a sign that Stalnaker's approach to content might be better equipped than other rival causal theories of content is provided by the fact that it manages quite efficiently with a handful of 'difficult cases' on which the idea of a NCC has been set up. I have in mind cases like John Perry's shopper that followed a trail of sugar on a supermarket floor, pushing his cart down the aisle on one side of a tall counter and back the aisle on the other, seeking the shopper with the torn sack to tell him that he was making a mess. Though with each trip around the counter the trail became thicker, the shopper took some time he realized that he was trying to catch up with himself.[7] It

---

[6] Evans' treatment of egocentric spatial thinking develops in the same spirit. See particularly *The Varieties of Reference*, pp. 153-156.

[7] "The Problem of Essential Indexical", *Noûs*, 13 (1979) 3-21. Collected in J. Perry, *The Problem of the Essential Indexical and Other Essays*, Oxford University Press, 1993.

has been pointed out that the content of the thought '*I* was making a mess' is not wholly conceptual; in other words, that it is (partially) non–conceptual.[8] The ground for such a diagnosis is that in order for content to be wholly conceptual, it has exclusively to be made up of descriptive and logical concepts. It is well–known, however, that there is no way for the shopper to reach at the disheartening discovery that does not deploy the first–person concept. He has to see himself as the origin of the mess. It seems to me that, if cases like Perry's represent a challenge for any theory of mental content, Stalnaker's approach has the resources to begin dealing with them. What makes me think so is Stalnaker's proposal[9] that in attributing representational content to a subject, we must bring into play not only causal and counterfactual dependencies of brain states to states of his environment, but also the proviso that these dependencies hold in normal conditions. When it comes to what normal condictions should be, Stalnaker mentions both conditions on the environment and conditions on the internal functioning of the representational mechanisms. It is indisputable that "conditions on the internal functioning of the representational mechanisms" is quite an intriguing label.[10] It is natural to suggest that in at least some cases the exercising of conceptual abilities might be among those internal conditions. Stalnaker's example, in the target paper, of the man that sees a Eucalyptus tree without being able to judge that it is a Eucalyptus tree is worth bringing up here, because it warrants the conclusion that in order for someone to normally be in a certain kind of high–level cognitive state, the deployment of conceptual resources is needed. Let us suppose we agree to this. Then it is also natural enough to extend the same principle to those cases in which information flows from the environment to a subject by virtue of the latter's exercising demonstrative conceptual abilities. (In this vein we would thus say that a necessary condition for Perry's shopper's becoming aware of having been making a mess is his ability to exercise the first–person concept on the occasion.) But, of course, the success of this analysis relies upon having firstly eluci-

---

[8] In A. Cussins, *op. cit.*

[9] *Inquiry* (Cambridge, MA: The MIT Press, 1984), *passim*; "Replies to Schiffer and Field", *Pacific Philosophical Quarterly*, 67 (1986) 113-123; "On What's in the Head", in J.E. Tomberlin (ed.), *Philosophical Perspectives*, 7: *Philosophy of Mind and Action Theory*, Atascadero, CA: Ridgeview Publishing Co., 1989; "Twin Earth Revisited", *Proceedings of the Aristotelian Society*, XCIII (1993) 297-311.

[10] Stalnaker uses it in "Twin Earth Revisited", *loc. cit.*, p. 302.

dated the idea of a demonstrative conceptual ability —a lack I have insisted on.[11]

The resort to normal conditions has a promisory tone, I have pointed out. However, it also seems to me it creates a tension with the naturalistic demands that Stalnaker seems to abide by. The tension lies in the fact that the notion of normal conditions does not easily lend itself to a complete naturalistic analysis. I do not deny that quite a lot of those conditions may have their own place in natural science —I endorse Stalnaker's confidence that it often corresponds to natural science to determine what conditions those are. But one cannot but expect that in trying to point out in what conditions high-level mental states causally (and normally) covary with states of the environment, we should refer to further contentful mental states and abilities. The above suggestion as to how to solve 'difficult cases' like Perry's shopper is a serious warning of the *impasse*. The remark, however, is a principled one. Stalnaker has persuasively argued that content adscription is a contextual affair, that the space of those states of the environment the subject tends to be sensible to cannot be fixed simply by consulting the environment; that the subject's history and presuppositions are determinant:

> The theorist, in describing the internal states of a representator in terms of informational content, has some choice in the range of alternatives relative to which content is defined. It may even be that for any possibility we can describe, there is a context in which we can ask whether the representator's beliefs distinguish that possibility from certain others. But this does not imply that there is an absolutely neutral context, a context free of all presuppositions about the environment, relative to which content adscriptions make sense.[12]

The recognition that content adscription is relative to a (high? very high?) number of presuppositions amounts to the recognition that a full-scale task of content naturalization is going to be very, very hard to culminate. In effect, if the naturalist demands of a theory of content that it be restricted to physical notions, as is sometimes

---

[11] A possibility that might be considered is whether Stalnaker would accept to identify a piece of demonstrative information with what he elsewhere calls a *propositional function*: a function from contexts to propositions, i.e. functions from possible worlds to truth values. (Propositional functions would perhaps have to be adequately modified to carry out this task.) See his "Indexical Belief", *Synthese*, 57 (1981) 129-152; "Semantics for Belief", *Philosophical Topics*, 15 (1987) 177-190. I wonder whether Stalnaker has found any fault in this notion that justifies his not having turned to it in arguing that there is no NCC.

[12] "On What's in the Head", *loc. cit.*, p. 306.

required, that it be put forward in non-intentional terms, then I see no hope of satisfying it by following the route Stalnaker and others have been exploring. The contextuality of mental content is the obstacle. This is not meant either as a criticism of Stalnaker's remark nor as something we should complain about. The naturalism I approve of does not require the reduction of content notions to non-intentional ones, but a clear understanding of how an evolutionary process is carried through, namely, one that begins with a newborn infant and leads to a mature person, a being endowed with plain thought and linguistic capacities. However, in making a detailed picture of such a process a causal and counterfactual view of content is undeniably useful. It not only gives us a clue as to the general features of the device by which very basic intentional states set up in normal conditions; it also help to draw a rough outline of the sketch that has to be filled out. But recognizing this does not even warrant the possibility of naturalizing NCC. I wonder to what extent Stalnaker would agree with this other way of endorsing naturalism.

Report of an Unsuccessful Search for Nonconceptual Content

Mario Gómez–Torrente

In his paper "What might nonconceptual content be?" (included in this volume) Stalnaker has given us a clear and concise account of his views on content and the role this notion should play in a theory of perception and thought. I, who know very little about this set of ideas, thank him very much for the expository effort. It has helped me, or so I hypothesize, to gain a clearer understanding of what the problems are in this area. I will rely on this hypothetical understanding acquired from Stalnaker's paper in the following comments.

According to Stalnaker, when we use certain statements involving sentential complements, for example, statements of the form "x believes that P", "it appears to x that P" and "x asserted that P", what we are doing can be usefully explained by supposing that we are asserting that certain relations hold between x and a certain abstract object denoted by the clause (of the form) "that P". These abstract objects denoted by clauses of the form "that P" must be objects which somehow have truth conditions; that is, there are possible conditions (of reality) under which they are true; and those conditions are described precisely by the embedded sentence P —i.e., P is true if the object denoted by "that P" is true, and vice versa. These abstract objects are called the (representational) "contents" of belief, appearance, assertion, etc.

There are many kinds of abstract objects that have the property characteristic of representational contents, says Stalnaker. The objects belonging to some of those kinds will have concepts as basic constituents (if there are such things as concepts), but still in such a way that the constituted object will have truth conditions; for example, on this construction the denotation of the clause "that the bone is under the tree" will be something constituted by the concept (or a concept) of "the", the concept (or a concept) of "bone", the concept (or a concept) of "is", and so on, arranged in such a way or according to such a law that the thing thus constituted by them "determines" the conditions under which the sentence 'the bone is under the tree' is true. Another kind of abstract objects with the property characteristic of contents are simply the truth conditions themselves, which Stalnaker identifies with sets of possible circumstances; the set of possible circumstances where P is true would, on this construction, be the denotation of the clause "that P", and hence the representational content of the appropriate beliefs, "appearings", assertions, etc.

The main purpose of Stalnaker's paper is, in his words, to "spell out my own assumptions about representational content, and ask how, given the way I understand this notion, a distinction between conceptual and nonconceptual content might be drawn, and what role it might play in the explanation of the relation between perception and thought" (p. 340). Given what we have said, we can see how Stalnaker draws a distinction between conceptual and nonconceptual content. According to this distinction, conceptual contents are abstract objects that have the property characteristic of representational contents and that have concepts as constituents; the abstract objects formed by "arrangement of concepts" would be examples of conceptual contents; and nonconceptual contents are abstract objects that have the property characteristic of representational contents and that do not have concepts as constituents; sets of possible circumstances would be examples of nonconceptual contents. (Perhaps nonconceptual contents in Stalnaker's sense can also have concepts as constituents, but not in the way that is relevant here —suppose that Peter is my favorite concept, and that I think that Peter is beautiful; then presumably the set of circumstances in which the object Peter is beautiful will involve Peter as a constituent.)

Stalnaker argues that when we use statements of the form "x believes that P", "it appears to x that P", "x asserted that P", etc., we are not attributing to x any specific capacity to deploy concepts. In particular, we do not attribute to x the capacity to "deploy" (any of) the concepts that we are supposedly deploying when we utter the clause "that P" that forms part of those statements. The argument for this claim seems to rely on the following premise: when we attribute representational content to a state of someone (a state of believing, of appearing to him, etc.), we are making a claim about a relation between that person and his environment, which is in part a claim about how the states of that person are disposed to reflect the properties of his environment. In Stalnaker's example, if I utter as an assertion "it appears to O'Leary that the zebra is striped", my assertion will be true, and hence O'Leary's state will have as its content the denotation of "that the zebra is striped" only if there is a zebra that O'Leary is looking at.

Now, from this remark alone it doesn't follow that we are not attributing to O'Leary the capacity to deploy the concept of a zebra —it only follows that something about the environment, and not just about O'Leary's mental state, must be true for the content attribution to be true. But I suppose that what Stalnaker means in this particular case (if in fact he is using these considerations to support the claim that I'm not attributing to O'Leary the capacity to deploy the concept of zebra) is that for the content attribution to be true it is sufficient that O'Leary be in a certain relation (code–named "appearing") to the zebra itself and to some other things (or, to be precise, to a set of possible circumstances in which the zebra and some other things appear somehow), a relation that can obtain without O'Leary having the capacity to deploy the concept of zebra (nor, perhaps, even the concept of striped).

Be this as it may, I find Stalnaker's claim that in content attributions we are not attributing "conceptual capacities" convincing —I find it convincing, that is, to the extent that I understand what concepts and conceptual capacities actually are (Stalnaker expresses the same reservation). From this claim Stalnaker concludes that the only kinds of contents that are needed to characterize content attributions are nonconceptual contents, in his sense of the term. Surely this conclusion is warranted if the premise is. (The premise could be disputed. I suppose that it's reasonable to think that typically when we make content attributions we do want to imply for our audience that the person to whose states we are attributing contents has the capacity to deploy the concepts that we are deploying by making our attributions. And the audience will generally accept that implication if they accept the attribution as true. Surely you will think that O'Leary has the capacity to deploy the concepts of "arithmetic" and "incomplete" if you believe me when I tell you that O'Leary believes that arithmetic is incomplete. But this phenomenon can be explained, I suppose, by appeal to pragmatic properties of our attributions, without need of postulating that the concepts are part of the content we are attributing. Perhaps O'Leary believes that arithmetic is incomplete, and the way he manages to do this is extravagantly different from ours (or mine), hard as it might be to imagine this.)

Let's go back to the beginning of Stalnaker's discussion. The reason Stalnaker wants to see how he could draw a distinction between conceptual and nonconceptual content is that a distinction employing those same words for the things distinguished was made and put to use by others. In particular by Gareth Evans, and later by other philosophers influenced by Evans, philosophers who typically claim that —under their sense of 'conceptual content' and 'nonconceptual content'— states of perception often or always have nonconceptual content and states of belief, assertion, knowledge and others always have conceptual content. Stalnaker says that he does not fully understand how these philosophers draw the distinction, and yet he wants to see if a similar distinction can be drawn and put to use in the context of his views about content. The discussion we have reviewed then follows, with the upshot that the distinction he makes turns out not to yield an interesting —or perhaps I should say useful— difference: we just don't need what Stalnaker calls conceptual contents.

But, of course, the worry will persist for Stalnaker that perhaps the distinction he makes is not the distinction the other philosophers make. Perhaps the fact that he has not been able to find an homonymous distinction with an interesting difference behind it is not too significant.

Interested in the question whether this conjecture might be true, I have skimmed through the pages of some of those philosophers who make a distinction between conceptual and nonconceptual content and put it to substantial use. And I have discovered that I also have great trouble understanding what these philosophers mean. However, I have reached the conclusion that I should try to comment on what they say. Perhaps the exegetical approach is better suited to a discussion of the question whether the distinction has an interesting or useful difference behind it. My exegetical foray will be of necessity very superficial, and perhaps wrong even in substantial ways. But I believe that a commentary on Stalnaker's paper that does a bit of exegesis will be more interesting than a commentary on the details of Stalnaker's views on content (views which I believe to be well known and to have been extensively discussed in the literature on the philosophy of mind —both with attention to their virtues and to the problems they face). And at any rate, such a reply will be more interesting towards an examination of the question that gives its title to Stalnaker's paper.

The distinction as drawn by Evans's followers responds to felt differences between perception on the one hand and belief on the other. The main one of these felt differences seems to be the following. When one is in a state of perception, one does not need to "have concepts" under which to subsume all the "parts" of his "perceptual state", even if one is able to discriminate them from other parts. However (it is claimed), when one is in a state of belief one is deploying conceptual capacities, in such a way that all the significant "parts" of the "belief state" reflect the deployment of a particular concept. For example, O'Leary has the zebra (or an appearance of the zebra) in his visual field, and he can (consciously) discriminate this part of what he is perceiving from other parts —the trees, the stripes, and so on—, without for that reason "having the concepts" of zebra, of tree, of stripe, and so on. However, in order for him to believe that the zebra is striped he has to be able to think of something —perhaps the zebra and stripes— as subsumed under some concepts or others (not necessarily, I take it, under the belief-attributer's concepts of zebra and striped). The question is then whether these intuitions support a claim that the contents of perception must be different in kind from the contents of belief; the first kind of contents would be nonconceptual, the second conceptual. (I'm not claiming to fully understand what all this means, but at the very least I'm under an illusion of partial understanding.)

The truth of these observations is compatible, it seems, with Stalnaker's claim that when we attribute content to a mental state (or a state in general) we are not thereby attributing the capacity to deploy particular concepts to the entity whose state is said to have content. In particular, in the case of belief states, it seems that we can say that someone believes that P without being thereby attributing to him the "possession" of any *particular* concepts, and at the same time we can say consistently that he must "have" some concept or other if he in fact believes that P. In fact, Stalnaker says precisely this towards the end of his paper. I'm not sure if the same claim has been held by any of the other philosophers, but it is not consistent with what some of those I have read say. For example, Tim Crane says: "When we describe the tree as representing its age, or as carrying the information that it is 70 years old, we do not suppose that the tree possesses the concept of a year —or indeed any other concept. However, we think that when someone believes that they are 70 years old, they presumably cannot believe this unless they possess the concept of a year" (Crane [1992], p. 141).

But even some of those who say that in belief ascriptions we attribute particular concepts to the believer say also that it cannot be the case that conceptual contents are objects that have concepts as constituents and nonconceptual contents are objects that don't. The reason some of them give is that perceptual and belief states "can share contents. When I believe that the sun is shining because I see that it is, then in an obvious way I believe what I see" (Crane [1992], p. 140). It follows that if the contents of perception don't have concepts as constituents then those of belief don't have them either, and the distinction evaporates, much as in Stalnaker's discussion.

However, the distinction is then sometimes drawn in a way different from Stalnaker's, and here is where I think the problems begin. For example, Crane offers the following as a "precise" definition of 'nonconceptual content': "For any state with content, S, S has nonconceptual content, P, iff a subject X's being in S does not entail that X possesses the concepts that canonically characterise P" (Crane [1992], p. 143).

I would like to point out that, *prima facie*, this definition leads quickly to an inconsistency with another claim of its proponent. By assumption, states of perception have nonconceptual content; this pretheoretical intuition seems to be respected by the definition: a state of seeing can have the content that the sun is shining without the subject of that state having the concepts of sun and shining. Also by assumption, states of belief have conceptual content; this pretheoretical intuition also seems to be respected by the definition: for a state of believing to have the content that the sun is shining, the subject of the state must have the concepts of sun and shining (we are not disputing this now, for the sake of argument). But according to Crane, as we have seen, perceptual and belief states can share contents, in particular the content that the sun is shining. Assuming that there is someone who sees than the sun is shining without having the concepts of sun and shining, the content that the sun is shining is nonconceptual. Assuming that there is someone who has ever believed that the sun is shining, that same content is conceptual. Under the apparently innocuous assumption that a content should not be both conceptual and nonconceptual, we have a contradiction.

Although I don't want to appear too picky, I also have to say that Crane's definition leaves something to be desired from the methodological point of view; if I say it, it's only because the point seems important for our discussion. It leaves something to be desired because one would have expected that it would define a subclass of the class of contents, namely the nonconceptual ones. Instead, it seems that it can be seen at most as a "definition" (a sloppy one) of a subclass of the states with content.

This is not a picky point, because it seems to me that when one uses the expressions 'nonconceptual content' and 'conceptual content' one should be using them to refer to two disjoint classes that fully exhaust a previously given class, the class of contents, and any other use will be philosophically misleading. The proposed "definition" quite obviously does not accomplish by itself a division of the class of contents into two mutually exclusive, jointly exhaustive classes of contents (as our little argument to contradiction shows). Rather, what the "definition" does is at most to define a predicate of states with content (namely, the only apparently semantically complex, and in fact atomic, predicate "to have nonconceptual content"), which applies with truth to them when a subject's being in them does not require the subject to "possess" certain concepts determined in some way ("canonically") by the content of the states (I won't enter into what this way might be). A better, non-misleading choice for the predicate that is (at best) being defined would be 'nonconceptualized' or something like that. According to the revised definition, then, some states would be conceptualized, others nonconceptualized, under suitable premises. If we accept the intuitions of Evans's followers, states of perception will often or always be nonconceptualized, and states of belief will always be conceptualized (in Crane the concepts involved in a state will be "determined" in some way by the state's content, but in other friends of the distinction as one between kinds of states I conjecture that this need not be the case).

Now, I don't know if the difference behind this distinction is an interesting or useful one. But one thing seems clear to me: it's not a distinction between kinds of content. Therefore, it does not vindicate the felt intuitions about a difference between perception and belief by means of a distinction between kinds of content.

But in other authors, specifically in Christopher Peacocke, I have found a more substantive way of vindicating those intuitions at the level of a distinction between kinds of content (see Peacocke [1992], ch. 3). I find Peacocke's discussion very hard to follow, but I'll try to comment on it and relate it to our main exegetical problem. According to Peacocke, there is a kind of abstract objects that are needed to characterize the contents of perceptual states, and that are essentially different from the other kinds of abstract objects that traditionally have been used to characterize the contents of belief states —for example, sets of possible circumstances, or Russellian propositions. We might call the latter 'propositions', and refer to Peacocke's distinction as a distinction between "nonpropositional" and "propositional" contents (observing that in this usage 'propositional' ceases to be synonymous with 'representational' or 'informational'). It seems that Peacocke thinks that the contents of belief are propositional (they are precisely abstract objects that have concepts as constituents). But I don't know whether he thinks that when we say that someone believes that P we are attributing to him the "possession" of particular concepts. I also don't know what he makes of the remark that in an obvious sense sometimes we believe what we see. But it seems clear that he thinks that the contents of perception are nonpropositional. And this is surely a substantive claim that Stalnaker is bound to disagree with.

For Peacocke, the contents of perceptual states seem to be, at least in some cases, certain abstract objects that he calls "positioned scenarios". A positioned scenario consists of three things. First, what Peacocke calls a "scenario". A scenario is something that consists in turn of two things: (a) an "origin" and "axes" ("for instance, one kind of origin is given by being the property of being the center of the chest of the human body, with the three axes given by the directions back/front, left/right and up/down with respect to that center" (Peacocke [1992], p. 62)); (b) a set of ways "of filling out the space around the origin" (Peacocke [1992], p. 63), ways of assigning to each point around the origin all relevant data from a certain range of possibilities: "whether there is a surface there and, if so, what texture, hue, saturation, and brightness it has at that point, together with its degree of solidity", etc. (Peacocke [1992], p. 63); this set of ways are those "ways of filling out the space whose instantiation is consistent with the correctness of the representational content" (Peacocke [1992], p. 63) of the state —I take it that there is no circularity here when Peacocke speaks of representational content in characterizing representational content: the former use refers to the pretheoretical notion of representational content, the latter to the technical notion he is aiming to introduce.

The second thing that a positioned scenario consists of is "an assignment to the labeled axes and origins of the scenario of real directions and places in the world that fall under the labels" (Peacocke [1992], p. 64), and the third thing is "an assigned time" (*loc. cit.*). For example, leaving technicalities aside, a positioned scenario for a state of seeing seems to be more or less the full state of the physical world around a point, at a given time, that would be "relevant" to someone seeing things from that point in a certain orientation. A positioned scenario has truth conditions, according to Peacocke, and therefore satisfies the property characteristic of contents enunciated by Stalnaker: a positioned scenario is true if "the volume of the real world" (Peacocke [1992], p. 64) around the place assigned to the origin "falls under the scenario at the assigned time, when the scenario is positioned there in accordance with the assigned directions" (Peacocke [1992], p. 65).

The important question for our concerns is why, according to Peacocke, one would need to introduce these complicated "positioned scenarios" as contents of perceptual states. His considerations on this matter are especially obscure to me, but the main (perhaps the only) claim he adduces in order to justify this need seems to reproduce a well-known point about so-called "indexical beliefs". He attacks the appropriateness of Russellian propositions, but probably he would give a similar argument against the appropriateness of propositions as sets of possible circumstances. Here is Peacocke's example. Suppose someone, A, is in a field and sees mist in a certain region to his north, while someone else, B, sees the same mist in the same region, which is in this case to his northeast. Someone may report on the content of A's perceptual state by uttering "A sees that R is misty" (where 'R' is a name of the misty region) and on the content of B's state by uttering "B sees that R is misty". Thus, observes Peacocke, the same Russellian proposition would be given in specifying the contents of both states. "But the region is clearly presented in perception in different ways to [A] and to [B]. Each of [them] sees it as being in a different direction relative to [himself], and [their] actions may differ as a result" (Peacocke [1992], p. 70). For example, A may walk towards his northwest and B may walk towards his north.

Now, to me this only seems to show that we did not report with sufficient detail on the contents of A and B's perceptual states. And this is what Peacocke seems to concede too. He considers the possibility that we should report (in A's case, say) uttering something like "A sees that R is located to the north of him and R is misty". And here is where Peacocke launches his criticism. In the Russellian scheme, the content of the new "that"–clause will contain A as a constituent (as the reference of 'him'). But it is a familiar point that the Russellian content of this clause and the content of the "that"–clause in, say, "A sees that R is located to the north of O'Leary and R is misty", will be the same if A is O'Leary. Yet A may not realize that he is O'Leary. The second attribution will then be apparently false and the first apparently true, despite the fact that they have the same Russellian content. The second attribution will then be apparently useless for explaining A's behavior, while the first will be explanatory, despite the fact that they have the same Russellian content. (This problem will not arise for Peacocke's account, since the positioned scenarios corresponding to states describable by the "that"-clauses in the first and second attributions (at the relevant time) will be intuitively different.)

This makes Peacocke say that the only alternative left to the propositional theorist is to "use the first-person way of thinking in giving the content of the visual experience" (Peacocke [1992], p. 71) (in order to explain the content of 'him' in the first attribution, I suppose); and then he gives a (to me) very obscure argument to defend the thesis that the propositional theorist just cannot do that. However, even without going into that argument, I think it's just not clear at all why the propositional theorist must "use the first-person way of thinking in giving the content of the visual experience". The Russellian propositional theorists may claim (and in fact I think some of them do claim) that the content of "R is located to the north of him and R is misty" and "R is located to the north of O'Leary and R is misty" when 'him' alludes to O'Leary *is* the same (and hence does not involve in either case "the first person way of thinking"; it just involves O'Leary, among other things), and therefore that the truth-value of the corresponding attitude ascriptions is the same, despite appearances. Those theorists may explain any differences in the behavior-inducing, and in general causal, powers of states with that same content in terms of non-representational (hence nonpropositional) features of those states: the states would be different in some way, even if not representationally different. No one can deny that non-representational features of mental states have behavior-inducing powers (unless it is denied *tout court* that there are non-representational features of mental states). Peacocke, it seems to me, has not discredited this possible reply of the propositionalist, at least anywhere I can see.

The preceding examination has the same upshot as Stalnaker's (although it has been reached through a different, exegetical, methodology): in the literature I have examined there seems to be no convincing defense of the claim that the felt differences between perception and belief are differences in the kinds of contents of the corresponding states. The significance of my claim is of course only proportional to the depth of my examination, which admittedly is not too great.

Why should one think that the felt differences between perception and belief are differences in the kinds of contents of the corresponding states? What do those intuitions respond to? In my opinion, it might be just a matter of sheer difference in the quantity of information of each kind of state. A rich perceptual state, if veridical, rules out many more possible circumstances than the average belief, if veridical. I truly do see a lot of things when I am in a state of seeing. I see that the sun is shining, but many things besides: that the grass is green, that my dog is searching for a bone, that the zebra is striped, and so on. But when I'm in the state of believing that the sun is shining, that's all I'm believing.

Consequently, the verbal specifications of the full contents of states of perception will on average be much more cumbersome, if possible at all, than those of the contents of belief states. But from this alone it's not clear why we should conclude that the contents belong to intrinsically different kinds. We know that there are many propositions which are very hard to specify verbally, and still many more which are not verbally specifiable at all. (This is especially clear under the view of propositions as sets of possible circumstances. But I think it's not hard to see that it holds also for Russellian propositions. That many Russellian propositions are not verbally specifiable at all can be seen from the fact that there are more objects and properties than names to name them; but also if we reflect that it does not seem to be a part of the theory of Russellian propositions that they be finite sequences: they may be just well–ordered sequences of any cardinality.) These propositions that are not verbally specifiable might be called "nonconceptual" in yet another sense of the word.

Acknowledgment: I thank Brom Anderson, Patricia Brunsteins, Maite Ezcurdia, Manuel García–Carpintero, Max Kölbel, Rupert Summerton and especially Ignacio Vicario for helpful comments. Thanks are also due to the Mexican CONACYT, project 3128P–H.

REFERENCES

Crane [1992]: T. Crane, "The nonconceptual content of experience", in T. Crane (ed.), *The Contents of Experience: Essays on Perception*, Cambridge University Press, Cambridge, 1992; pp. 136-157.

Peacocke [1992]: C. Peacocke, *A Study of Concepts*, M.I.T. Press, Cambridge, Mass., 1992.

Stalnaker [1997]: R. Stalnaker, "What might nonconceptual content be?", included in this volume.

Information and Content

David Pineda

I take it that in his contribution, Stalnaker is arguing for the claim that all there is to content is nonconceptual content, and that he reaches his conclusion basically from two premises: the first premiss says that all there is to content is informational content, and the second says that informational content is nonconceptual content. So then, in my comments I will focus on the central notion of "informational content" with the hope that the discussion of them will help me to clarify this key notion in Stalnaker's approach to content.

Informational content, we are told, is individuated by truth conditions, propositions as sets of possible worlds or alternative possibilities (in the metaphysical sense of "alternative possibilities".) This is, as Stalnaker stresses, the most coarse-grained or minimal sense of "content" you can get if you endorse the very reasonable assumption that, whatever content turns out to be, if something or a state of something has content then this something has truth conditions (or, in a somewhat more neutral fashion, "conditions of satisfaction") and it has them in virtue of having content. What Stalnaker wants to argue for, then, is that this minimal sense of content is all there is to the notion, including mental content.

Informational content is an abstract object, in particular it abstracts away from the means of representation, whether linguistic or mental. Thus, when we attribute to an object X the belief that P, we are attributing to X a relation to the proposition denoted by the term "that P". This is to say that we are attributing to a natural object X a relation to an abstract object, a proposition, a set of possible worlds, and the problem for someone willing to give a naturalistic account of intentionality, as is Stalnaker's case, is to characterize in nonintentional terms such a relation between a natural object and an abstract object. The relation, besides being nonintentional and nonmysterious, must also of course explain why something X instantiating it represents thereby the world as being a certain way, if it is to serve as an explanation of the phenomenon of intentionality. Here is where Stalnaker relies on some version of an information–theoretic account, the essentials of which are that to attribute an informational content P to X is to attribute to X a certain counterfactual or causal dependency to its environment, is to say that X carries the information that P, where all that this says is that X is in some state it would not be in if P were not the case.

Now in this sense of informational state, it is true that something can instantiate informational states without having, or using, any concepts. So, the second premiss of Stalnaker's argument seems to be true, so far. The problem is that in this same sense of informational state, informational states seem to be veridical. As Stalnaker himself acknowledges, it turns out that X cannot carry the information that P unless it is true that P. This is a characteristic problem for any information–theoretic account of intentionality, and it is not a minor fault on the part of the theory, since central to the phenomenon of intentionality is the idea of representation, and central to the idea of representation is that whatever has the power of representation it also has the power of misrepresentation. When we say that an object represents something it makes perfect sense to ask whether it represents it correctly or not, moreover it is a requisite of representation that it can be done correctly or wrongly. Therefore, an information–theoretic account of intentionality should also account, to be considered as such, for the phenomenon of misrepresentation. The traditional way of doing so is by giving theoretical shape to the intuitive idea that when misrepresentation occurs something has gone wrong. One introduces the notion of "normal conditions" and proposes the following ammendment to the theory sketched above: X carries the information that P when and only when X is in an state which would depend counterfactually or causally on P if normal conditions obtained. The explanation of misrepresentation is then simply that it occurs when X is in the right state but the normal conditions have not obtained. So, in spite of the fact that X carries the information that P, when the normal conditions doesn't obtain P might not be the case.

The problem with this solution is that there seems to be no easy, nonintentional and noncircular way of telling the normal conditions from the abnormal ones (the problem that Fodor labelled "the disjunction problem", Fodor, 1984), as Dretske's successive efforts to deal with it I think that have shown (Dretske, 1981, 1986, 1988). Now, I will sketch very briefly a familiar solution to this problem, the teleological account of content, and contrast it with Stalnaker's notion of information–carrying states (or informational states, for short.) In spite of some acknowledged virtues of this account, I remain skeptical to it, and I will also offer the reasons of my skepticism.

Let me state very briefly what I take to be the core idea behind these teleological proposals. What they do is to resort to a non–dispositional concept of function. I will capitalize the 'F' to distinguish this sense from the purely dispositional one. According to this capitalized sense, an instantiation of a type of state S belonging to a system has the function F when and only when:

(1) S brings about F, and

(2) The explanation of that particular instantiation of S involves the fact that past instances of S brought about F. (Wright, 1973)

The second clause gives to the notion its teleological sense. In the case of natural systems, it is supposed that the explanation needed to satisfy the clause will be given in terms of evolutive selection, while in the case of artifacts the explanation will be in terms of the conscious intentions of the designers of the artifact.

The idea then is to spell out the normal conditions by saying something as follows. An state X of a system carries the information that P when there are certain intermediate mechanisms or states of the system whose Function —in this teleological sense of the term— is to cause an instantiation of X when P is present in the environment of the system. Now the conditions are normal when these intermediate states are Functioning properly, that is, when they help to correlate instantiations of P in the environment with instantiations of X in the system; and the conditions are abnormal when they are misFunctioning.

No doubt this account should be refined in a number of ways to cope with a number of problems, but the essentials of the account, I think, are as described and, in any case, this sketchy formulation is enough for my purposes. Before contrasting this teleological account of information and informational states with Stalnaker's views let me highlight some of the virtues of the account. Firstly, it looks as a promising way of spelling out in a nonintentional way the "normal" conditions and, therefore, of giving a naturalistic account of the phenomenon of misrepresentation, which is, as I said, of the essence of the phenomenon of intentionality. Secondly, it underwrites a treatment of perceptual hallucination which I feel intuitively more plausible than the one offered by Stalnaker, because the account allows us to say that a perceptual hallucination carries the same information as the corresponding correct perception, only that in the first case the information is wrong and in the second it is correct. And thirdly, the account retains one of the chief motivations behind Stalnaker's notion of an informational state, namely that it avoids "the dreaded myth of the given", in Stalnaker's words, since it follows from the teleological notion of informational state that an informational state depends on the environment in such a way that it is endowed with "objective content".

Still, as far as I can tell, one cannot say that the pattern of light and dark on the ground on a sunny day carries information, in this teleological sense of "carrying information", of the shape of the tree; and one cannot certainly say that Swampthermometers or Swampcameras are informational systems in this teleological sense. So, it looks as if Stalnaker doesn't have in mind this sort of teleological solution to the misrepresentation problem. However, after discussion, he admits to be prepared to embrace any information–theoretic solution to the misrepresentation problem, including the teleological solution.

The problem, of course, is whether there exists such a solution. On my part I would like to finish with this issue of the possibility of misrepresentation by stating what I take to be two sources of discomfort towards the teleological account. The first is that I'm prone to get convinced by Fodor's reasons (Fodor, 1990) to the effect that after all a teleological account, however the details of the account are settled, doesn't solve the problem of misrepresentation: you get indeterminacy of Functional content right where the disjunction problem arises. My second source of discomfort is the Swampman's case. I accept that it is a conceptual point that it makes no sense to attribute rememberings to the Swampman at the very moment of its coming into existence, since it is a conceptual fact that in order to attribute a remembering to something you have also to attribute to this something past experiences, and it is clear that you cannot attribute past experiences to the Swampman at the very moment he comes to live. However, I doubt whether there is any conceptual impossibility to the attribution to the Swampman of other intentional states, like desires, beliefs and perceptions, at the moment of its coming into existence, assuming as it is assumed in the thought experiment, that the Swampman exhibits complex intelligent behavior from the first moment. So I doubt, in short, that the teleological account can be read as a conceptual analysis of the notion of informational or intentional state in general.

One final point about the Swampman. If someone is prepared to look at him not merely as a conceptual possibility, but also as a nomological one, then I think that he will confront an annoying problem, if he is also prepared to accept the physicalistic assumption that two physically identical things have the same causal powers. Because if he accepts this piece of physicalism and endorses the teleological account of intentionality, then it seems *prima facie* that the intentional would become causally idle (unless one is willing to endorse the odd metaphysical view that mental states somehow supervene on the "history" and the environment of the system).

I turn very quickly to the first premiss of Stalnaker's argument. I take it that his notion of informational content is somehow based on the distinction between what is thought and how it is thought, and the corresponding distinction between what is said and how it is said. This intuitive distinction is after all, I suppose, the deep motivation for the Fregean distinction between sense and reference. But I have doubts that all there is to intentional content is informational content, that something like fregean senses or concepts should not be built into intentional content somewhere. Let me give some reasons for these doubts.

Firstly, I do not find conclusive Stalnaker's only reason in his paper for this strong conclusion (at least the only reason I have been able to find in his paper). He seems to derive his conclusion from the following premiss: "If your concepts are different from mine — Stalnaker writes—, then I would be unable to use my concepts to attribute beliefs to you if in doing so I were saying that you had beliefs with those concepts as constituents" (p. 352). I think this is absolutely correct. But I do not see that this shows that the contents of the beliefs attributed are devoid of concepts. It could be, for example, that in order to attribute beliefs to someone there has to be a large (maybe not a total) overlaping between the concepts of the attributer and the concepts of the attributee. Or, alternatively, a certain theory of belief attribution could be true according to which when I use my concepts to attribute beliefs to you, I'm not saying that these concepts are constitutive of your beliefs, but they are somehow related to the concepts which constitute the content of your beliefs. I'm not endorsing these possibilities, my claim is simply that one has to argue against them to reach the conclusion that the content of beliefs is conceptless. And to do that one needs more premises.

Secondly, there is the well-known fact that two propositional attitudes towards two necessarily equivalent propositions have the same content, according to the notion of informational content that Stalnaker defends. Let me state what I take to be a problem for any theory which understands content as "what is thought" as opposed to "how it is thought", which is closely connected to this fact. Perhaps, as Stalnaker himself suggests, it all is a matter of what assumptions about content you are prepared to retain as central and what other assumptions you are prepared to dismiss, so I will set my criticism in the form of a couple of assumptions about content that it seems *prima facie* that you have to dismiss if you stick to the claim that intentional content is informational content "all the way up".

The first assumption says that a set of beliefs is consistent, and coherent, or not in virtue of the content of their members, and the second assumption says that what rationalizes an intentional action is on the one hand the content of the mental states attributed to the agent and on the other hand the psychological mode of those states (if you individuate them, as usually and as Stalnaker does, precisely by their role to determine rational action.) The reason for abandoning these assumptions is that there seems to be *prima facie* counterexamples to them, if we stick to the thesis that content is just informational content. Take for example Pierre-like cases. There we have Pierre's belief that Londres is nice and Pierre's belief that London is not nice, and in spite of the fact that they involve contradictory informational contents they do not strike us —assuming Kripke's story— as contradictory at all. Again we have Pierre's belief that Londres is nice and his belief that London is nice, and in spite of the fact that they involve the same informational content, it turns out that they rationalize different actions of Pierre's. Notice that nothing hangs on the peculiarities of Kripke's Pierre, since we could construct lots of similar counterexamples easily. For example, surely there are counterexamples involving, for instance, a desire for water and a desire for H_2O.

On view of these counterexamples one can, of course, decide to give up these assumptions or even to dismiss them as wrong assumptions. The problem with this strategy, of course, is that, to put it in a Fregean way, when finally Pierre comes to believe that London is Londres one would say that he acquires new information he hadn't got before, if it ever made sense at all speaking of someone acquiring new information. So, one would say that there is a difference in information between his belief involving Londres and his belief involving London, and the thing is how to account for this sense of information. One possible reaction on the face of this problem, not the only one, is what I take to be Stalnaker's reaction. The idea is to account for this sense of information in terms of content in such a way that the informational content of Pierre's relevant beliefs —and in general the informational content of the mental states involved in such *prima facie* counterexamples to these two assumptions— is, to put it roughly, metalinguistic; that is, it concerns the expressions which we use to attribute these beliefs and states. Now, my closing remark is that I do not find this poposal entirely satisfactory, since I share the view of those who think that Pierre's beliefs are not metalinguistic in any sense.

REFERENCES

Dretske, F., 1981: *Knowledge and the Flow of Information.* Cambridge, Mass: MIT Press.
———, 1986: "Misrepresentation", in *Belief,* R. Bogdan (ed.), Oxford: Oxford U.P.
———, 1988: *Explaining Behavior.* Cambridge, Mass MIT: Press.
Fodor, J. , 1984: "Semantics, Wisconsin Style", *Synthese,* 59, pp. 231-250.
———, 1990: *A Theory of Content.* Cambridge, Mass: MIT Press.
Kripke, S., 1979: "A Puzzle About Belief", in *Meaning and Use,* A. Margalit (ed.). Dordrecht: Reidel.
Wright, L., 1973: "Functions", *Philosophical Review,* 82, pp. 139-168.

Replies to Comments

Robert Stalnaker

Let me start by thanking my four commentators for their stimulating comments. I cannot adequately respond to all of their points, but I will make a few remarks about some of the many issues they have raised: first, on the distinctions between conceptual and nonconceptual states and contents, second on the subject–centered character of perception and thought, third about naturalism and reduction, and fourth about the identity conditions for contents.

1 Kinds of States and Kinds of Content

The sound bite that I threw in at the end of my paper gets much of the attention from my commentators. Stephen Neale refers to my "overt claim that all content is nonconceptual", Juan José Acero says that I reject a distinction between two kinds of content, and David Pineda takes me to be "arguing for the claim that all there is to content is nonconceptual content". I do not want to disown my concluding suggestion that content is "nonconceptual all the way up", but I also do not want to deny that there may be various abstract objects, some of which might be appropriately thought of as conceptual contents, that are useful for describing intentional mental states. My main point was not to argue for a restrictive thesis about content, but only to raise questions about what sorts of objects conceptual and nonconceptual contents might be, and about the role of a distinction between them in the debate between McDowell and Evans about the relation between perception and thought. I continue to be puzzled about just what background assumptions underlie the debates between Evans, McDowell, Peacocke, and others who distinguish conceptual from nonconceptual content, even though Neale tells me that "the debate in which they are engaged is clear".

I posed my questions as questions about the nature of the objects —conceptual and nonconceptual contents —since I was suspicious, as Neale notes in his comments, that there is in this debate "slippage between talk of mental states as conceptual (nonconceptual) and talk of the contents of such states as conceptual (nonconceptual)" (p. 354). Neale thinks that this suspicion shows that I have "not fully appreciated the antecedently Fregean nature of the conceptual–nonconceptual debate" (p. 354), but I am not sure why he thinks this, or what the relevant Fregean assumptions are. In fact, Neale's own discussion reinforces my suspicion that the waters of this debate have been muddied by a conflation of a distinction between two kinds of content with a distinction between two kinds of mental states. To my suggestion that one might regard Fregean thoughts (a kind of sense that consists of senses) as conceptual contents and Russellian propositions (composed of properties and objects) as nonconceptual, Neale responds that "this is not the sense of 'conceptual' that is meant to be at issue: the representational content of a belief or judgment is said to be 'conceptual', according to Evans, in the sense that entertaining a belief or forming a judgment involves the exercise of conceptual capacities" (p. 356). But this is not a *sense* in which content is conceptual; one cannot just assume that a fact about forming judgments and beliefs —that these activities involve the exercise of a certain kind of capacity— is reflected in a distinctive feature of the contents of judgments and beliefs. A theory might hypothesize that a distinction between representational acts and states —those that involve the exercise of conceptual capacities and those that do not— corresponds to a distinction between the kinds of representational content used to characterize those states, but one still has to say what the corresponding difference in content is.

Perhaps Neale is suggesting that I have misconstrued the nature of the debate by taking it to be about a distinction between kinds of content at all. He attributes to *me* the belief that the contrast between conceptual and nonconceptual states "can best be answered by reflecting on what kinds of objects can serve as these different types of content" (p. 357), (that is, as the contents of these different types of states). But in fact my belief is just the opposite of this: I think it is a mistake to think that differences between perceptual and belief states are reflected in differences in the contents of those states —a mistake that has distorted the debate between Evans and McDowell about the relation between the information received in perception and the contents of judgments and reasoning about what is perceived. But I think it is clear that Evans, McDowell, Peacocke, Tim Crane, and others have taken it for granted that they are arguing about different kinds of content.

The slippage from a distinction between kinds of state to a distinction between kinds of content in the writing of those who talk of nonconceptual content is brought out in Gomez–Torrente's helpful discussion of Tim Crane's way of drawing the distinction, which quite explicitly defines a difference in content in terms of a difference in the states with content. Gomez–Torrente's arguments show some of the problems with this kind of definition. I agree with him that "this is not a picky point".

2   The First Person Point of View

As Juan Acero says, "most of the information we gain and use wears a first–person dress" (p. 364). Both perception and thought involve the perceiver and thinker in the contents of what is perceived and thought about. Both Acero and Gomez–Torrente discuss an example that Peacocke uses to argue that differences in perspective must be included in any adequate description of the contents of perceptual experience. If I see the mist to the north while you see it to the northeast, then things appear differently to us, even if we don't disagree about the way things appear to be. Similarly with Acero's example of the difference between his perspective on the items on his desk and that of the visitor facing him. Now I would agree that we need to account both for the sense in which the contents of our experience (the way things appear to be) are different in such examples, and for the way that they are the same. And I would agree that neither Russellian propositions, Fregean thoughts, or sets of possible worlds are suitable, in themselves, for representing the perspective of the perceiver.(Gomez–Torrente seems to want to resist Peacocke's argument that there is an ineliminable perceiver perspective in the content of perception, but I find Peacocke's argument persuasive.) But I don't think that the essentially perspectival character of perception can be used to motivate a distinction between conceptual and nonconceptual content, or that it is relevant to the difference between perception and thought. It is a familiar fact that judgments and beliefs can be essentially indexical; the fact that I believe the dictionary is to my right, while you believe it is to your left, can explain why we behave differently whether or not those beliefs are based on perception. And despite what Acero suggests, I don't think that Peacocke's point that differences between experiencers' perspectives must be reflected in the contents of their experiences indicates a conflict between his approach and mine. Peacocke's notion of a positioned scenario (as a candidate for a kind of content) is close in spirit to the more abstract notion of a set of possible situations (or, to include the perspectival element, a set of centered possible situations) —a candidate for the contents of judgments and thoughts as well as perceptual experience.

3 Naturalism and Normal Conditions

In the paper I sketched the outlines of a familiar account of the facts that give content to the states of what Evans called "the informational system". According to this account, the content of a state is determined relative to some notion of *normal conditions*. David Pineda and Juan Acero both raise questions about how the normal conditions presupposed by attributions of informational content are to be specified. One kind of account, discussed by Pineda, is an evolutionary or teleological account. Normal conditions are defined in terms of the functions of a system, and functions are defined in terms of how the system came to be disposed to behave as it does. I think such a teleological account might appropriate for some applications of the information theoretic story, but I would resist the idea that this kind of account is essential, in the general case, to the concept of normal conditions. I take the information theoretic story to be one that explains how content is determined relative to any given account of the normal conditions —conditions that may vary from one context in which the story is applied to another. If one finds an object (such as swampman, or swampcamera) that tends, under certain conditions, to vary systematically with variations in some features of its environment, then whatever the origins of the thing, and whatever the explanation for the fact that such a systematic causal correlation exists, one may correctly say that it's internal states tend (under those conditions) to carry the information. So I agree with Pineda's doubts that the teleological account should be "read as a conceptual analysis" (p. 385) of what it is for a state to carry information. And since I don't think that the abstract account of information, because it takes normal conditions as given, can provide a naturalistic *reduction* of intentionality, I would agree with the kind of naturalism that Acero endorses —a naturalism that "does not require the reduction of content notions to non–intentional ones" (p. 367). I take it that what is required for a defense of naturalism is an explanation of how it is possible for physical objects that are part of the natural order to have the capacities (such as the capacities for perceiving, remembering, reasoning and communicating) that we human beings have. If we can give such explanations without an eliminative reduction of the intentional to the physical, then we can have a nonreductive naturalism.

4 Identity Conditions for Contents

The minimal notion of content that I defended —content as truth conditions, represented by the set of possible situations in which the truth conditions are realized— faces a familiar and daunting problem: since the account holds that necessarily equivalent propositions are identical, it is seems to be committed to the view that for any equivalent P and Q, the property of perceiving or believing that P is the same as the property of perceiving or believing that Q —a consequence that seems intuitively to be obviously false. Informational content, it seems, is just too coarse–grained to be a plausible candidate for the kind of content that we attribute when we describe either a person's judgments or her perceptions. I have elsewhere floated various ideas about how to reconcile this account of content with the phenomena. Here I want just to make some general remarks about this problem, and about some of the examples that Neale and Pineda use to raise it. First, I want to emphasize that in a sense, the most coarse–grained concept of content is a neutral concept —one that all parties, at least all those who are willing to talk of representational content at all, should admit can be used to characterize perceptual and intentional states. Representational contents, whatever they are, *have* truth conditions, and so states with any kind of representational content are states that can be characterized with coarse–grained informational content. Perhaps they can also be characterized, more informatively, with a finer–grained concept —for example Russellian propositions or Fregean thoughts— but for the characterization to be more informative, one needs to be able to say how the difference in structure between different but necessarily equivalent fine–grained propositions is reflected in differences between the representational states. It is not difficult to describe notions of content that are more fine-grained than the minimal notion of informational content (although if such objects contain concepts or senses as constituents, one has to say what concepts or senses are); what is more challenging is to give a plausible account of the role of the distinctions that the finer grained notions of content allow for in distinguishing between different intentional states.

Mathematical belief (distinguishing, for example, the belief that $2 + 2 = 4$ from the belief that there is no greatest prime) indeed presents a serious problem for the coarse-grained conception of content, but I am in any case independently puzzled about what mathematical beliefs are about. The other examples that Neale and Pineda mention seem to me much easier to deal with. One can, using only coarse-grained contents, distinguish the belief that Hesperus is a planet from the belief that Phosphorus is a planet if one assumes, with the Fregean, that "Hesperus" and "Phosphorus" have different senses that might have determined distinct referents. On this assumption, "Hesperus is a planet" and "Phosphorus is a planet" may be only contingently equivalent. This kind of example, which is a problem for the Russellian, but not necessarily for the defender of simple truth-conditional content, points to an oversimplification in Neale's characterization of the "descending order of fineness of grain" of the different notions of content (most fine-grained, Fregean thoughts, next Russellian propositions, most coarse-grained, informational contents). It is true that Fregean thoughts are more fine-grained than Russellian propositions in the sense that different Fregean thoughts may correspond to the same Russellian proposition, and it is also true that distinct Russellian propositions may have the same truth conditions. But these correspondences are not transitive. Different Fregean propositions that correspond to the same Russellian proposition may in some cases have different truth conditions. A problem (such as is posed by the Hesperus-Phosphorus example) for the Russellian is not necessarily a problem for the defender of purely truth-conditional content.

Whether one believes such names have senses or not, it seems intuitively natural to say that the person who believes Hesperus is a planet, while disbelieving that Phosphorus is a planet, is a person who recognizes the possibility that the thing he refers to as "Phosphorus" (or at least the thing presented to him in one of the ways —the "Phosphorus" way— that Venus is actually presented) is a different thing from the thing he calls "Hesperus". I think one can say the same kind of thing about the informational difference between water attitudes and H_2O attitudes, and between Pierre's different beliefs. Pineda objects to my strategy (spelled out in other places) for responding to these examples, which he regards as unacceptably metalinguistic. I agree that the relevant beliefs of Pierre, of the Babylonian who denies that Hesperus is Phosphorus, and of the chemical innocent who is ignorant of the composition of water are beliefs about urban aesthetics, astronomy and chemistry, respectively, and not about language, and I don't think the response to the counterexamples that I am defending needs to deny this. But this is a large issue for another occasion.

Contributors

Juan José Acero, Universidad de Granada
George Bealer, Colorado University
Paul Boghossian, New York University
Josep Corbí, Universitat de València
M Ezcurdia, Universidad Nacional Autónoma de México
Jerry Fodor, Rutgers University
Mario Goméz Torrente, Universidad Nacional Autónoma de México
Richard Grandy, Rice University
James Higginbotham, Oxford University
Terence Horgan, Memphis State University
Paul Horwich, University College London
Pierre Jacob, CREA
Jaegwon Kim, Brown University
Brian Loar, Rutgers University
Ruth Millikan, University of Connecticut
Josep Maciá, Universitat de Barcelona
Eric Margolis, Rice University
Genoveva Martí, California State University
Carlos Moya, Universitat de València
Stephen Neale, University of California
Eleonora Orlando, Universidad de Buenos Aires
Christopher Peacocke, Oxford University
David Pineda, Universitat de Girona
Georges Rey, University of Maryland
Stephen Schiffer, New York University
David Sosa, University of California
Robert Stalnaker, Massachussetts Institute of Technology
James Tomberlin, California State University, Northridge
Josefa Toribio, University of Washington
Stephen Yablo, University of Michigan

Enrique Villanueva is now Research Fellow at the Centro de Neurobiología in the Universidad Nacional Autónoma de México in Juriquilla, Querétaro, México, a University where he has been doing research and teaching since he completed his Graduate Studies at the University of Oxford in 1972, and where he is currently doing research on the philosophy of mind. He has published more than seventy essays and reviews in metaphysics, philosophy of mind, philosophical history and political philosophy. Besides editorship of the present series he has edited the series *Simposio Internacional de Filosofía* and the volumes *Information, Semantics and Epistemology, El argumento del lenguaje privado* and coedited *Mente y Cuerpo*. He is author of *Lenguaje y Privacidad, Ensayos de Historia Filosófica, Las Personas,* and *¿Qué son las Propiedades Psicológicas?*